ROUTLEDGE LIBRARY EDITIONS:
THE HISTORY OF SOCIAL WELFARE

Volume 15

A TREATISE OF THE LAWS FOR THE RELIEF AND SETTLEMENT OF THE POOR

A TREATISE OF THE LAWS FOR THE RELIEF AND SETTLEMENT OF THE POOR

In two volumes
Vol. I

MICHAEL NOLAN

Routledge
Taylor & Francis Group
LONDON AND NEW YORK

First published in 1805 by J. Butterworth, London
Published in 1978 by Garland Publishing, Inc.

This edition first published in 2017
by Routledge
4 Park Square, Milton Park, Abingdon, Oxon OX14 4RN
605 Third Avenue, New York, NY 10017

Routledge is an imprint of the Taylor & Francis Group, an informa business

British Library Cataloguing in Publication Data
A catalogue record for this book is available from the British Library

ISBN: 978-1-138-20330-3 (Set)
ISBN: 978-1-315-45977-6 (Set) (ebk)
ISBN: 978-1-138-20759-2 (Volume 15) (hbk)
ISBN: 978-1-138-20760-8 (Volume 15) (pbk)
ISBN: 978-1-315-46169-4 (Volume 15) (ebk)

Publisher's Note
The publisher has gone to great lengths to ensure the quality of this reprint but points out that some imperfections in the original copies may be apparent.

Michael Nolan

A TREATISE OF THE LAWS FOR THE RELIEF AND SETTLEMENT OF THE POOR

In two volumes
Vol. I

Garland Publishing, Inc.
New York & London • 1978

Bibliographical note:
This facsimile has been made
from a copy in the British Library
(1381.d.1)

*The volumes in this series are printed
on acid-free, 250-year-life paper.*

Library of Congress Cataloging in Publication Data

Nolan, Michael, d. 1827.
A treatise of the laws for the relief and settlement of the poor.

(Classics of English legal history in the modern era ; 68)
Reprint of the 1805 ed. published by J. Butterworth, London.
Includes index.
1. Poor laws--Great Britain. I. Title. II. Series.
KD3310.N6 1978 344'.41'0325 77-89221
ISBN 0-8240-3167-9

Printed in the United States of America

A

TREATISE OF THE LAWS

FOR THE

RELIEF AND SETTLEMENT

OF THE

POOR.

By MICHAEL NOLAN,

OF LINCOLN'S INN, ESQ. BARRISTER AT LAW.

IN TWO VOLUMES.

VOL. I.

LONDON:

PRINTED BY A. STRAHAN,

LAW-PRINTER TO THE KING'S MOST EXCELLENT MAJESTY;

FOR J. BUTTERWORTH, LAW-BOOKSELLER, FLEET-STREET.

1805.

ADVERTISEMENT.

THE importance of that fyftem of our laws, which refpects the civil œconomy and comforts of the poor is fo obvious, that it is hoped an attempt to offer fome facilities to the perfons concerned in the adminiftration of them, will be received with indulgence.

For this purpofe, it has been thought convenient, inftead of giving the numerous cafes on every branch of the fubject, to reduce the fubftance of the decifions into the form of a treatife. The words of the judgment of the court are preferved as much as poffible, but it is difentangled from thofe circumftances of an individual nature, which could be of no ufe in illuftrating the principle upon which the determination is founded. When, however, a more minute ftatement of the cafe feemed neceffary, it has been given in the language of the report.

The prefent work differs, not only in its outline, from thofe of Dr. Burn, and Mr. Conft, but alfo in its general arrangement; and it will be found to treat of fome fubjects, which are either omitted altogether, or but flightly touched upon in thofe valuable productions.

The object has been not only to unfold the theory and doctrine of the law, but to fupply in fome degree the want of perſonal experience, by pointing out the manner in which that theory is to be applied in practice. The mode of proof, neceſſary to eſtabliſh the different kinds of ſettlement, is ſet forth with ſome minuteneſs ; and ſuch a general ſtatement is given of the manner of conducting appeals before courts of quarter-ſeſſions, as is conſiſtent with the various rules of practice, which are different in different courts. An account is likewiſe added of the practice on the crown ſide of the court of King's-Bench, as it reſpects the orders of magiſtrates removed thither by *certiorari*.

A few caſes connected with the ſubject of this work, have been determined in the court of King's-Bench, ſince it was committed to the preſs. They are annexed, with references to thoſe pages in each volume to which they ſeverally belong, and will be found to include the deciſions of laſt Michaelmas Term, taken from a manuſcript copy of Mr. Eaſt's notes, which he kindly furniſhed for the purpoſe.

5. King's-Bench Walks, Inner Temple,
January 28, 1805.

CONTENTS

OF

THE FIRST VOLUME.

CHAPTER VI.

CHAPTER VII.

CHAPTER VIII.

CHAPTER IX.

CHAPTER X.

CHAPTER XI.

CHAPTER XII.

CHAPTER XIII.

CHAPTER XIV.

CHAPTER XV.

Origin

Origin and History of the Law of Settlements.

CHAPTER XVI.

CHAPTER XVII.

CHAPTER XVIII.

CHAPTER XIX.

CHAPTER XX.

CHAPTER XXI.

INDEX

INDEX

OF THE

NAMES OF CASES

CITED IN THE FIRST VOLUME.

*** Thoſe printed in *Italics*, are inſerted in the *Addenda*.

Brazier's

Edge-

Lord

Rex

Rex

Rex

Temple

ADDENDA

TO

THE FIRST VOLUME.

PAGE 22, note (3), add "But see the opinion of Lord Mansfield, C. J. Rex. *v.* Beeding, Cald. 92."

Page 30, line 19, dele "*therefore,*" add "each being of a sufficient number of overseers."

Page 50, note (3), add "But where one entire rate was made upon the tolls of a canal, part of which were rateable, and part exempt by statute, the court quashed the rate, it being the business of those who made it to apportion it." Rex. *v.* Leeds and Liverpool Canal Company, 5 East, 325. and see Rex *v.* Cunningham, *post*, Vol. II. 370. addenda.

Page 52, note (3), add "Lord Bute *v.* Grindall, 1 Term Rep. 338. 1 H. Black, 267. 1 Bott, 195. Pl. 190."

Page 54, line 35, after "judgment" insert, "And in a recent case Lord Ellenborough C. J. seemed of opinion, that a common in gross is rateable." Rex. *v.* Watson, Mich. 45 Geo. 3. 5 East, 480.

Page 61, insert as a note to the last sentence, "See the opinion of Lord Ellenborough, C. J. Rex. *v.* Terrot, 3 East, 513."

Page 60, note (4), add, "Rex. *v.* Richard Cunningham, Mich. 45 Geo. 3. where, upon a case from

 sessions,

sessions, whether an iron-mine was rateable, the court held it to be too clear for argument, that it was not rateable, and quashed the rate."

Page 63, after line 21, add, "The particular use to which the produce of a coal-mine is applied, by the owner of the lands, does not exempt it from this tax. Thus, if the coal is used for smelting the ore of his iron-mine, the coal is rateable, although the ore is not. For, there is no difference whether it is thus applied by the owner, or sold by him to another, who uses it in an iron foundery, Rex. *v.* Cunningham, and others, 5 East, 478. Mich. 45 Geo. 3."

Page 65, at the end add, "By 10 Geo. 3. the incorporated company of the proprietors of the canal navigation from Leeds to Liverpool are enabled to make a navigable canal, and take a certain sum per mile, for the tonnage and wharfage of goods navigated thereon, and so in proportion for any greater or less quantity. It is also enacted, "that the said tolls, rates and duties, should at all times thereafter *be exempt from the payment of any taxes, rates, assessments, or impositions whatsoever*, any law or statute to the contrary notwithstanding, *other than such taxes, rates, and assessments, as the land which should be used for the purpose of the said navigation would have been subject to, if this act had not been made.*" The meaning of this exemption is, that the company shall not be liable to any other taxes than those which the land they make use of in their undertaking was previously subject to. As the land, therefore, was not before liable to be rated for tolls, the proprietors shall not be liable to a poor's-rate on tolls in respect of it, when converted into a canal. Rex. *v.* The Leeds and Liverpool Canal Company, 5 East, 325.

"The land will be rated in the same manner as it was before the act. *Per* Le Blanc, J. *Ib.*

"Another

Another part of the canal is exempted altogether from assessment for tolls, by 20 Geo. 3. *Ib.*"

A case was sent up from the court of quarter-sessions in Devonshire, concerning the validity of a poor rate. The statute 7 Geo. 3. for building *Stonehouse bridge* by s. 19. exempted it from "the land tax or any other public or parochial rate or tax whatsoever;" and by s. 20. provided, that certain persons, and their heirs, should stand seized of the tolls of the bridge, "to the same uses, trusts, and estates, and subject to the same wills, settlements, limitations, remainders, *charges*, tenures, rents, and incumbrances," as the ferry was, in lieu of which the bridge was erected; and held, that the word *charges* only extended to private charges on the estate. Case of Stonehouse bridge, 5 East, 356. n. *a*.

At a sessions holden for the city and county of Norwich, Ann Sutcliffe appealed against an assessment of 100l. stock, charged upon her for the relief of the poor. It appeared by the case, stated for the opinion of the court of King's-Bench, that the appellant was assessed for 100l. stock, or personal property, charged upon her by a rate for raising 137l. 11s. 10d. for maintaining the poor, made by virtue of a local statute of the 10th of Anne, for erecting a work-house in Norwich, for the better employment and maintaining the poor there; under which act, the church-wardens, and overseers of the poor of the said parish, were, according to the directions and words of the said act of parliament, authorized and required "to rate and assess the said sum (of 137l. 11s. 10d.) on the inhabitants, and on every parson and vicar, and on all and every the occupiers of lands, houses, tenements, tithes impropriate, appropriations of tithes, and on all persons having and using stocks and personal estates in the said parish (of St. John's, Maddermarket), *or having money out at interest*, in equal proportion, as near

as

as máy be, according to their ſeveral and reſpective values and eſtates." And, on hearing the ſaid appeal, it appeared to the ſaid court, that ever ſince the paſſing ſaid ſtatute, lands, houſes, tenements, ſtocks, and perſonal eſtates, within the ſaid city and county, and money out at intereſt, as well without as within the ſaid city and county, of the reſpective inhabitants within the ſeveral pariſhes of the ſame, have been conſtantly aſſeſſed to the poor's rates, according to the circumſtances of ſuch inhabitants. That the appellant had not any ſtock or perſonal eſtate in the ſaid pariſh of St. John's, Maddermarket, or in any other pariſh or hamlet within the ſaid city and county of Norwich, *nor had any money out at intereſt* on real or perſonal ſecurity; but that ſhe was poſſeſſed of money *veſted in the public funds*, or on government ſecurity, and then ſtanding in her name in the books of the governor and company of the bank of England in the 5 *per cent.* bank annuities: and, therefore, the appellant admitted, that the ſaid aſſeſſment was juſt, if the ſaid laſt mentioned money was liable to be rated. The court of quarter-ſeſſions being of opinion, that money veſted in the public funds, or on government ſecurity, was not by virtue of the aforeſaid act liable to be rated to the relief of the poor, allowed the appeal. The court of King's-Bench were of opinion, that government ſtock was not money out at intereſt, within the meaning of this local ſtatute, and therefore not taxable under it; and alſo, that it was not taxable under the 43 of Eliz., not being local viſible property within the pariſh. Rex *v.* St. John's, Maddermarket, in Norwich. Hil. 45. Geo. 3.

Page 79, after line 14 inſert, "But no lodger, though poſſeſſing the principal part of the houſe, was ever rated; but the owner, how ſmall ſoever the part reſerved for himſelf, is, in the eye of the law, the tenant of the whole, and is rated as the occupier. *Per* Buller, J. Rex. *v.* Eyles, Cald. 414."

Page

Page 80, after line 20 insert, " In another case it was found that the mayor, aldermen and burgesses of a borough, were the owners of a large tract of land within the borough, used as a common of pasture, and stocked by the resident burgesses, in right of their burgherships, according to a stint annually fixed by the leet jury, who are burgesses of the borough, under the control of the mayor for the time being. That of the resident burgesses, who have rights of common, some stock to the full of their rights, others partially, and some not at all, and that those who do not stock receive an annual payment of 19s. 4d. from those who do. In was held, upon this statement, that this is not properly a right of common; and that the corporation are the owners in fee, but not the occupiers of the land; and the burgesses who turn out stock are the occupiers, as tenants in common, who may each maintain trespass for an injury done to his occupation in common, and who are rateable for it to the poor. Rex. *v.* James Watson, Mich. 45 Geo. 3. 5 East, 480."

Ibid, note (6), add, " And see Rex. *v.* Terrott, *post* 82."

Page 82, after line 9 insert, " The true criterion, in all cases, of the occupier's liability to be rated is, whether he derives some emolument from his occupation, in a personal and private respect.

The appellant was a lieutenant-colonel in the artillery, and the premises in which he resided, and for which he was rated, were the property of the crown and part of a barrack. They were fitted up for a field-officer, under the direction of the board of ordnance, and at a considerable expence. The building consists of two stories, with four rooms on each floor, besides attics. The rooms on the ground floor are thus appropriated; one room as a store-room; another as a quarter for the adjutant, a third as an office for a commanding officer to transact the business of the regiment,

and

and the fourth as the appellant's kitchen. The whole of the first floor, and the attics, are the residence of the commanding officer of the artillery *for the time being* (which the appellant then was), together with a kitchen, wash-house, and other offices, coach-house, stable-yard, and small garden or drying-ground. The appellant resides there with his wife, family, and servants; two of the latter, a man-servant, who is one of the private soldiers of the artillery, and his wife, who is cook to the colonel, sleep in the attic, and the other female servant sleeps in one of the rooms on the first floor. The part used by the appellant is in every respect separate and distinct from the rest, there being no communication between it and any other apartment. At the time of fitting up the building, chairs, tables, fire-grates, and the usual barrack furniture, were supplied by the crown; beds, and the residue, by the appellant. The court were of opinion, that the appellant was rateable as the occupier of these premises, and confirmed a rate made upon him as such.

By Lord Ellenborough, C. J. who delivered the judgment of the court.—" The principle to be collected from all the cases on the subject is, that if the party rated have the use of the building, or other subject of the rate, as a mere servant of the crown, or any public body, or in any other respect for the mere exercise of public duty therein, and have no beneficial occupation of, or emolument resulting from it, in any personal and private respect, then he is not rateable. The property of the crown, *in the beneficial occupation of a subject*, whether he be a *civil* officer of the crown, as in Lord Bute's case (who was ranger of the new park near Richmond), and in the case of the comptroller of Chelsea Hospital, Eyre *v.* Smallpace, 2 Burr. 1059; or as a *military officer*, as in Hurdis's case, he is in each case equally rateable. For, in these cases, each of the persons rated had a degree of personal benefit and accommocommodation from the property enjoyed by him, *ultrà* the mere public uſe of the thing; and which exceſs of perſonal benefit and accommodation, *ultrà* the public uſe, may be conſidered as ſo much of ſalary and emolument annexed to the office, and enjoyed in reſpect of it by the officer for the time being. But if the uſe of, or reſidence upon the property, be either *as the ſervant* of the crown, and for public purpoſes only, as in Lord Somers's caſe, or as a mere public officer or ſervant, or of any other deſcription, ſuch as the ſuperintendant of the Philanthropic Society, Rex. *v.* Field, 5 Term Rep. 587, the truſtees of a meeting-houſe, the ſervants at St. Luke's, the maſters in chancery, in reſpect of their public offices (1); in all ſuch caſes, the parties having the immediate uſe of the property, merely for ſuch purpoſes, are not rateable, becauſe the occupation is throughout that of the public, and of which public occupation the individuals are only the means and inſtruments. It is ſaid, that if the commanding officer be rated for the degree of private accommodation he enjoys in a building of this deſcription, why not the ſoldiers in their barracks for the accommodation they enjoy there? I am not aware that private ſoldiers have any accommodations in barracks beyond what are required for the mere ordinary uſes and purpoſes of animal nature, I mean for ſleeping and eating, and the like; but if their barracks ſhould ſupply even them with any accommodation of a beneficial and valuable, and not ſtrictly of a neceſſary nature, the analogy between the two caſes would rather afford perhaps a ground for including them, under ſuch circumſtances, in the rate, than for excluding an occupier of the preſent deſcription from it. The reaſon of the thing, and the ſound and eſtabliſhed conſtruction of the ſtatute, ſubjects every perſon, who has the beneficial uſe of any local viſible property in a pariſh, to this ſpecies of public contribution. The pariſh is liable to be

(1) See Holford *v.* Copeland, 3 Boſ. and Pull. 129.

1 burthened

burthened with ſettlements of them and their children: a part of the property antecedently contributing to the poor-rate is, by being thus built upon, and appropriated to ſuch public purpoſes, effectually withdrawn from its liability to contribute, unleſs the nature and quality of the occupation thereof reſtores and throws it back again, either in the whole or in part, within the ſcope and reach of this ſpecies of parochial contribution. And the immediate occupant has, in fact, nothing to complain of; for I believe it never has occurred in experience, that the *quantum* of the mere rate upon an occupier of this kind has exceeded, in amount, the benefit and advantage derived to him from his occupation. Whether the commanding officer could withdraw himſelf from the rate, by contracting his occupation in ſome proportionable degree, within the ſame narrow limits of merely neceſſary enjoyment with the ſoldier in his barracks, will be a queſtion to be decided when it ſhall occur. It is enough for us to ſay at preſent, that upon the principles laid down and acted upon, in the caſes already referred to, the commanding officer, in queſtion, has ſuch a beneficial occupation of theſe appartments, and other conveniencies, as to render him rateable for the ſame, and that this rate of courſe ſhould ſtand, and the rule for amending the ſame be diſcharged." Rex. *v.* Terrot, 3 Eaſt, 506.

Ibid, note (2), add, "But ſee Rex. *v.* Terrot, *ante*, 82."

Ibid, note (4), add, "See alſo the opinion of Lord Ellenborough, C. J. in Rex *v.* Terrot, *ante*, 82."

Page 85, note (6), add, "*Per* Lord Ellenborough, C. J. Rex. *v.* Terrot, 3 Eaſt, 513."

Page 85, note (7), add, "*Per* Lawrence, J. Rex *v.* Aberavon, *poſt*, vol. II. 298."

Page 86, note (1), add, "Rex *v.* Watſon, 5 Eaſt, 480."

Page

Page 89, add, in a note upon line 12, "Rex *v.* Terrot, *ante*, 82."

Page 94, after line 18 insert, "Goods may likewise be carried along two lines of canal under one contract, the tolls arising from one of which are exempted by statute from being rated, while those of the other continue liable. In this case, as well as in the preceding, the tolls are only taxable at the place where the voyage terminates. If it end, therefore, at any place within the line of canal, the tolls of which are not exempt from rate, the toll arising from this carriage is taxable there, yet not upon its total amount, but for so much only as accrued within the unexempted line. For in such a case, *per* Le Blanc, J. "The tolls will be rated where they become due; but in calculating the *quantum* of toll, which is the subject of rate, allowance must be made for so much of the toll as accrued in respect of the line exempted. For instance, if two thirds of the line are exempted, then tolls (of goods), which have come along the whole line, will only be liable to be rated in the proportion of one third: so, if the goods have been carried 15 miles, five of which are not exempt, they must be rated only for those five miles; and so in proportion." Rex *v.* The Leeds and Liverpool Canal Company, 5 East, 325.

Page 95, line 20 add, "Nor for money laid out in the public funds." Rex *v.* St. John's, Maddermarket, in Norwich, *ante*, 65.

Page 125, after line 17 add, "But if the object be to commit him to prison as an offender, in default of a distress, it will be the safest way to serve it upon him in person."

Page 153, line 4, after "from her" insert, "or being unable to maintain her, consent to the removal." Rex *v.* Eltham, 5 East, 113.

Page 159, add "A marriage licence is subjected to a stamp duty of 10s. and a marriage certificate to one of 5s. by 44 Geo. 3. c. 98." But a certificate of the marriage of any common seaman, marine, or soldier, is exempted. *Ib.*

Page 176, after line 15 insert, "A fourth exception seems to be, where the child is born in a work-house belonging to parishes united, under 9 Geo. 1. c. 7. and which is situated in a third parish. Here it shall be considered as settled in the parish to which the mother belongs." See the opinion of Buller, J. Rex. *v.* St. Peter and St. Paul, Cald. 213, *post*, vol. II. 235.

Page 205, at the end, insert, "The pauper hired himself for eight weeks, at 5s. *per* week; and at the expiration of that time, for three months, at 4s. *per* week. He then entered into a new agreement with the same master, to live with him, the master finding him board and lodging, and paying him 2s. 6d. *per* week; but no time was fixed, or talked of, by the master or servant, for the duration of the contract. When the summer season arrived, the pauper said to his master, "I must have more now, I believe, master." The master said, "How much more?" and his wages were increased. And so as the winter or summer succeeded, his wages were accordingly reduced or encreased. The alterations of wages took place at the beginning of the week. He entered and left his service on the same day, being Sunday. He served in the whole five years and a quarter, and received money on account of wages; but there was no general settlement of wages till he and his master parted, at which time one took place.

He gained no settlement, for the first and second hiring were for definite periods, short of a year. No time was mentioned at the third hiring, but it was at weekly wages; and this being the only circumstance from which

which the duration of the contract was to be collected, it must be taken to be only a weekly hiring. Besides, if there were any doubt, a circumstance confirmatory of this construction is, that the servant in the middle of the year required an advance of wages, which the master acceded to without any question, and he left his master at the end of the week in the middle of the year. Rex *v.* Pucklechurch, 5 East, 382."

Page 295, note (2), add, "Declared to be a settled rule. Rex *v.* Pucklechurch, 5 East, 386."

Page 302, note (5), insert at the beginning, "Of facts happening during the coverture."

Page 303, line 2, after "rates" insert, "and omitted for the purpose of bearing testimony in that particular case." Rex *v.* Kirdford, 1 East, 559.

Page 305, note (1), add, "J. H. while on his death-bed, told his wife that she and her children would belong to, and prove their settlement in, the parish of R. *Per* Buller, J.—"No argument has been urged against receiving the declarations of the husband on his death-bed. From the awful situation in which the party speaks, such testimony is uniformly received in criminal cases, and is consequently admissible here." Rex *v.* Bury, Cald. 486. And see Wright *ex dem* Clymer *v.* Littler, 3 Burr. 1244. 1 Black. Rep. 345, S. C. But where, as in this case, the person speaks to his settlement in the abstract, his declaration includes a question of law as well as a matter of fact."

Page 312, line 14, after "old" insert, "or put out by the officers into another parish. Rex *v.* St. Nicholas, Nottingham, *post*, 213, (3)."

ADDENDA

TO

THE SECOND VOLUME.

PAGE 27, after line 20 insert, " But there muſt be an agreement to depaſture the cows upon ſome particular ground, and by that means a taking of the profits of the land. A contract to feed the cows generally, under which they might be fed with green tares bought in the market, would not be a tenement within the act. *Per Lawrence*, J. Rex *v.* Diſbury, Mich. 45 Geo. 3."

Page 76, note (1), add, " Doe *v.* Wroot, 5 Eaſt, 132. Weakley *v.* Rogers, *ibid*, *n. a.* and the caſes there cited."

Page 131, note (1), line 1, col. 2, after " 131" inſert, " Their wives and families, 43 Geo. 3. c. 47. ſect. 8."

Page 133, note (1), col. 1, line 7, after " ſo" inſert, " It is laid down in Waltham *v.* Sparks, Skinn. 566. Comb. 321. 1 Bott, 374. Pl. 432. that a father, who is by nature bound to maintain his children, being unable to do ſo, is in that reſpect impotent and chargeable to the pariſh."

Page 134, line 3 from the bottom, after " 2d" inſert, " Children of the age of nurture 3d."

Page 136, after line 11 inſert, " 2. Upon the ſame principle, children within the age of nurture cannot be removed from their parents, whether legitimate (1) or otherwiſe (2).—(1) Rex *v.* Cuckfield, Burr. S. C. 290.

 (2) Rex

(2) Rex *v.* Hemlington, Cald. 6. *Post* 228, 229, and the cases there cited."

Page 138, after line 16 insert, "As to persons made irremoveable by statute, see 44 Geo. 3. c. 47. and *ante*, 131."

Page 141, after line 2 insert, "An order of removal is usually under hand and seal. This seems necessary, as it is called "a warrant to remove," in 13 & 14 Car. 2. c. 12. & 3 W. & M. c. 11. and the better opinion seems to be that all warrants should be thus executed. 1 Hal. H. P. C. 577. 3 Hawk. book 2. chap. 13. p. 181. Ed. 7. 2 Inst. 591. Dalt. Just. Peace, chap. 169. p. 579. Ed. 1727.

It is likewise usual and proper to specify the day upon which the order is signed. But this omission does not vitiate it, unless some damage is proved to result from the neglect. An order of removal purported to be executed thus, "given under our hands and seals the day of April in the year of our Lord 1804;" upon appeal the sessions were of opinion, that the day of the date being left in blank, rendered the order defective; and that they had no power to amend it, or receive evidence of the date of the order, or of the time of the removal; and they quashed the order. But the court of King's-Bench quashed their order, and confirmed that made by the two justices. Rex *v.* Brimpton, Hil. 45 Geo. 3."

Page 142, at the end insert, "5th, Two justices cannot make an order to remove the same paupers whilst an appeal against a prior order for their removal is pending at sessions." Rex *v.* Hedingham, Sible, Burr. S. C. 112.

Page 154, note 4, col. 2, line 4, after "order" insert "or warrant."

Page

Page 154, line 5, insert "It is to be noted, however, that in 13 & 14 Car 2. c. 12. & 3 W. & M. c. 11. what is now usually called *an order of removal*, is denominated a warrant of removal."

Page 156, note (2), add, "But in Capel *v.* West Pecham, where there was a similar lapse of four years, the court said, they could intend nothing as to a new settlement, and quashed the order. Fortes, 327. 2 Sess. Cas. 81."

Page 157, line 15, after "the order" insert, "It seems to contain sufficient powers to enable the persons to whom it is directed to convey them by force, but at all events,

Page 175, after line 17, add, "One Stable quitted his place of abode in the parish of Corney, leaving his wife chargeable to the parish. The overseers applied to two justices of the peace, who made an order, which after stating that Stable had gone away and left his wife chargeable, and that he had some estate whereby to ease the parish of their charge, &c. "thereby authorized and commanded the church-wardens and overseers, &c. of Corney *to receive the annual rents and profits of the lands and tenements* of the said Stable at B. in the parishes of B. and W. in the said county, *for and towards the discharge of the said parish of Corney for the providing for the said Stable's wife*: and that with the said warrant the said church-wardens and overseers should appear at the next quarter-sessions for the county, and certify then and there what they should have done in pursuance of the said warrant." This order was confirmed at the next quarter-sessions, in pursuance of the statute; and the court did then and there order the said church-wardens and overseers, &c. to receive 7l. 16s. part of the rents and profits of the lands and tenements of Stable's at B. in the parishes of B. and W. &c. for and towards the discharge of the said parish of Corney

Corney for the providing for the wife. The tenant of the premiſes at W. made two annual payments of 7l. 16s. each to the pariſh officers of Corney, by virtue of this order, during Stable's abſence. Stable afterwards brought an action of covenant for the entire rent of the premiſes againſt the tenant, the object being to recover this ſecond yearly payment of 7l. 16s. The above facts were ſet forth by the pleadings; and the queſtion, as to the validity of theſe orders, came on by demurrer, when judgment was given for the plaintiff.

The court doubted whether the ſtatute meant to give the two juſtices power to direct what sum ſhould be taken *proſpectively* under their order. Yet ſuppoſing them to have such a power, ſtill they were to aſcertain by their order how much was to be ſo taken; for an order to levy indefinitely a ſum in diſcharge of the pariſh would be bad. But aſſuming that the original order was ſo far valid as to be the ground-work of appeal to the ſeſſions, the ſeſſions appear to have defined the ſum to be taken, and more having been paid by the defendant, viz. a farther ſum of 7l. 16s. he could not ſupport this latter payment againſt his landlord the plaintiff. For if the order, as amended by the ſeſſions, was unlimited, it was bad, [*i. e.* would juſtify neither payment;] if limited to 7l. 16s. that limited ſum had been already paid. Stable *v.* Dixon, Hil. 45 Geo. 3."

Page 239, at the end add, "But the method of relieving the families of militia men is altered by 43 Geo. 3. c. 47. for which ſee Appendix."

Page 240, note (2), add, "Atkins *v.* Banwell, 2 Eaſt, 505.

Page 277, line 17, after "adjournment" add, "as is uſual when a county is ſubdivided, and the ſeſſions adjourn from one diviſion to another."

Page

Page 370, after line 5, add "The appellant was rated "*for the farm and lands* 32l.; *for the iron and coal-mine* 70l." The iron mines not being rateable, the court of King's-Bench was pressed to send the case back to sessions to ascertain the proportion at which they had been rated with the coal-mines, and to amend the rate by deductnig it from this conjoint assessment. But the court thought, that not having any means to ascertain the several proportions at which the iron and coal-mines had been rated, they could do nothing else than quash the order of sessions, which, having confirmed the rate generally, was wrong at all events. Rex *v.* Cunningham *et al.*' 5 East, 478, and see Rex *v.* Leeds and Liverpool Canal Company. *Ante*, Addenda, xxiii.

Also, where the sessions quashed a rate, and it appeared to the court of King's-Bench, that a large tract of rateable land was not assessed therein, the order of sessions was confirmed. Rex *v.* Aberavon, 5 East. 453, *ante*, vol. II. 301. But where the sessions confirmed a rate, and the court of King's-Bench was of opinion, that certain burgesses, who occupied lands as tenants in common, had been improperly omitted; the rate (*i. e.* the order of sessions) was sent back to have the rate amended by the insertion of the burgesses occupying the land. Rex *v.* Watson, 5 East, 480."

COR-

CORRIGENDA.

VOL. I.

Page 24, line 20, *for their* read *its*.
56, — 23, after *is* insert *in*.
73, — 20, for *made* read *taxed*.
99, — 23, after *several parishes* add, *and resides in all*.
104, — 26, for *when* read *a tax*.
105, — 15, for *rents* read *receipts*.
126, — ult. insert *issue* before *one*.
127, — 2, for *it* read *the warrant*.
141, — 23, for *of* read *against*.
145, — 1, for *freehold* read *by*.
150, — 9, after *him* read *against his consent*.
151, — 2, dele *rented*.
—— — 3, for *a freehold* read *an*.
160, — 8, for *it* read *their evidence*.
166, — 6, for *nature* read *nurture*.
214, after SECT. IV. add PART I.
217, note (1), for VI. read SECT. IV. PART II.
296, last line but two, after *residences* insert *in* A.
379, line 20, for *stopped* read *estopped*.
380, — 2, after *unnecessary* insert *for the respondents*.
381, — 21, for *obligee* read *other*.
384, — 3, for *lessee* read *lessor*.

VOL. II.

Page 64, line 4, after *value* insert *is*.
207, — 8, after *settlement* insert *only*.
—— — 9, for *it* read *the order*.
—— — 15, after *contract* add *originally*.
—— — 16, for *the old contract* read *which as it could not be dissolved by the justice's adjudication still*.
211, note (6), col. 2, line 8, for *or if he* read *he may also*.
222, — ult. after *servants* add *whose masters reside under certificates*.
223, last line but three, for *resided* read *who come into and reside*.
—— last line but two, for *were* read *are*.
233, note (1), col. 1, line 3, for *no* read *but one*.
234, line 5 from the bottom, for *two* read *three*.
236, line 12, for *other* read *remaining*.
255. For SECT. IV. read SECT. VI. and correct the numerals of the subsequent sections of the chapter, by advancing the series so as to correspond with this alteration.
284. For SECT. II. read SECT. III. and correct the numerals of the subsequent sections of this chapter, by advancing the series so as to correspond with this alteration.
212, line 2 from the bottom, instead of *for* read *by*.
295, 2d marginal abstract, line 12, for *conferred* read *confirmed*.
363, insert part of note (2), beginning, *This seems*, &c. at the end of note (3), *Ibid*.
366, line 12, for *A* read *The*.

A TREA-

A TREATISE ON THE LAWS OF THE POOR, &c. &c. &c.

CHAPTER I.

Of the Manner of providing for the Poor previous to the Statute 43d Elizabeth, *cap.* 2.

THE duty of maintaining the poor is ſaid to have devolved upon the clergy for ſome ages after the introduction of chriſtianity into England. Originally a fourth, and afterwards a third of their tithes was devoted to this charitable purpoſe, and adminiſtered by the incumbent under the ſuperintendance of his biſhop (1). The churchwardens and principal inhabitants are ſuppoſed to have taken ſome ſhare in making a judicious application of this parochial fund (2). But if ſuch interference ever did take place, it was by the rector's permiſſion, for they had no power to direct the expenditure, or control the miſuſe.

(1) Kennet. Impropr. 14, 15. 1 Black. Com. 359. Burn's Hiſt. of the Poor Laws. 1, &c.

(2) 3 Burn. Tit. Poor.

The period is not aſcertained at which this portion of tithes was applied to other purpoſes. We may conjecture that it was gradually re-aſſumed, from the increaſe of monaſtic inſtitutions. The principal or rectorial tithes of many pariſhes, being appropriated to the uſe of religious orders, they undertook a ſhare of the burthen, as they retained the funds originally ſet apart for the poors' ſupport.

The legiſlature did not interfere with this appropriation of the eccleſiaſtical revenues, except in a ſolitary inſtance. In the 15 of Richard the ſecond an act paſſed, requiring, "that in every licence to be made "in the chancery of the appropriation of any pariſh "church, it ſhall be expreſſed that the dioceſan ſhall "ordain, according to the value of ſuch church, a con- "venient ſum of money to be paid and diſtributed yearly, "of the fruits and profits thereof, to the poor pariſhion- "ers, in aid of their living and ſuſtenance for ever." (1).

Until the firſt attack made upon monaſtic property at the dawn of the reformation, the clergy were permitted to deal with their revenues in other reſpects according to private diſcretion, the ſtatutes of thoſe by whom eccleſiaſtical corporations were founded or endowed, and the ſuperintending control of their ſuperiors. Several ſtatutes paſſed between theſe periods to regulate the internal œconomy of religious houſes; but they were directed to a different object. To eaſe them of oppreſſive viſits from the great, and a tributary hoſpitality exacted by the powerful, which abſorbed their revenues and uſurped the portion of charity and the dues of the indigent (2).

The alms given by theſe houſes, together with hoſpitals and other inſtitutions founded and endowed for the purpoſe, conſtituted the chief but not the ſole reſources

(1) Chap. 6. enforced by 4 Hen. IV. chap. 12.

(2) 3 Edw. I. chap. 1. 35 Edw. I. ſt. 1. c. 1. 9 Edw. II. ſtat. 1. c. 11. 5 Hen. V. c. 1.

of

of thoſe who fell back upon their fellow-creatures as unable to ſuſtain themſelves (1). The effects of perſons dying inteſtate were veſted in the ordinary, to be applied, among other pious uſes, to relieve the poor of his dioceſe; and private charity derived vigour and energy beyond the common impulſe of humanity, from the ſuperſtitious notion that prayers purchaſed by donations to the poor, contributed to the eternal happineſs of the dead.

The aged and impotent poor had no other ſources of ſupport, until the reign of Henry the VIII.; for ſince the conqueſt, neither the common nor ſtatute law made any direct proviſion for the purpoſe, unleſs permitting the poor to beg by licence can be deemed an exception.

The author of the Mirror ſtates indeed, (2) that by the common law, " the poor were to be ſuſtained by parſons, " rectors of the church, and the pariſhioners, ſo that none " of them ſhall die for default of ſuſtenance." But no method is pointed out by which the performance of this duty could be enforced, or its omiſſion puniſhed (3). Such abſtinence from regulation on the part of our civil government, is no ſlight teſtimony that the clergy devoted a ſufficient portion of their immenſe property to diſcharge their truſt (4). If any objection can be made to their conduct, it is, that their charities were laviſhed with inconſiderate humanity, detrimental to the induſtry and police of the country.

The various and highly penal laws made during this period againſt vagrants and ſturdy beggars (5), a deſcrip-

(1) Perk. ſect. 485.

(2) Mirr. c. 1. ſect. 3.

(3) 1 Black. Com. 359.

(4) A third, and ſome ſay a greater proportion of the entire property of the kingdom was veſted in the clergy at the time of the conqueſt, and in the reign of Richard II. they held a fourth. At the commencement of the reformation, the regular or monaſtic clergy are calculated to have poſſeſſed what amounted to a fifth of the revenues of the kingdom. See 2 Burn's Ecc. Law. Tit Monaſteries, and the authorities there cited.

(5) See them collected, Burn's Hiſt. of the Poor Laws. chap 3. p. 22.

tion of perſons who ſprung from and were nouriſhed in their way of life by the largeſſes of miſguided piety, gives ſome countenance to this opinion.

But a more direct proof of the fidelity with which the clergy adminiſtered the truſt repoſed in them, ariſes from obſerving, that the firſt legiſlative attempt to provide for the impotent poor, was made in the very year when the property of the religious houſes was veſted in the crown. The firſt great act of diſſolution 27 Hen. VIII. c. 28. affords a deciſive teſtimony, not only of their hoſpitality, but of their efforts to promote the induſtry of the country. It enacts, that all perſons to whom the king ſhall demiſe the ſites and demeſnes of any of the diſſolved houſes, ſhall keep an honeſt continual houſe and houſehold there; and for that purpoſe occupy yearly as much of the demeſnes in plowing and tillage of huſbandry, as the ſaid religious had done before, on pain of 6l. 13s. 4d. a month, and the juſtices in ſeſſions were to inquire thereof. This regulation continued until 21 Jac. I. when the clauſe was repealed.

The 27 Hen. VIII. c. 25. contains the firſt proviſion by which particular diſtricts are directed to ſupport their poor, ſo that none of them of very neceſſity ſhall be compelled to go openly in begging. The act was enforced by a trivial penalty of 20s. per month. Many ſchemes were propoſed and enforced by ſubſequent ſtatutes to accompliſh this object (1). They are collected in the fourth chapter of Dr. Burn's hiſtory of the poor laws, and it is ſufficient for the preſent purpoſe to point out their general tendency in the words of that reſpectable author.

" It is curious," (ſays he) (2) " to obſerve the pro-
" greſs, by what natural ſteps and advances the compul-

(1) 12 Ric. II. c. 7. 11 Hen. VII. c. 2. 19 Hen. VII. c. 12. 22 Hen. VIII. c. 12. 27 Hen. VIII. c. 25. 1 Edw. VI. c. 3. 3 & 4 Edw. VI. c. 16. 5 & 6 Edw. VI. c. 2. 1 & 2 Ph. & M. c. 5. 5 Eliz. c. 3. 14 Eliz. c. 5.

(2) Ch. 5. p. 105.

" ſory

" ſory maintenance became eſtabliſhed. Firſt, the poor " were reſtrained from begging at large, and were con- " fined to beg within certain diſtricts. Next, the ſeveral " hundreds, towns corporate, pariſhes, hamlets, or other " like diviſions, were required to ſuſtain them with ſuch " charitable and voluntary alms, as that none of them of " neceſſity might be compelled to go openly in begging. " And the churchwardens, or other ſubſtantial inhabi- " tants, were to make collections for them, with boxes " on Sundays, and otherwiſe by their diſcretions. And " the miniſter was to take all opportunities to exhort and " ſtir up the people to be liberal and bountiful. Next, " houſes were to be provided for them by the devotion " of good people, and materials to ſet them on ſuch work " as they were able to perform. Then, the miniſter, " after the goſpel every Sunday, was ſpecially to exhort " the pariſhioners to a liberal contribution. Next, the " collectors for the poor, on a certain Sunday in every " year, immediately after divine ſervice, were to take " down in writing, what every perſon was willing to " give for the enſuing year; and if any ſhould be obſti- " nate and refuſe to give, the miniſter was gently to ex- " hort him; if ſtill he refuſed, the miniſter was to cer- " tify ſuch refuſal to the biſhop of the dioceſe, and the " biſhop was to ſend for and exhort him in like manner; " if he ſtood out againſt the biſhop's exhortation; then " the biſhop was to certify the ſame to the juſtices in " ſeſſions, and bind him over to appear there: And the " juſtices, at the ſaid ſeſſions, were again gently to move " and perſuade him; and, finally, if he would not be " perſuaded, then they were to aſſeſs him what they " thought reaſonable towards the relief of the poor. And " this brought on the general aſſeſſment in the fourteenth " year of queen Elizabeth."

This ſtatute underwent ſome modifications during the government of that excellent princeſs (1). But in the 43d 43 Eliz. c. 2.

(1) 18 Eliz. c. 3. 35 Eliz. c. 4. 39 Eliz. c. 3. c. 4. c. 5. c. 21.

year of her reign (2), another act was framed upon those which had passed previously. Under this statute, with a few alterations to be noticed hereafter, the fund for setting the poor to work, and maintaining those who are unable to do so, is raised at this day.

(2) C. 2.

CHAPTER

CHAPTER II.

Of the Divisions by which the Poor are to be maintained.

THE more ancient ſtatutes were enacted to repreſs vagrancy in the poor, not to provide for their maintenance; and they refer to the civil diviſions of the kingdom into townſhips and hundreds, and not to that of pariſhes which reſpects our eccleſiaſtical inſtitutions (1). Origin of maintaining the Poor by pariſhes.

But the firſt direct mode of raiſing a fund for their relief after the ſuppreſſion of monaſteries, was by collecting alms in the church. This may be attributed to the former liberality of the clergy, and their influence upon the charitable feelings of their pariſhioners; and the conjecture is ſtrengthened by obſerving that the original means of enforcing contributions as ordained by ſtatute were by eccleſiaſtical exhortation. The manner of collecting money, neceſſarily pointed out the limits within which it ſhould be diſtributed. The 43d of Eliz. c. 2. made no alteration in this reſpect, but applied a more effectual method of raiſing the fund in pariſhes, by which the poor were ſupported when the ſtatute paſſed.

It enacted, that "the churchwardens of every pariſh, "and four, three, or two ſubſtantial houſeholders there, "as ſhall be thought meet, having reſpect to the propor-"tion and greatneſs of the ſame pariſh and pariſhes, to "be nominated yearly in Eaſter week, or within one "month after Eaſter, under the hand and ſeal of two or "more juſtices of the peace in the ſame county, whereof 42d Eliz. c. 2. ſ. 1.

(1) 12 Ric. II. c. 7. 11 Hen. VII. c. 2. c. 19. 22 Hen. VIII. c. 12.

"one to be of the quorum, dwelling in or near the ſame "pariſh or diviſion where the ſame pariſh doth lie, ſhall "be overſeers of the poor of the ſame."

Sect. 9. provided, that where any pariſh extends into more counties than one, or into different liberties the magiſtrates of which poſſeſs an excluſive juriſdiction, that each ſet of magiſtrates ſhall nominate overſeers within their reſpective juriſdictions, who are to execute the office through the entire pariſh.

Confined to pariſhes.

By this act therefore, the appointment of overſeers, and every proviſion for the management of the poor, was confined to pariſhes.

Or reputed pariſhes.

It was decided indeed, that a village having a church of its own, and being held and reputed a pariſh prior to the 43d Eliz. c. 2. and having diſtinct churchwardens, is entitled to the ſeparate government and maintenance of its poor within the meaning of the act, although it in fact conſtitutes part and parcel of a rectory (1) or pariſh (2), to the parſon of which the tithes are payable. For the ſtatute entruſts the adminiſtration of the poor to the churchwardens and overſeers; but the churchwardens of the pariſh are not in theſe inſtances churchwardens of the village; the act, therefore, muſt be ſuppoſed to refer to ſuch places as were reputed pariſhes at the time it was enacted, the churchwardens of which were to meddle with the church *there*, and by conſequence with the poor.

Dont extend to vills, not pariſhes by reputation.

But the conſtruction of the ſtatute could go no further; ſo that a vill not being a pariſh by reputation prior to 43d Elizabeth, and having no diſtinct churchwardens, but performing its parochial rites, ſuch as marriages, burials, &c. ſubſequent thereto in the pariſh

(1) 1 Hilton *v.* Pawle. Cro. Car. 92. W. Jones, 356. *p.* c. 1 Bott. 27. Pl. 48.

(2) Nicholas *v.* Walker, Cro. Car. 394. 1 Bott. 28. Pl. 49.

church,

church, was adjudged to be within the parish, although it had made poor rates since the statute, and had possessed a chapel previous to the act being passed. For making rates will not make it a parish without all other parochial rites (1).

Two inconveniences followed from the provisions of the statute, being confined to parishes :—

1. Many considerable districts in the kingdom, more especially forest and abbey lands, were not situated within any parish; and consequently their poor could reap no benefit from the act. No settlement could be gained there, no rate made, and those who became chargeable to other parishes without having acquired a settlement, could not be removed back to be there supported (2). Inconveniencies of 43d Eliz. c. 2.

2. Several parishes, especially in the northern parts of the kingdom, were of such great extent as to be unable to fulfil the purposes of the act within their extensive limits. The overseers being appointed for the whole parish, could neither inspect the wants nor the conduct of a numerous poor, spread over a district, many miles in circumference. The same circumstances threw considerable difficulty in the way of making and collecting an equal rate.

To remedy this, it was provided by 13 & 14 Car. II. c. 12. s. 21. which, after reciting, that " whereas the in- " habitants of Lancashire, Cheshire, Yorkshire, Northum- " berland, the Bishoprick of Durham, Cumberland, and " Westmorland, *and many other counties in England and* " *Wales*, by reason of the largeness of the parishes, can- " not reap the benefit of the said act of the 43d Eliz." enacts, " that all and every the poor, needy, impotent, " and lame persons, within every township or village " within the several counties aforesaid, shall be maintained, Remedied by 13 & 14 Car. 2. c. 12.

(1) Rudd *v.* Foster. 4 Mod. 157. 1 Bott. 29. Pl. 50.

(2) Dolting *v.* Stokelane. Fort, 219. Bridewell *v.* Clerkenwell. 2 Salk. 486. Dean *v.* Linton. Ib. 487.

" provided

" provided for, and set on work within the several and " respective townships and villages wherein he shall in- " habit, or wherein he was last lawfully settled; and " there shall be yearly chosen and appointed two or more " overseers, within every of the said townships or villages " respectively."

Extends to all counties.

This act, from the superadded words, " many other " counties," was held to extend throughout the kingdom, notwithstanding the particular enumeration in the preamble, and a reference to them in the enacting clause, the counties specified being considered as put by way of instances (1).

2d, To extraparochial places.

By a liberal and remedial construction of the words " every township and village," it was held to apply to extraparochial places, as well as to the subdivisions of parishes of an inconvenient magnitude (2).

But only to vills or townships.

Under the words of the statute, overseers can only be appointed for places which are either actually or by reputation a vill or township (3), or for an hamlet which is considered as synonimous in common acceptation (4). An appointment therefore of overseers " for the precinct of " the Tower, *otherwise called* the parish of St. Peter's, " *ad vincula* within his majesty's tower of London," was quashed as bad. For the name or description which precedes an " *otherwise called*," is to be considered as the true one, and not the name and description which follows it;

(1) Dolting *v.* Stokelane. Fort. 219. Rex *v.* Justices of Middlesex. 1 Bot. 34. Pl. 56. Clifton *v.* Churcham. Andr. 314. But the contrary has been decided so early as 27 Car. II. in Skillington *v.* Norton. 2 Lev. 142.

(2) Dolting *v.* Stokelane. Fort. 219. 1 Bott. 30. Pl. 51. Rex *v.* Rufford. 1 Str. 512. 1 Bott. 31. Pl. 52.

(3) Rex *v.* Justices of Bedfordshire. Cald. 167. 1 Bot. 44. Pl. 63. Rex *v.* Showler & Atter. 3 Burr. 1391. 1 Bott. 36. Pl. 58. and several other cases. But Liddleston *v.* Mayor of Exeter. 1 Bott. 75. Pl. 20. Foley 19. seems contra.

(4) Rex *v.* Morris. 4 Term Rep. 550. But see the opinion of Probyn J. Rex *v.* Welbeck. 1 Bott. 34. Pl. 55.

and

and the court ought not to intend that it is a townſhip or vill, in order to make an appointment good that is not warranted by the ſtatute (1). So an order of removal to " a certain extraparochial place called Brewcomb's " Lodge," is bad, for the court cannot intend it to be a vill (2).

What is a township? If there is a conſtable.

Some queſtions have ariſen as to what is a townſhip or vill within the meaning of the act. Mr. J. Buller ſtates one criterion to be, " that where there is a conſtable " there is a townſhip; for there may be a conſtable for a " larger diſtrict, but not for a ſmaller, and that the doubt " in many of the caſes has ariſen where there was no " conſtable (3)." Mr. J. Lee expreſſed a ſimilar opinion in a former caſe (4). But earlier caſes ſtate, that in order to render an extraparochial place ſubject to the poor laws, it muſt conſiſt of more than two houſes (5).

The number of houſes.

For the definition of a vill or townſhip, is a place conſiſting of many manſions and many neighbours, or according to Lee J. it corresponds to the legal notion of a tithing (6). The judges in forming this opinion, ſeem to have regarded the ſtate of the place at the time when overſeers are to be appointed, as the material circumſtance, inſtead of its ancient condition, and they aſſign as a reaſon why there muſt be more than two houſeholders to bring the place within the act, that otherwiſe the ſame perſons would be overſeers for life (7).

(1) Rex *v.* Severn and Arnold. Say. 278. 1 Bott. 35. Pl. 57. But ſee Liddleſton *v.* Mayor of Exeter, *ut ſupra.*

(2) Dolting *v.* Stokelane. *ut ſupra.*

(3) Rex *v.* Sir Watts Horton. 1 Term Rep. 374. 1 Bot. 50. Pl. 66.

(4) Rex *v.* Denham. Bur. ſet. ca. 35. 1 Bott. 32. Pl. 53.

(5) Per Lord Hardwicke C. J. Ib.

(6) Ib.

(7) Dolting *v.* Stokelane. Fol. 98. 1 Bott. 32. *notis.* Rex *v.* Denham. Burr. ſet. ca. 35. 1 Bott. 32. Pl. 53. Mr J. Page ſtates his opinion in this latter caſe, " that a " ſingle houſe or two houſes cannot " amount to the notion of a townſhip " or village. If it had been formerly " a town, and the houſes were in " fact decayed and gone, it would " ceaſe to be a town or village."

But

But the court in more recent determinations seem to consider the ancient condition of the place as that to which the act meant to refer and overrule the former opinion (1).

Townships, &c how proved.

Towns and vills, are ancient divisions of the country, which may be proved by different sorts of evidence, like any other facts. The true point being, whether the place in question has been treated, as a vill or township, or at least reputed to be so? If a place has a constable, it is decisive evidence that it was so considered from time immemorial. But it is not the sole proof, because the appointment of a constable is not essentially incident to the existence of a township. The number of houses, or rather of families, may have been the original reason for giving this denomination to a particular place. But though the fact may be used as a ground from which the existence of a township may be inferred, it is not equally decisive with the appointment of a constable, for the number of houses may have increased or diminished from accidental circumstances long after the division had taken place. Therefore a place may be deemed a vill, though consisting of only two houses (2), or adjudged not to be so, although it comprehends many mansions (3).

Determinations.

Thus an extraparochial manor, once consisting of a capital mansion and three keepers lodges in the park; the park being since converted into farms, of which there are five; each having a dwelling-house in the occupation of five different tenants, was held not to be a vill, never having been reputed as such, or having had an

(1) Rex *v.* Eyeford. 1 Bott. 490. pl. 65. Rex *v.* Ronton Abbey. 2 Term Rep. 207 1 Bott. 53. P. 67. Rex *v.* Stubbs 2 Term Rep. 406.

(2) *Ut supra.* n. 1.

(3) Rex *v.* Justices of Peterborough. Cald. 238. 1 Bott. 46. Pl. 64.

overseer

overſeer (1). In adherence to the ſame rules, an hamlet, conſiſting of one houſe and three or four hundred acres of land (2); an extraparochial place, conſiſting of two houſes and three hundred acres of land, belonging to and in the occupation of ſeveral perſons (3); one conſiſting of a farm, and capital meſſuage, inhabited by the tenant of the whole, with three cottages under let by him to his labourers (4); a capital manſion houſe and large farm houſe thereto belonging, of the value of 200l. per year, with three other farm houſes and farms belonging to each, worth together 500l. a year, and containing within it four ſubſtantial houſeholders, but being extraparochial, and never reputed a vill, nor having a conſtable belonging to it (5). The ſites and areas of ancient cathedrals and colleges—inns of court, though conſiſting of many tenements (6), never having appointed overſeers, nor been reputed townſhips, do not come within the operation of the poor law.

Townſhips, &c. how erected into independent diſtricts.

To erect a vill into an independent diſtrict, which ſhall maintain its own poor, nothing is required but the appointment of overſeers. This may be done in the firſt inſtance by two magiſtrates, in the ſame manner as they are appointed for diſtricts which have ſuſtained their poor ſince the paſſing of the ſtatute. Where a vill or townſhip is extraparochial, it is a matter of courſe (7). But the appointment muſt expreſsly call it a townſhip or vill, or the court will not intend that it is ſo (8).

When extraparochial places.

(1) Rex *v.* Grafton. Bur. ſet. ca. 101. 1 Bott. 33 Pl. 54. This caſe was decided without argument, and is ſo referred to by Lee C. J. Rex *v.* Welbeck. 1 Bott. 33. Pl. 55. But it is cited as law by Aſton J. Rex *v.* Tamworth. Cald. 28. 1 Bott. 40. Pl. 61.

(2) Rex *v.* Tamworth. Cald. 28. 1 Bott. 40. Pl. 61.

(3) Rex *v.* Denham. Burr. ſet. ca. 35. 1 Bott. 32. Pl. 50.

(4) Rex *v.* Showler & al. 3 Burr. 1391. 1 Bott. 36. Pl. 58.

(5) Rex *v.* Juſtices of Bedfordſhire. Cald. 167. 1 Bott. 44. Pl. 63.

(6) Rex *v.* Juſtices of Peterborough. Cald. 238. 1 Bott. 46. Pl. 64.

(7) Rex *v.* Ronton Abbey. 2 Term Rep. 207.

(8) Rex *v.* Severn and Arnold. Say. 278. 1 Bott. 35. Pl. 57. But ſee Dolting *v.* Stokelane. Fort. 213. Fol. 58. 1 Bott. 30. Pl. 51. 52 n.

But

To divide a parish.

But to divide a parish into districts, two things are necessary: 1st, It should consist of two or more vills or townships, such as have been described. 2d, It must appear that the parish cannot otherwise conveniently enjoy the benefit of the 43d Eliz. c. 2. (1).

For where a parish had two overseers appointed for the whole parish, and but one rate; each overseer collected and payed within his own division; at the end of the year if there was a surplus in the hands of either, so much was paid over to the other as to make both equal; and there was but one workhouse which the overseers looked over by turns weekly. The court refused a *mandamus* to appoint separate overseers for a township, constituting part of the parish. For what is stated shews that the parish can do very well under 43 Eliz. c. 2. without resorting to 13 and 14 Car. II. c. 12. "To bring it within the latter statute, "they must shew it to be a distinct vill; we expected "they would have shewn that they had separate overseers, "had maintained their poor separately, and had a separate "rate."(2)

Inability as a parish must appear.

This inability is a fact which should be distinctly stated, and may be ascertained by various circumstances, of which the customary appointment of more than four overseers is a material ingredient though not a decisive criterion (3).

Doubts as to policy of 13 and 14 Car. 2. c. 12.

In some cases the court expressed an opinion that the policy of 13 and 14 Car. II. c. 12. was mistaken, and that the divisions ought rather to be enlarged than diminished.

Inability when not sufficiently shewn.

Thus where it was found by a special verdict, that the parish of Stanhope in the county of Durham, being 26 miles long and 8 broad, maintained its own poor jointly, and had one joint appointment of four overseers, which,

(1) Per Lord Mansfield. Peart *v.* Westgarth. 3 Burr. 1610. 1 Bott. 37. Pl. 59. Rex *v.* Uttoxeter. Doug 246 Cald. 84. S. C. 1 Bott. 41. Pl. 62. Per Grose J. Rex *v.* Newell. 4 Term Rep. 266. 1 Bott. 58. Pl. 69.

(2) Rex *v.* Justices of Middlesex. 1 Bott. 34. Pl 56.

(3) Per Buller J. Rex *v.* Sir Watts Horton. 1 Term Rep. 374. 1 Bott. 50. Pl. 66. Per Lord Kenyon, C. J. Rex *v.* Newell, 4 Term Rep. 266. 1 Bott 58 Pl. 69.

with

with the four churchwardens, (one of each being respectively nominated out of each of four quarters or districts into which the parish was subdivided,) collected the poor rates in the districts where they severally resided but under one entire assessment for the whole parish, and carrying it to one general fund for the joint relief of all the poor. This practice continued from 43 Eliz. until the midsummer quarter sessions for the county, 9 Geo. I. when the sessions ordered upon motion, that "the four "several townships or constableries within the parish "should separately maintain their own proper poor." Since which time each district had overseers separately appointed, and separately maintained its poor; and orders of removal were made from one quarter to another, and appeals heard and decided thereon. But about 12 years before the present question arose, two townships or constableries separated themselves from one of the four into which the parish had been divided by this order, and of which they had previously constituted component parts. The question was, whether the several places or districts were one entire parish, or whether being divided into six separate constableries, they constituted four distinct and separate townships or villages, within the meaning of 13 and 14 Car. II. c. 12. The court were of opinion after two arguments, that to subdivide a parish it should appear that there was an inability in the parish to have the benefit of the act of 43 Elizabeth; that no such inability appeared, but quite the contrary for a great number of years, so that there is no foundation for the division: that the acquiescence under the division by the order of sessions, was upon a false notion that the sessions had power to make it, which they had not; for it was a mere nullity, not being made upon appeal, but upon a motion on behalf of one of the quarters and opposed by the other; and there is no inconvenience in setting right this wrong usage which had obtained for 40 years, but cannot vary the right (1).

(1) Peart v. Westgarth. 3 Burr. 1610. 1 Bott. 37. and see Rex v. Beeding. Cald. 90.

So

Inability not shewn.

So where a parish five miles in length and five in breadth, contained five townships, Uttoxeter, Crakemarsh, Creighton, Stramshall and Loxley, which jointly maintained their poor until 1730. From 1643 to 1703 two overseers were elected for Uttoxeter, one for Loxley, one for Crakemarsh, Creighton and Stramshall, and one for Woodlands, which is part of the township of Uttoxeter. From 1703 to 1737 only, two were elected for the parish. In 1733 a *mandamus* issued, directing the appointment of two or more overseers for the parish; and in 1734 two overseers were appointed by separate appointments for each township. These appointments were removed the next term by *certiorari* and affirmed, no opposition being made; since when separate overseers had been appointed for each township, and they had separately maintained their poor. An appointment of distinct overseers for these townships was confirmed at sessions, subject to a case, which stated these facts. Being removed into the king's bench, the court quashed the order of confirmation. For the confirmation of the appointments in 1734 was of no authority, the question not having been raised, and the inability to receive the benefit of the act must appear, which is not here shewn (1).

A parish consisted of two separate districts, each of which had always made a separate rate in a stipulated proportion, but blended the expence when incurred in one integral sum, the overseers for each, after relieving their own poor, accounting with the other reciprocally for any surplus or deficiency in the proportion of the rate. They had for 150 years distinct overseers, and more than four in number, and each had a constable of its own; yet it not being found in the case stated for the opinion of the court that the parish could not enjoy the benefit of the statute, the court of king's bench confirmed a rate made for the whole parish (2).

(1) Rex *v.* Uttoxeter. Doug. 246. 1 Bott. 41. Pl. 62.

(2) Rex *v.* Newell. 4 Term Rep. 266. 1 Bott. 58. Pl. 69.

Recent

It appears from these cases, that a recent separation between the component townships of a parish, is not so convincing a proof of its inability to reap the benefit of the statute, as the antecedent maintenance of its poor as a parish before and after the 13 and 14 Car. II. c. 12. is, that it may still continue to do so without having recourse to the latter act.

To enable the townships of a parish, therefore, to separate from each other, where it appears that the parish has had the benefit of the 43 Elizabeth, it must be shewn, that from an increase of population, or some other cause, it is impossible that they can continue to reap the benefit of that statute (1).

But a long separation of distinct vills, and their being in the habit of managing and supporting their poor exclusive and independent of each other by distinct officers, and by a separate rate is the best and most decisive evidence of the necessity of recourse to the 13 and 14 Car. 2. c. 12.

Thus where a township for 60 or 70 years *(and before for any thing that appeared to the contrary)* had separate overseers, a separate constable, and separately maintained its own poor, and in one case a pauper was removed from the parish to the township without an appeal, the court affirmed an order of sessions quashing a rate made for the entire parish (2).

Recent opinion as to policy. 13 and 14 2 Car. 2. c. 1, 2.

The judges in a recent case intimated, that notwithstanding what had been laid down in Peart *v.* Westgarth (3), that the 13 and 14 Car. 2. proceeded upon an erroneous policy, it was their opinion that the poor were better maintained in small districts, where officers are more attentive to their duty than in large ones (4).

(1) Per Ashurst J. Rex *v.* Leigh. 3 Term Rep. 746. 1 Bott. 55. Pl. 68.

(2) Rex *v.* Leigh. 3 Term Rep. 746. 1 Bott. 55. Pl. 68.

(3) *Ante* 14.

(4) Rex *v.* Leigh. Ib.

Pariſhes may be ſtill ſubdivided.

They remarked alſo in furtherance of this principle, that wherever pariſhes come within the reaſon of 13 and 14 Car. 2. they may be ſtill ſubdivided without regard to their former ability to reap the benefit of the 43 Eliz. except ſo far as it may affect the proof of their preſent inability, in the manner already ſtated. Or as it is expreſſed by Mr. J. Buller, "Though it ſhould appear that "a pariſh had enjoyed the benefit of the 43 of Eliz. yet "if they could not now conveniently maintain their own "poor jointly, we would permit them to divide themſelves "if it contains ſuch legal diviſions as will admit of it."(1)

And where a pariſh conſiſts of ſeveral townſhips, ſome of which are actually ſeparated, and have diſtinct overſeers under 13 and 14 Car. 2. the court will conſider the remainder as entitled to have diſtinct officers appointed, whenever they think proper to apply (2).

But the court won't diſturb the diviſion when made.

But on the other hand, the court will not diſturb the ancient ſeparation of pariſhes into townſhips, although a reunion might enable the pariſh to ſupport its poor with more convenience. Lord Kenyon ſtating that "the "queſtion is, whether at the time of paſſing the ſtatute "of Charles the 2d, the diſtrict was in a ſituation to "receive the benefit of the 43 Eliz. c. 2.; for if the "pariſh were properly divided at that time, nothing which "has happened ſince will induce the court to make any "innovation;" and Mr. J. Buller obſerving, "that though "it was found that it was formerly inconvenient to the "pariſh at large to maintain their own poor, and though "it was convenient to do ſo now, yet they would not "aſſiſt in overturning the old practice, which might "operate to the diſcouragement of individuals in reducing "the poor rates in ſmall diſtricts." (3)

(1) Rex *v.* Leigh. Ib.

(2) Rex *v.* Sir Watts Horton. 1 Term Rep. 374. 1 Bott. Pl. 66.

(3) Rex *v.* Leigh. 3 Term Rep. 746. 1 Bott. 55. Pl. 68.

When

When a pariſh has been thus ſubdivided, the ſeparate diviſions are to be conſidered with reſpect to the poor laws as ſeparate pariſhes (1).

Effect of the diviſion.

Where overſeers are appointed improperly, either for an extraparochial place not being a vill; or for a vill conſtituting part of a pariſh, when it ſhould be for the whole; or when there is one appointment for the entire pariſh, inſtead of ſeveral for the component townſhips; ſuch perſons as are aggrieved may diſcuſs the validity of the order in ſeveral ways.

Remedies for not, or for improperly appointing overſeers under 13 & 14 Car. II. c. 12.

Thoſe who wiſh to *annul* it, may bring the point *directly* forward.

1, *By Appeal* to the quarter ſeſſions, for the juſtices in ſeſſions have an appellant (2), but no original juriſdiction in appointing overſeers (3). If the magiſtrates entertain any doubts upon the legality of the appointment, they ſhould ſtate the facts in a caſe, and make their order ſubject to the opinion of the ſuperior court thereupon. But if the doubt be whether the place for which the appointment is made, be a *vill or townſhip*, the ſeſſions muſt not adjudge it to be a *vill* even *by reputation*. For the court will hold themſelves concluded by that finding, and will not exerciſe any judgment whether the ſeſſions have rightly deduced the fact, from the circumſtances ſet forth in the caſe (4).

1. Appeal, againſt the appointment.

2d, By removing the order of appointment into the court of King's Bench by writ of *certiorari*; when the court will quaſh it not only for ſuch defects as appear on

2 Removal, by *certiorari*.

(1) Rex *v.* Kirkby Stephen. Burr. S. C. 664 1 Bott. 40. Pl 60.

(2) Rex *v.* Morris 4 Term Rep. 550. 1 Bott. 63 Pl. 70.

(3) Peart *v* Weſtgarth. 3 Burr. 1610. 1 Bott. 37. Pl. 59. Chilmerton & Flagg. 1 Seſſ Caſ. 260. Fol 7. 1 Bott. 13. Pl 30

(4) Rex *v.* Eyford. Cald. 542. 1 Bott. 49. Pl. 65. Rex *v.* Renton Abbey. 2 Term Rep. 207. 1 Bott. 53. Pl. 67.

the face of the order (1), but upon a sufficient statement of facts disclosed by affidavit (2).

But the court will not quash such an order after the year for which it was made has expired (3).

3. Mandamus.

3d, By motion for a writ of *mandamus*, to be directed to two neighbouring justices, commanding them to appoint overseers for a district different from that for which the existing appointment is made, *viz.* for a township within the parish, where overseers are appointed for the entire parish (4), or the reverse, where the appointment is reversed. For wherever justices refuse to appoint overseers for a place which ought to have them, the proper remedy is by *mandamus* commanding them to do so, and if the case fall within the 13 and 14 Car. 2. a *mandamus* is a writ of right, and the court must grant it (5).

This motion should be founded on affidavit making out a proper case to call for such an extraordinary interposition by the court, and must state an application to the justices to whom the writ is to be directed, and a refusal by them to make the order; for it is not to be presumed that compulsory means are necessary to oblige magistrates to do their duty.

The Court in granting or refusing this rule on the merits, must determine whether one appointment should be made for the entire parish, or whether there should be distinct overseers for the several vills which are compre-

(1) "Quashing an appointment "where the fault does not appear "on the face of it, is *ex debito justitiæ*. But where the fault does "appear on the face of the appointment, then the party has another "remedy by action, and quashing is "not *ex debito justitiæ*." Per Cur. Rex *v.* Butler. 1 Bott. 13. Pl. 31.

(2) Rex *v.* Great Marlow. 2 East. 244. and the cases there cited. Post 32.

(3) Rex *v.* Butler. 1 Black. Rep. 632. 1 Bott. 1 Pl. 3. 31. S. C.

(4) Rex *v.* Justices of Middlesex. 1 Bott. 34. Pl. 56. Rex *v.* Sir Watts Horton. 1 Term Rep. 374. 1 Bott. 50. Pl. 66. But this proceeding dont apply to improper appointments for extraparochial places

(5) Per Curiam, *supra* note (4).

hended

hended within it. And where the material facts are sufficiently manifest from the affidavits, they will at once pronounce their judgment on the rule; but if there is any doubt or contradiction respecting them, the Court will, by consent of parties, direct the question to be tried in a feigned issue (1).

When the *mandamus* is ordered to go, it must be served on the magistrates to whom it is directed, and they may either return that they have appointed overseers as they were commanded, or else set forth those facts upon which they submit to the Court that they cannot lawfully obey the writ. If they adopt the latter method, and state in their return a sufficient ground of defence for non-obedience, the Court interferes no farther, however false that return may be. Yet if it be untrue, the party aggrieved is not without remedy. He may have an action for a false return against those who made it, in which the truth or falsehood of what is alleged, will be controverted before a jury, and if found to be false by the jury, he shall recover damages equivalent to the injuries sustained, and shall have a peremptory *mandamus* to the defendants to do their duty (2).

Those who wish to *enforce* the appointment, may do so;

4th, By prefering *an indictment* against the party who is appointed and refuses to take the office upon him. When this indictment is tried, if any difficulty should arise in point of law, the jury will under the judges direction find a special case or verdict, for the opinion of the superior court (3); or if the defendant is found guilty by the judges direction, the law permits that the propriety of his opinion should be discussed before the court in a motion for a new trial, upon the facts which appear from the judges' report of the evidence (4).

4. Indictment.

(1) Peart *v.* Westgarth *ut supra.* Rex *v.* Justices of Gloucester, cited Hooper *v.* Carr. 7 Term Rep. 270. 1 Bott. 257. Pl. 243.

(2) 3 Black. Com. 111.

(3) Peart *v.* Westgarth. 3 Burr. 1610.

(4) Rex *v.* Wa ner. 8 Term Rep. 375. 1 Bott. 707. Pl. 699. They may first remove the order into K. B., and have it confirmed. Post. 32.

It

It may be brought *collaterally* into question;

5. Appeal against a removal. 5th, By *an appeal* against an order of removal; for the district that removes a pauper must take care that the place to which it sends him maintains its own poor (1), and that a settlement is to be gained there (2).

6. Against the rate. 6th, *By Appeal* against the poors' rate. For it is a good ground of appeal, that the poors rate is made for part of the parish, when it should have been made for the whole; or *e converso* for the whole, when it should only include a township (3); and the objection is equally fatal, that it is made for a extraparochial place for which none ought to be made.

7. Action. 7th, By action of trespass(4) or replevin (5), where the rate is attempted to be enforced by distress; for the rate being made for an improper district, is altogether void, and consequently the distress is illegal, being taken without due authority.

(1) Dolting *v.* Stokelane. Fort. 219.

(2) Rex *v.* Denham Burr. S. C. 35. 1 Bott. 32 Pl. 53. Rex *v.* Tamworth. Cald. 28. 1 Bott. 40. Pl. 61.

(3) Rex *v.* Leigh. 3 Term Rep. 746. 1 Bott. 55. Pl. 68. Rex *v.* Newell. 4 Term Rep. 266. 1 Bott. 58. Pl. 69.

(4) Hilton *v.* Pawle, Cro. Car. 92. 1 Bott. 27. Pl. 48.

(5) Rudd *v.* Foster. 4 Mod. 157. 1 Bott. 29. Pl. 50. Lord Bute *v.* Grindall. 1 Term Rep. 338. 2 H. Black. 267.

CHAPTER III.

Of appointing Overſeers, and their Duties.

THE appointment of overſeers for pariſhes (1) or townſhips (2), is to be made in counties by two or more juſtices of the peace. By whom appointed in pariſhes and vills.

In towns and places corporate and cities, it is to be executed by the mayors, bailiffs and other head officers, being juſtice or juſtices of peace, and no other juſtices of peace, to enter or meddle there (3). But it cannot be made by the head officer alone if there are other corporate juſtices, the ſignature of two magiſtrates being neceſſary in that caſe, as well as in counties. For the ſtatute only meant to give juſtices, in corporations and head officers where there are no juſtices, the ſame power as juſtices in counties; in ſeſſions (where there are juſtices) as well as out of it (4). In places corporate.

But an alderman of London has this power expreſsly by the ſtatute (5). In London.

When a pariſh extends into more counties than one, or part lies within the limits of any city, town, or place corporate, the juſtices of the county and head officers of the city, ſhall within their ſeveral limits, wards and juriſdictions, execute the ordinances reſpecting overſeers; but the churchwardens or overſeers, or the moſt part of them of the ſaid pariſhes, ſhall, without dividing themſelves, execute their office in all places within the ſaid pariſh (6). In pariſhes extending into more counties than one.

(1) 43 Eliz. c. 2. ſ. 1.
(2) 13 & 14 Car. II. c. 12. ſ. 21.
(3) 43 Eliz. c. 2. ſ. 8.
(4) Rex v. Butler. 1 Black. 649. 2 Bott. 13. Pl. 31.
(5) 43 Eliz. c. 2. ſ. 8.
(6) Ibid. ſ. 9. Ante, p. 8.

This

When to be appointed.

This appointment is to be made yearly, in Easter week, or within one month after Easter (1); and if neglected, the justices dwelling within the division, and every mayor, alderman and head officer, of city, town, or place corporate, where the default shall happen, is to forfeit 5l. for every such default, to the relief of the poor, to be levied by the parish officers by distress, under a warrant from the quarter sessions (2).

5l. penalty for default.

But subsequent appointment good.

But the statute is only directory, in commanding the justices to appoint within the month, and imposing the penalty on those who neglect it. The court of king's bench will not quash an appointment because subsequently made. For the act has no negative words restricting the power to a month after Easter, and should be construed so as to destroy the mischief and advance the remedy which was to have proper officers set over the poor. But if a subsequent appointment was to be void, it would subject the parish to the inconvenience of wanting overseers, by default of the justices, which it was not in their power to prevent (3).

Mandamus to compel an appointment after the month.

After the month is expired, and no officer appointed, the court upon application will grant a *mandamus* to compel the magistrates to make one.

Where an overseer dies, or removes power to appoint another.

If an overseer dies, or removes from the place for which he is appointed, or becomes insolvent, two justices may, on oath thereof, appoint another in his stead to continue till new ones are appointed (4).

This power discretionary in the justices.

The appointment of fit persons for the discharge of this office, is a discretionary power vested in the justices, who are to select such householders as they think most proper, having respect to the circumstances of the place and condition of the individual (5). To enable them to make a fit selection, it is usual for the existing

(1) 43 Eliz. c. 2. f. 1.
(2) Ibid. f. 10.
(3) Rex *v.* Sparrow. 1 Bott. 21. Pl. 39. 2 Str. 1123.
(4) 17 Geo. II. c. 38. f. 3.
(5) Rex *v.* Chardstock. 16 Vin. Abr. 415. Rex *v.* Stubbs. 2 Term Rep. 395. 1 Bott. 10. Pl. 21. Rex *v.* Forrest. 3 Term Rep. 38. 1 Bott. 14. Pl. 32.

overseers,

overseers, some time before the expiration of their year, to form a list of a sufficient number of substantial householders within the parish, proper to succeed to the office. Where this is not done voluntarily, the justices generally issue a precept to the high constable of the division, or constablewick, commanding him to issue his warrant to the petty constables of those places in which it has been omitted, requiring them to give the overseers notice, that they shall forthwith deliver the same (1).

Number of overseers.

The 43 Eliz. directs that the overseers for parishes "are to be four, three, or two substantial householders, having respect to the proportion and greatness of the parish," (2) and 13 & 14 Car. 2., that there shall be "two or more for townships or villages;" (3). More than four (4), and less than two (5), can not be appointed. For the number descending in the act of Elizabeth, shews that it was the intent of the legislature, to prevent the appointment of a greater number to a burthensome office, not likely to be better executed by many than by few. This construction is strengthened by reference to sect. 18. which empowers the justices to appoint such a number of overseers for the island of Fowlness, as the exigence of the place shall require (6).

Appointment of five.

An appointment therefore of five overseers is void for the whole, for being entire and relating to all equally, none of those chosen are entitled to preference, and it must be good or void altogether (7).

Appointment of one overseer.

But though there must be more than one overseer, yet an appointment of one is not bad on the face of it, or unless

(1) See 3 Burn's Justice. Tit. Poor (overseers).

(2) 43 Eliz. c. 2. s. 1.

(3) 13 & 14 Car. II. c. 12. s. 21.

(4) Rex *v*. Harman. 1 Bott. 16. Pl. 33. Rex *v*. Loxdale. 1 Burr. 445. 1 Bott. 18. Pl. 35.

(5) Per Lord Hardwicke, C. J. Rex *v*. Denham. Burr. S. C. 35. 1 Bott. 32. Pl. 53. Per Lord Kenyon, C. J. Rex *v*. Morris. 4 Term Rep. 550. 1 Bott. 20. Pl. 36. Decided Rex *v*. Clifton. 2 East. 168. But doubted by Lord Mansfield, Rex *v*. Eyford. 1 Bott. 49. Pl. 65. Cald. 542.

(6) Ut in n. (4).

(7) Ut in n. (4). Rex *v*. Wymondham. 6 Term Rep. 552. and the opinion of Lawrence J. Rex *v*. Clifton. 2 East. 175.

unless it appears that no other is appointed by some other order (1); for there is no law which says that there shall be an appointment of two or more overseers *uno flatu*, or at the same time (2), much less by one and the same instrument (3).

Their condition. Substantial householders.

They are to be substantial householders. But the word *substantial* is a relative term. The appointment therefore in an extraparochial place of Mrs. Stubbs, who occupied the greatest part of the land there, and of one Miles, who occupied a small house which he rented, with something more than an acre of land, he *being poor and a servant* to Mrs. Stubbs; together with one Keeling, who *was a labourer and poor*, but the house in which he lived being his own property, was held a good appointment of substantial householders to serve the office, there being no other persons in the township. "If there were a great many opu-" lent farmers, the appointment of a day-labourer might " be improper; but being both householders, and no other " persons to serve, no better can be had than the place af-" fords, and the want of them is no reason why the poor " should not be provided for (4)."

A woman may be appointed.

It was also held in the same case, that a woman was not incompetent to the office by reason of her sex, and that her appointment was good from necessity, where there was not a sufficient number of male householders to execute it. But where there are a sufficient number of men qualified to serve, they are more proper, and the justices being vested with a discretionary power of approbation, are not likely to approve of a female appointment where there are other proper objects (5).

Who are exempt from the office by common law.

Some persons are exempted from the burthen of this office by their necessary attendance on other public duties: such as practising barristers (6) and attornies (7). A clergyman,

(1) See Rex *v.* Clifton, *ut supra.*

(2) Per Denison J. Rex *v.* Besland. 1 Bott. 17. Pl. 34.

(3) Rex *v* Morris. 4 Term Rep. 550. 1 Bott. 20. Pl. 36.

(4) Rex *v.* Stubbs. 2 Term Rep. 395. 1 Bott. 10. Pl. 21.

(5) Ibid. Rex *v.* Chardstock. 16 Vin. Abr. 415.

(6) Pordage's Case. 1 Mod. 22.

(7) Rex *v.* Prowse. Cro. Car. 389. 1 Bott. 8. Pl. 16.

man, though he has no cure of ſouls (1); an officer of the cuſtoms, though he have not his writ of privilege at the time of his appointment (2); and all revenue officers, as officers of the exchequer (3).

It is alſo ſaid that occaſional reſidents in the pariſh, if not abſolutely inelegible, are at leaſt improper to be choſen (4). It has been made a queſtion likewiſe, whether an acting juſtice of the county who was alſo a lieutenant of marines on half-pay, is exempt. The Court gave no decided opinion on the point, but ſeemed to conſider the ſituation as a good ground for ſelecting ſome more eligible perſon, and that it did not amount to an exemption (5).

Some perſons are exempted by ſtatute, ſuch as the Preſident, Commons, and Fellows, of the College of Phyſicians within the city of London (6). Freemen of the company and corporation of Surgeons in London, who are examined and approved; while they exerciſe the art (7). Apothecaries exerciſing the art within the city of London, and ſeven miles thereof, if free of the apothecaries company; and thoſe who uſe and exerciſe it elſewhere, if they have ſerved ſeven years apprenticeſhip (8). Thoſe who apprehend perſons guilty of burglary, or privately ſtealing to the value of five ſhillings in a ſhop, warehouſe, coach-houſe or ſtable, and proſecute to conviction, ſhall have a certificate, which ſhall diſcharge them or their reſpective aſſignees from all pariſh and ward offices in the pariſh where the felony is committed (9). By ſtatute.

(1) Per 3 Juſt. but Holt. C. J. contra, Anon. 6 Mod. 140. 1 Bott. 8. Pl. 18.

(2) Rex *v.* Warner. 8 Term Rep. 375. 1 Bott. 707. Pl. 999.

(3) Raymond *v.* Botolph's, Aldgate. 2 Chan. Rep. 196. Cawthorne *v.* Campbell and others. 1 Anſtr. 205. 216.

(4) Rex *v.* Moor. Carth. 161. 1 Bott. 9. Pl. 19. 3 Com. Dig. Tit. Juſtices of the Peace. (B. 64).

(5) Rex *v.* Gayer. 1 Burr. 245. 1 Bott. 9. Pl. 20 Poſt. 30.

(6) 32 Hen. VIII. c. 40.

(7) 18 Geo. II. c. 15. ſ. 10.

(8) 6 & 7 W. III. c. 4.

(9) 10 & 11 W. 3. c. 4.

Serjeants,

Serjeants, corporals, drummers, and privates, in the militia, from the time of their enrollment till their regular discharge (1), are excused from serving as overseers; as are dissenting ministers taking the oaths, and subscribing the declaration and articles of the church of England required by the toleration act (2). But other dissenters who are appointed and scruple to take the office upon them, have no further privilege than that of serving by deputy, provided the said deputy is allowed and approved of by such person and persons, in such manner as the principal should by law have been allowed or appointed (3).

Form of the appointment, should name their "Overseers."

As to the form of the order of appointment, it must be under hand and seal, and therefore in writing (4). It should pursue the words of the act, and appoint the persons named "overseers" *eo nomine*. An order, setting forth that such persons by name "were appointed to set the "poor to work, &c." mentioning the several duties imposed by the act, but not appointing them *overseers* in express terms, was quashed for this defect (5). It must also state them to be "substantial householders;" and no other description seems equivalent; for where an order described them as "*principal inhabitants*," it was held bad (6). It must further express, that they are "substantial house-"holders there, or in the parish (7); and that the appoint-"ment is for a parish (8) or township, or what is syno-"nymous, an hamlet (9), as the case may be." The order must likewise set forth, that the district for which it is made is within the county or corporate place over which the magistrates who make it possess jurisdiction (10).

"Substantial householders."

"In the parish, and for it, &c."

(1) 26 Geo. 2. c. 107. s. 130.

(2) 1 W. & M. c. 18. s. 11.

(3) 2 W. & M. c. 18. s. 7.

(4) Rex *v.* Arnold. 1 Str. 101. 1 Bott. 69. Pl. 78.

(5) Rex *v.* St. George. Fort. 320. 1 Bott. 4. Pl. 9.

(6) Rex *v.* Sherringbrooke. 2 Ld. Raym. 1394. Case of the overseers of Weobly. 2 Str. 1261. 1 Bott. 4. Pl. 10 & 12. and the cases there cited.

(7) Case of the overseers of Weobly, *ut supra*.

(8) Rex *v.* Severn and Arnold. Say. 278. 1 Bott. 5. Pl. 13.

(9) Rex *v* Morris. 4 Term Rep. 550. 1 Bott. 6. Pl. 15.

(10) Rex *v.* Houlditch. 1 Bott. 4. Pl. 11.

But it is not neceſſary that it ſhould mention the juſtices to be for the diviſion, for the words of the ſtatute are only directory (1); nor that the perſons named are appointed overſeers of the pariſh "together with the churchwardens thereof," for where overſeers are legally appointed, they are by operation of law joined with the churchwardens (2).

The time for which made. The order muſt expreſs the time for which theſe officers are appointed. But though they can only continue in office until the Eaſter enſuing their appointment, and muſt not be appointed for a longer period; yet if the order appoint them "for the preſent year," (3) or "for this "preſent year 1766," (4) or "for a whole year," (5) or "for one year then next enſuing," (6) or "then next en-"ſuing the date thereof," (7) it is ſufficient; for where the expreſſion admits of a two-fold conſtruction, that ſhall be given to it by which the order may be ſupported, and therefore the *year* in theſe orders was underſtood to mean the *overſeers' year*.

How executed. The appointment is not only to be under the hand and ſeal of two juſtices, but they muſt ſign and ſeal in the preſence of each other, or it will not be good (8). **Executed on Sunday.** Though executed on Sunday, yet if done *bona fide* it is ſufficient, as being a work of charity (9). But it is ſaid in a ſubſequent caſe, that the impropriety of the day, renders it *prima facie* clandeſtine and bad (10). Thus where two adverſe ſets of borough juſtices met before midnight of

(1) Rex *v.* Sparrow. 2 Seſſ. Caſ. 140.

(2) Regina *v.* Searle. 1 Bott. 3. Pl. 8.

(3) Rex *v.* Sparrow. 1 Bott. 21. Pl. 3,.

(4) Rex *v.* Helling. 3 Burr. 1904. 1 Bott. 24. Pl. 41.

(5) Rex *v.* Jones. 1 Bott. 24. Pl. 40.

(6) Rex *v.* Burder. 4 Term Rep. 778. 1 Bott. 27. Pl. 46.

(7) Rex *v.* Stubbs. 2 Term Rep. 395. 1 Bott. 26. Pl. 45.

(8) Rex *v.* Forreſt. 3 Term Rep. 38. 1 Bott. 24. Pl. 32. Rex *v.* Great Marlow. 2 Eaſt. 244.

(9) Rex *v.* Clerkenwell. Fol. 4. 1 Bott. 21. Pl. 38. Rex *v.* Merchant and Allen. 1 Bott. 25. Pl. 43.

(10) Rex *v.* Butler. 1 Black. Rep. 649. 1 Bott. 25. Pl. 42. where Lord Mansfield doubts of the caſe of Rex *v.* Clerkenwell. But the 43 Eliz. c. 2. requires, that the churchwardens ſhall meet once a month on Sunday after ſervice, to confer reſpecting the objects of the act.

Eaſter

Easter Eve, and begun making appointments of overseers the instant the clock had struck twelve, and kept on renewing the same appointments for an hour or two; and one set made a fresh appointment on Sunday morning, supposing that there would be a contest concerning the validity of the appointment made soon after midnight, and perhaps all of them bad. The appointments being removed into the king's bench by *certiorari*, and these facts disclosed by affidavit, Lord Mansfield delivered it as his opinion, in which the other judges concurred. "I dont know that there is any authority which "says that an appointment made on Sundays is good: it "certainly is not a day for such purposes, and I will not "give my sanction to any of these. Let them be set aside, "and a mandamus directed to the justices to make a new "appointment, and let the mayor give two days notice of "the time and place of meeting for it" (1).

When the appointment is made, other justices cannot alter it.

When an appointment is once legally made, the magistrates are *functi officio*. If two appointments therefore are made on the same day, that which is prior in time is good (2), and the second void. And other magistrates are not only disabled from making a new appointment (3), but if a person who has been appointed applies to them to be exempted, upon sufficient cause, they cannot remove him and substitute another in his place, but he must appeal to the sessions for his discharge (4).

Appeal against appointments.

If any "person or persons are aggrieved" by the appointment, they may appeal to the next quarter sessions, whose jurisdiction extends over the place for which they are appointed (5).

(1) Rex *v.* Overseers of Bridgewater. Cowp. 139. 1 Bott. 26. Pl. 44.

(2) Reg. *v.* Searle. 1 Bott 21. Pl. 37. Rex *v.* Merchant and Allen. Ib. 25. Pl. 43.

(3) *Ut* in n 2.

(4) Rex *v.* Great Mallow. 2 East. 244

(5) 43 Eliz. c. 2. f. 6. 17 Geo. 2. c. 38.

This

This right is not only given to thoſe who are appointed, but alſo to the pariſhioners, for they may be "perſons ag-"grieved" by the choice of an improper perſon (1). In this appeal, the parties may go into evidence of whatever can ſhew a want of juriſdiction in the magiſtrates making the order (2), or point out the impropriety of their choice. **Given to the pariſhioners.**

The ſeſſions, on appeal, have a right to exerciſe the ſame latitude of diſcretion in judging who are fit to be nominated as overſeers, as the two juſtices had when making the original order. "They are not obliged to give any reaſon "for their opinion, becauſe the legiſlature has inveſted "them, on appeal, with the power and authority of ap-"pointing overſeers." **Power of Seſſions.**

The order which they make may be removed by *certiorari* into the Court of King's Bench; and though the juſtices are not bound to ſtate their reaſons for making it, yet, they may, if they think proper, either give them as *rationes decidendi* in the body of the order, or ſeparately in the ſhape of a caſe. If they appear in the body of the order, and are wrong, the Court will quaſh what is manifeſtly made by miſtake: but the bad reaſon ought to appear to have been their only inducement for making it; for the execution of a diſcretionary power ſhould be ſupported, unleſs the whole reaſon is ſet forth, and is manifeſtly wrong. If there may have been other grounds, they ſhall be preſumed to be ſufficient.—Thus, where, on an appeal againſt an appointment of a Mr. G., the ſeſſions ſtated in their order, "that G. "was and is an acting juſtice of the peace for the county, "and alſo a lieutenant of marines on half-pay, and that "there are other ſufficient and ſubſtantial houſeholders "within the pariſh, and therefore vacate the warrant of "appointment;" the Court of King's Bench confirmed their order, on the foregoing principles:—"For the whole "reaſon is not given; they ſay there were other perſons **Removal of order from Seſſions by certiorari.** **When the Court will quaſh.**

(1) Rex *v.* Forreſt. 3 Term Rep. 38. 1 Bott. 68. Pl. 77.

(2) Albrighton *v.* Skipton. 1 Stra. 301. Rex *v.* Stotfold. 4 Term Rep. 601. Rex *v.* Fliſher. 1 Bott. 67. Pl. 76.

" qualified, and supposing Mr. G. liable to serve the " office, they might think him not so proper as many " others (1).

Original removal into B. R.

There is also a power of removing by *certiorari* into the King's Bench the original appointment, without appealing to the sessions, and when removed, the Court will quash it, not only for defects appearing in the order itself, but upon facts stated by affidavit where they imply a want of jurisdiction in the justices by whom it is made (2).

When to be removed.

The party aggrieved by the order, who moves to *quash* it, may remove it previous to the *next sessions* after it is made (3), unless an appeal is actually lodged, in which case it cannot be done until the sessions have made a determination upon the appeal. If a *certiorari* should be granted for the purpose by mis-apprehension pending the appeal, the Court will quash it on motion, *quia erronicè emanavit* (4). But as this appointment may be removed likewise by those who wish to have it *confirmed*, they cannot bring it up in order to move for its confirmation, until the next sessions has been held, to which the appeal must be made. At least the court will not allow it to be done, when attempted for the purpose of taking away the benefit of appeal from those who are entitled thereto (5).

Punishment of those not performing their duty.

If those who are appointed do not take one of these steps to get freed from the office; or if doing so, the original order is confirmed, they are liable to an indictment where they refuse to undertake or execute the duty (6).

Their duties.

The care of the poor is intrusted to them in conjunction with the churchwardens, where there are any.

(1) Rex *v.* Gayer. 1 Burr. 245. 1 Bott. 9. Pl. 20.

(2) *Ante* 29, and per Lawrence J. Rex *v.* Great Marlow. 2 East. 247.

(3) Rex *v.* Harman. And. 343. 1 Bott. 65. Pl. 74.

(4) Case of the borough of Warwick. 2 Stra. 991. 1 Bott. 65. Pl. 73.

(5) Rex *v.* Houlditch. 1 Bott. 66. Pl. 75. Rex *v.* Jones. 2 Stra. 1146.

(6) See the cases cited, *ante* 21, and *per* Lawrence J. Rex *v.* Great Marlow. 2 East. 249.

They

They are required to meet at leaſt once a month in the church on Sunday after divine ſervice in the afternoon, under the forfeiture of 20s. to the uſe of the poor, by every one who abſents himſelf from theſe meetings without lawful cauſe (1); and if negligent in their office, they are ſubject to the like penalty for every default. The forfeitures to be levied by ſome or one of the churchwardens and overſeers, by warrant of diſtreſs from two juſtices; and in defect of diſtreſs, any two ſuch juſtices may commit the offender to the common gaol, there to remain without bail or mainprize, till the forfeiture ſhall be paid. But the perſon aggrieved may appeal to the quarter ſeſſions, whoſe order ſhall bind all parties (2). The power of acting is veſted in the major part (3), and they are to continue in office until the Eaſter enſuing their appointment, when others are to be elected (4).

The moſt prominent points of their duty are: 1ſt, To make a rate in order to raiſe a fund for the maintenance of the poor. 2d, To aſcertain what poor the pariſh is bound to maintain. 3d, To remove ſuch perſons as it is not liable to ſupport ſo ſoon as they become actually chargeable. 4th, To inſpect the œconomy, and adminiſter to the wants of their proper poor. 5th, and laſtly, Upon going out of office, to make up and paſs their accounts, and deliver over any balance in their hands to their ſucceſſor, together with the property and documents of the pariſh. Theſe form the great outlines of the law which reſpects the relief of the poor, and will be treated of in the remainder of the work.

(1) But the penalty for not meeting in the church ſhall never be inflicted on the overſeers of the poor of extra-parochial places, as they have no church to meet in. Rex v. Rufford. 8 Mod. 39; and query if in the caſe of townſhips?

(2) 43 Eliz. c. 2. ſ. 2.

(3) Ibid. ſect. 2.

(4) Per Lee C. J. Rex v. Sparrow. 2 Bott, 21. Pl. 463. *ante* 29.

OF THE POOR's RATE.

CHAPTER III.

Of making, allowing, and publiſhing the Rate.

Under what acts the rate is made.

THE fund raiſed for the general relief of the poor, is called the Poor's Rate.

In counties.

It is made and levied in pariſhes within the juriſdiction of County Magiſtrates, by 43 Eliz. c. 2. ſ. 1.

In corporate places.

Within that of corporate towns, places, and cities, including the city of London by the ſame act, ſect. 8.

In townſhips.

And by 13 and 14 Car. 2. chap. 12. ſect. 22. for extraparochial townſhips, and thoſe ſubdiviſions of pariſhes for which ſeparate overſeers are appointed under the ſame ſtatute.

By whom made.

The power of making a rate is veſted entirely in the churchwardens and overſeers, or the major part of them, and the concurrence of the inhabitants is not neceſſary (1).

But as the ſtatute requires that it ſhould be made by the major part of the pariſh officers, a rate cannot be made by one overſeer (2).

Overſeers, how compellable to make it.

If the officers refuſe to make a rate, the court of King's Bench will, if a caſe is laid before them upon affidavit,

(1) Per Holt C. J. Tawney's caſe. Salk. 531. 2 Lord Raym. 1013. Per Eyre J. Rex v. St. Michaels, Cornhill. 16 Vin. 425. 1 Bott 75. Pl. 91. (2) Semb. Rex v. Atkins. 4 Term Rep. 12. 1 Bott. 284. Pl. 276.

hear

hear both parties, and, if neceſſary, compel them to do ſo by mandamus (1). But they will not intermeddle with the equality of aſſeſſment, or interfere even ſo far as to command them to make an equal rate (2). For the overſeers are to take care of that in the firſt inſtance, and the court of quarter ſeſſions upon appeal in the ſecond (3).

Allowing the rate.

The act preſcribes, that the rate ſhall be made "with "the conſent of two or more juſtices of peace dwelling "in or near the ſame pariſh, or diviſion where the pariſh "doth lie, whereof one to be of the quorum." The firſt ſtep therefore to be taken after making the rate is, to carry it to two juſtices for their conſent, or, as it is uſually termed, "their allowance." This allowance is in their individual capacity of Magiſtrates, and not as a court of ſeſſion, which has no original juriſdiction reſpecting rates (4).

Juſtices' power not diſcretionary.

Whatever might have been the legiſlature's intention in requiring neighbouring juſtices' conſent, it has been often decided that they are to act miniſterially, and muſt allow the rate as a matter of form, without exerciſing any diſcretion to refuſe where they think it unjuſtly and improperly made (5). But if two rates are preſented to them by different officers of the ſame pariſh, they are ſaid to have an election of ſigning that which they conſider as moſt equitable (6).

Though the juſtices are required by the act to dwell in or near the diviſion, it is not neceſſary that this ſhould be ſtated in their allowance (7).

(1) Liddleſton *v.* Mayor of Exeter. Fol. 18. 1 Bott, 75. Pl. 90. Rex *v.* Overſeers of Weobly. 1 Bott. 265. Pl. 262.

(2) Rex *v.* Weobly, *ut ſupra*; and ſee Butler *v.* Cobbet. 1 Bott, 265. Pl. 258. the caſe of a mandamus to make an equal aſſeſſment of the land-tax.

(3) Ibid.

(4) 1 Bott, 75. Pl. 89.

(5) Rex *v.* Uttoxeter. 1 Bott. 76. Pl. 93. Rex *v.* Juſtices of Dorcheſter. Ib. Pl. 94. 2 Str. 393. Rex *v.* Edwards. 1 Black. 637. 1 Bott. 77. Pl 97.

(6) Rex *v.* Anon. Comb. 479. 1 Bott. 99. Pl. 122. It is ſtated in the report, that the rate which they ſigned, was brought to them by one of the overſeers; but whether it was made by a majority of the pariſh officers does not appear.

(7) Cobbet *v.* Mary St. Lincoln. 16 Vin. Abr. 425. 1 Bott. 75. Pl. 92.

 But

Confined within their jurisdiction.

But the place for which they allow a rate must be within their jurisdiction. An allowance by county justices of a rate for a whole parish within a borough, having Magistrates of its own who possess an exclusive jurisdiction, or for the part of a parish being so situate, is void (1).

Publication.

It is required by 17 Geo. II. c. 9., that the churchwardens and overseers, or other persons authorised to take care of the poor, shall give public notice of the rate on the Sunday after it has been allowed by the justices, otherwise it is null and void. It must be published therefore in the church, and on the Sunday ensuing the allowance. Where notice was given on the third Sunday after allowance, it was held a radical defect in the rate itself, which nothing could cure (2). But the publication need not be set forth in a special case stated for the opinion of the court of King's Bench, respecting the validity of the rate in other particulars. It is sufficient if it aver that the rate was duly made; for the court, with respect to an order of justices, will intend every thing to be right which does not appear to be otherwise (3).

(1) Rex *v.* Folly. 1 Bott. 76. Pl. 96.

(2) Rex *v.* Newcombe. 4 Term Rep. 368. 1 Bott, 77. Pl. 98.

(3) Rex *v.* Aire and Calder Navigation. 1 Bott, 73. *n. a.* But this remark does not seem to apply to what is necessary to be set forth to shew their jurisdiction.

CHAPTER IV.

Of the Time for which the Rate is to be made.

THE time for which rates are to be made, is declared in the statute of Elizabeth to be " weekly or *otherwise*." Upon the discretion evidently given by these words, Lord C. J. Holt was of opinion, that poor rates ought to be made monthly, that being the period at which the same act requires the parish officers to meet in vestry to consider matters for the relief of the poor (1). The same Judge was also of opinion, that they were not empowered to make one for a quarter of a year in advance, since a man could not move in the middle of it without being charged twice (2). This inconvenience is remedied by 17 Geo. II. c. 38., which enacts, that persons are to pay the poor's rate only in proportion to the time that they occupy.

Lord Holt's construction of " weekly or otherwise."

Great inconveniences would ensue from making rates for short periods. It is impossible to foresee and provide for every expence that may arise. The legislature appear to have seen the necessity of extending the rate beyond one week in particular cases, and therefore added the general words " or otherwise," to empower those who make the rate to adapt it to the situation of the parish. The Court of King's Bench has for these reasons determined, that without any reference to usage in the particular parish, a rate may be made prospectively, not only for a quarter of a year (3), but for six months (4). Neither

May be for a quarter,

or six months.

(1) 43 Eliz. c. 2 s. 2.

(2) Tracey *v.* Talbot. Salk. 532. 2 Bott, 77. Pl. 99. Rex *v.* Littleport. 6 Mod. 97. 1 Bott. 78. Pl. 100.

(3) Rex *v.* Overseers of St. George, Middlesex. 2 Black. 694. 1 Bott, 78. Pl. 104.

(4) Durrant *v.* Boys. 6 Term Rep. 580. 1 Bott, 79. Pl. 105.

do the judges seem to point out in these decisions any definite time short of a year, for which a rate is to be made. They merely lay it down as a principle, that it should not be done wantonly, but on a scale adapted to the probable exigencies of the parish (5).

(5) Durant v. Boys. 6 Term Rep. 580. 1 Bott, 79. Pl. 105.

CHAPTER V.

Of the general Purposes to which the Rate is to be applied.

For what purposes it is to be levied.

THE general purposes for which this rate is to be raised, as stated in the act of Elizabeth, are, for setting to work those who are able; relieving such as are not; and for apprenticing the children of parents unable to maintain them; also by 9 Geo. I. for purchasing work-houses (1). 18 Geo. III. c. 19. enacts, that money shall be taken from this fund to repay constables, &c. what they expend for the relief and removal of paupers and vagrants, which the 13 and 14 Car. 2. chap. 12. sect. 18. (2), had directed to be raised by a separate rate. It is applicable to no other purpose, except defraying such law expences as are necessarily incurred by the overseers in the discharge of their office (3), at least when the proceedings are directed by the vestry (4). Thus the salary of an assistant overseer appointed by a vestry meeting cannot be paid out of it (5), nor a sum of money borrowed by the parish to rebuild a work-house (6).

Law expences.

For what not.

Not to reimburse former overseers.

Where an overseer disburses money out of his private funds to relieve the poor, he may make a rate during his continuance in office, and re-imburse himself

(1) 9 Geo. I. c. 7. s. 4.

(2) Rendered perpetual by 12 Ann. c. 18.

(3) Per Buller J. Rex v. Micklefield. Cald. 507. 1 Bott, 91. Pl. 116. Rex v. Inhabitants of Essex, 4 Term Rep. 591.

(4) Per Willes J. Rex v. Micklefield. Ib.

(5) Rex v. Welch and others. Cald. 504. 1 Bott, 318. Pl. 339.

(6) Rex v. Wavell. Doug. 116. 1 Bott, 91. Pl. 115

from

from the produce (1); or if the rate is unpaid at the expiration of his year, the succeeding overseers are directed by statute (2) " to levy such arrears, and reimburse " their predecessors all sums expended for the use of the " poor, and allowed to be due to them in their ac" counts (3)."

But it was formerly necessary, that the parish officers should in all cases make a rate during their continuance in office, and obtain re-payment of the money advanced out of the produce. For a rate could not be made by new churchwardens and overseers to reimburse their predecessor what he had applied for the poor's support although he had been turned out of office before the end of his year, and thereby lost the opportunity of making a rate to repay himself (4); nor for law expences incurred by former officers (5). For the act of Elizabeth is express, that they are to raise a fund for the relief of the poor only, and an overseer is not bound to expend money until he receives it (6). So if an overseer continues in office for successive years, he cannot reimburse himself the outlays of former years, by a rate made in the last, although the rates made in antecedent years were either quashed on appeal, or could not be collected as being informal; for all the items of his accounts are to be confined to the particular year for which the act directs they shall be passed (7).

(1) Tawney's case. Salk 531. Rex v. Ware. Fol. 10. 1 Bott. 90. Pl. 113.

(2) 9 Geo. I. c. 7. s. 4.

(3) 17 Geo. II. c 38. s. 11. Rex v Overseers of Rotherhithe. 8 Mod. 338. 1 Bott, 90. Pl. 114.

(4) Tawney's case, *ut supra*. Ld. Raym. 1011.

(5) Case of the Overseers of Chichester. 1 Bott, 90. *n. b.* s. 6. Ib. 317. Pl. 330.

(6) Tawney's case, *ut supra*.

(7) Rex v. Goodcheap. 5 Term Rep. 159. 1 Bott, 97. Pl. 118. This objection is usually made matter of appeal against the overseers accounts, as being an improper application of the money raised by the rate, and not against the rate itself. Rex v. Goodcheap, *ante*. It is only, when the rate appears from the title to be made for this purpose, that it forms a ground of appeal against it. But it may come under discussion, as matter connected with making a rate, either in that way, or upon a motion for a mandamus to the parish officers to make a rate for that purpose. Tawney's case, *ut supra*.

Considerable

Considerable inconvenience occurred in particular cases from this restriction. Unhappily the makers of the the statute of Elizabeth, did not foresee those enormous burthens which their humanity has thrown upon posterity, and the number of appeals which originate in the hope of escaping from a supposed inequality of taxation. Many things occur to prevent the officers from making a rate during their continuance in office. When made, an appeal might render it ineffectual, not only against those who dispute the rate, but against such as do not object to the assessments. For overseers were afraid to collect, as they might be harrassed with actions to refund money which they received under a void authority. If the rate was quashed at sessions, the office might expire before a new one could be made; and if another was previously allowed, the collection might be again suspended by a fresh appeal. In the mean time the poor must either starve or be supplied by the humanity of those officers, who, if prevented from making a rate for their reimbursement, had nothing to trust to, but the uniform honesty of every rateable inhabitant of the parish, to allow, in their accounts, sums of which they had no legal means to enforce payment.

Inconvenience of this rule.

The cases already cited, shew that they could not rely with safety upon the expectation at all times; and particular circumstances which gave rise to 41 Geo. III. c. 23. proved, that a system of mischief and oppression might receive effect from a rigorous application of the law, as it then stood.

To remedy which, section 9. of this act provides, that succeeding churchwardens, overseers, and guardians of the poor shall repay and reimburse those who precede them, such sums as they have advanced or expended for the relief of the poor during the time that no rate or assessment has been made for that purpose; or that any appeal has been depending which affected the whole of such rate, or upon hearing of which the same might be wholly quashed.

Remedied by 41 Geo. III. c. 23. where no rate made, or it is quashed.

The inconveniencies enumerated, ſeem removed by this proviſion. The law remains in other caſes as it previouſly ſtood, in order to compel attention from pariſh officers in collecting, and enforcing payment of the neceſſary rates during their continuance in office.

CHAPTER VI.

Of Persons and Property to be rated.

THE 43 Eliz. c. 2. enacts that competent sums to be levied for the purposes therein specified, shall be raised, "by taxation of every inhabitant, parson, vicar and other, "and of every (1) occupier of lands, houses, tithes im-"propriate, propriations of tithes, coal mines, or saleable "underwoods in the said parish, for, &c., to be gathered "out of the same parish according to the ability of the "same parish." 43 Eliz. c. 2. s. 1.

This is the only statutory provision which regulates the description of persons and property to be included in the poor rate. The 13 and 14 Car. II. c. 12. s. 22. extends the operation of the 43 Eliz. to villages and townships, but makes no alteration in the manner of imposing the tax. 13 and 14 Car. II. c. 12. s. 22.

Rate to be on the occupiers.

By this clause, the assessment is to be made upon the inhabitants and other occupiers of lands, &c. according to the ability of the parish, and the tax is levied upon the person in respect of some particular property possessed or occupied by him (2). All persons who inhabit the district for which the rate is made, being able to contribute; and all who occupy real property there, although dwelling elsewhere, come within the act (3). A corporate body is rateable (4), as well as a private individual. The king

Who rateable.

(1) The word "*other*" is inserted here as the statute is recited in Bott. But all the editions of the statutes have it as above. See Rex *v.* Andover. Cowp. 559.

(2) Theed *v.* Starkey. 8 Mod. 314. 1 Bott, 118. Pl. 155. Sir Anthony Earby's case, 2 Bulst. 354.

(3) Jeffrey's case, 5 Co. 66. establishes the principle in the case of a church rate. 1 Bott, 112. Pl. 138.

(4) Rex *v.* Corporation of Wickham. 3 Keb. 540. 1 Bott, 115. Pl. 145. Rex *v.* Gardner. Cowp. 79. 1 Bott, 138. Pl. 172.

is

is alone exempt by reason of his prerogative, as not being mentioned in the statute (1).

Principles of rating property.

1. On real and personal.

Two great principles were laid down by all the judges very soon after the 43 Elizabeth was passed, respecting the rateability of property. First, the assessment is to be made according to the visible estate of the inhabitants, both real and personal (2). For the statute renders inhabitants liable to this tax, as a distinct class from occupiers of real property, and must therefore affect their personal estate.

2 Within the parish.

Second, No inhabitant is to be taxed to contribute to the relief of the poor, in regard of any estate he hath elsewhere in any other town or place (3). For the statute expressly limits the tax by "the ability of the parish itself," as it might otherwise fall with inequality upon persons of equal substance. Because those who reside or have property in several districts, would be taxed otherwise, not in proportion to their actual ability, but to the number of places in which they lived or had property, acting upon its total value, for they would contribute in each upon the full value of what they possessed in all (4).

All

(1) Semb. Rex *v.* Matthews. Cald. 8. 1 Bott 148. Pl. 175.

(2) Sir Anthony Earby's case. 2 Bulst. 354. 1 Bott, 114. Pl. 141. Rex *v.* Churchwardens of Andover. Cowp. 550. 1 Bott, 151. Pl. 176. Rex *v.* White. 4 Term Rep. 771. 1 Bott, 208. Pl. 205.

(3) Ib. In Atkins *v.* Davis. Lord Mansfield says, "By constant usage, "(and I know not upon what other "ground it is) ability to pay is mea- "sured by the local rateable property "in the parish." Cald. 336. But the resolutions in Earby's case are reported 9 Car. I. only 33 years after the act passed, and the opinions of this great judge respecting the importance of usage in construing the 43 Eliz. c. 2. seems overruled by subsequent decisions.

(4) The question is very distinctly put in the resolutions of the Judges of assise 1633. 18. Qu. "Whether the "law for the relief of the poor upon "th statute of 43 Eliz. shall be made "ꞏyability, or occupation of lands, or "both; and whether the visible ability "in the parish where he lives, or general "ability whatsoever; and whether his "rent received within the parish shall "be accounted visible ability, and "whether he shall be taxed for them "only, and for any rent received from "other parishioners; and what shall be "said visible ability?"

The resolution in answer is not so precise, viz: "The land within each "parish is to be taxed to the charges in "the first place equally and indifferent- "ly, but there may be an addition for "the

All estate or property within the parish is divided by these resolutions into real and personal. These terms, when applied to the subject of rating, are not intended to denote the quantity of estate, or to distinguish between a freehold and chattel interest. Such distinctions are immaterial with reference to statutes which, in rating real property, lay the tax upon the occupier according to the actual value of the thing occupied, without regard to the extent or quantity of his interest (1).

Real property defined.

The meaning of *real property* in the poor-laws, appears to have been confined in many cases to immoveable things, which are the direct object of sight and touch, and to be synonymous to what is understood by lands and tenements. More recent decisions seem to consider it as extending likewise to all incorporeal rights which issue out of lands and tenements (2), and perhaps (though never directly decided) it is to be understood as comprehending all that

"the personal visible ability of the pa-"rishoners within that parish, accord-"ing to good discretion; wherein if "there be any mistaking, the sessions, "&c. or the justices must judge between "them." Dalt. Just. tit. Poor, chap. 73. p. 234, 235. ed. 1727. It is remarked in Dalton, 231. that the authority of these resolutions is not very great. Some country gentlemen coming to Sir Robert Heath when chief justice on the circuit, put him these several queries, to which he subscribed his opinion, then brought the same into Serjeant's Inn-Hall, and proposed the same to the rest of the judges; but they differing from him in opinion in many things, they never came to a resolution, and so were no more than his private opinion, which some clerk getting, has published the same, as Justice Twysden declared in the court of King's Bench in East. Term. 28 Car. II. as I heard and observed: and afterwards a gentleman of the bar using these resolutions to the third, fourth and eighth questions, touching putting out apprentices as an authority to his purpose, Justice Twysden said, "why do you use that as an authority "which all the judges disclaimed?" They are however evidence of what the chief justice took the law to be in 1633, and the legislature seems to have had them in contemplation when regulating the poor by statute, in more instances than one.

(1) Sir Anthony Earby's case, *ut supra*.

(2) Lord Bute *v.* Grindall. 2 H. Black. 265. and post; sect. 2.

is signified by the term *hereditament* (1), which, to follow the definition given by Judge Blackstone, includes " not only " lands and tenements, but whatsoever may be inherited, " be it corporeal or incorporeal, real, personal, or mixed.(2)

Personal defined.

" By *personal property* is understood stock in trade, " goods, money, and all other moveables, which may " attend the owner's person wherever he thinks proper " to go."

Requisites to render property rateable.

In shewing how far and when these two kinds of property can be assessed, for the poors' relief, it may render the subject more intelligible, briefly to specify those general principles or canons upon which its rateability depends in each particular district.

1st, It must not be excepted out of the statute. 2d, It must yield a profit. 3d, It must be occupied. 4th, It must not be rated twice. 5th, It must be situated within the parish or township for which the rate is made.

All these qualifications must concur in order to render the rate upon a particular subject valid.

SECT. I.

Of rating Land, Houses, and Profits annexed thereto.

THE first kind of real property mentioned in the statute is " *land and houses*." They are put by way of example, and not as excluding every kind of real property of the same nature; for, not only lands and houses, but shops, sheds, and all things real which render an annual revenue, are subject to the rate (3).

(1) Per Lord Kenyon. Rex *v.* Mayor of London. 4 Term Rep. 21. 2 Bott, 201. Pl. 202.

(2) 2 Black. Com. book 2. chap. 2. p. 16.

(3) 4 Com Dig. tit. Justices of the Peace, B. 66 p. 565. 4th edit. The resolution of the judges of assize in 1633, accords with this opinion. It being taken perhaps from the 19 Qu. Whether shops, salt-pits, sheds, profits of a market, be taxable to the poor, as well as lands, coal-mines, &c. expressed in the statute? Resol. " All things " which are real, and in yearly reve- " nue, must be taxed to the poor." Dalt. 235.

1. Though

1. Though the tax is laid upon the land or house, it is in respect of the revenue or annual profits which issue from them, and that whether they are produced by nature or by means wholly artificial; for, things very distinct from the natural profits of land are rateable under that name; the land being considered as the principal, the profits of which are augmented by the annexation of the accessary.

1. Natural profits of land, &c.

2. Thus where certain lands and buildings at Cheltenham, containing four acres and a well of mineral water thereout arising, were let at the yearly value of 100l.; the lands and buildings, independent of the well, being of the value of only 20l. *per annum*. The rent paid for the mineral water of the well was 80l. The tenant was rated upon 100l. *per annum* for the premises, and the rate was held to be good. For, it is not a rate upon the profits of the well, but upon four acres of land let at 100l. *per annum*, the value of which arises partly from the buildings, and partly from the spring that produces the mineral water; therefore the profits of the spring are part of the produce of the land, and as such ought to be rated (1). In Worcestershire and Cheshire, where there are salt-springs, the rent of the land is increased considerably on that account (2).

2. Natural productions connected with land; as a mineral spring.

3. By 17 Geo. III. c. 18. passed for more effectually completing the navigation of the river Thames, the city of London purchased an ancient barge-way or towing-path, with certain ancient tolls thereto belonging, situate within the hamlet of Hampton Wick, which maintains its own poor. In pursuance of the act they discontinued the old tolls and collected new ones, authorised by the statute, and let the annual herbage and pasture of the barge-way at a yearly rent. It was held that the corporation was assessable to the poor rates of the hamlet, for such tolls as became due there; for, the rate

3. Artificial profits of land; as of a towing-path.

(1) Rex v. Miller. Cowp. 619. 2 Bott, 155. pl. 179. Per Lord Mansfield, C. J. Atkins v. Davis, Cald. 338.

(2) Per Lord Mansfield, Rex v. Miller, *ut supra*. Resolution of Judges, 1633, *ut supra*, n. 2. p. 36.

is made upon "the barge-way and the toll-gate," and the corporation have the inheritance and ownership of the soil, which is the subject matter of the rate; and being occupiers, notwithstanding the demise of the herbage, they are liable to be rated (1).

4. Of a dock.

4. So lands purchased by a company, and converted into a dock by statute, which declares that the shares of the proprietors shall be considered as personal property, is rateable for the amount of its annual profits, under the appellation of a dock, although personal property is not rated in the parish; for, it is landed property lying there and was liable as such before the act passed; the legislature in declaring the shares personal property, did not mean to exempt this land which was rateable and rated before, but only to declare that it should go to executors instead of heirs (2).

5. So the occupier of land, who is possessed of a way-leave or waggon-way over it, for the purpose of carrying coals from his mine, is rateable for the value of the waggon-way (3).

6. Incorporeal hereditaments annexed to land there.

6. Incorporeal hereditaments have been deemed rateable as an adjunct profit when annexed to lands and houses, although not issuing from thence. Thus an estate may be rateable in a higher proportion, on account of a right of common being appendant to it (4), and, as it is said, although the common land itself is situate in another parish (5).

7. Personal chattels annexed to it; a machine affixed to the building.

7. In the same manner a real subject is rateable according to its annual value, although that value be derived from the annexation of a personal chattel. As where a corporation, being possessed of a house, erected a machine in the street leading by the said house, for the purpose of weighing

(1) Rex *v.* Mayor of London, 4 Term Rep. 21. 1 Bott, 201. pl. 202.

(2) Rex *v.* Dock Company of Hull, 1 Term Rep. 219. 1 Bott, 174. Pl. 189.

(3) Rex *v.* Bell, 7 Term. 598. 1 Bott, 232. pl. 215.

(4) Per De Grey. C.J. Kemp *v.* Spence. 2 Black. 1245. 1 Bott, 81. Pl. 108.

(5) Eod. Jud. ibid. But the learned judge only states that "possibly" the law may be so.

waggons,

waggons, carts, &c. loaded with coal, &c. at 2d. a ton, the steelyard part of the said weighing machine was, and always had been, in the said house. The corporation was rated for the *machine house*, according to the annual value not only of the house itself, but of the clear profits of the machine. The rate is good, for they are one entire thing, and the house is rendered much more valuable from the machine's being appurtenant thereto (1).

Some reliance seemed to have been placed by the court in this case upon the machine being affixed, and as such constituting part of the freehold.

But where a building, called the engine-house, consisted of a bay of building 18 feet long and 19 wide, in which there was a carding machine for manufacturing cotton, not fixed to the premises, but capable of being moved at pleasure. The building, independent of the machine, was worth only two guineas *per annum*. The building and machine together, were rated at 36l. It was not the usage of the place to rate personal property (2). The engine is generally worked with water, but frequently by the hand. The building was not a dwelling-house, nor erected for the purpose of receiving the engine. There was in the same building another carding and a tumming machine (3). All the engines were placed on the floor, and no ways annexed or fastened to the same, but might be moved at pleasure, and carried out and worked in any other place, 8. Personal chattels let with it, though not fixed. A carding machine.

(1) Rex *v.* St. Nicholas Gloucester, Cald. 262. 1 Bott, 165. pl. 185.

(2) This was the substance of the case as originally stated by the court of quarter sessions. But the court of king's bench sent it back to be re-stated, requiring them to return answers to the following inquiries? "Whether the engine mentioned in "the said order is worked with water "or with horses? and whether the "house wherein the said engine stands "is a dwelling-house, or built for the "purpose of receiving the engine? "and in what manner the engine is "put up in the engine house, and "what is its size and bulk? and also, "whether the owner of the building "has contracted to discharge the occupier of all the taxes?" The remainder of the above case is the return to this order. Cald. 266.

(3) These were not rated; nor, so far as can be conjectured from the case, demised with the building.

 either

either by means of water or manual labour, and were not adapted to any particular building. The frame in which the engine stood was 12 feet long, 3 feet 11 inches broad, 2 feet 9 inches high; the semi-diameter of the largest cylinders, with a small roller at the top, rising 20 inches above the frame; the engine sinking in the frame 17 inches. One L. W. was lessee of the premises under the owners, and subject by his lease to discharge the premises from taxes; the appellant was the under tenant, but L. W. paid the taxes.

The court were of opinion, that though it did not clearly appear whether the carding-machine was actually fixed to the building or not (1), yet being demised with it and forming one entire subject, and the rate being on the building, it was properly rated for the entire profits, the house acquiring a greater value from the use to which it was put, and that it fell exactly within the case of Rex *v.* St. Nicholas, Gloucester (2).

Two of the judges were also of opinion, that the engine was rateable as personal property, and that the finding by the justices "that it was not usual to rate personal "property in the place," made no difference upon that question.

The remaining judge said, it was enough to enable the court to confirm the rate, that part was rateable, viz. the house, and the rate being on the house, the court would not interfere with the quantum of the rate (3).

(1) "It seems to me that this case "is still imperfect: for it is not "stated negatively, that this engine, "while it is in a state of working, is "not some way or other fixed to the "house. It is only stated that it is "not fixed to the *floor*. But it may "be fixed to the walls of the building "without being fixed to the floor. "We can assume no facts on "either side; but one should suppose "that it must be fastened in some "way, otherwise, as it is worked by "water, the weight of the water must "displace it." *Per* Ashurst. J. Cald. 273.

(2) Rex *v.* Hogg. Cald. 266. 1 Term Rep. 721. 1 Bott, 180. pl. 191.

(3) *Ibid.*

Se

So a tenement of little or no value, fitted up as a malt-house, and let together with a malt-mill, though ſuch malt-mill is removeable at pleaſure, is not only rateable as real property under the denomination of a malt-houſe, but alſo to the full extent of the annual amount of the profits which ſuch a mill might have added to the building (1). Machinery of a malt-houſe.

It is alſo laid down by another judge, that "if a billiard-table ſtand in a houſe, and the houſe ſhould in reſpect of ſuch table let at a higher ſum, it is rateable while the table continues there, and it is ſo let at the advanced rent (2). A billiard-table.

SECT. II.

Incorporeal Hereditaments per ſe.

THAT theſe profits are rateable when the right or thing from which they accrue is annexed to lands or houſes, is fully ſettled by the foregoing caſes; but whether an incorporeal right yielding an annual profit, is rateable in the hands of one who has no poſſeſſion of the ſoil out of which it ariſes, and to which it can be conſidered as annexed, has formerly created conſiderable doubt among the judges. Doubts to incorporeal hereditaments being rateable *per ſe*.

(1) *Per* Groſe J. *Ib.* Cald. 275.

(2) *Per* Willes J. arguendo. Rex *v.* St. Nicholas, Glouceſter, *ut ſupra.* If this caſe proceeds on the ſuppoſition that the billiard-table need not be affixed to the floor; or if Rex *v.* Hogg goes the length of eſtabliſhing, that things let together with a houſe in the ſame demiſe, and yielding a profit, are rateable whether fixtures or not; a houſe leaſed out ready furniſhed, or a farm demiſed ready ſtocked, ſeem rateable. But furniture is not rateable as perſonal property. Rex *v.* White. 4 Term Rep. 771. 1 Bott. 208. pl. 205. Nor the ſtock neceſſary for the culture of a farm. Queen *v.* Barking. 2 Ld. Raym 1280. 16 Vin. Abr. 426. 1 Bott. 216. pl 150, 151.

 The

As incapable of occupancy.

The act speaking of rating real property, directs the assessments to be laid on the occupier, and the doubt was, whether this kind of property lies in occupancy. It was contended, that it did not according to the common law sense of the word, since actual possession could not be delivered. No ejectment would lie to recover the thing itself, nor could trespass be brought against those who infringed the right (1).

It was said therefore, that a right of common cannot be rated, as not being the subject of occupation (2). It was doubted among the judges for the same reason, whether the privilege of taking herbage and pannage is rateable (3). The annual profits of a fair have been incidentally held not to be so (4): and according to one report it seemed intimated by the judges, that the tolls of a light-house were not rateable, only because the light-house was not made the subject of the rate (5). In a recent case also it was held, that a mere easment in the soil of another, such as a right of passage for which a certain annual rent is payable, is not rateable. Therefore, where a person is possessed of a waggon-way, and another agrees with him for the use of it for carrying his coals at so much *per* ton, the latter at least is not liable to be assessed (6).

Contrary opinion.

But the general principle upon which these cases are said to depend, has been much doubted; and property has been considered as capable of being *occupied* within the meaning of the statute of Eliz. although not so according to the strict common law sense of the word.

(1) Jones *v.* Maunsell, Doug. 302. 1 Bott, 157. Pl. 181.

(2) *Per* De Grey, C. J. Kemp. *v.* Spence. 2 Black. 1245. 1 Bott, 81. Pl. 108.

(3) Jones *v.* Maunsell. Dougl. 302. 1 Bott, 157. Pl. 181. See Rex *v.* Minchin-Hampton. 3 Burr. 1310. 1 Bott, 271. Pl. 265.

(4) Rex *v.* Brograve. 4 Burr. 2291. 1 Bott, 133. Pl. 169.

(5) Rex *v.* Rebowe. Dougl. 118. n. 1 Bott, 138. n. a.

(6) Rex *v.* Jolliffe. 2 Term Rep. 90. 1 Bott, 184. Pl. 192. *Per* Lord Kenyon, C. J. Rex *v.* Bell. 7 Term Rep. 600. 1 Bott, 235.

Sir

Sir Robert Heath C. J. was of opinion ſo early as 1633, that the profits of a market might be taxed to the poor(1).

In 27th Car. 2. the tolls of a corporation were held rateable; but it does not appear from the reports, what the nature of theſe tolls were, or for what they were paid (2). In more recent caſes, the profits ariſing from tolls paid for paſſing a particular ſluice (3), or bridge, being private property (4), and alſo thoſe from tolls payable for carriage of goods on navigable canals, have been adjudged liable to this aſſeſſment (5). 1. Tolls.

Turnpike and other tolls paid for the public benefit, and not of private individuals, are not ſubject to this tax; but this is not upon the principle that they are not in their nature rateable, but under another already alluded to; that there is no beneficial occupier (6). When not rateable.

It has been urged however, that theſe inſtances are not deciſively in point to impugn the principle relied on. That in thoſe of tolls of a ſluice or bridge, the perſons rated might have ſome property in the ſoil on which they ſtood (7); and in the caſe of navigable canals, the land is always purchaſed by the proprietors of the canal, ſo that Doubts.

(1) *Ante*, 46. n. (3).

(2) Rex *v.* Corporation of Wickham. 3 Keb. 540. Freem. 419. 16 Vin. Abr. 425 Aſhurſt J. ſuppoſed it might be for piccage, which is, in nature of a rent for land, for it is an acknowledgment payable to the owner of the land in reſpect of the uſe made of the ſoil; *i. e.* breaking the ground for the erection of booths and ſtalls in a fair or market. Atkins *v.* Davis. Cald. 382. But Willes and Buller J. held it to be good law as a common caſe of toll. *Ib.* 328. *Ib.* 333.

(3) Rex *v.* Cardington. Cowp. 58. 1 Bott, 152. Pl. 177. But Aſhurſt, J. denied this caſe to be law. Atkins *v.* Davis. Cald. 332.

(4) Jones *v.* Maunſel, Doug 302. n.

(5) Rex *v.* Page. 4 Term Rep. 543. 1 Bott, 83. Pl. 109. Rex *v.* Aire and Calder Navigation. 2 Term Rep. 660. 1 Bott, 190. Pl. 194. Rex *v.* Proprietors of Staffordſhire Navigation. 8 Term Rep. 340. 1 Bott, 696. Pl. 598.

(6) *Per* Lawrence J. Rex *v.* Staffordſhire Navigation. *Ib* & *poſt*. 8c.

(7) But ſee the opinion of Buller J. Atkins *v.* Davis. Cald. 320.

it resembles lands converted into a dock, which are held rateable for the profits (1).

Refuted.

But these grounds of distinction may be justly repelled. The cases respecting profits accruing from the tolls of a fair and light-house, are directly over-ruled by subsequent determinations deciding that they are rateable. Herbage and pannage of a park or forest, is a privilege of a singular nature. He who has the grant of it cannot take any but of surplusage, over and above the competent and sufficient pasture and feeding of the game; it is entirely casual, as it depends upon the will of the proprietor in stocking his park; and by disafforesting, it may be extinguished. The judges only doubted as to its rateability, and were divided on the question. It was admitted also by Lord Mansfield, that the case of tolls, if clearly established, would tend considerably to shake the opinion against its rateability; and that point, although doubted at the time when the question of herbage and pannage was agitated, is now settled beyond dispute by numerous decisions.

As to herbage and pannage.

A way-leave.

The case of the way-leave depends upon different principles. The person who paid so much a ton for the passage of his waggon, occupied nothing. The profits, if any, arose from the land over which the coals passed, and consequently to him who occupied the ground, who must be the person liable, supposing them rateable at all. To rate the other would be to rate the consumer directly who paid for vegetables, instead of the gardener, who occupied and enjoyed the profits of the ground from whence they sprung.

A common.

There is no other case but that of a common, which favours the contrary principle. It rests upon the opinion of a very great judge, but given before the rateability of herbage and pannage had been discussed, and not directly connected with the point in judgment. Neither is the case of tolls unsupported by others, which depend on the same principle.

(1) *Ante*, 48. In Rex *v*. The Proprietors of the Staffordshire Canal, it was taken for granted that the rate was not upon the land, but upon the tolls. See the opinion of Le Blanc J. *Ib*.

Rents

Rents are not ufually rateable *eo nomine*, but this is not, as being a fpecies of property exempted by ftatute, but upon a principle to be explained hereafter, that they are rated in the land (1), for ground rents have been adjudged liable (2).

Rents why not ufually rat able.

2. Ground rents.

Quit rents, and the cafual profits of a manor, have been held not rateable (3); but if this decifion is maintainable, it is upon the principle of excluding a double rate (4). Lord Holt declared, that they were determined to be rateable (5), and though it was afterwards decided otherwife, it was upon the ground of ufage, as never having been rated before. For ufage was confidered by Lord Mansfield, as a cotemporaneous, or rather confuetudinary expofition of the ftatute, and relied upon as a rule of decifion, in this and other cafes. But befides that, the determination referred to by Lord Holt precluded the prefumption of general ufage: it is now fettled, that ufage cannot be reforted to, in order to limit the exprefs meaning of this modern ftatute.

3. Quit rents.

A leffee for years from the crown, of all thofe mines of lead with their appurtenances, within the foke and wapentake of W. with lot and cope; the firft of which is a duty of every 13th meafure of lead ore dreffed and made merchantable; and the latter a duty of 6d. for every load, or nine difhes of lead ore raifed at all mines within the faid foke, &c.; both being received without any rifk or expence of working the mines, are rateable according to their annual value, and as that varies; for it is partof the owner's vifible real property in the parifh; not a cafual profit, but an annual revenue, and the immediate leffee of the lead mine not being rateable, it is not twice rated (6).

4. Lot and cope of a mine.

(1) *Per* Eyre C. J. Lord Bute *v.* Grindall. 1 Term Rep. 338. 2 H. Black. 265. 1 Bott, 175. Pl. 190. Sir Anthony's Earby's cafe, 2 Bulft. 354.

(2) Rex *v.* Gibbs. Comb 62. 1 Bott, 115. Pl. 147. opinion of Blackftone J. Lowndes *v.* Horne, 2 Bl. 1252. 1 Bott, 156. Pl. 180.

(3) Rex *v.* Vandewall. 2 Burr. 991. 1 Bott, 122. Pl 161.

(4) *Per* Lord Kenyon C. J. Rex *v.* Alberbury, 1 Eaft. 535. *Et per* Eyre J. Comb. 264.

(5) Hull's cafe, Carth. 14. *et per* Holt C. J. Comb. 264.

(6) Rowls *v* Gells, Cowp. 451. 1 Bott, 146. Pl. 174.

 So

5. Farm tin.

So the proprietor of a certain dish or measure arising out of certain lands and tin bounds in the parish, called toll and farm tin, which is paid free and clear of all risk and deductions, was upon the same principles adjudged rateable for all annual profits, although the amount of the toll varies, and is uncertain (1). These cases are in the nature of rents paid to the owners (2), and depend upon the same principle; for whether it is a return in kind, or money, makes no distinction; and it makes as little, whether a reversion is annexed to the rent or not.

General principle.

In the lot and cope case, the lessee of the mine was the landlord; the persons rated were not occupiers in either, but they were considered as being so, for the purpose of an assessment *quoad* these profits. They were in possession, and occupiers of profits arising immediately from the land, and as such, rateable (3); or to state the general position as laid down by the Chief Justice, whose judgment is here referred to, and which he professes to deliver as the opinion of all the Judges in the Exchequer Chamber:—"We think it may be stated as a general proposition, that "the immediate profits of land (some mines excepted) "are a proper subject of assessment; or to speak more cor- "rectly, that the person who is possession of the imme- "diate profits of land, may be taxed to the relief of the "poor in respect of these profits (4)."

6. Rents when rateable.

The statute having directed the rate to be laid on the occupier of the land, cases will rarely occur in which rent is rateable. It is only so where the thing out of which it is paid, is from the particular nature of its occupation exempt from being rated in the hands of the occupier, as in the case of lands or buildings held by the king or the public.

(1) Rex *v.* St. Agnes, 3 Term Rep 480. 1 Bott, 192. Pl. 197.

(2) Per Lord Mansfield, Atkins *v.* Davis, Cald. 337.

(3) *Per* Eyre C. J. Lord Bute *v.* Grindall, *ut supra.*

(4) *Eod. Just. Ibid.*

Whether

Whether the rents of premiſes thus occupied are rateable, has never been directly decided (1): but the caſe may be explained in the words of a late moſt able Judge: "A warehouſe, &c. may be rated to the "proprietor or occupier, according to the uſe to which it "is applied. If it be let for inſtance to the exciſe or "cuſtom-houſe for public purpoſes, the burthen muſt "be borne by the proprietor, but if it be afterwards "converted to a private uſe, the occupier of it will be "liable to the rate." His Lordſhip's words, however, cannot be drawn into an authority upon the ſubject, for he was interpreting a local ſtatute, which declared, that public buildings ſhould be liable to a particular tax, and the tax paid by the proprietor (2).

Ill conſequence if incorporeal rights not rateable *per ſe.*

From theſe deciſions and opinions of the Judges, it may be concluded, that incorporeal rights which ariſe out of lands and tenements, and are enjoyed diſtinct from the ſoil, are equally rateable as when annexed to the occupation of the land itſelf, and are ſubject to the ſame reſtrictions. The contrary interpretation would produce an inequality of taxation for which it is not eaſy to aſſign a reaſon. If a right of common be appendant to a farm, it is admitted that the rate on the farm may be increaſed by the value of the common; yet, if the ſame perſon hold the ſame farm, and have a right of common in groſs of equal value, he is not liable to aſſeſſment. If the proviſions of a ſtatute are explicit, courts of law are bound by them, however inequitable; but when they admit of a more rational conſtruction, the Judges will decide in its favour (3).

(1) The anſwer to 18 qu. in the reſolutions of the Judges of aſſize, 1633, ſeems to take it for granted, that rents are rateable as part of the viſible ability: but it does not directly decide the point. See *ante.* 44. n. (4).

(2) Per Lord Kenyon C. J. Eckerſall *v.* Briggs, 4 Term Rep. 6. 1 Bott, 197. Pl. 201.

(3) See the opinion of Buller J. Rex *v.* Hogg, Cald. 274. 1 Term Rep. 721. 1 Bott, 180. Pl. 191.

SECT.

SECT. III.

Tithes.

Tithes,

THE next ſpecies of property mentioned in the ſtatut is " tithes impropriate," and " propriations of tithes." This kind of tithes uſually exiſt in vicarages, but ſometimes elſewhere. They are generally the great tithes ſevered from the benefice, and due to ſome other perſon than the vicar. They originated from the practice of annexing benefices to ſome ſpiritual corporation, either ſole or aggregate, which was conſidered as the perpetual parſon of the living (1). This corporation provided a clergyman to officiate in its room, to whom the vicarial tithes were aſſigned for ſubſiſtence; and the benefice, with the remaining tithes, were appropriated to its own uſe. The latter ſhare is what is called in the ſtatute " propriations," or more correctly " appropriations of tithes." Advowſons, amounting to more then one third of all the pariſhes in England, got into the poſſeſſion of religious houſes during the times of popery, by theſe means. Upon the ſuppreſſion of monaſtries, the 27 Hen. VIII. c. 28 and 31. Hen. VIII. c. 13. gave their benefices to the king, to hold as they held them. Many of them were afterwards granted to the ſubject; and as they are called *appropriations* while they continue in ſpiritual hands, they are called *impropriations* in thoſe of the laity; and tithes payable to theſe lay impropriators, are called " *tithes impropriate* (2)."

1. Appropriate.

2. Impropriate.

3. Property of the clergy.

Tithes in the hands of the efficient incumbent, whether parſon or vicar, are not expreſsly mentioned in the ſtatute.

(1) 1 Black. Com. 384. Grendon v. Underwood Plowd 496. Terms de la Ley, voc. Impropriation; and Cowel's Law Dict.

(2) Sir H. Spelman of Tithes, ch. 29. Cow. Dict. voc. Impropriation.

But

But as it directs that the " parson or vicar" is to be taxed, it must intend that it shall be for that property which constitutes the chief subject of their occupancy; tithes being deemed a tenement by our law.

Not only parsonage houses and glebe lands are rateable in the hands of the occupier (1), but both rectorial and vicarial tithes have been always deemed so, whether due by common law (2), or by custom. Such are the tithes of fish caught in the sea; for it is a certain annual profit received within the parish without any risk run (3). **4. Tithes rectorial and vicarial.**

A modus, or other composition paid in lieu of tithes, is equally liable to this tax. Thus where by an inclosure act, an allotment of common field land was made to the rector in lieu of the tithes issuing out of the old inclosures in the parish; and it was provided, that when the owners of such inclosures had none, or not sufficient land in the common field to make such allotment, they should pay an annual sum to the rector, with power to distrain in case of non-payment, and sell the distress in such manner as landlords are by law authorised to distrain for rent. This being a sum of money payable in lieu of the tithes of the old inclosures, is liable to be rated as the tithes themselves previously were (4). So also a rate or assessment directed by statute to be made in lieu of all tithes and **5. A modus.** **6. Other ecclesiastical dues.**

(1) Rex *v.* Turner. 1 Bott, 116. Pl. 152. *Per* Lord Kenyon, Rex *v.* Catt. 6 Term Rep. 332. 1 Bott, 226. Pl. 211.

(2) The parson or vicar presentative shall bear according to the reasonable value of his parsonage, having consideration to just deductions. 33 resol. Judg. 1633. Dalt. 237. Rex *v.* Turner, *ut supra.* Rex *v.* Shingle. 1 Str 100. 1 Bott, 117. Pl. 153.

(3) Rex *v.* Carlyon, 3 Term Rep. 385. 1 Bott, 150. Pl. 195. The question made, respected a rate upon the lay impropriator's tithe of pilchards; but the vicar was also rated for his share, and no objection made. As to when fish is titheable or otherwise, see Gould *v.* Arthur, 1 Roll. Abr. 636. Pl 7. Anon. Cro. Car. 264. Ib. 234. Anon. Het. 13. Guavas *v.* Kelynac. Bunb. 256. 3 Com. Dig. tit. Dismes (H. 13.) (H. 16.) Williams *v.* Baron. 3 Wood's Decr. 130. 3 Gwillim on Tithes, 931.

(4) Lowndes *v.* Horne, 2 Black. 1252. 1 Bott, 156. Pl. 180.

other

other ecclesiastical dues, is rateable, unless exempted by express provision (1), as are likewise oblations or other offerings which constitute the rectorial or vicarial dues (2).

SECT. IV.

Coal Mines.

THE next species of property mentioned in the statute are coal mines. These are rateable within the words of the act (3). But it has been held, that as other mines were known in the country when the statute passed, the mention of this inferior species of mine amounts to a tacit exemption or exclusion of all others, such as lead, tin and copper mines, or any other but coal mines. The reasons assigned for this are "that these other "mines are governed by particular laws, the worker of "them is not always the owner of the soil; a local law "gives the right of working under certain regulations and "conditions to other persons than owners or lessors, or "persons having any right of property in them." It is also said, "that there is an infinite expence and anxiety "in finding lead mines, and the finder is obliged to pay "certain proportions to the owner of the land; and there "is a much greater risk in the search after them, even "so much as that a man may be ruined by it instead of "succeeding (4)."

Metal mines not rateable.

It has been already shewn, that the owners of duties arising out of metallic mines, such as the lot and cope of lead mines (5), the toll and farm tin of tin mines (6), are

(1) Rex *v.* Toms, Doug. 401. 1 Bott, 159. Pl. 182. Rann *v.* Pickering. Cald. 196. 1 Bott, 164. Pl. 184.

(2) Per Lord Kenyon, Rex *v.* Carlyon, *ut supra*, 59. (n. 3.)

(3) Rex *v.* Parrot, 5 Term Rep, 593. 1 Bott, 220. Pl. 208.

(4) The Smelting Company *v.* Richardson, 3 Burr. 1341. 1 Bott. 127. Pl. 164. *Per* Lawrence J. 2 East. 167.

(5) Rowlls *v.* Gells, Cowp. 451. 1 Bott, 146. Pl. 174.

(6) Rex *v.* St. Agnes, 3 Term Rep. 480. 1 Bott, 192. Pl. 197.

I rateable

rateable when they are paid clear of deduction, and freed from the hazards of working.

Lime works and slate works rateable.

Neither does the exception extend beyond mines properly so called. Lime-works are not comprehended within it, but their profits are rateable in the hands of the occupier, although uncertain in their amount, owing to the expence and risk of working (1).

Upon the same principle, the occupier of a slate quarry is held rateable, though the quarter sessions stated in the case, that the working of such quarries is a thing of great expence and risk, and is always considered as a matter of uncertainty and speculation, and that the "slate *mines*" had never been rated before. For the word "mine having slipped in at the end of the case, cannot "alter the nature of the thing, which is no mine in the "proper sense of the word; and if every substance which "is raised from under the surface of the soil is to be "considered as the produce of a mine, and therefore that "the profits of it are not rateable, the exception will "equally extend to gravel, sand, marle, stone and the like, "none of which were ever considered as the produce of "mines (2)."

Why mines and casual profits excepted.

Some of the reasons assigned by the court for not rating other mines, seem to favour the conclusion, not only that the legislature by the expression of one species of mine designed to exclude the remainder by reason of their peculiar laws, but that it was never intended to rate mere casual profits of a similar nature, from whatever subject they arise.

The 43 Elizabeth enacts, that the rates shall be made for short periods, and manifestly refers to the profits which accrue according to the common course of affairs during that time. It purports to raise at all times the necessary

(1) Rex *v.* Alberbury. 1 East. 534. Davis, Cald. 338. *Per* Lord Mansfield arg. Atkins *v.*

(2) Rex *v.* Woodland. 2 East. 164.

necessary funds upon the usual income of the parish. It makes the rate prospective, so that the former return of profit must constitute the foundation of the ensuing assessment. This cannot be unless the amount admits of an average certainty, which is not to be affected by an irregular swell or diminution from casual profits or subsequent losses.

It is further observable, that the statute does not tax capital, but the produce of capital. If a man builds a house, the occupier is rateable for its yearly value as soon after it is built as it is occupied (1); for the amount of the capital exists in the house itself, and the annual produce of that capital is the fair subject of rate. But where a shaft is sunk for a metal mine, the capital is in the first instance consumed; it rises again only in the ore. To rate the entire ore, deducting the expence of raising the specific quantity, would be to rate the capital itself, instead of its produce; and the uncertainty attending such works, renders it doubtful whether the profits will ever repay the expence. The whole property is in constant hazard, and its value may alternately sink or rise beyond the costs of the adventure, just as the buckets do by which the mineral is raised. The adventurer would be taxed for a year of profit, but he could have no allowance for a losing year, although it might draw the former profit back again into the mine, and sink much additional capital with it.

There is a great distinction also between the uncertain amount of profit; and the uncertainty of profit altogether, which is attended with risk of capital. Every object of human care and culture is subject to the first. Uncertainty in the amount, while the capital or direct subject of the tax is permanent, forms no ground for a general exemption from the rate, although it may for particular abatements proportioned to the diminution of profits. But

(1) Per Willes J. Atkins v. Davis, Cald. 333.

uncertainty

uncertainty of profit puts the capital in hazard, and is a matter of ſpeculation and chance: if any thing is derived from the riſk, it is not properly an occupiers profit, at leaſt of an occupier for that ſhort period which the ſtatute has in contemplation. It may be ſaid indeed, that both are uncertain, and that the loſs of profit on a farm may ultimately diminiſh the actual capital employed, as it does in a copper mine. But the probable riſk of capital is the characteriſtic of the latter undertaking, and is the ground of diſtinction.

Coal mines are of a mixed nature: the working is attended with a degree of certainty, and therefore the mine itſelf may be conſidered as the capital, and the coals at the pit's mouth as its annual return. The principle explained here ſeems to be that which is meant by what the books call a "permanent value (1)." The recent deciſions of the rateability of lime and ſlate works, do not overturn it (2). Theſe are not mines in any ſenſe of the word, and although the working may be attended with hazard, it is only as to the amount of the return, but not of a conſiderable capital.

SECT. V.

Saleable Underwoods.

THE 43 Eliz. points at theſe principles more manifeſtly by the laſt ſpecies of property, which it mentions as rateable in the hands of the occupier, viz. *Saleable Underwoods*. Woods, conſiſting of what is called great wood or timber trees, are exempt from contributing to the poor, as they are freed from tithes (3). For they are not the profits of the occupier conſidered as ſuch, but parcel of the inheritance itſelf (4). By confining the rate alſo to

Timber exempt.

(1) Per Lord Loughborough, Atkins *v*. Davis, Cald. 337, 338. And ſee the opinion of Lord Mansfield. Rowls *v*. Golls. Cowp. 451. 1 Bott, 146, Pl. 174.; and of Aſhurſt J. Atkins *v*. Davis. Cald. 330.

(2) But what is ſaid by Buller J. Atkins *v*. Davis, Cald. 325. is *contra*.

(3) Com. Dig. Tit. Diſmes (H. 3.)

(4) Herlakenden's caſe, 4 Rep. 62. a. Robert Liford's caſe, 11 Rep. 466. 1 and ſee other authorities, 2 Com. Dig. tit. Biens (H.).

ſaleable

ſaleable underwoods, the legiſlature ſhews, that it meant to tax property only, at the time when a periodical profit could be fairly and ſeaſonably made.

Timber by cuſtom.

This exemption of wood is not confined to trees coming within the ſtrict legal deſcription of timber, ſuch as oak, aſh, and elm; it is ſufficient if the trees in queſtion are deemed ſo by the cuſtom of a particular diſtrict. Thus woodlands, the trees growing thereon conſiſting chiefly of *beech*, and ſome oak and aſh trees, there being no coppice wood, and the underwood being left to grow as ſtandards, were held not rateable, *beech* being found by the ſeſſions to be *timber*, by the cuſtom of the country (1). And it retains the privilege, although it be put to the uſes of underwood, being cut and made up in parcels for firing (2); in which reſpect this law ſeems to differ from that of tithes (3).

(1) Rex *v.* Minchin-Hampton. 3 Burr. 2310. 1 Bott, 271. Pl. 265.

(2) *Ibid.*

(3) Greenaway *v.* Earl of Kent, Bunb. 98. and the caſes cited. *Ibid.* in the note.

CHAPTER VII.

Of real Property exempted by particular Statutes.

THE principles which have been detailed, respect real property, as it is affected by the 43 Eliz. c. 2. But particular things, which would be liable to the tax under that act, may claim exemption by a subsequent statute. In some instances, they have been considered as exonerated by general words.

Thus, where houses and lands given to charitable uses, were by a private act declared "*freed, discharged, and acquitted of and from the payment of all and every manner of taxes, charges, and assessments, civil or military whatsoever;*" and that the occupiers shall not at any time hereafter be rated, &c., *for or towards any manner of public tax, assessment, or charge whatsoever*, they were held exempt from the poor's rate, it being considered *a public tax*, or levy of the parish, within 3 W. & M. c. 11. s. 6 (1). So where 7 Geo. III. c. 3. enacted, that *lands* to be enclosed and embanked from the Thames, shall vest in the owner, &c. *free from all taxes and assessments whatever:* houses erected upon this ground, are not liable to the poor's rate, for this act being subsequent to 43 Eliz. c. 2., and the lands themselves being exempted thereby, so must also the houses built thereon (2).

Likewise, where by 19 Geo. III. c. 60., the parish officers of the parish of St. Michael's, in Coventry, are to raise yearly by a pound rate, any sum not exceeding 300l. nor less then 280l., and to pay the same to the vicar, by equal quarterly payments, "clear of all taxes, deductions, charges, and extras whatever, *parochial*, parliamentary, or otherwise howsoever"; which said sum is to be in full satisfaction of all the vicar's claims under the act; and is "in lieu and full discharge of all ancient payments, Easter offerings, *tithes*, and other ecclesiastical dues, claims, and demands whatsoever, except surplice fees." This salary is not liable to the poor's tax (3).

(1) Rex *v.* Scott, 3 Term Rep. 602. 1 Bott, 193. Pl. 198. Williams *v.* Pritchard, *Ib.* 195. Pl. 197.

(2) Eddington *v.* Borman, 4 Term Rep. 1 Bott, 196. Pl. 200.

(3) Rex *v* Toms, Dougl. 401. 1 Bott, 159. Pl. 182.

CHAPTER VIII.

Of the Ratcability of Perſonal Property.

THE ſtatute makes no ſpecific mention of any other kind of property than thoſe which are treated of in the foregoing chapters. But as it requires that the ſeveral inhabitants ſhould be taxed according to the ability of the pariſh, it renders them liable to the extent of that ability, however conſtituted (1). The pecuniary funds, or ability of the inhabitants, when referred to their ſources, are diviſible into three kinds: 1ſt, What ariſes from real property. 2d, What ariſes from capital ſtock, or as it is here called, perſonal property. And, 3d, The produce of perſonal labour, or in other words, " what ariſes from " the ingenuity of a man's head, or the work of his " hands (2)." The reſolutions of the judges already cited, by deciding that the tax is uponthe perſon in reſpect of his real and perſonal property, excluded the produce of perſonal labour, as a direct object of aſſeſſment. Their opinion ſeems to have been framed upon the ſyſtem of taxation by ſubſidy, which at that time was in uſe. A ſubſidy being a tax not immediately impoſed upon property, but upon perſons in reſpect of their eſtates (3), " which was to be levied of every ſubject of his lands or " goods, after the rate of 4s. in the pound for lands, and " 2s. and 8d. for goods; and for aliens, for goods, double(4).

Of parochial ability.

Perſonal labour exempt.

(1) Lord Kenyon expreſſes it thus: " The legiſlature intended that when " rates are made for the relief of the " poor, every perſon ſhould contribute " according to the benefit which he " receives in the pariſh". Rex *v.* Carlyon, 3 Term Rep. 385. 1 Bott; 190. Pl. 195.

(2) *Per* Willes J. Atkins *v.* Davis, Cald. 334. and Buller J. Rex *v.* Hogg. *Ib.* 275.

(3) 1 Black. Comm. 310.

(4) 4 Inſt. 33. See alſo Raſtall's Abridg. tit. Taxes, Tenths, Fifteenths, Subſidies, &c. There is, however, this difference eſtabliſhed at leaſt by ſubſequent determinations: that in a ſubſidy, the tax was impoſed on the ſuppoſed value of the goods; in a poor rate, it is laid upon the profit which they yield.

Lord

Lord Mansfield was of opinion, that the words of the 43d Eliz., considered merely of themselves, would bear a more extended construction then has been given to them, if they had not been explained and narrowed by usage. "The words of the statute," said he, "are very loose "and very general, and they may be construed into any "latitude; even to make all a man has, and all a man "gets in any way, the measure of his ability: for truly "and substantially it is so; but usage has explained it "and narrowed it. I know nothing of any usage that "says, a man shall pay according to his ability in the "obvious common sense of the word, *i. e.* all he gets or "makes by his efforts or abilities. If this were the rule, "every profession would be liable to be taxed for all they "get upon an average. If we don't find it there (*i. e.* in the usage), "I know nothing in the words of the statute "to prevent taxation being carried to that extent (1)."

Sir Anthony Earby's case is reported in the ninth year of Charles I., and the resolution of all the judges, upon which it is founded, was some time previous. Nothing entitled to the name of usage could have sprung up between the 43d of Elizabeth and the date of the report; and this opinion of the learned judges, to which he leaned with peculiar predilection (2), has been overruled (3).

But his opinion, that the profits of personal labour are not rateable *eo nomine*, or in the moment in which they are made, is confirmed by several decided cases (4).

Salaries not rateable.

Thus an officer in the salt office; (5), or in the customs; (6), a captain in the navy; or merchants' service; (7), and a clerk to a merchant (8), have been held not rateable

(1) Atkins *v.* Davis, Ca'd. 336.

(2) See 1 Bott. 132. Pl. 168. *Ib.* 155. Pl. 178. *Ib.* 162. Pl. 183.

(3) *Ib.* 151. Pl. 176. *Ib.* 208 Pl. 205, &c. Ca'd. 315.

(4) *Per* Buller J. Rex *v.* Hogg. Ca'd. 275. *Per* Lord Mansfield, Rex *v.* Andover. Cowp. 550. 1 Bott, 151. Pl. 176.

(5) Rex *v.* Shalfleet, 1 Bott, 129. Pl. 165.

(6) Rex *v.* White, 4 Term Rep. 771. 1 Bott, 208. Pl. 205.

(7) *Ibid.*

(8) *Ibid.*

for

for their refpective falaries; (1) nor an attorney for the profits of his profeffion (2), for it would be to tax labour, and not pecuniary ability.

Perfonal property rateable.

As it was unufual to affefs perfonal property for near two centuries fubfequent to the ftatute, the court felt confiderable reluctance to decide upon its rateability, notwithftanding Sir Anthony Earby's cafe. Such an univerfal agreement to omit it, was confidered as ftrong evidence to fhew that it was impoffible it fhould be rated: but it was held at length, that it is clearly rateable where its value can be afcertained (3). That a clothier, therefore (4), and a draper or fhopkeeper (5), are rateable for their ftock in trade; a butcher for capital employed in his bufinefs (6). The owners of fhips are rateable to that parifh in which the fhips lie, if the port is their home (7). In one cafe the court feemed of opinion, that the ftock in trade of a brewer was not rateable; but this was before the general queftion refpecting the rateability of perfonal property was determined; the decifion turned upon another point, and there feems no principle upon which it is to be diftinguifhed from any other ftock in trade yielding profit.

Stock in trade, fhips, &c.

Profits of labour when rateable.

Though the profits of labour are not immediately rateable, yet, when the produce has accumulated, and is vefted in property that is liable, it is of courfe to be affeffed; for the court cannot go into the inquiry whether fuch profits were the profits of a trade or a profeffion, or how they were acquired; the queftion whether rateable or not, muft depend upon the form that has been given them, *the thing that vifibly exifts*. Thus, fifhermen are not rateable for

(1) Rex *v.* White, 4 Term Rep. 771. 1 Bott, 208. Pl. 205.

(2) Rex *v.* Startifant, 7 Term Rep. 60. 1 Bott, 231. Pl. 213.

(3) Rex *v.* Canterbury, 1 Bott, 132. Pl. 167. Rex *v.* Whitney. *Ib.* 134. Pl. 170. and in Rex *v.* Barking, it was decided that a tradefman was rateable for his ftock in trade. 2 Ld. Raym. 1280.

(4) Rex *v.* Hill, Cowp. 613. 1 Bott, 155. Pl. 178.

(5) Rex *v.* Andover, Cowp. 550. 1 Bott, 151. Pl. 176.

(6) Rex *v.* Rodd, Cald. 147. 1 Bott, 162. Pl. 183.

(7) Rex *v.* White, *ut fupra.*

(8) Rex *v.* Ringwood, Cowp. 326. 1 Bott, 144. Pl. 178.

the

the fiſh caught; but if they pay tithes to the clergyman whoſe profit is certain, and who runs no riſk, they aſſume a new ſhape, and are, as has been already obſerved, directly rateable under the words of the ſtatute (1).

Of rateable property, which is doubtful, whether to be claſſed as real or perſonal.

Reaſon for this diſtinction.

A difficulty, however, ſtill remains behind, even where the ſubject of the rate is clearly rateable. Moſt pariſhes have confined themſelves to rating real property, and the judges ſeem inclined to approve their conduct (2). In many inſtances where this mode is followed, it becomes neceſſary to determine, whether a particular ſubject is real or perſonal property, in order to decide whether it ſhall be aſſeſſed with the firſt, or ſtand exempt where the ſecond is exempted. This may be likewiſe neceſſary, where perſonal property is rated; for the aſſeſſment upon real and perſonal eſtate may require very different deductions to render the tax an equal burthen upon the proprietors; and wherever different deductions are made upon the two ſpecies of property, it becomes equally neceſſary to aſcertain the particular nature of each ſubject aſſeſſed, in order to ſettle the deduction that is to be made from it (3).

The court of King's Bench will not entertain this queſtion, unleſs expreſsly ſtated for their opinion.—They decide, whether the property ſet forth in the caſe is in its nature rateable; but without reference to the fact, whether property of the ſame ſpecies, in the hands of other perſons, is included in the rate, for that relates merely to the quantum of the aſſeſſment, which the ſeſſions, acting in the nature of a jury, can moſt properly determine (4).

Atkins *v.* Davis. Profits of water works.

The great caſe of Atkins *v.* Davis, furniſhes an apt illuſtration of this difficulty (5). It was an action of treſ-

(1) See Rex *v.* Maſt, 6 Term Rep. 154. 1 Bott, 224. Pl. 210. *Per* Buller J. Rex *v.* Hogg, Cald. 275. Rex *v.* Carlyon, 3 Term Rep. 385. 1 Bott, 190. Pl. 195.

(2) Rex *v.* Canterbury, 4 Burr. 2290. 1 Bott, 132. Pl. 167, 168. Rex *v.* Whitney. *Ib.* 134. Pl. 170. Rex *v.* Ringwood, Cowp. 326. 1 Bott, 144. Pl. 173.

(3) See *poſt*.

(4) Rex *v.* Hogg, 1 Term Rep. 721. 1 Bott, 180. Pl. 191.

(5) Cald. 315.

pass, in which the *trustees of the London Bridge water-works* were plaintiffs, and the constables of the ward were defendants. A verdict was found for the plaintiffs, subject to the court's opinion upon a case, stating the following circumstances:—The defendants had taken goods of the company by way of distress, pursuant to an order of the London sessions made under the riot act, upon the inhabitants of that city, to make good the damages recovered against them by actions brought in consequence of the riots in 1780. The company were not incorporated, and the defendants had, as constables for the ward of Bridge Within, rated them for, 1st, Their offices, with the wheels and works for raising the water. 2d, A wharf. 3d, A house for their secretary, detached from their works and wharfs. 4th, A fire-engine used for raising the water to a proper height, also detached. And, 5th, The pipes, trunks, branches, &c. laid and dispersed in the different streets, not only in the city of London, but in the county of Middlesex, and borough of Southwark, for the conveyance of the water. The whole property is within the ward of Bridge Within, except the works, with their pipes, trunks, and branches on the Southwark side of the river; and except such parts of the pipes, trunks, and branches, as are a continuation from the pipes, trunks, and branches within the said ward, and which are from thence dispersed in the different streets out of the said ward, and out of the said city of London, *but are all originally derived from*, and connected with the pipes, trunks, and branches within the said ward. The profits arising from the water-works consist of rents paid by persons supplied with water from the works, and amount to 2500l. per annum; but of which 276l. 10s. is collected within the ward of Bridge Within, the remainder in Southwark, London, and Middlesex. All these receipts are accounted for by different collectors at the abovementioned office, where the books and accounts of the company are kept, and all business transacted; but the money collected is paid to the treasurer without the ward.

The

The proprietors are rated to the land tax for their ſhares, under 21 Geo. III. c. 3. ſ. 57. The plaintiffs paid their aſſeſſments in reſpect of the wharf, the fire-engine and ſecretary's houſe; and the queſtion was, whether they were liable to the rate for the 1ſt and 5th articles, which conſtitute their water-works.

It was not ſtated in the caſe, whether the proprietors had any property in the land, under or over which the wheels, trunks, and pipes are laid. But it was obſerved by Lord Mansfield C. J., that "it is moſt probable, that "though their title was not ſtated, nor any thing con-"cerning it, that they had only the liberty to lay them." The point turned upon the meaning of the ſtatute of hue and cry, 27 Eliz. c. 13. ſ. 5., to which the riot act, 1 Geo. I. ſt. 2. c. 5. ſ. 6. refers: by 27 Eliz. c. 13., two juſtices are to aſſeſs the towns, pariſhes, villages, and hamlets; and after ſuch taxation, "the conſtables ſhall have "power to aſſeſs, *according to their abilities, every inhabitant* "*and dweller* towards the payment of ſuch aſſeſſment as "ſhall be ſo made by the juſtices."

The caſe, however, was argued in the court of King's Bench, as if it had depended upon 43 Eliz. c. 2. reſpecting the poor's rate. The judges of that court were equally divided in opinion. Lord Mansfield, and Aſhhurſt J., holding, that theſe water-works were not rateable; Willes and Buller Juſtices, that they were. Judgment in B. R.

It was argued againſt rating them, 1ſt, That this kind of property never had been rated before, and that uſage ought to prevail in a doubtful caſe. 2d, That ſuch things only ſhould be rated as yielded a certain profit, and the profit here is uncertain, and depends upon conſtant labour and expence. 3d, No part of the property is rateable; not the pipes and trunks, for they cannot by any cultivation be made to yield a produce, and they are mere tools with which the plaintiffs labour; not the fire-engine, or the water, or the arch of the bridge, for the leave to make uſe

 of

of the arch does not give any property in it, and the fire-engine which raises the water, is rated separately. It is therefore a rate on the profits made merely by the ingenuity of a man's head, the work and labour of his hands; which, whether done with or without mechanical tools, are not rateable property within 27th or 43d Eliz.

The judges, who were of opinion on the other side, that these water-works were rateable, stated, 1st, That usage of a particular district cannot make law against an act of parliament. 2d, These works were not attended with greater risk, expence, or uncertainty than farms or tolls, which are rated; and in assessing houses, the expence of building is never considered, but the house is rated as soon as *built* (1). 3d, That this is not a tax upon the pipes (a mechanical instrument), but upon the water, which, from yielding a profit, becomes a rateable subject. 4th, Being a personal visible property yielding profit, it constitutes part of a man's "*ability*", for which he is to be rated.

In Exchequer Chamber.

The judges being equally divided, the case was turned into a special verdict; judgment was given for the plaintiff "*pro forma*," and being removed into the Exchequer Chamber, it was twice argued. The judges here gave no opinion, whether the works were rateable under 43d Eliz., but confined themselves to the 27th Eliz., to which the riot act referred, and which they considered as distinguishable in many particulars from the 43d Eliz. They were of opinion that these works, being property of a permanent, visible, annual, real value, were rateable under the 27th Eliz., which directs the constables to assess towards it, *according to their abilities, every inhabitant and dweller*. The judgment of the court of King's Bench therefore was reversed.

Water-works rateable:

As the 43d Eliz. directs the poor's rate to be laid upon all inhabitants, in proportion to the *ability* of the parish,

(1) Qu. "*Occupied*?"

this

this ſpecies of property might be equally conſidered, as a criterion of ability under that act, as under the 27th Eliz., unleſs the former is ſuppoſed to exclude all property from aſſeſſment, which is different in genus and deſcription from thoſe which are there enumerated. It ſeems now ſettled, although it was by no means ſo when Atkins *v.* Davis was decided, that perſonal property is rateable to the poor, and conſequently, that the enumeration in 43 Eliz. was not deſigned by the legiſlature to reſtrict aſſeſſments to the enumerated claſſes. Perhaps, therefore, it may be inferred upon the authority of this caſe, that theſe water-works are at all events rateable to the poor, if not as real, at leaſt as perſonal property; juſt as the ſhips of a merchant, or the capital of a butcher (1).

Whether as real or perſonal property?

It may be neceſſary, however, for the reaſon already aſſigned, to determine under which kind of property they are to be claſſed. The judges who argued for the rateability, conſidered the water, when collected by means of the fire-engine and works, as the thing ſubject to the rate. Upon this principle they held, that it was rightly made in the diſtrict where the water was collected; and the judges in the Exchequer Chamber intimated a ſimilar opinion, although not directly called upon to decide the point. Lord Loughborough, who delivered their determination, ſtated, "that the proper place where the value of the "whole (*i. e.* water) is to be taken, is to be ſure at the "fountain head, from which the whole is diſtributed." Water, whenever it becomes property, falls as truly within the definition of perſonal property, as hay when ſtacked in the farm-yard; corn ſevered from the ground; or wheat extricated from the ſtraw for market.

Mr. J. Buller gives the following opinion in anſwer to a caſe put from the bar:—Whether if the water was carried in carts, inſtead of pipes, the pump could be rated for the value of all the water carried from thence?

(1) *Ante*, 68.

"Whether

"Whether the water is carried in pipes or in carts to the "place where it is consumed, is quite immaterial. I hold "in the case put, that the pump would be rateable to "the value of all the water carried from thence: for the "pump is the permanent visible property, and the quan- "tity of water carried from thence constitutes its "produce (1)."

The water in the case of the works, as well as of the pump, is to be considered as produce, which fixes the amount of the rate, and the place in which it is payable; but is not that which is the subject of the rate. It resembles the hay and corn, or other crop which ascertains the quantum of the yearly assessment to be laid upon the land upon which it grows; the latter being the direct object of tax.

In following this principle, it may be difficult to ascertain to what class of property the works which convert the water, which is the direct source of profit, into a thing of private ownership, are to be referred; especially if the proprietors have, as was supposed by Lord Mansfield, no farther interest in the soil than the liberty of laying their trunks and pipes which pass through it. But the profits themselves resemble the rent of houses more than any other species of productive return: a portion of the annual profits is necessary to keep them in repair, and the remainder is the fair object of taxation, as the produce of the capital originally expended in the scheme. With that repair they seem to be of a nature not less permanent than buildings, and are fixed to the freehold as much as the sluice or turnpike gate, of which the tolls are rateable (2).

There is no principle applicable to rating real property, which is not equally applicable to them; and it is even possible that a real estate may be created out of a thing in its nature personal. Such is the case of corodies and an-

(1) Cald. 387. (2) *Ante.*

nuities,

nuities, in which a man may have an intereſt in fee, notwithſtanding his ſecurity is merely perſonal (1). So that this property, though of a very ſingular nature; may perhaps be ranked as an hereditament, and rated as ſuch.

(1) 2 Black. Com. 40.

CHAPTER IX.

Of the Profit neceſſary.

AS the aſſeſſment is in fact laid upon the profits, the ſubject aſſeſſed muſt yield ſome return to the occupier, or it is not rateable (1).

1. Real property exempt Meeting-houſes.

Therefore the preacher of a meeting-houſe is not rateable as the occupier, unleſs he lets out the pews ſo as to reap a profit from it (2). Neither is an houſe converted into a conventicle, and uſed for no other purpoſe, rateable to the poor's tax (3). So where a quakers meeting-houſe was ſolely appropriated to charitable and religious purpoſes, the baſement ſtory being divided into a number of ſmall rooms; one occupied by a door-keeper, with a ſmall ſalary payable out of the quakers' donations; the remainder by a number of their poor, who are likewiſe maintained out of the ſame fund; the meeting-houſe or upper part being alſo appropriated ſolely to religious and charitable purpoſes, no pecuniary advantage being made thereof: the court was of opinion, that neither the truſtees nor any other perſon was rateable, for there was no occupier, *nor any profit made of the premiſes* (4).

But immaterial whether profit certain.

But where a profit does exiſt, it is immaterial whether the return is annual, and in a fixed unvarying proportion (5); or whether it is uncertain in the amount, and ſubject to riſk and expence (6).

(1) Lord Bute *v.* Grindall, 1 Term Rep. 338. 1 H. Black. 267. 1 Bott, 195. Pl. 190. *Per* Buller J. Atkins *v.* Davis, Cald. 325.

(2) Rex *v.* Southwark, 2 Stra. 745. 2 Bott, 119. Pl. 156.

(3) Anon. *Ib.* Pl. 157.

(4) Rex *v.* Woodward, 5 Term Rep. 79. 1 Bott, 214. Pl. 206.

(5) & (6) Jones *v.* Maunſell, Dougl. 302. 1 Bott, 147. Pl. 181. Rowls *v.* Gells, Cowp. 451. 1 Bott, 146. Pl. 174. In Atkins *v.* Davis, per Buller J. Cald. 325. Rex *v.* Alberbury, 1 Eaſt. 534. Rex *v.* Woodland, 2 Eaſt. 164.

Perſonal

Personal property must also yield a profit to him who is rated, or it cannot be assessed (1). Upon this ground a sum of money in a man's possession (2), and the furniture of his house, have been held not rateable (3). **2. Personal property exempt; Money; Furniture.**

It was laid down by one judge, in an early case upon the rateability of personal property, that if liable, at all, it must at least be ascertained, and not fluctuating and uncertain (4). If the observation was designed to extend to all such profits generally which are of a fluctuating nature, it is inaccurate, for it would exclude almost every kind of personal property, except monies lent out at interest (5). But it is self-evidently true, so far as it respects each particular rate; since in order to impose the tax, the profits out of which it is to arise must be first liquidated and ascertained. **Uncertainty of its profits.**

SECT. I.

Of the Occupation necessary.

The thing rated must be actually occupied, not only because the statute in cases of real property directs the tax to be laid upon the occupier; but because otherwise it yields no profit to lay the rate upon. Thus, if an house be untenanted, and kept shut up without being put to any use, it is not rateable. **1. It must be occupied.**

But it is not necessary that the possessor should be in the habit of using every part of the house to render him liable to an assessment for the whole. Where a gentleman **Occupation of houses, &c.**

(1) Rex *v.* Canterbury, 1 Bott, 132. Pl. 168. Rex *v.* Andover, *Ib.* 151. Pl. 176. Cowp. 550. Rex *v.* Dursley, 6 Term Rep. 53. 1 Bott, 223. Pl. 209.

(2) Rex *v.* White, 4 Term Rep. 771. 1 Bott, 208. Pl. 205. But judgment was originally given, with considerable scruples, by two of the three judges then in court: and in a subsequent case, Lord Kenyon says, "If a person chuse to keep his property in money, and the fact of his possessing it be clearly proved, he is rateable for that." Rex *v.* Mast, 6 Term Rep. 154. 1 Bott, 225. Pl. 210.

(3) Rex *v.* White, *ut supra.*

(4) Per Willes J. Rex *v.* Canterbury, *ut supra.* n. (1)

(5) Atkins *v.* Davis, Cald. 337.

purchased

purchased a house of the value of 24l. a year, and frequently, for amusement, he used a throw or lathe, and other turning instruments in one of the rooms; he had a table and three chairs there, and now and then a fire, but no other household furniture in the house; he kept corn for his horse in another room, and occupied the garden, keeping a gardener to take care of that and another garden; but no person ever slept or lodged in the dwelling-house, except a poor person whom he permitted to live rent-free in the kitchen, the communication being stopped up between it and the remainder of the house. The court were of opinion, that he occupied the whole house, and was properly rated for the whole (1).

Of incorporeal hereditaments.

When the thing is from its nature incapable of direct possession, as in the case of incorporeal hereditaments, such as tolls, the receipt of the profits is the occupancy, which subjects the party to the rate.

Therefore the herbage and pannage of a park belonging to the ranger, which is (as we have seen) a right or privilege to take by his beasts and swine, the surplusage of the feed and mast, over and above a sufficient pasture and feeding for the game, is not rateable when he does not put cattle and swine in to take it; because they yield no profit, by the taking of which the right can be alone occupied (2). It would seem also, that where the ranger is entitled to put beasts upon a certain part of the land in the king's park laid open to park pasture, that he is not liable to be rated for it if he has not received any profit at all from thence. But upon this point, the judges gave no opinion (3).

(1) Rex *v.* St. Mary the Less, 4 Term Rep. 477. 1 Bott, 206. Pl. 203.

(2) Lord Bute *v.* Grindall, 1 Term Rep. 338. 1 Bott, 175. Pl. 190. It is not settled whether herbage and pannage are rateable at all, the Judges having differed upon that question. Jones *v.* Maunsell, Doug. 302. 1 Bott, 157. Pl. 131. *ante.* But the judges, both in B. R. and the Exchequer Chamber, were clear that it should not be rated on the above ground.

(3) See n. 1.

 The

The rate should in strictness be laid upon the occupier, and no other person; and if laid upon the landlord instead of those who are in possession, it is bad (1). So if a person who farms tithes, agrees with the tenant of the land, that in consideration of his paying a particular sum, he shall retain the tithes, and gather the whole crop without dividing; the person who farms the tithes is the occupier, and shall be rated: the tenant is not liable (2). 2. And rate should be made upon the occupier.

In the case of tolls, it is not he who pays, but he who receives the tolls that is rated (3).

If one tenement be divided by a partition, and inhabited by different families, the owner in one, and a stranger in the other, they are several tenements, and severally rateable while thus inhabited (4).

3. The occupation must be absolute.

A rateable occupier is a person in actual possession, with powers of exercising such control and dominion over the subject, as implies freedom from any paramount occupation or direct interference by any other with his domestic arrangements and internal management; such as a farmer enjoys over his farm, and the master of a family over his house.

Therefore a laundress is not rateable.

For if a gentleman, having a coach-house or a laundry at a small distance from the mansion-house, permits the coachman to live in one, and the laundress in the other, they are not to be considered as occupiers of these tenements, so as to be rated for them (5).

Nor the housekeeper of the Philanthropic Society.

So a woman who covenanted with the Philanthropic Society to become their servant in the capacity of matron or mistress to superintend the children, at annual wages, take apprentices and instruct them; and to have a dwelling free from taxes, with certain other perquisites: she had no distinct apartment in the house provided by the society, except a bed-chamber, and her family were not allowed to live there; and she was liable to be dismissed at a month's

(1) Milward *v.* Caffin, 2 Black. 1330. 1 Bott. 250. Pl. 238. *Per* Eyre C. J. Lord Bute *v.* Grindall, *ante.*

(2) Rex *v.* Lambeth, 1 Str. 524. 1 Bott, 118. Pl. 154. *Et vide* Rex *v.* Turner, *Ib.* 116. Pl. 152.

(3) *Per* Buller J., Rex *v.* Jolliffe, 2 Term Rep. 90. 1 Bott. 284. Pl. 192; and see the principle of that case, *ante* 54.

(4) *Per* Holt C. J. Tracey *v.* Talbot, Salk. 531. 1 Bott, 116. Pl. 149.

(5) *Per* Lord Kenyon, Rex *v.* Field, 5 Term Rep. 587. 1 Bott, 215. Pl. 207.

month's notice, or an allowance of three month's wages instead thereof. She is a mere servant in the house, and as such is not liable to be rated as occupier (1). So the servants attending an hospital for the reception of lunatics, much less the poor wretches who are the objects of the charity, are not such occupiers as are intended by the statute (2).

Nor prisoners in the Fleet, nor soldiers.

Neither are the prisoners in the Fleet Prison considered as such, although they pay a weekly rent to the warden (3). Nor are soldiers living in a barrack (4).

But if the occupation is complete, the occupier is rateable, though a servant; as a keeper in the king's park for his house, &c.

But where the head of the family possesses this right of control, he is to be considered as occupier, although he stands in the relative situation of servant to his landlord in other respects. Therefore a keeper of the king's park, appointed by the ranger to continue during pleasure, and occupying a lodge and two acres of land within the parish in right of his appointment, is subject to the rate; for he occupies an house and two acres of land, and whether he pay for them by rent or by service, can make no difference as to his being rated (5).

Officers of Chelsea Hospital for their apartments.

So where the comptroller of Chelsea Hospital, or officers of that or other charitable foundations, have large distinct apartments appropriated to the use of their respective offices, where they and their families reside, they are to be charged not as servants of such hospitals, or as inhabitants and occupiers of the ordinary rooms and lodgings, but as having separate and distinct apartments, which are considered as their dwelling-houses (6).

4. Must be a beneficial occupation.

And as it is required that the property should yield a profit, it must also be received immediately by the occupier, and subject to his private disposition, otherwise he

(1) Rex *v.* Field, *ante* 75 (n 5). Rex *v.* Hurdis, 3 Term Rep. 497.

(2) Rex *v.* St. Luke's Hospital, 2 Burr. 1053. 1 Bott, 123. Pl. 162.

(3) Rex *v.* Eyles. 1 Bott, 169. Pl. 198.

(4) *Per* Lord Kenyon, Lord Amherst, *v.* Lord Somers, 2 Term Rep. 372. 1 Bott, 187. Pl. 193. 1 Bott, 191. Pl. 196. Eckersall *v.* riggs *Ib.* 197, 201. 4 Term Rep. 6.

(5) Rex *v.* Mathews, Cald. 1. 1 Bott, 148. Pl. 175. Rex *v.* Hurdis, *Ib.* n. 2.

(6) Ayr *v.* Smallpiece, 1 Bott. 121. Pl. 159. *Ib.* 126. *Ib.* 192.

would

would be called upon to contribute in consequence of a nominal and supposed ability, when his possession was destitute of advantage. Thus the trustees or governors of an hospital are not rateable for the hospital itself, although part of the area or site had paid poor rates before its appropriation to the present use (1). **The trustees of an hospital exempt.**

So where Mr. Waldo provided an house previously rated in the parish of M., and placed ten poor girls in it, some being taken from the parish of M. and some from other parishes, who were educated, maintained, and brought up on his charity. He provided and paid a woman, as his servant, to superintend and instruct them in reading and working, and qualify them for service. This woman and the children were the only persons resident in the house, which was solely appropriated to the purpose, all vacancies being supplied from time to time at W.'s discretion. Mr. W. was held not to be an occupier rateable for this house, for he makes no profit of the building (2). **The founder of a charity.**

The tolls of a sluice in a navigation were vested in commissioners by statute, "to be applied and disposed of to the "uses and purposes of the said act, and to no other whatso-"ever," these uses, &c. being for improving the navigation and draining the land. The commissioners cannot be rated for these tolls, because they are mere trustees to superintend the execution of the act, without any personal advantage (3). **The trustees of a sluice, the profits being dedicated to public use.**

Where a colonel of the troop of horse guards, by order of the crown, under the sign manual, took a lease of stables and a riding-house for the use of the troop, at a certain rent, the lease to be binding on the captain and colonel of the troop for the time being, and the rent being stopped out of the pay of all the troop, except the colonel, chaplain, and surgeon. The only use made of the stables was to keep the troop horses, with the accoutrements **The lessee of a stable for the horse guards.**

(1) Rex *v.* St. Bartholomew's Hospital, 4 Burr. 2405. 1 Bott, 131. Pl. 166. Rex *v.* St. Luke's, 2 Burr, 1053. 1 Bott, 123. Pl. 162.

(2) Rex *v.* Waldo, Cald. 358. 1 Bott, 168. Pl. 187.

(3) Rex *v.* Salter's Sluice Navigation, 4 Term Rep. 730. 1 Bott, 207. Pl. 204.

 belonging

belonging to them, except the horses and accoutrements belonging to the captain and colonel of the troop, which never have been kept there. The colonel, with whom the agreement was made, died before the time at which the term was to commence, and possession was delivered to his successor, upon whom a rate was made. But he was held not liable as the occupier; for although he is the lessee of the stables, he derives no benefit from them: they are used for a public purpose, and as such are not rateable (1).

But the execution of profit immaterial.

But where there is an occupier for the purposes of profit, the law only looks to the productive value of the thing occupied, without reference to whether the person occupying enjoys an actual share in those profits or not: for if there is an occupier such as the act requires, the tax is not laid upon his profits, but upon those which the land yields, to whomsoever they are payable (2).

Thus, if a landlord makes a hard bargain with his tenant, so that he derives no profit from his farm, the tenant is notwithstanding rateable to the poor (3). So where the lessees of a coal-mine paid as a rent one sixth part of the price of the coal raised from the mine, without deduction of the expence of working, and incurred a loss thereby. But they embarked in this losing adventure knowingly, as the cheapest way of getting at their own adjoining coal, when they had worked out this colliery which they rented. The lessees were held liable to the rate, for they are occupiers of rateable property yielding a clear profit: the court cannot inquire whether the tenant has made an unprofitable bargain (4).

Or being occupied for charitable purposes, if beneficial.

Neither will the charitable purposes for which land is given in occupation excuse an occupier who is otherwise

(1) Lord Amherst *v.* Lord Somers, 2 Term Rep. 372. 1 Bott, 187. Pl. 193. Eckersall *v.* Briggs, 4 Term Rep. 6. 1 Bott, 197. Pl. 201.

(2) Rex *v.* Parrot, 5 Term Rep. 593. 1 Bott, 220. Pl. 208.

(3) Per Lord Kenyon, arg. ib.

(4) Ibid. It does not appear from the report, whether they were rated upon the full amount of the rent paid, or only upon the profits actually yielded by the mine. But from the following expressions of Lord Kenyon; "It appears in this case that there has "been a clear profit of 1000l. a year," &c. it may be inferred that the rate was upon the clear profits.

within

within the act. Land or houses granted to a charity, not less useful than the maintenance of the parochial poor, or even operating collaterally for their relief and assistance, and so far applied in exoneration of the rate, are notwithstanding liable.

As where the master of a free-school was appointed by the minister and inhabitants of the parish under a deed of indenture, whereby a house and garden were assigned "for the habitation of the master, and for the use of him "and his family freely, without payment of any rent, "income, gift, sum of money, or other allowance what-"soever, for or out of the same, which, together with "certain lands and annuities, were given for the teaching "of ten boys, sons of the meaner sort of the inhabitants "of the parish;" it was held, that the master being found the occupier of the house and gardens, was rateable for them. For there is no exception of property given for charitable purposes, in the act respecting rates of the poor. Lands appropriated for the establishment of the religion of the country, are, in one sense of the word, lands given for charitable pnrposes; but parsonage houses, glebe lands, &c. are rateable in the hands of the occupiers (1).

School-master occupying a free-school.

So where Lord Rich, having founded a corporation in the parish of F. for the relief of the poor there, granted to the corporation and their successors a messuage, twenty acres of land, and four of wood; and appointed the messuage for an alms-house for the dwelling and lodging of five poor and impotent persons, with a grave woman to attend them: the said six persons to have freely during their lives, by the permission of the corporation, their dwelling-chambers and lodgings in the said alms-house, with the hall, kitchen, buttery, cellars, barns, and all profits and commodities to the said alms-house belonging; and also that the said corporation should permit them to have and occupy the said land for their cattle, and a rood of wood each year for firing: the persons elected, in case of non-conformity to the regulations of the charity, being liable to be put from his

Beneficial occupiers of lands under a charity.

(1) Rex v. Catt, 6 Term Rep. 332. 1 Bott, 226. Pl. 221.

or her room and place, lodging and living, &c. as if the party so refusing were dead. Six persons who had not been previously parishioners, where the premises lay, possessed the said messuage, land, and wood, being of the annual value of 15l. which were never rated before; keeping up a stock of cows according to the founder's directions, and paying a labourer for making their hay and cutting their wood, both of which they disposed of to their own use. The visitor of the said alms-house having frequently granted them additional relief. The King's Bench was of opinion, on a case stated by the sessions, that they are liable to assessment, if the parish officers think it prudent to rate them. For the property comes within the general description of rateable property in the statute; and these persons ploughing, sowing, and reaping for their own benefit, have every sort of occupation which any other person can have, and the smallness of the benefit cannot constitute an exemption (1).

Nor application of the rent to charitable uses.

Upon the same ground, the application of the rent paid by the occupier to charitable purposes, does not exempt him, although his liability must necessarily diminish the amount of the fund which is to be so applied. Thus hospital lands are rateable in the hands of a beneficial occupier (2).

A private building always used for the performance of divine service according to the rites of the Church of England, and by covenant between the lessor and lessee *never to be used for any other purpose*, is rateable in the hands of the lessee who lets the pews and receives the rent thereof for his own use and benefit, although the rent paid by him had always been applied to the public and charitable purposes of another parish.

Some stress seems to have been laid in this case upon the building not being a chapel or consecrated place, but a mere private room let out for the purposes of religious

(1) Rex *v.* Munday and others, 2 East. 584.

(2) Anon. 2 Salk. 526. 2 Bott, 215. Pl. 148. Rex *v.* Gardner, Cowp. 79. 2 Bott, 138. Pl. 172.

worship,

worship, which the owner might apply at his pleasure to any other use, in-as-much as the restriction by covenant could not vary the nature of the property. Mr. Justice Buller however intimated a strong opinion, that a member of the established church, parson, or vicar, who has the profits of the pews of his church given him by the parish, *in increase of his benefice*, is rateable for such profits(1).

Charities, where rateable. The distinction therefore as to where charities are rateable, and where they are not so, seems to depend upon this; whether there is any body who can be rated as *occupier*. The trustees are not rateable when they intermeddle with the property merely as trustees, *because their occupation is not beneficial.* Neither are the poor, where they are mere inmates without power or control over the premises which they inhabit, as in the case of St. Luke's and Bartholomew's hospital, Mr. Waldo's alms-house, and the other cases cited, *for they are not occupiers* (2). But where the objects of a charity are *occupiers*, as in Lord Rich's charity (3), or where another is *a beneficial occupier* for their benefit, as in those of hospital lands (4), the occupier is rateable, without considering the charitable purpose to which the profits are dedicated, although the rate must ultimately come from thence. Nay, where the charity is appropriated to assist the parochial poor for whose support the rate is raised, the property seems liable to the rate if occupied, although the assessment may be nugatory in some instances, and highly improper in others (5).

Occupier's title or interest immaterial. Where lands or other hereditaments are beneficially occupied, the quantity of the occupier's interest, or the validity of his title to the possession, are immaterial (6). He is rateable during his occupation, although he holds at will (7), or may be turned out for misconduct (8), or if his

(1) Robson *v.* Hyde, Cald. 310. 1 Bott, 166. Pl. 186.

(2) *Ante*, 81. (3) *Ante*, 81.

(4) *Ante*, 84. n. (2).

(5) Rex *v.* Catt, *ante*, 83. Rex *v.* Munday, 1 East. 584.

(6) Per Buller J. Lord Bute *v.* Grindall, 1 Term Rep. 338. 1 Bott, 178. *ib. Per* Lord Mansfield, Jones *v.* Maunsell. Doug. 302. 1 Bott, 157. Pl. 181.

(7) *Per* Buller J. Lord Bute *v.* Grindall, n. (6). Rex *v.* Mathews, Cald. 1. 1 Bott, 148. Pl. 175. Rex *v.* Hurdis, 3 Term Rep. 497. 1 Bott, 191. Pl. 296.

(8) Rex *v.* Munday, 1 East. 584.

title

title is altogether defective. As where the dean and chapter of Durham granted leases for 21 years of land, reserving a right to them and their successors, of laying, making, and granting waggon-ways, paying reasonable damage; the dean and chapter granted a waggon-way over lands thus demised, and the grantee inclosed and occupied the soil of the line of way, erecting houses and putting up gates thereon, thereby excluding the lessees and their undertenants. The court were of opinion, that the grantee of this waggon-way was rateable for the land, "as a piece or "parcel of ground called a waggon-way," so long as he occupied it; for the question is, whether the defendants are, or are not *possessed* of property that is rateable to the poor? And though nothing more passed than a way-leave by the grant from the dean and chapter, for they could grant no more, not having reserved a right to grant the land, yet as the person rated occupied the land, it is sufficient; for the court are not to inquire into the title of occupiers. If a desseisor obtain possession of land, he is rateable as the occupier of it (1).

Of joint, several, and particular occupation.

The occupation also may not only be joint (2) or several (3), but as it were special and particular. The occupation may be considered as particular, where the person occupies so far as to receive immediately some particular profits thereout for which no other person is rateable as occupier, although some other is, for distinct pruposes, in possession of the subject from which they issue. Thus the warden of the fleet is rateable for that part of the prison which he lets out in rooms to his prisoners at a weekly rent, although the rooms are in the actual possession of the prisoners (4). The corporation of London was held rateable for the tolls of the barge-way, of which the herbage and pasture was demised to a lessee who was rated for them (5). The lessee of the lot and cope of a lead-mine is liable, although the mine itself is in the possession of those who work it, and who are not

(1) Rex v. Bell, 7 Term Rep. 598. 1 Bott, 232. Pl. 215.

(2) Rex v. Munday, *ante* 85. n. (8).

(3) *Ibid.*

(4) Cald. 407. Rex v. Eyles, 1 Bott, 169. Pl. 188.

(5) Rex v. Mayor of London, 4 Term Rep. 21, 1 Bott, 201. Pl. 202.

subject

ſubject to the tax (1). So the ranger of a park is aſſeſſable for his ſhare of the profits of the land; yet the crown, who permits a ſort of community of poſſeſſion as to the *uſufruct*, is exempt from aſſeſſment (2).

Of exempted occupation: 1. The king.

Property is in two caſes exempt from the rate on account of the particular nature of the occupation; namely, when occupied by the crown, or for public uſe. Thus the royal palaces are not liable, and never have been rated (3). It ſeems taken for granted in the caſe, that this is a kind of preſcriptive exemption of lands which have been veſted in the crown ever ſince paſſing the act, and have never paid the tax, and that it does not properly ariſe from the king's prerogative. For the caſe ſent from ſeſſions for the court's opinion, ſtated as facts proved before them, that his majeſty is rated to the poor's rate for the mews in the pariſh of New Windſor, and that the ſame is paid by the maſter of the horſe to his majeſty; and that his majeſty is rated for the mews in the pariſh of St. Martin in the city of Weſtminſter, and Lord Mansfield ſeemed to ſanction the propriety of rating the crown in theſe inſtances, by obſerving, that "as to the mews in "St. Martin's pariſh, that part of it only is rated which "was taken in of late years, and which was before that "time ground belonging to ſome adjacent pariſh (4)." This opinion proceeds partly upon the ground, that the mews are extraparochial; but if that were ſo, they could not be rated to an adjoining pariſh, unleſs in aid (5), whether they belonged to the crown or to a private individual: and it ſeems difficult to maintain that they are exempt upon the ground of preſcription, for it has been often held, that no cuſtom, preſcription, or uſage, can have any power in reſtraining the operation of a ſtatute which is ſo modern as 43 Eliz. (6) The true reaſon therefore ſeems to be that already given, viz. that the king not being

(1) Rowls *v.* Gells, Cowp. 451. 1 Bott, 146. Pl. 174.

(2) Lord Bute *v.* Grindall, 1 Term Rep. 338. 1 Bott, 175. Pl. 190.

(3) *Per* Lord Mansfield, Rex *v.* Matthews. Cald. 1. 1 Bott, 150.

(4) *Ibid.*

(5) See *poſt.* chap. xiii.

(6) *Ante.* 67. n. (2), (3). and Cald. 414.

being named in the act, is exempted by virtue of his prerogative.

Does not extend to occupiers under him.

But upon whatever principle the sovereign's immunity from this tax depends, it does not extend beyond his actual occupation. It has been decided not only that when the site of a palace is demised to a subject for a certain permanent interest, that the grantees who occupy are rateable (1); but also that those who beneficially occupy part of the royal parks, and (perhaps for the same reason) of the palaces to their own use, are liable to assessment (2), although the premises are to be considered in all other respects as in the hands of the crown.

Thus the crown lessee of certain duties payable out of lead mines, is rateable (3).

The ranger of Richmond park is, by virtue of his office, entitled to certain profits arising out of land inclosed in the park, the meadows of which are mowed at the king's expence for the use of the deer, and the overplus applied for the use of the king's and ranger's horses; the arable lands are manured, ploughed, and sown by the king's servants, and with his horses, but the seed is found and the corn reaped by and for the ranger's use. It was found also by the verdict, that the profits arising to the ranger for the whole of the said lands, were worth 100l. a year, and he was held rateable for the same; but the court doubted at first whether his occupation was sufficiently stated (4). So a keeper of a royal park appointed by the ranger during pleasure, and occupying a lodge and two acres of land within the parish, is rateable for what he occupies (5). The master of the rolls, and the auditors and tellers of the Exchequer, are rateable for houses which they occupy, in respect of their offices as servants of the crown (6).

(1) Duke of Portland's case, 1 Bott, 122. Pl 160. And Mr. Caldecott's note in page 158 of his Reports.

(2) Rex *v.* Mathews, *ut supra.* 85. n. (7).

(3) Rowls *v.* Gells, *ut sup.* 87. n. (1).

(4) Lord Bute *v.* Grindall, *Ibid.* n. (2).

(5) Rex *v.* Mathews, *Ibid.* n. (3.)

(6) *Per* Lord Kenyon, Rex *v.* Hurdis 3 Term Rep. 497. 1 Bott, 191. Pl. 196.

Provided

Property occupied merely for public use, is also exempted from the rate. Of occupancy by the public.

Thus stables rented by the colonel of a regiment by order of the crown, for the use of his regiment of horse guards, in which the troop horses with the accoutrements were kept, are not liable to be rated for the poor's relief (1). So turnpike and navigation tolls paid for the benefit of the public, are exempted from rate (2). But these cases come perhaps most properly under the class of exemption for want of a beneficial occupier, and the actual possessions of the crown are the only just exceptions from the statute, where a beneficial occupation exists.

The question of who is to be considered as the occupier, is generally a matter of fact, and when actually found by the sessions, the court of King's Bench will hold themselves concluded by the finding, unless that question be expresly submitted to them, although the circumstances of the case would have warranted a contrary deduction (3). The occupier, if found by the session, conclusive.

The master-gunner of the fort or battery of Seaford, is a warrant officer appointed and removeable at pleasure by the master-general of the ordnance, though his office is usually considered as a provision for life, and he was rated as the occupier of the battery-house. The sessions found in their case, that being so employed in the fort, he occupied the whole of the house except one room, which is allotted to the under governor by direction from the ordnance, and that the furniture of the house belonged to the master-gunner. The court held, that upon this statement he was properly rated; for the statute subjects every occupier of " lands, houses," &c. to be rated, and the sessions having expresly stated that he is the occupier, they have by that finding concluded the question of his rateability (4). The master-gunner of Seaford battery.

(1) Lord Amherst *v.* Lord Somers, Eckersall *v.* Briggs, *ante* 81.

(2) *Per* Lawrence J. Rex *v.* Proprietors of Staffordshire Navigation, 8 T. Rep. 340. 1 Bott, 696. Pl. 998.

(3) Rex *v.* Turner, 1 Bott, 116, Pl. 152.

(4) Rex *v.* Hardis, 3 Term Rep, 497. 1 Bott, 191. Pl, 196.

To

Occupation of personal property.

To render personal property rateable, it must not only be in the possession of the person rated; but when distinctly assessed as moveables, it should be his actual property (1). For the tax is not imposed, as in the case of real property, in respect of occupancy, but upon the person's ability as an inhabitant, of which, ownership, and not possession, is the criterion. But possession of personal property is evidence upon which the sessions ought to conclude, that the possessor is the proprietor, unless the the contrary is proved (2).

(1) *Per* Lord Mansfield, Rex *v.* Ringwood, Cowp. 326. 1 Bott, 144. Pl. 173. Rex *v.* Dursley, 6 Term Rep. 53. 1 Bott, 223. Pl. 209.

(2) *Ibid.*

CHAPTER X.

Of Rating double.

REAL property is not to be rated twice: the affeffment is to be levied on the occupier according to the total profit, every perfon who has an intereft therein, paying his proportion of the tax. So that the occupier is the receiver of the whole produce, who, after defraying all charges, diftributes a fixed fhare of the net profits to thofe under whom he holds, and retains the remainder in remuneration of his trouble. 1. Real property.

Upon this principle, rents are not rateable in the hands of the landlord, for it would be a double affeffment (1). So quit-rents, and the cafual profits of a manor, fuch as fines paid upon renewal of copyholds, heriots, &c. are not affeffable; the leffees being refpectively affeffed to the entire value of the lands out of which thefe interefts arife (2). Rents, &c.

It is faid to have been decided, that ground rents are fubject to the rate (3): but to reconcile this determination with the cafe of quit-rents juft cited, it feems neceffary to fuppofe that the annual value of the houfe was rated, after deducting the rent payable for the ground on which it ftood (4).

Perfonal property is alfo exempted, where it has been taxed in another fhape (5). Thus the ftock neceffary for cultivating 2. Perfonal property. Stock on farm.

(1) *Per* Lord Mansfield, Rowls *v.* Gells, *ante*, 87. n.(1). Rex *v.* Toms, Doug. 401. 1 Bott, 161. *Per* Eyre C. J. Lord Bute *v.* Grindall, *ante*, 87. n. (2).

(2) Rex *v.* Vandewall, 2 Burr. 991. 1 Bott, 122. Pl. 161. *Per* Ld. Kenyon, Rex *v.* Alberbury, 1 Eaft. 536.

(3) Rex *v.* Gibbs, Comb. 62. 1 Bott, 115. Pl. 147.

(4) *Ante*, n. (2).

(5) Regina *v.* Barking, 2 Ld. Raym. 1280. 1 Bott, 116. Pl. 150, 151. 16 Vin. Abr. 426.

cultivating and rendering a farm productive, is not rateable, because the annual profits of the land being rated, the profits of the stock are assessed in those of the farm. In rating land therefore, the annual loss of capital laid out in purchasing stock, with the expence of maintaining it, and the damage arising from wear and tear, operates in diminution of the profits of the land, and should be deducted in assessing the land, instead of forming a separate article for taxation (1).

But, if a farmer keeps stock, the profits of which cannot be counted in those of his land; as if he fattens cattle upon food purchased from other persons, and sells them with a profit, he seems not less liable to be taxed for this profit, where personal property is rated, than the butcher is for what he makes by killing the stock when bought from the farmer. Keeping them in his farm-yard, cannot exempt him, for he resembles a tradesman, who is rateable for his stock in trade, and also for his dwelling-house, although he converts part of it into a shop, the rent of which forms a drawback upon the net profit of his goods (2).

(1) Post. Chap. 12 p. 97. (2) *Ut* in 91. n. 5.

CHAPTER XI.

Property, in what Place rateable.

PROPERTY, whether real or perſonal, or rather the produce upon which the rate is laid, muſt ariſe in the diſtrict for which the aſſeſſment is made. In lands or tenements, this muſt of courſe be in the place where the thing itſelf is ſituate. Thus, if a gardener contracts to ſerve twenty families, and carries all his crop to their different houſes (which are ſituate in different pariſhes), he is rateable for the whole of his garden where it lies (1). In lands, &c.

So in the caſe of the water-works, it was held, that the whole profits were aſſeſſable in the pariſh where the water was collected by means of the fire-engine and other works fixed there, as it there firſt becomes property. For when water is once collected by means of a fire-engine, and brought within lands or buildings, for the purpoſe of ſupplying houſes at a certain ſtipend, it is as much private property as the land itſelf. Whatever is done afterwards, is only done for the purpoſe of vending that property to greater advantage (2). So when fiſh caught at ſea are titheable, the tithe is rateable in the pariſh by being brought into, which they yield a profit payable to the clergyman (3). Water-works.

The caſe of tolls is in ſome inſtances of more apparent difficulty, but is aſcertained upon the ſame principle. Such as are paid *for paſſing* a bridge (4), a ſluice (5), or a turnpike-gate (6), are evidently rateable where theſe things are ſituated; for it is there only that they become productive, as it is from paſſing there that the duties accrue. Tolls of a bridge, &c.

(1) *Per* Buller J. Atkins *v.* Davis, Cald. 327.

(2) *Ib.* & *per* Ld. Loughborough, 357.

(3) Rex *v* Carlyon, 3 Term Rep. 385. 1 Bott, 190. Pl. 195.

(4) (5) (6) See *ante*, 53.

of a navigation,

But the caſe of profits ariſing from inland navigations, which run through ſeveral pariſhes, has produced more diſcuſſion. They might be rated either in each pariſh through which the goods are carried in proportion to the number of miles they float in each; or at the place only where the tolls are actually collected, whether it be appointed at the diſcretion of the proprietors, or by direction of the ſtatute by virtue of which they are taken: or, finally, they might be rated where the tolls become due. The Court determined in favour of the latter mode, in conformity to the deciſions already ſtated in the caſe of other tolls. Even where the tolls were directed by ſtatute to be taken "at ſo much per mile upon all goods;" it was held, that they were aſſeſſable only in thoſe pariſhes where the ſeveral voyages are completed, and to the amount of the profits ariſing thereon. For unleſs the voyage is completed, the contract being entire, nothing can be due from the owner of the goods (1).

of a light-houſe.

The profits of tolls and duties payable to the Harwich light-houſes, ſeem to have been adjudged not aſſeſſable upon the ſame principle. They were payable by all ſhips paſſing or coming into that harbour, only part thereof being received at the port of H., the remainder at many different parts of the kingdom. The collections were caſual as ſhips paſs by, or come into the harbour, and there was no other advantage ariſing to the proprietor from the light-houſes. It is taken for granted in the argument, but not ſtated as a fact in the caſe, that the light-houſes were ſituated within the pariſh for which the rate was made. But whether the tolls became due in an extra-parochial place, or where elſe, is not expreſly mentioned. The court were of opinion, that the tolls were not locally ſituated within the pariſh, and therefore not rateable there (2).

(1) Rex *v.* Air and Calder Navigation, 2 Term Rep. 660. 1 Bott, 107. Pl. 133. Rex *v.* Page, *ib.* 83. Pl. 109. 4 Term Rep. 543. Rex *v.* Proprietors of Staffordſhire Navigation, 8 Term Rep. 340. 1 Bott, 696. Pl. 998.

(2) Rex *v.* Rebowe, 1 Bott, 139. Pl. 171.

By

Marsh lands, when drained.

By 17 Geo. II. c. 37. when waste lands, which were formerly fens and marsh, are drained and improved, and the parish to which they belong cannot be ascertained, the occupier thereof, or of houses built thereon, tenements, tithes arising therefrom, mines therein, and saleable underwoods thereon growing, or hereafter to grow, are to be rated to the parish that lies nearest to such lands; and if any dispute shall arise as to what parish or place they ought to be rated to, the justices in quarter sessions shall, after due notice given to the persons interested, and to the parishes and places abutting and adjoining the said lands, cause them to be assessed in such place as they think meet, and their determination and allotment is to be final and conclusive.

Personal property, when rateable;

To render the profits of personal property rateable, they must arise in that parish for which the rate is made. Upon this ground the owner was adjudged not rateable in the parish where he resided, for money which he had vested in real securities upon lands lying without the parish (1).

how far visible.

The resolution in Sir Anthony Earby's case states, that personal property to be rateable, must not only be locally situated within the parish, but *visible* there. Several opinions of the judges in subsequent cases are to the same effect (2), and in determining, whether principal money in the custody of the owner was rateable, Mr. J. Buller relies upon it as an argument in the negative, that the rate must be confined to visible property, yielding profit in the parish (3). But other judges have found it difficult to affix a determinate meaning to the term, visible property (4).

That it must be to a certain degree visible, or more properly perceptible, is manifest, since, otherwise the parish

(1) Rex *v.* White, 4 Term Rep. 771. 1 Bott, 208. Pl. 205.

(2) Rex *v.* Canterbury, 1 Bott, 132. Pl. 168. Rex *v.* Andover, Cowp. 550. 1 Bott, 151. Pl. 176.

(3) Rex *v.* White, *ante*, n. (1).

(4) Lord Mansfield, Rex *v.* Ringwood, Cowp. 326. 1 Bott, 144. Pl. 173.

parish officers will be unable to support by competent proof, that the property which they have rated is actually possessed (1). But there are several kinds of property which are liable to the rate, and yet not generally and sometimes not even the possible subject of occular inspection. Lord Mansfield defines visible property to be "something local in the place where a man inhabits (2);" adding the qualification of residence by the owner to what is implied by the term local, as applied to the thing rated. Lord Kenyon observes on the same subject; "it "is said that only property which is *visible* should be rated; "but I think that is carrying the rule of exemption too far; "for oblations and other offerings which constitute the "rectorial or vicarial dues, are rateable (3)." And in a case subsequent to that in which principal money was held not rateable, the same learned judge intimated an opinion which seems to the contrary (4).

(1) *Per* Lord Kenyon, Rex *v.* White, 4 Term Rep. 771. 1 Bott, 214.

(2) Rex *v.* Ringwood, 95. n. (4).

(3) Rex *v.* Carlyon, 3 Term Rep. 385. 1 Bott, 190. Pl. 195.

(4) Rex *v.* Mast, 6 Term Rep. 154. 1 Bott, 225. Pl. 210.

CHAPTER XII.

Of the Principles upon, and Proportions in which the Rate is to be made.

THE sums raised for the poor's relief should be assessed upon the productive value of all property occupied in the district for which the rate is made, for the tax has reference to the present local ability and situation of those who are to pay it. A parish therefore cannot have a standing rate, neither should an old one be confirmed, for the proportions must vary with the fluctuations of property (1). It will be bad likewise, if made according to the land tax (2). But the assessment in the old rate may be a good reason for making one similar in the new, unless there is some increase or decrease of value (3). Rate on actual value.

It has been already shewn (4), that the pecuniary ability of each district arises from three sources: 1st, The product of labour; 2d, Of capital or personal property; and, 3d, Of real property, such as lands, houses, and the like. It has been also stated, that the first species of property is not directly assessable (5). 1. Rate on product of labour.

Personal property, with reference to this statute, is defined by Lord Mansfield, "the surplus of a man's estate "and effects, after payment of debts, the maintenance of "his family, and necessary expences (6)." But it has never been decided, whether such indefinite quantums, as maintenance and necessary expences, can be deducted. 2. On personal property.

(1) Rex v. Audley, 2 Salk. 526. 1 Bott. Pl. 123.

(2) Rex v. Clerkenwell, Ib. 100. Pl. 125. Fol. 12.

(3) Rex v. Wrexham, 1 Bott, 102. Pl. 126.

(4) *Ante*, p. 66.

(5) *Ibid.*

(6) Rex v. Shalfleet, 1 Bott, 129. Pl. 125.

Analogy to the tax of ſubſidies in uſe when the 43 Eliz. paſſed (1), and the manner in which the poor's rate is impoſed on real property, imply that it is to be levied on the clear profits of the productive ſubject, without further drawback. Lord Kenyon ſeems alſo to have conſidered that the ſole queſtion neceſſary to determine its rateability is, " whether or not it produced a profit, or was liable " to incumbrances equal to the value of the property " itſelf (2)."

The principles upon which this kind of property ſhould be aſſeſſed, have not been ſettled by judicial deciſions. But it is laid down, that if a perſon be rated for ſtock in trade, and virtually ſubmits to his aſſeſſment by not appealing againſt the rate, it is *primâ facie* evidence, that he is aſſeſſable in the enſuing year to the like amount (3). It has been likewiſe remarked, that perſonal property is not to be rated at random, or the party left to get off as he can; but the officer making the rate, muſt be able to ſupport what he has done by evidence (4).

What deductions from product of perſonal property.

It may be obſerved on this ſubject, without the guidance of caſes, that as the tax is laid upon the net profits, the proprietor is entitled to deduct the prime coſt, the expences of clerks, warehouſe-room, inſurance, and whatever elſe the tradeſman or merchant ſubtracts, as conſtituting the difference between the groſs and net produce of ſtock, ſo far as they operate in diminution of his perſonal ability to contribute.

It is not ſettled whether he can deduct the value of his individual labour, upon the ſame principle which exonerates the profits of perſonal labour in profeſſions and mechanical trades, or whether it is to be conſidered as merged in the profits of ſtock, and rateable therewith.

(1) *Ante*, 66.

(2) Rex *v.* Durſley, 6 Term Rep. 53. 1 Bott. 223. Pl. 209.

(3) Rex *v.* Darlington, 1 Term Rep 468. 1 Bott, 228. Pl. 212. See alſo Rex *v.* Brograve, 4 Burr. 2491.

(4) *Per* Lord Kenyon, *citing the* opinion of Yates J. Rex *v.* White, 4 Term Rep. 771. 1 Bott, 208. Pl. 205.

But

But a trader may ſubſtract the intereſt of borrowed capital, for it is in the nature of an incumbrance upon the goods (1). Yet he cannot allow intereſt for his own, becauſe though it forms no part of the net profits of his trade, it is rateable in another ſhape, namely, as the direct produce of his capital.

Deduction of debts.

It is ſaid, that the total amount of a man's debts (2) is to be deducted, and the tax laid upon the profits of his ſurplus property. This principle, which is highly equitable, may give riſe to ſome difficulty when it operates in conjunction with another rule, *viz.* that perſonal eſtate is only rateable where it is locally ſituated. If, on the one hand, no other property of this deſcription is aſſeſſable within the pariſh for which the rate is made than what exiſts there (3), and if the debts are to be conſidered, on the other hand, as following the perſon, ſo that their total amount, whereſoever contracted, are to operate not againſt the entire perſonal ability of him who is rated, but againſt his particular local ability in that pariſh; it gives a great advantage to thoſe whoſe property is diſtributed in ſeveral diſtricts.

Thus, for example, if the perſon to be taxed has 100,000l. diſtributed in ten ſeveral pariſhes, viz. 10,000l. in each, and his total debt amounts to ten thouſand pounds; this debt operating to its full amount in every pariſh, and the 10,000 l. property which he has in each pariſh, being the whole of what is rateable there, he eſcapes from the tax in all, though poſſeſſed of a clear perſonal eſtate of 90,000 l., yielding an annual return. But if this 100,000 l. is ſituated in one pariſh, he is rateable for the profits of 90,000 l., which is the real amount of his property, deducting his debts.

(1) Rex *v.* Durſley, 6 Term Rep. 53. 1 Bott. 223. Pl 209.

(2) Rex *v.* Canterbury, 1 Bott, 238. Pl. 168. Rex *v.* Sha'fleet, 1 Bott, 129. Pl. 125. 4 Burr. 2031. *Per* Lord Kenyon, Rex *v* White, 4 Term Rep. 771. 1 Bott, 214.

(3) *Ante*, 95.

Perſonal property is not uſually rated. It is difficult to aſcertain its actual amount, unleſs by uſing thoſe arbitrary means, which are neither provided by the poor laws, nor permitted by the ſpirit of our conſtitution. Sometimes, a fair diſcloſure of his effects is ſuppoſed to injure a commercial man, and he would rather chuſe to ſubmit to the impoſition of an exorbitant aſſeſſment, than ſeek redreſs at the hazard of his credit. Theſe, and other reaſons, have induced moſt pariſhes to refrain as it were by common impulſe, from aſſeſſing perſonal property ſince the 43d Elizabeth. Its liability is no longer queſtionable; but the apprehenſion of miſchievous conſequences has uſually prevented its being rated even in manufacturing countries, where the omiſſion preſſes upon the landed proprietor with conſiderable hardſhip.

3. Rate on real property.

The fund for maintaining the poor is therefore chiefly raiſed by a pound rate upon real property. The great principle upon which it is to be rated is, that *the tax ſhall be impoſed on the actual productive value at the time of making the rate, whether that is more or leſs than what it had been when the former rate was made* (1).

If a houſe to day is let for 30*l. per annum*, and tomorrow, if turned into a ſhop, would let for 50l.; when it is turned into a ſhop it ſhall be rated at 50l. (2). If a perſon has a ſmall piece of land in the heart of a town, which is only of ſmall value, and he afterwards build on it, he muſt be rated to the poor upon its *improved value* with the building upon the land (3).

The circumſtances and manner in which that property became ſo valuable are not to be conſidered (4); whether the perſon rated occupies as proprietor or leſſee, he can obtain

(1) See the opinion of De Grey, C. J. Kemp *v.* Spence, 2 Black. 1245. 1 Bott, 81. Pl. 103.

(2) *Per* Buller J. Rex *v.* St. Nicholas Glouceſter, Cald 262. 1 Bott, 156.

(3) *Per* Lord Kenyon C. J. Rex *v.* Maſt. 6 Term Rep. 154. 1 Bott, 224. Pl 210.

(4) *Per* Aſhurſt J. *Ibid.*

tain no abatement from the actual value, as increased by his improvements, however beneficial they may be to the parish, permanent in their nature, or laudable in their object.

Thus where a gentlemen had purchased an estate, which he kept in his own possession, and rendered of greater value by various improvements, it was held by the court of King's Bench, that he must be rated according to the improved, and not the original value or first cost (1). Improvements.

So where it appeared that a farm was let on lease at a reserved rent, which was then its annual value, and neither fine nor other premium or consideration was paid to the landlord, beside; but during the progress of the term, the farm rose in value beyond the rent. It was thought a question too clear to admit of argument, that the rent was not conclusive evidence of the value, but that the farmer must be rated according to the actual improved worth of what he occupied (2).

More difficulty arises in determining by what method this present value is to be ascertained. In the case of lands and houses, the rate is usually imposed in one of three ways: 1. Upon the actual rack-rent, when they are in the hands of a lessee. 2. On a supposed rent formed on valuation; which is done where they are occupied by the proprietor, or by a tenant who pays less rent than the premises are worth. 3. On an annual per centage calculated upon the purchase money, with a just allowance for necessary outgoings. 3. Modes of rating lands and houses.

All these modes of valuation proceed upon the assumption, that the rack-rent is the criterion of that actual value upon which the tax is laid: but this principle is fallacious, rent 1. On the rack rent.

(1) Rex *v.* Mast. *Ante*, 100. n.(3).
(2) Rex *v.* Skingle, 7 Term Rep. 549. 1 Bott, 231. Pl. 214.

being only so much of the actual value as the tenant can afford to pay his landlord, deducting the expence of cultivation, and a reasonable remuneration for trouble and time. The rent therefore is the landlord's profit, the reasonable remuneration is the tenant's profit. Both come from the land, and form parts of its productive value. When land is occupied by the proprietor, he receives both these profits; when it is demised to a tenant, they are divided.

Deductions thereon.

Deductions for expences of labour and capital necessary to render the subject productive, should be considered in both cases as drawbacks upon the profit, and due allowance should be made, upon the same principle, for every part of the produce which belongs to another person, and may be rated in his hands; such as tithes. So also if lands, subject to a right of common, are rated in the hands of the proprietor, a deduction ought to be made proportioned to the value of this right, as it takes from him so much of the benefits of the soil (1). But the net produce after these deductions, whether it goes to the landlord in the name of rent, or to the tenant as profit, or to the occupant proprietor who stands in the place of both, is the legitimate object of tax in the hands of him who occupies the land.

Inconvenience of rating by the rack rent.

If no other property but land was rateable, there seems but one objection to this mode of fixing the rate by the rack-rent; namely, that the tax would fall principally, if not altogether, upon the owner of the inheritance. But as every sort of real property is rateable, some mines excepted, this practice produces great inequality, and violates the grand rule of rating, which is, "that whatever be the "poportion of rating in a parish, whether to the full "value or otherwise, the rate must be equally made on "all persons (2)."

(1) *Per* De Grey C. J. Kamp *v.* Spence, 2 Black. 1245. 1 Bott, 81. Pl. 108.

(2) *Per* Lord Kenyon C. J. Rex *v.* Mast, 6 Term Rep. 154. 1 Bott, 224. Pl. 210.

 Thus

Thus tithes, coal-mines, tolls, water-works, and faleable under-woods, are affeffed according to the net annual amount of profits, deducting all expences; or, in other words, they are rated at their full value; but land, when rated upon the rack-rent, is only affeffed according to the landlord's profits, or *minus* the productive value, by whatever the farmer's profit amounts to. As to tithes, &c.

Let it be fuppofed, by way of example, that the fair principle for dividing the annual produce of a farm between landlord and tenant, is, that after deducting all expences, each fhould take one-half, and that the annual average of this moiety is the rack-rent ftipulated to be paid; it is obvious, that if the farm is affeffed upon its rent, the occupier is rated only for half the actual value of the land, while the clergyman, and thofe who occupy tolls, coal-mines, &c. are rated at the full value of the property, or in a twofold proportion.

But the principle is ftill more unequal when applied to buildings. In general they yield no direct profit to the tenant, mere convenience not being the fubject of rate. The rent therefore is the total annual produce; but as buildings are fubject to decay, the rent fhould be divided into two parts; one to be laid by for the purpofe of repair, or, in other words, to reproduce the capital, which has been expended on a perifhable fubject. This portion is not affeffable, becaufe capital is not directly taxed to the poor's rate. The remainder is the annual produce of the capital thus originally laid out, and is the only fair object of affeffment. A houfe therefore, yielding a certain rent, is, by this method, not only affeffed double what land yielding the fame rent is, but fo much more as the fum amounts to, which the proprietor ought to lay by out of his rent, for the re-production of his capital. As to houfes.

Such a divifion is nearly made by the landlord and tenant, when the latter agrees to make thofe fubftantial repairs which he would not otherwife be compellable to do.

Where that takes place, the rent paid to the landlord is the true profit which ſhould be taxed, the tenant not being rateable for theſe repairs, although they are in effect a rent payable to the landlord in kind. But where the landlord is to make theſe repairs, and receives in conſequence a greater rent, an adequate deduction ſhould be made on that account, and the occupier aſſeſſed only for the reſidue.

3. By a *per centage.* Calculating a *per centage* on the purchaſe money, hath this advantage in common with that of calculating upon the rack-rent, *viz.* that where the price is fairly diſcloſed, the mode of aſcertaining the rate is certain. But as the clear rack-rent is always the ground upon which the price of land is calculated, it is at beſt but another method of rating upon that rent. A further objection may be made, where both are practiced, namely, that they introduce into the ſame pariſh three diſtinct modes of valuing the ſame ſpecies of ſubject in the ſame rate: 1ſt, That of price when an eſtate is bought; 2d, Of rent where it is farmed; and, 3d, Of valuation as to the fair rent, where it is occupied by the ancient proprietor, or by a tenant paying leſs rent than it is worth.

Independent of theſe objections to rating by a *per centage* on purchaſe money (which applies to all caſes, even where the fee is acquired), it is in its nature more inaccurate than when impoſed upon the rent; for it aſcertains the value upon the judgment or good fortune of the purchaſer, inſtead of the actual worth of the thing. The rate is diminiſhed in proportion as the real value exceeds the price paid, and increaſed in the ſame *ratio* where it is leſs: thus taking the burthen from him who has made a lucrative bargain, to impoſe it upon him who has made one that is unprofitable.

But if an intereſt ſhort of a fee is purchaſed, this mode of calculation becomes more complicated, and is therefore in danger of being ſtill more fallacious.

Where

Of ascertaining the actual value for a particular rate.

Where it is agreed that the entire profits ſhall be rated by whomſoever enjoyed, it ſtill remains to ſettle how they are to be aſcertained.

According to ſtrict theory, the rate ſhould be raiſed upon the actual value of the taxable ſubject during the period for which, according to reaſonable intendment, the ſum levied will ſupply the poor.

If this principle was purſued, the farmer (ſuppoſing the rates to be made half yearly) would be aſſeſſed at a higher proportion during autumn, in which his harveſt is gathered, than in ſpring, when his land is more expenſive in its cultivation, and leſs productive in return. The owners of houſes at watering places would pay more during the ſeaſon in which the influx of occaſional ſojourners increaſes their rent, than when the town is left to its uſual inhabitants.

But the application of a theoretical principle muſt be limited by the convenience of ſociety, or it defeats the object for which it is introduced. The natural deficiencies and diverſities of human ſenſe and intellect, and the variety of our avocations and habits, render it impoſſible for practice to follow to its utmoſt verge, that clear and ſteady outline which is marked out by the eye of ſpeculation. The period for which the fund raiſed ſhall laſt is uncertain, as it depends upon the uncertain demands of the poor. The inceſſant inveſtigation of pariſh officers can not always lead to a certain concluſion, and the expences of litigation would exceed any benefit which might reſult from a more accurate aſſeſſment, if it could be attained.

On annual average value.

The beſt method therefore ſeems to be, that the annual value of the property ſhould be aſſumed as the foundation of the aſſeſſment. That value alſo ſhould be eſtimated, not according to the productive return of the particular year in which the rate is made, but according to the fair average thereof, as compared with other lands in the pariſh of a ſimilar quality. Thus lands cultivated with hops or teazel,

teazel, which do not yield an annual crop, ſhould be taxed upon a yearly average ſtruck between the producing and unproductive years; lands ſown with graſs, corn, or ſuch roots and vegetables as give an annual return, ſhould be aſſeſſed upon the ſame average annual value, without reference to the crop of the particular year.

Objection to this mode of valuing.

One objection may be reaſonably made to this mode of calculating the tenant's profit of land. It is not founded upon what he actually makes, but upon what it is ſuppoſed that he ought to make according to ſober principles of calculation, having reſpect to the actual ſtate and condition of his farm. It makes no allowance for the difference of induſtry, ſkill, and capital, in different farmers.

An aſſeſſment on the rent is exempt from this inconvenience, for ſuch deductions are made from the tenant's profit, which is not included in the rate when made upon that principle. But in neither method is there any allowance for extraordinary deficiencies, from the calamities of a particular ſeaſon, or the accidental failure of crops.

A ſcrutiny of this ſort would lead to all that difficulty and inconvenience, which is felt in rating perſonal property. Extraordinary contingencies muſt always give riſe to particular relief; but the moſt effectual remedy againſt the general objection, will be found in making the valuation moderate; rather below than at the rate of profit which a tenant uſually receives. This will compenſate for any accidental exceſs of the rate beyond the due proportion, and as it can rarely occur, the occupier will rather acquieſce, than riſk the expence and trouble of an appeal. If by this means alſo, ſome perſons are in a ſlight degree under rated, it will be ſuch as deſerve the bounty, by rendering their farms more productive than thoſe of their neighbours, through ſuperior ſkill or activity.

It has been already ſeen, that the rate is to be made upon the preſent value, and has no reference to ſpeculative improvements, or the poſſible application of property to a more lucrative purpoſe.

And

And as the value, if enhanced, ſhould be rated; ſo due allowance ſhould be made where it is leſſened, annihilated, or new created, by culture or neglect, by pulling down ancient buildings, or erecting new ones, for that is no injury to the pariſh, though the taxes thereby become heavier to the reſt of the pariſhioners(1). But where land has found an actual value, which is afterwards diminiſhed by the *voluntary* act of the occupier for *his particular pleaſure*, it ſeems doubtful what deduction he ſhould obtain on that account. **Premiſes falling in value.**

It is unreaſonable that men who from opulence are enabled to devote conſiderable portions of their land to gardens, hot-houſes, deer-parks, and other pleaſureable purpoſes, ſhould not be rated according to the actual value of the ſame extent of land in the ſame pariſh of ſimilar quality, which the farmer devotes to the more beneficial object of providing articles of the firſt neceſſity for mankind. The principle already ſtated, that the rate is to be impoſed upon the average annual value, and not the particular produce of the land, may apply in ſome degree, but not ſo ſtrongly as it does to the inſtances of hops and teazel which have been mentioned. In thoſe caſes, the occupier is content to forego the profits of one or two years, in order to receive them with advantage in the ſecond or third. But pleaſure grounds are not laid out with a view to a profitable return to the occupier at any time. **Profits of pleaſure-grounds.**

The only caſe which bears upon this difficulty is; where the fellows of a college purchaſed five houſes of the annual rent of 55l., pulled them down, and erected ſome apartments for ſtudents, and houſes for their butler and porter on part of the ſite. The remainder was turned into the college court, and an area planted with trees for ornament; and they were rated not only for the apartments and houſes they had built, but for the court and area, according to the former value of the houſes. When

(1) *Per* De Grey C. J. Kemp *v.* Spence, 2 Black. 1245. 1 Bott, 81. Pl. 108. By *injury*, the chief juſtice means *legal injury*.

this

this caſe was litigated, no objection ſeems to have been taken at the ſeſſions as to its being an over rate, although it appeared that the value of the court and area was eſtimated at 43l. 15s. out of 50l. (1) This caſe furniſhes at leaſt ſomething like a rule for overcoming the difficulty. For the college having converted ground which was productive to the amount of 43l. 15s. to ſuch a purpoſe, amounted to ſtrong evidence that it was at leaſt of ſo much value to the body in its preſent ſtate.

Of tolls and water-works, &c.

In taxing other hereditaments, ſuch as tolls, water-works, and coal-mines, of which the produce is tolerably certain, the profits of the laſt form a fair ground to eſtimate thoſe of the riſing year, unleſs reaſons are given to increaſe or reduce it.

Uncertain Profits.

But there is a difficulty where the profits are dubious, and the amount uncertain, inaſmuch as they are rateable notwithſtanding (2). Such are the ranger's profits from the king's park; for the rate is proſpective (3), and the thing is rateable only when it produces profit (4). The aſſeſſment muſt therefore be either made on paſt profits, contrary to the manner of rating lands and tenements, or elſe thoſe which are accruing muſt be eſtimated by the average production of former years.

The rate muſt be proportionate on different kinds of property.

In pointing out the inconvenience of rating real property by the rack-rent, it has been ſhewn that the value o each kind of property ſhould be juſtly eſtimated, not only with reference to its own ſpecies, but with regard to all other kind of property exiſting in the pariſh, and included in the rate. The ſame principle which applies there, applies equally to a rate on real and perſonal where the latter is aſſeſſed.

(1) Rex v. Gardner, Cowp. 79. 1 Bott, 138. Pl. 172. See alſo the caſe of St. Bartholomew's hoſpital, *Ibid.* 131. Pl. 166; and the opinion of Lord Kenyon as to the rateability of money, Rex v. Maſt, *ante*, 96.

(2) Jones v. Maunſell, Doug. 302. 1 Bott, 157. Pl. 181.

(3) Durrant v. Boys. 6 Term Rep. 580. 1 Bott, 79. Pl. 105. and ſee 17 Geo. 2 c 38. ſ. 12.

(4) Lord Bute v. Grindall, 1 Term Rep. 333. 2 H. Black. 267. 1 Bott, 175. Pl. 190.

Dalton

Dalton lays it down, that the moſt reaſonable way of taxing land is according to a pound rate; and where perſonal eſtate, as goods, money, &c. are taxed, it ought to be in the ſame proportion as the land, *viz.* the value of every hundred pounds at 5 *per cent. per annum* (1).

But as the actual value of different ſpecies of property may be affected by very unequal drawbacks on the ground of neceſſary expenditure, and as the general return of profit varies in different parts of the kingdom, no ſuch rule can be laid down with ſafety as applicable to all pariſhes (2).

The relative value of houſes and lands in the ſame pariſh, vary with local circumſtances, even where the rent is the ſame, for (as has been already ſtated) ſome drawbaks of expence may diminiſh the annual value of the one, which do not affect the other.

K. B. will not preſume relative inequality.

The court of king's bench will not preſume that a rate is unequal; yet they will interfere and quaſh one, when framed upon an erroneous principle, and the inequality is ſelf evident on its face (3). But a mere difference in the proportional aſſeſſment of lands and houſes, or of real and perſonal property, will not induce the court to infer inequality, or intermedle with the peculiar province of the quarter ſeſſions, who are to judge of the equality of the rate (4).

Thus the court of king's bench ſuſtained a rate, which appeared by the title to be made "upon all occupiers of "lands, at three fourths of *the yearly value* of the lands, "and upon all occupiers of houſes, at the rate of one "moiety of the yearly value of their reſpective houſes." For though the yearly value might mean the clear yearly value after all deductions, in which caſe the rate would

(1) Dalton Juſt. 123. 1 Bott, 99. Pl. 120.

(2) Rex *v.* Sandwich, Dougl 562. 1 Bott, 104. Pl. 131.

(3) Rex *v.* Audley, 2 Salk 526. 1 Bott, 100. Pl. 123. Rex *v.* Brograve, *Ib.* 102. Pl. 128. 4 Burr. 2491. S. C. Rex *v.* Lakenham. *Ib.* 105. Pl. 132.

(4) Rex *v.* Weobly, *Ib.* 101. Pl. 127. Rex *v.* Barnſtable, *Ib.* 99. Pl. 121. Fol. 26. and the caſes n. 3.

be

be unequal, it may with propriety mean the yearly rent without these deductions, in which case it will not be manifestly unequal, and the court ought to put such a construction upon the title of the rate as will make it good (1).

So where it appeared by a case stated, that a rate was made upon real property, by assessing a moiety or half part of the rack-rent or yearly value of farms; and upon personal, by taking the 20th part of the stock, personal estate, or money, out at interest, and valuing the interest of such 20th part at and after the rate of 4 *per cent. per annum*, and then rating one moiety of such 20th part equally, or as near thereunto as may be; this is not such an inequality as will induce the court to quash the rate (2). Likewise, where it had been customary to make a distinction in the proportion of the rate between farms, which were assessed at 1d. in the pound, and dwelling-houses and cottages only three farthings in the pound; the court of King's Bench on a case, stated, affirmed the judgment of the sessions confirming a rate which assessed them all equally at the rate of 1d. in the pound (3), and the next year confirmed their order for quashing one in the same parish, because made upon the ancient principle of different proportions (4).

When K.B. will quash for it.

But, on the other hand, it was decided in one case, that where the relative proportion which one species of property

(1) Rex *v.* Brograve, *supra* 109. n. 3. The reason, as given here, is made out of both reports, which are not very clearly stated.

(2) Rex *v.* Hardy, Cowp. 579. 1 Bott, 102. Pl. 129.

(3) Rex *v.* Butler, Cald. 93. 1 Bott, 103. Pl. 136.

(4) Rex *v.* Sandwich, Doug. 562. 1 Bott, 104. Pl. 131. In this case Lord Mansfield lays it down, that "the proportion in which lands and "houses respectively contribute, must "ever depend upon local circum- "stances; and if nine-tenths of the "burthen arise from the houses, such "circumstance was sufficient to in- "fluence the judgment of the court "below in adjusting that proportion." This latter position, that the particular species of property which gave rise to the greatest burthens upon the rate, should be taxed in a higher proportion, seems never to have been followed. It is laid down more equitably in the following resolution of the judges of assize, 1683: "35. Qu. If a pa- "rishioner, or owner within a parish, "do

property bears in value to another is, ſtated to be the foundation of the aſſeſſment, and is groſsly and manifeſtly unequal, the court of King's Bench will quaſh the rate. Thus where a rate was made upon a moiety of the yearly value or rack-rent of the real eſtate, and a 40th part of the intereſt on the perſonal, calculated at 4 *per cent.* they quaſhed the rate on the ground of apparent inequality, although the quarter ſeſſions had confirmed it, and found in a ſpecial caſe that this mode of rating contained a relative equality (1).

It has never been expreſsly decided whether a rate muſt be made upon the full value of the property in the pariſh, or whether it may be laid upon a portion of that value, ſuch as two thirds or one half, provided the relative proportions of value are preſerved in all. It appears, however, in the caſes juſt cited, and in ſome others, that ſuch rates have been queſtioned upon other grounds, and ſuſtained, without any objection made on this account. Such a practice is collaterally ſupported likewiſe by the opinion of Lord Kenyon, who ſays, "whatever the proportion of rat-"ing in a pariſh, *whether to the full value or otherwiſe*, the "rate muſt be equally made on all perſons (2)," putting it hypothecally that a rate, though not made upon the full value, may be good if relatively equal. There is in reality no difference in reſpect to the aſſeſſment, which ever method is purſued; whether the ſame ſum is raiſed upon one half, or upon the entire property, the calculation in the pound muſt increaſe or diminiſh in the inverſe *ratio* of the ſum upon which the fund is calculated.

Rates on a portion of the value.

"do bring into the pariſh (without the "conſent of the pariſh) a ſtranger of "another pariſh, which is, or apparently is likely to be burthenſome "unto the pariſh, how may they eaſe "themſelves?

"*Reſol.* By taxing ſuch a one to "the charge of the rates of the poor, "not only having reſpect to his ability, or the land he occupies, but "according to the damage and danger "he bringeth to the pariſh by his "folly." Dalt. Juſt. tit. Poor, c. 73. p. 237. ed. 1727.

But neither rule ſeems ſanctioned by practice, or by any determination.

(1) Rex *v.* Sellers and others, Inhabitants of Lackenham, 1 Bott, 105. Pl. 132. Cald. 522.

(2) Rex *v.* Matt, 6 Term Rep. 154. 1 Bott, 224. Pl. 210.

CHAPTER XIII.

Of rating Pariſhes in Aid.

43 Eliz. c. 2 ſect. 3. within the hundred.

THE poor are to be ſuſtained by pariſhes in the firſt inſtance; but they may ſometimes be too numerous and burthenſome for a particular pariſh to ſupport. The 43 Eliz. c. 2. ſect. 3. provided therefore, that if the juſtices perceived that the inhabitants of a pariſh are unable to levy among themſelves ſufficient ſums of money for the purpoſes of the act, the ſaid two juſtices ſhall tax, rate, and aſſeſs as aforeſaid, *any other* of other pariſhes, or out of any pariſh, within the hundred where the ſaid pariſh is, to pay ſuch ſum and ſums of money to the churchwardens and overſeers of the ſaid poor pariſh, for the ſaid purpoſes as the ſaid juſtices ſhall think fit.

Out of it.

But if the ſaid hundred ſhall not be thought by the ſaid juſtices able and fit to relieve the ſaid ſeveral pariſhes unable to provide for themſelves as aforeſaid, then the juſtices of the peace at their general quarter ſeſſions, or the greater number of them, ſhall rate and aſſeſs as aforeſaid, *any other* of other pariſhes, or out of any pariſh *within the ſaid county* for the purpoſes aforeſaid, as in their diſcretion ſhall ſeem fit.

By two juſtices within the hundred.

Whenever there is any perſon or pariſh within the hundred in which the pariſh unable to maintain its poor is ſituate, of ability ſufficient to ſupply the deficiency, the rate in aid is to be made by two juſtices. They have power to determine the inability of the pariſh which applies for aſſiſtance, and the capacity of thoſe upon whom they make an order to contribute. Reported caſes furniſh no rules to guide their diſcretion, further than that in one pariſh, where the rates amounted to 25s. in the pound,

pound, and were gradually on the increase, and the parishes called upon to contribute were moderately assessed, it was taken for granted at the bar to be a case in which two justices might interfere (1).

In aid of a vill.

According to the words of the statute, this rate could be made only in aid of a parish; but it has been determined, that since the 13 & 14 Car. II. chap. 12. it may be likewise made in favour of a vill which maintains its poor, as being within the equity of the act (2).

Made upon a vill, or extra-parochial place.

But although it was doubted whether a vill which sustained its proper poor, could call upon other districts to contribute, it is evident from the words of the act that a vill (3), or tithing (4), or extra-parochial place (5), which is within the hundred, and of competent ability, may be rated in aid of a parish unable to support its poor.

Justices may rate within what is substantially an hundred, though called by another name.

The jurisdiction of two justices extends not only over an hundred, when so denominated expressly, but also over any other division which is called by a name synonymous or equivalent, as being equally within the intention of the act, although it uses the word "hundred" only. Thus, where two justices made an order for rating the tithing of Milland, in aid of the parish of St. Peter's in the same county, which was confirmed at the sessions, who stated upon their order, "that "the tithing of Milland lies in the same liberty of the "soke with the said parish of St. Peter's;" it was objected in the court of King's Bench, that it does not appear that the places are within the same hundred, as required by 43 Eliz. c. 2., for liberty and soke are vague terms, not equivalent to the known legal term "hundred,"

(1) Rex *v.* Holbeach, 4 Term Rep. 778. 1 Bott, 359. Pl. 409.

(2) Anon. *Ib.* 358. Pl. 405. Fol. 25. *Per* Lord Kenyon and Buller J, Rex *v.* Holbeach, *sup.* n. 1.

(3) *Ib.*

(4) Rex *v.* Milland, 1 Burr. 1 Bott, 359. Pl. 408.

(5) Rex *v.* Clarendon Park, 16 Vin. Abr. 431. Rex *v.* Boroughsen, Fol. 37. 1 Bott, 357. Pl. 407.

 and

and a liberty may extend into ſeveral hundreds. The court ſent the caſe back to the ſeſſions to be more particularly ſtated: but it appearing on the return to be ſubſtantially an hundred, though called by another name, they confirmed both orders (1).

But not where no hundred,

But two juſtices can make no order in aid of pariſhes upon places where there are no hundreds or equivalent diviſions. Such an order of ſetting forth that the two pariſhes were within the county of the city of Norwich, without ſtating that they were within the hundred, was quaſhed for this defect (2).

or the poor pariſh out of their juriſdiction.

Neither can they rate a pariſh within their juriſdiction in aid of one that is not, although both are ſituate within the hundred. As where a rule called upon two juſtices for the county of Worceſter, to ſhew cauſe why a mandamus ſhould not iſſue, commanding them to tax and aſſeſs ſome pariſh within the hundred of Half-Shire, within the ſaid county, in aid of the inhabitants of that part of the pariſh of Dodderhill which lies in the borough of Droitwich, in the ſaid hundred and county, to the ſupport of their poor. It appeared on the affidavits, that part of the pariſh is within the borough and part without, but that both are within the hundred of Half-Shire, and the county of Worceſter. It was admitted, that the borough of Droitwich is an excluſive juriſdiction, with a non-intromittant clauſe as to the juſtices of the county, who therefore had no authority to enter the borough (3). That the part of the pariſh of Dodderhill within the borough, had immemorially maintained its own poor, and had diſtinct overſeers, and was at preſent unable to maintain its poor. But the court diſcharged the rule, being of opinion that the magiſtrates had no juriſdiction to do what was required of them.

(1) Rex *v.* Milland, 1 Burr. 576. 2 Bott, 359. Pl. 408.

(2) St. Benedict *v.* St. Peters, 11 Mod. 269. Fol. 43. 2 Bott, 355. Pl. 399. 406.

(3) Talbot *v.* Hubble, 2 Stra. 1154. Rex *v.* Sainſbury, 4 Term Rep. 45.

For "the ſection of the act ſays, that if the juſtices "perceive that any of the inhabitants of any pariſh are "not able to levy among themſelves ſufficient ſums, &c. "the ſaid two juſtices ſhall and may tax, rate, and aſſeſs "any other of other pariſhes", &c. Having the allowance of all aſſeſſments, and the ſuperintendance of the overſeer's accounts, the legiſlature preſumed, that the juſtices would have the means of knowing the neceſſities of all the pariſhes within their juriſdiction; but they cannot have the opportunity of knowing the circumſtances of thoſe diſtricts which lie out of their juriſdiction. And therefore to provide for all caſes that might happen, the eighth ſection of the act was introduced, which gives the ſame power to borough juſtices, that was before given to county juſtices. So that in all caſes, the acts of magiſtrates are to be confined within the limits of their reſpective precincts.

There is one difficulty indeed, in a caſe where a borough conſiſts only of one pariſh. But the argument drawn thence, to ſhew that the county magiſtrates muſt of neceſſity interfere, proves too much, for there are inſtances of ſuch towns being counties in themſelves; *e. g.* the borough of Caermarthen; but in ſuch a caſe it is impoſſible to ſay that the juſtices of the adjoining county can interfere (1).

Where one pariſh in an excluſive juriſdiction, it is out of the act.

When the aſſeſſment is judged neceſſary, it may be impoſed in two ways: "the juſtices may tax particular "perſons in aid to that pariſh which cannot relieve its "own poor (2); or they may aſſeſs the whole pariſh in a "certain ſum, and leave it to the churchwardens to levy "the ſame on particular perſons (3)."

Rate, on whom made.

The

(1) Rex *v.* Holbeach, 4 Term Rep. 778. 1 Bott, 359. Pl. 409.

(2) Anon. 1 Vent. 250. Skin. 259. Fol. 40.

(3) Caſe of St. Rumbald's Pariſh, Skin. 258. 1 Bott, 351. Pl. 387. Rex *v.* Eaſtchurch, 2 Salk. 480. 1 Bott, 356. 400. Rex *v.* Boroughfen, *Ibid.* 401. Rex *v.* Knightly, *Ib.* 352. Pl. 389. Comb. 309. Rex *v.* Holbeach, *ante*, n 1. and *per* Buller J. *Ibid.* The words in the text

The last is recommended as the least harsh and unreasonable, and is equally applicable to parishes and extra-parochial places (1).

Justices are to assess the quantum.

The justices are themselves to make the rate, and cannot delegate their power to others. An order of two justices, directing the churchwardens of St. Peter and St. Paul to assess, raise, and levy sixty pounds for the maintenance of the poor of the other parish, was quashed on this account (2). But if they had assessed the particular sum, it would have been good. As where two justices made an order that two parishes in Colchester should pay relief to the poor of a third, viz. the one five shillings a week, and the other eight shillings a week; and that the overseers should collect it. This order was held well enough, and according to the right course; for the justices are only to assess the quantum, and the rate is to be made by the overseers of the poor of the parish (3).

Overseers may make the rate.

Form of the order. Sum specified.

The order must therefore state a sum certain (4), and one requiring the contributory parish to make a rate at sixpence in the pound, was held ill for uncertainty on that account (5).

(1) Rex *v.* Boroughsen, 1 Bott, 356. Pl. 401.

(2) Case of Parish of St. Peter and St. Paul, 2 Str. 1114. 1 Bott, 354. Pl. 397.

(3) Case of St. Rumbald's Parish, Skin. 258. 1 Bott, 351. Pl. 387.

(4) Rex *v.* Knightly, *Ib.* 352. Pl. 389. Comb. 309. Case of Parish of St. Peter and St. Paul, *supra*, n. 2.

(5) Rex *v.* Telscombe, 1 Stra. 314. 1 Bott, 353. Pl. 394.

text are given to Lord C. J. Holt, Rex *v.* Eastchurch. But it seems hard, if the rate cannot be made upon the entire ability of the contributing parish, as is done in making its own poor's rate, but that it must in all cases be made upon particular persons. In Rex *v.* Boroughsen, *ut supra*, the judges were of opinion, that an order on particular persons would be hard and unreasonable, since particular persons of other parishes would be much exposed to the mercy of the justices; and that such a power was hardly to be trusted with them; for they may rate some, and excuse others altogether as well able to pay. But the words of the statute are very strong.

This

This contribution is to be made only ſo long as the inability continues; an order therefore for the pariſh of St. Peter to pay to the officers of St. Mary, twenty pounds weekly " till we the ſaid juſtices ſhall ſee fit to " order the contrary," is bad, for it may be a perpetual order, which the juſtices have no authority to make; ſince, if one of the juſtices die, or is removed, no other can alter it (1). But if made for a ſpecified ſum *per* week (2), or ſo much yearly (3), or a ſum in groſs to be levied for the whole year, it is ſufficient (4). Time ſpecified.

It ſhould appear on the face of the order, that the pariſh which prays aid of another is unable to maintain its poor; and there muſt be an aſſertion and adjudication, that it appeared ſo to the juſtices who make it (5). Therefore, where there were two vills in one pariſh, and the order recited that one of the vills was very rich, and the other very poor, and that the vill that was rich did not pay half ſo much to the poor as the poor vill did, it was quaſhed for uncertainty (6). But it need not purſue the very words of the ſtatute, where the allegation is ſubſtantially the ſame. Thus an order of ſeſſions, ſtating that the pariſh " *was oppreſſed,*" was adjudged well enough, for it implies inability (7). Liability adjudged.

It has been decided alſo, that it ſhould appear by the order, that the place on which the rate is made is not within the pariſh in aid of which it is aſſeſſed, and that this is neceſſary, although the names of both appear on the

(1) Caſe of the Borough of Marlborough, 16 Vin. Abr. 431. 1 Stra. 700. 1 Bott, 354. Pl. 396.

(2) Caſe of St. Rumbald's Pariſh, *ſupra*, n. 2.

(3) Rex *v.* Little Glen, Comb. 241. 1 Bott, 352. Pl. 388.

(4) Rex *v.* Knightly, *ut ſupra*, n. 3. Rex *v.* Boroughſon, 1 Bott, 356. Pl. 401.

(5) Conbet *v.* St. Mary Lincoln, 16 Vin. Abr. 431. 1 Bott, 352. Pl. 390. But ſee caſe of Borough of Marlborough, 16 Vin. 431. 1 Bott, 354. Pl. 396.

(6) Anon. Fol. 25. 1 Bott, 353. Pl. 393.

(7) Rex *v.* Little Glen, Comb. 241. 1 Bott, 352. Pl. 388.

face of the order, and are different (1). So alſo, that both pariſhes are within the ſame hundred (2).

Several perſons, who reſide in different pariſhes, or ſeveral pariſhes, if within the ſame hundred, may be rated at the ſame time by diſtinct orders to the relief of the ſame diſtrict. It may be ſuppoſed from the expreſſions uſed in ſome caſes, that the juſtices can rate the entire hundred; but what ſeems meant is, that they may, when neceſſary, rate every pariſh, vill, or extra-parochial place, which conſtitute the hundred, if of ability to contribute, for it is no where ſtated that they can rate the hundred generally *eo nomine*.

Rate, by the ſeſſions.

The juſtices, at their general quarter ſeſſions, are to aſſeſs any other of other pariſhes, or of any pariſh within the ſaid county, where the hundred is unable to contribute to the relief of the incapable pariſh. They have juriſdiction, not only when the hundred is thus incompetent, but where the place praying aid is not ſituated within any hundred or equivalent diviſion.

Thus an order was made by two juſtices to aſſeſs the pariſhes of St. Stephen and St. Magdalen in Norwich, in aid of the pariſh of St. Benedict, which was not able to maintain its own poor. It was objected, that the pariſhes being in Norwich, where there was no hundred, the juſtices had no juriſdiction; and for this reaſon the order was quaſhed. But *per* Powell J., this is not a *caſus omiſſus* out of the ſtatute; and though the two juſtices have not power, here being no hundred, yet the ſeſſions have a juriſdiction,

(1) Rex *v.* Boroughfen, Fol. 36. 1 Bott, 354. Pl. 395. *Ib.* 356. Pl. 401. But query this caſe? In Rex *v.* St. Helen's, Trin. 42. Geo. III. it was cited to this point, when Lord Ellenborough C. J. obſerved, that the diverſity of name, imports a diverſity of place, unleſs the contrary is ſhewn, MSS. And if it were a vill maintaining its own poor, although within the pariſh, the order would be good if that was made to appear. See *ante*, and 1 Bott, 358. Pl. 405.

(2) Caſe of Boroughfen, Fol. 37. 1 Bott, 353. Pl. 592. St. Benedict *v.* St. Peter's, 11 Mod. 269. 1 Bott, 355. Pl. 399.

juriſdiction, and may tax the county of the city in part, or at large; to which the reſt agreed (1).

As the power of two juſtices is confined within the hundred, the original juriſdiction of the quarter ſeſſions is limited to places out of it.

Therefore, where the ſeſſions made an original order to this effect; "it appearing to this court that the pariſh "of Dunchurch, in the hundred of Worth, being over-"burthened with poor; and that the pariſh of Eaſtbridge, "within the ſame hundred of Worth, having no poor "relievable within the ſaid pariſh, it is ordered, that the "ſaid pariſh of Eaſtbridge be from henceforth annexed "to the ſaid pariſh of Dunchurch; and that the occu-"piers of lands and tenements within the ſaid pariſh of "Eaſtbridge be chargeable and contributory towards the "relief of the poor of the ſaid pariſh of Dunchurch, the "the ſum of twenty pounds a year, ſo long as the ſaid "pariſh ſhall be overburthened, and no poor within the "ſaid pariſh of Eaſtbridge." It was moved to quaſh this order on two grounds: 1ſt, That it is an original order, which the ſeſſions cannot make; 2d, That juſtices have no power to annex pariſhes one to the other, which is in the nature of an act of parliament: and the order was quaſhed for the firſt reaſon (2).

Seſſions can't make an original order upon a pariſh within the hundred,

nor annex one pariſh to another.

As the power of aſſeſſment is granted to two juſtices, and to the quarter ſeſſions in the ſame words, the exerciſe thereof ſeems governed by the ſame rules in both caſes; and deciſions reſpecting the former, equally apply to caſes occurring under the latter. Thus, where a rate is made by the quarter ſeſſions upon pariſhes of another hundred than that in which the incapable pariſh is ſituated,

Governed by ſame rules in making orders without the hundred, as juſtices within.

(1) St. Benedict's *v.* St. Peter's, 11 Mod. 269. 1 Bott, 355 Pl. 399.

(2) Rex *v.* Eaſtchurch, 5 Mod. 397. 2 Salk. 480. 1 Bott, 352. Pl. 391. *Ib.* 356. Pl. 400. According to the report in Salkeld, the court were inclined to conſider "ſo "much as concerned the annexing of "pariſhes void, and the reſt good;" but they took time to adviſe.

 the

the pariſhes within the hundred muſt appear to be, and muſt be adjudged by the ſeſſions, unable to contribute.

But they may make their order, "taxing certain "pariſhes in the hundred of A. in aid of the pariſh "of B. in the hundred of C.," although two juſtices have not previouſly inquired whether any pariſh in C. can contribute; notwithſtanding that the act gives power to the ſeſſions only, if the hundred ſhall not be thought by the ſaid juſtices able and fit to relieve, &c. "For the inquiry would be uſeleſs, ſince, if two juſtices "made ſuch an adjudication, the ſeſſions muſt ſtill in- "quire into the truth of it. If no order appear, charg- "ing any pariſh within the hundred, it is a ſufficient "ground for the ſeſſions to act. If two juſtices had "charged any pariſh within the hundred, it would have "ſtopped the ſeſſions from proceeding. If two juſtices "ſhould adjudge the hundred not able, yet if other two "juſtices adjudge the contrary, their charge would be "good, and the ſeſſions be ouſted of their juriſdiction (1); "notwithſtanding the firſt determination (2)."

Appeal to ſeſſions.

But though the ſeſſions have no original juriſdiction within the hundred, an appeal lies there from the juſtices order, in which the propriety of that adjudication may be queſtioned.

Caſe for B. R.

The ſeſſions may ſtate a caſe for the conſideration of the ſuperior court, not only upon any point ariſing in an appeal, but alſo where they act by virtue of their original juriſdiction.

Power to appoint, if original order quaſhed.

And it ſeems, that if they quaſh an order of juſtices, they have power to make a new one within the hundred, in the ſame manner as they were enabled to make a new parochial rate prior to 17 Geo. II. (3).

(1) *Id eſt.* "*original* juriſdiction."

(2) Rex *v.* Percival, 2 Str. 56. 2 Bott, 357. Pl. 403.

(3) Rex *v.* Inhabitants of Little Glen, Com. 241. 1 Bott, 352. Pl. 388. But the caſe is reported in a very ſlovenly manner, as moſt of the caſes upon this part of the poor laws ſeem to be.

Should

Should the justices in or out of quarter sessions refuse to make an order of this kind, the remedy is by application for a writ of mandamus to the court of King's Bench; and it is immaterial, although the rule to shew cause command them to rate and assess a particular parish, instead of commanding them to hear the complaint. But the form of the mandamus, if it is granted, should be to compel them to inquire, in the first place, whether the parish stands in need of any assistance, and to act accordingly (1).

Mandamus to make a rate.

Its form.

To this mandamus, as a writ of right, there must be a return (2), the propriety and truth of which may be examined by the court in the manner already discussed, when treating of the appointment of overseers (3).

The return.

(1) Rex *v.* Holbeach, 4 Term Rep. 778. 1 Bott, 359. Pl. 409.

(2) Rex *v.* St. Mary's in Marlborough, 2 Shaw's Pract Just. 47. 16 Vin. Abr. 416.

(3) *Ante*, p. 20.

CHAPTER XIV.

Of levying and distraining for the Poor's Rate.

43 Eliz. c. 2. f. 4.

BY 43 Eliz. c. 2. f. 4. if the rate and all arrearages be not paid voluntary, present and subsequent churchwardens and overseers may levy them by distress and sale of the offender's goods; and in defect of such distress, he may be committed to the county gaol. By 17 Geo. II. c. 38. f. 11. succeeding overseers were empowered to levy arrears previously incurred, and to reimburse their predecessors out of the money levied, such sums as they had expended for the poor's use, and which are allowed to be due to them in their accounts.

17 Geo. 2. c. 38.

Demand of rate.

Before any step is taken to enforce payment under these statutes, the rate must be lawfully demanded (1). And if the person liable should die after such demand, and before further proceedings, it seems the better opinion and safer practice to demand it likewise from his personal representatives (2). If the money is tendered by any other than the person rated, as by the landlord on his tenant's account, it must be received (3).

Application to magistrates.

Where payment is refused, the overseers should apply to two magistrates of the county or place in which the

(1) *Semb. per* Holt, C.J. East India Company *v.* Skinner, 1 Bott, 242. Pl. 230. and see *post.* A summons to appear before the magistrates, may possibly amount to a sufficient demand, if the party attends and refuses payment, or neglects to appear before them. But it is unnecessary to add, that it is more humane at least to make a previous demand, without which, the justices do not seem called upon to issue their summons. The form of the warrant of distress in 3 Burn Just. tit. Poor (Rate), states a demand made before the summons issues.

(2) Stevens *v.* Evans, 2 Burr. 1152. 1 Bott, 249. Pl. 237. Wallis Adm. *v.* Hewit, cited *Ib.*

(3) Rex *v.* Cozens, Doug. 426. 1 Bott, 252. Pl. 239.

district

district is situated for which the rate is made. This is usually done at what is called a petty sessions, which are periodical meetings of magistrates who reside within a convenient extent of country, subject to their jurisdiction, and are held weekly or otherwise for the discharge of such duties as require the conjunction of at least two magistrates to perform.

Justices having property in the parish, empowered to act.

According to the universal principle of the common law, a magistrate, who possessed property in the parish, was prohibited from interfering in its concerns, as being incidentally connected with his private interests. But the interest being remote and trifling, and the inconvenience of sending parties from their homes in search of other magistrates very great, the 16 Geo. II. c. 18. s. 1. enables justices to act (among other things appertaining to their office, so far as the same relates to the laws, for the relief, maintenance, and settlement of poor persons), in all matters concerning parochial taxes, levies, or rates, in any parish, notwithstanding that they are rated to or chargeable with the taxes, levies, or rates, within such parish, &c.; but it excepts the power to act in the determination of appeals at the quarter sessions, in matters relating to the parish.

16 Geo. II. c. 18.

It was formerly necessary, that magistrates should not only be in the commission for that particular county or place for which they act; but also, that they should be locally present within the limits of their jurisdiction at the time of acting.

Not residing in the county, 28 Geo. III. c. 49.

But the latter part of this rule is dispensed with, for the purposes of general convenience, by a modern statute (1). Where a justice *acts* for two or more counties, *being adjoining counties*, and personally resides in one of them, any magisterial act of his, done in any one of them, shall be as valid as if done in that county to which it particularly relates

(1) 28 Geo. III. c. 49. s. 1.

If

Mandamus. If the magistrates should refuse to hear the overseers' information or complaint, the court of King's Bench will direct a mandamus to compel them to do so (1), or they will grant a criminal information where they have corruptly refused (2).

If the mandamus is disobeyed, the court will enforce obedience by attachment.

Summons. When the justices entertain the information, their first duty is to summon the party, or in case of death, his personal representative, to hear them upon the complaint (3).

This summons should state the nature of the charge, and require the parties to appear at some certain place, and at such convenient time, as is sufficient for them to make appearance and defence (4). It was the practice formerly to grant a conditional warrant in the first instance to distrain in case of non-payment (5); and in a reported case, a mandamus was directed to justices to sign a warrant of distress for levying the poor's rate without summoning the party (6). It was conceived, that granting such a warrant was a ministerial act, like the allowing a rate; and that it would be useless for magistrates to call a party before them, and hear a defence which they had no power to allow. Besides this case, many similar writs of mandamus were shewn to have issued from the Crown-Office in the first instance, neither stating the parties to have been summoned, nor requiring the justices to do so. But the court of King's Bench, upon mature deliberation, disregarded these precedents; because a distress to levy this rate is in the nature of an execution. The justices must, therefore, exercise a discre-

(1) Rex *v.* Benn, 6 Term Rep. 198. 1 Bott, 255 Pl. 241.

(2) Rex *v.* Cozens, Doug. 426. 1 Bott, 252. Pl. 239.

(3) Rex *v.* Benn, *ut supra*, n. 1. Stevens *v.* Evans, 2 Burr. 1152, 1 Bott, 249. Pl. 237.

(4) See the form, 3 Burn's Just. tit. Poor (Rate).

(5) Rex *v.* Boroughsen, Foley, 37. 1 Bott, 359. Pl. 407.

(6) Rex *v.* Justices of Middlesex, *Ib.* 243. Pl. 235.

tion

tion of inquiring into the circumſtances, and it is of courſe neceſſary, that a ſummons to the perſon who refuſed to pay, ſhould precede it: "For it is an invariable maxim "in our law, that no man ſhall be puniſhed until he has "an opportunity of being heard; whereas, if a warrant "of diſtreſs were to be iſſued without any previous ſum-"mons, the party would have no opportunity of ſhewing "cauſe why the warrant ſhould not iſſue againſt him (1).

As magiſtrates are civilly anſwerable where they iſſue a warrant of diſtreſs illegally (2): this rule is not leſs for their benefit, than it is for that of the perſon whoſe goods are liable to diſtreſs, where he neglects to pay his rate.

Service of ſummons.

The proceedings before the magiſtrates being in the nature of a civil execution (3) for the purpoſe of levying the aſſeſſment, perſonal ſervice of the ſummons ſeems unneceſſary; and it is ſufficient to leave it with ſome *inmate* at the houſe where the defendant uſually reſides.

When party does not appear.

The party being thus ſerved, either refuſes to obey, or appears in conformity to the tenor of the ſummons. If he does not appear, or offer ſuch a ſatisfactory excuſe as ought to induce the magiſtrates to poſtpone the hearing until another time, the warrant of diſtreſs ſhould iſſue upon proof of ſervice of the ſummons. But if there be any juſt reaſon to ſuppoſe that granting the warrant may ſubject the juſtices to an action, ſuch as, that the rate is void for any cauſe; as, for inſtance; that the place for which it is made is without their juriſdiction; they may require

(1) Rex *v.* Benn, 6 Term Rep. 198. 1 Bott, 255. Pl. 241. Harper *v.* Carr, 7 Term Rep 270. 1 Bott, 257. Pl. 243. The form of the rule for the mandamus, as ſettled in Rex *v.* Benn, was "To receive "ſuch information and complaints as "have been or ſhall be duly laid be-"fore them, againſt ſuch perſons as "have neglected or refuſed, or ſhall "neglect or refuſe to pay the ſums "reſpectively aſſeſſed on them by a "certain rate or aſſeſſment, made on "——— laſt, for the relief of the "poor of———, in the county of "———, and to proceed thereupon "to levy the ſaid ſeveral ſums."

(2) Harper *v.* Carr, *ſupra*, n. 1. Nutting *v.* Jackſon. Loft, 249. 1 Bott, 333. Pl. 364.

(3) *Ante*, n. 1.

the

the parish officers, to shew that their act in granting the warrant will not be illegal. But they can inquire no further than is necessary for this purpose, since they are civilly answerable in no other cases to persons who may be aggrieved by their warrant.

Causes to be shewn against granting the warrant: 1. Payment.

If the defendant appears, he may shew for cause why the warrant should not issue, any thing which amounts to payment, as, that the sum at which he stands rated has been tendered by him, or by some person on his behalf, and refused, and that he or they are still ready to pay it (1). That he has paid the assessment to one of the parish officers, who has not accounted for it (2).

2. Nullity of rate.

He may also urge any circumstances which shew the rate to be a nullity, into which the magistrates might inquire of their own accord. Such as, that public notice has not been given of the rate in the church on the *next* Sunday after it was allowed by the justices (3). That the place for which it is made is not within their jurisdiction, or that it is not made for the proper district (4). That the subject for which he is assessed is not by law rateable (5). That he is not liable to the rate, either as not being the occupier at all (6), or as not being a rateable occupier (7). For if the rate is void, those who are rated may treat it as a nullity; and the warrant being illegal where the assessment is so, the magistrates are not compellable to one even by mandamus; and the court will not grant one

(1) Rex *v.* Cozens, Doug. 426. 1 Bott, 252. Pl. 239.

(2) *Per* Lord Kenyon, Rex *v.* Benn, 6 Term Rep. 198. 1 Bott, 255. Pl. 241.

(3) Rex *v.* Newcombe, 4 Term Rep. 368. 1 Bott, 253. Pl. 240.

(4) Nicholas *v.* Walker, Cro. Car. 394. 1 Bott, 28. Pl. 49. Rudd *v.* Foster, 4 Mod. 157. 1 Bott, 29. Pl. 150. Peart *v.* Westgarth, 3 Burr. 1610. 1 Bott, 37. Pl. 59. Rex *v.* Justices of Gloucester, cited in Harper *v.* Carr, 7 Term Rep. 270. 1 Bott, 257. Pl. 243.

(5) Jones *v.* Maunsell, Doug 302. 1 Bott, 157. Pl. 181. Lord Bute *v.* Grindall, *Ib.* 175. Pl. 190. 14 Term Rep. 338. 2 Hen. Black. 267.

(6) Milward *v.* Caffin, 2 Black. 1330. 1 Bott, 250. Pl. 238.

(7) Lord Amherst *v.* Lord Somers, 2 Term Rep. 372. 1 Bott, 187. Pl. 193.

for

for the purpoſe, ſince it would be no juſtification in an action of treſpaſs brought for a diſtreſs taken under it (1).

But no other circumſtances can be inquired into at this hearing, excepting ſuch as amount to payment, or prove that the rate is a nullity. The quantum, or any overcharge in the rate, is only to be controverted by an appeal to the quarter ſeſſions. If the defendant omits to diſpute it there, he is ſuppoſed in legal conſtruction to have acknowledged the propriety of his aſſeſſment; neither can the magiſtrates refuſe their warrant, from the perſon's utter inability to diſcharge his quota.

But not an overcharge.

Formerly, if notice of appeal was given, it took away the magiſtrate's juriſdiction to diſtrain until the appeal was either abandoned or decided; but now, by 41ſt Geo. III. c. 23. ſ. 1. the juſtices may proceed to recover by diſtreſs, ſo much only as the perſon then rated, or any other occupier of the premiſes was rated in the laſt effective rate (2).

Of granting warrant pending an appeal.

Where no ſufficient cauſe is ſhewn againſt granting the warrant, the magiſtrates muſt iſſue it.

The aſſeſſments in a legal rate become due from the moment that it is allowed and publiſhed; and may be demanded, and the warrant granted before the time has expired for which the rate is made (3).

When warrant may be granted.

(1) Rex *v.* Newcomb, 4 Term Rep 368. 1 Bott, 253. Pl. 240.

(2) The act, which is drawn with great care and accuracy, extends to rates upon perſonal as well as real property. The former can be laid only on the perſon, and is comprehended under the firſt proviſion, "than the "perſon ſo rated ſhall have been rated "in the laſt effective rate." But as real property may have been occupied before making the rate appealed againſt, it requires the appellant to pay the contribution to which his predeceſſor ſubmitted or was adjudged liable, but exempts him from an immediate advance of any ſurplus which may be ſuppoſed the fair ground of his appeal.

(3) Charlwood *v.* Beſt, 1 Bott, 243. Pl. 234. But it is not uſual to expreſs any time in the title of the rate.

A ge-

Its substance.

A general warrant of distress is not sufficient (1). It must state specially the name of the person upon whose goods the levy is to be made, the rate upon which it is granted, and the sum assessed and directed to be levied (2). The sum will either be, 1st, The whole assessment in the rate: 2d, A part of it proportioned to the time of occupying the premises, by 17 Geo. II. c. 38. s. 11.: 3d, Under 41 Geo. III. c. 28. s. 2. in case of notice of appeal, the amount of the last effective rate on the person appealing, or upon the premises for which he is assessed: Or, 4th, The sums at which the several parties stand assessed in the amended rate, if the appeal has been heard and allowed before the warrant issues.

Of the time of sale.

By 27 Geo. II. c. 20. in this and all other cases where the justices have power to levy by distress, the warrant must direct the goods and chattels so distrained, to be sold within a certain time limited therein, not less than four, nor more than eight days; unless the sum for which the distress is made, together with reasonable charges of taking and keeping it, be sooner paid.

One for two rates.

One warrant may be granted to compel payment of two assessments under different poor's rates due to the same parish by the same person; but it is more prudent to make separate warrants, since, otherwise, if one of the rates is illegal, the warrant which enforces payment of the aggregate sum is bad (3).

Of the levy.

When the warrant is thus issued, it becomes the duty of those to whom it is directed, to levy under it, and they are alone answerable for their conduct, if it is good in its form, and properly granted (4).

(1) Tracey v. Talbot, 2 Salk. 531. 1 Bott, 243. Pl. 232.

(2) See the form, 3 Burn's Just. tit. Poor (Rate).

(3) Admitted in Milward v. Caffin, 2 Black. Rep. 1330. 1 Bott, 250. Pl. 238.

(4) Hutchins v. Chambers, 1 Burr. 579. 1 Bott, 244. Pl. 236. Durrant v. Boys, 6 Term Rep. 580. 1 Bott, 256. Pl. 242.

As

As to the place in which this levy is to be made, the moſt obvious is the pariſh for which the aſſeſſment is made.

But where the offender had no chattels within the pariſh, a levy under the warrant in the adjoining pariſh where he had goods and reſided, was held well, without the help of ſtatute, both pariſhes being ſituated in the ſame county, within the magiſtrates' juriſdiction (1).

But now, by 17 Geo. II. c. 38. ſ. 7. the goods of any perſon aſſeſſed and refuſing to pay, may be levied by warrant of diſtreſs, not only in the place for which the aſſeſſment is made, but in any other within the ſame county or precinct. 17 Geo. 2. c. 38.

If ſufficient diſtreſs cannot be found in the ſaid county or precinct, on oath made thereof before ſome juſtice of *any* other county or precinct, (which oath ſhall be certified under the hand of ſuch juſtice on the ſaid warrant,) ſuch goods may be levied in ſuch other county or precinct by virtue of ſuch warrant or certificate. In a different county.

Any perſon aggrieved by the diſtreſs, may appeal to the next quarter ſeſſions of the county or precinct for which the aſſeſſment is made, who are required finally to hear and determine the ſame. Appeal.

And by 33 Geo. III. c. 55. ſ. 3. in all caſes where any penalty, forfeiture, fine, or other money, may by the warrant of any juſtice or juſtices of the peace be directed to be levied by diſtreſs and ſale of the goods and chattles of any perſon or perſons; if ſufficient diſtreſs cannot be found within the limits of the juriſdiction of the juſtice granting ſuch warrant of diſtreſs; on oath thereof made by one witneſs, before any juſtice of the peace of any other county, riding, diviſion, city, borough, town corpo- 33 Geo. 3. c. 55.

(1) Hampton *v.* Lammas, *coram* Bott, 243. Pl. 272. Holt C. J. Lord Raym. 735. 1

rate, or place, (which oath ſhall be by him certified by indorſement on ſuch warrant,) ſuch penalty, forfeiture, fine, or other money, or ſo much thereof as may not have been before levied or paid, ſhall and may, by virtue of ſuch warrant and indorſement, be raiſed and levied by the perſon or perſons to whom ſuch warrant of diſtreſs ſhall have been originally directed, by diſtreſs and ſale of the goods and chattels of ſuch perſon or perſons, in ſuch other county, riding, diviſion, city, borough, town corporate, or place; and the money ariſing by ſuch diſtreſs and ſale, ſhall be applied and diſpoſed of for ſuch purpoſes, and in like manner, as if ſufficient goods and chattels of ſuch perſon or perſons had been found within the juriſdiction of the magiſtrate originally granting ſuch warrant; and if no ſuch diſtreſs can be found, ſuch offender or offenders ſhall and may be forthwith proceeded againſt according to law: provided always, that no juſtice who ſhall endorſe any certificate upon, or authoriſe the execution of any ſuch warrant of diſtreſs which may not have been granted within his juriſdiction, ſhall be anſwerable or accountable for any irregularity which may have been committed or done, in or about the obtaining or granting of ſuch warrant of diſtreſs.

27 Geo. 2. c. 20.

When the officer executes the warrant, he is required by 27 Geo. 2. c. 20. to ſhew it *upon demand* to the perſon whoſe goods and chattels are diſtrained, and to ſuffer a copy of it to be taken.

In taking goods under a warrant of diſtreſs, the law gives a power in ſome reſpects different from that which obtains in diſtreſſes made by landlords for recovery of rent.

Goods exempt from diſtreſs.

Under the ſtatutes relating to levying a poor's rate, two ſorts of things found on the premiſes of the perſon diſtrained, are protected from this ſtatutory execution. 1ſt, Such as are not the actual property of the perſon rated, and refuſing to pay; the act of Eliz. expreſsly requiring,

requiring, that the sum due shall be levied by distress and sale "*of the offender's goods.*"

2d, Things affixed to the freehold, and which therefore do not come properly under the legal denomination of "goods," as they are called by the act of Eliz.; or "goods and chattels," as by the subsequent statutes (1).

Goods partially exempted.

Perhaps things in actual custody and use cannot be seized as a distress; such as an axe in a man's hand (2); the horse on which he is riding (3); or the loom that he is working at; since to permit them to be taken away from the possessor, must perpetually tend to a breach of the peace (4).

And although this point has only been determined with respect to distresses for rent, and not for poor rates; yet the same tenderness for life, and respect to the intemperate passions of mankind seem to require that it should not extend to them, at least when there is a sufficiency of other goods on the premises to satisfy the warrant (5).

Things not privileged.

The goods of the offender are in other respects less privileged, than where the remedy is applied for the recovery of rents. For as things distrained may be sold, the proceeding, though called a distress, resembles more nearly an execution. Things therefore which are holden privileged by common law, at least *sub modo* in the case of rent (6); that is, which are exempt from being distrained upon, while a sufficiency in value of other goods remains on the premises, obtain no such privilege here.

(1) Gorton *v.* Falkner, 4 Term Rep. 569.

(2) *Ibid.*

(3) Storey *v.* Robinson, 6 Term Rep. 138.

(4) *Ibid.*

(5) There is however a considerable distinction between the cases of distress for rent, and for a rate. The latter is in the nature of an execution by a warrant granted by a public magistrate, to which the party is bound to pay obedience; but a distress for rent is a summary remedy permitted to the landlord, who is interested in the question.

(6) See Gorton *v.* Falkner, 4 Term Rep. 569.

Beaſts of plough.

Thus it has been held, that beaſts of the plough may be taken as diſtreſs for the poor's rate, although there is at the time more than a ſufficiency of other goods upon the premiſes to ſatisfy the demand (1). Hence it may be ſafely relied upon as a general poſition, that all goods which can be taken as a diſtreſs for rent, may be taken alſo in ſatisfaction of the poor's rate.

Money, tools, &c.

So money may be diſtrained (2), or the working tools of a cooper lying in his ſhop for the purpoſe of carrying on his trade (3); nay, the very wearing apparel of his wife and children, if taken while not in actual uſe; as, when thoſe who wore them are in bed (4).

Goods to be ſold, &c.

The goods are to be publicly ſold at the time directed in the warrant, unleſs the ſum due, with reaſonable charges for taking and keeping the diſtreſs, is previouſly paid.

When ſold, the officer who makes the diſtreſs is empowered by 27 Geo. II. c. 20., to deduct the reaſonable charges of taking, keeping, and ſelling the diſtreſs out of the money ariſing by the ſale; and the overplus, after fully ſatisfying and paying theſe charges, and the ſum directed to be levied, is to be returned on demand to the owner of the goods and chattels diſtrained.

Where a ſecond diſtreſs.

If the officer does not take ſufficient goods by his firſt diſtreſs to ſatisfy the exigence of his warrant, he may make a ſecond under it for that purpoſe (5), although he could have taken enough upon his firſt coming on the premiſes (6). This is beneficial to the perſon diſtrained upon, as it enables the officer to act with moderation and tenderneſs, in not taking too much, which he muſt

(1) Hutchin *v.* Chambers, 1 Burr. 579. 1 Bott, 244. Pl. 236.

(2) Eaſt India Company *v.* Skinner, *Ibid.* 242. Pl. 230.

(3) Edgecomb *v.* Sparks, 2 Show. 126. 1 Bott, 242. Pl. 229. Gorton *v.* Falkner, 4 Term Rep. 569.

(4) Biſſet *v.* Caldwell, 1 Bott, 242. n. a.

(5) Hutchin *v.* Chambers, 1 Burr. 579. 1 Bott, 244. Pl. 236.

(6) *Ibid.*

other-

otherwise do in order to secure himself, if he could not come a second time to make good the deficiency (1). On the other hand, it seems advantageous to the person levying, since although it has been determined, that a general action of trespass cannot be maintained against him for taking an excessive distress, where the goods levied upon are of arbitrary and uncertain value; yet the party injured might have a special action against him upon the statute of Marlbridge (2).

If there should be no distress, the party may be committed by warrant of two justices to the common goal, there to remain without bail or mainprize, until he discharges the sum at which he is assessed; and perhaps, when it is intended to proceed to this extremity, the summons to appear before the magistrates should be served upon the defendant in person. But no parish ought to take this course, unless by way of punishment, where the defendant has fraudulently concealed or disposed of his goods. Commit party to prison.

Formerly, if payment was enforced even from those who did not appeal, and the rate was afterwards quashed; the justices who granted the warrant of distress, and the officers who acted under it, were liable to an action of trespass, as having entered the premises of the person distrained upon, and taking his goods without lawful powers; and those who had voluntarily paid their proportion, might in many cases harass the collector by an action for money had and received under a void authority. Of payment where the rate is afterwards quashed.

These mischiefs were remedied by the act for the better collection of the poor's rates, 41 Geo. 3. c. 23. It provides, that when it is necessary for the relief of the persons appealing, the sessions shall quash the rate; but that all and every sum of money charged by such rate on any person, may be levied by such means, and in such manner, as if no appeal had been made against it; and all sums charged therein, which any person charged therein 41 Geo. 3. c. 23.

(1) Hutchin *v.* Chambers, 1 Burr. 579. 1 Bott, 244. Pl. 236.

(2) *Ibid.*

ſhall pay, or which ſhall be levied or recovered from him, ſhall be taken as payment on account of the next effective rate.

Sect. 2. It has been already ſeen, that the ſum at which the perſon rated and appealing, or any former occupier of the premiſes, was rated in the laſt effective rate, may be recovered by diſtreſs notwithſtanding the appeal, but no more.

Sect. 4. Sect. 4. provides further, in conſideration both of thoſe who are to enforce, and thoſe who are to pay the rate, that where it is quaſhed on appeal, the ſeſſions may order any ſum charged in and by ſuch rate, or any part thereof, not to be paid, and then no proceedings ſhall, after the making ſuch order, be commenced, and if previouſly commenced, they ſhall be no farther proſecuted to enforce payment in any ſum which ſhall be ſo ordered not to be paid.

Provided alſo, that no juſtice, conſtable, peace-officer, or other perſon, ſhall be deemed a treſpaſſer, or liable to any action, for any warrant, order, act, or thing, which ſuch juſtice, &c. ſhall have granted, made, executed, or done, for the purpoſe of enforcing payment, before he ſhall have *had notice in writing* of the order for non-payment.

CHAPTER XV.

Of ascertaining what Poor the Parish are bound to maintain.

Origin and History of the Law of Settlements.

IT is difficult to trace the law of parochial settlements with precision to its original foundation. Of the settlement of vagrant poor.

The poor, as regulated by act of parliament, were originally distinguished into two classes: beggars able to work, whom it punished with severity as criminals; and beggars, who being unable to maintain themselves from age or bodily infirmity, were compelled to live by the alms of charity.

The settlements provided for this latter class of unfortunate people, are easily followed through the statute-book. The earliest act directs, that beggars impotent to serve, shall abide in the place where they be dwelling at the time of the proclamation of the statute; and if the cities or other towns will not, or may not suffice to maintain them, then they shall draw themselves to other towns within the hundred, or to the towns where they were born, within forty days after the proclamation made, and there shall continually abide during their lives (1). 12. R. 2. c. 7.

But as it frequently happened that the indigent had, from accidental circumstances, least means of exciting compassion in the place of their nativity; 11 Hen. VII. c. 2. conceded to the unfortunate beggar a more ample circuit for the exercise of his sole and fortuitous means of subsistence, by declaring that all beggars shall go and abide in that hundred where last he dwelled or where he is best known, or born. The restriction to the hundred 11 H. 7. c. 2.

(1) 12 Ric. 2. c. 7.

"where the person was best known," was too indiscriminate to determine any thing, and nearly amounted to a general licence to beg throughout the kingdom. The 19 Hen. VII. c. 12. therefore, limited this vague description, by enacting that they shall go and abide in the city, town, or hundred, where they were born, or else to the place where they made last their abode for the space of three years; and this continued to be the rule of settlement in subsequent statutes passed against vagrancy, in the reign of Henry VIII. his son Edward, and daughters Mary and Elizabeth (1).

19 H. 7. c. 12.

14. Eliz. c. 5.

The 14 Eliz. c. 5., after enacting that the justices shall appoint within their divisions neat and convenient abiding places to settle the aged and impotent poor, for their habitations and abidings; directs, that the mayor of London, and the mayor, sheriffs, bailiffs, and other head officers, of every other city, borough, or town corporate, and the constables, or tithing-men of the several hundreds within all and every the said shires in England and Wales, in all and every such abiding places within their hundreds, limits, and precincts, as shall be appointed to settle the poor people in, shall once a month make search of all the aged, impotent, and lame persons within the precincts of their jurisdiction; and all such as they shall find not being born within that division, nor dwelling within the said three years, (except leprose and bedrid people,) shall cause to be conveyed on horseback, cart, or otherwise, to the next constable, and so from constable to constable, till they be brought to the place where they were born, or most conversant by the space of three years next before, and there to be put in the abiding place, or one of the abiding places appointed for the habitation of the poor people of that country.

(1) 22 H. 8. c. 12. 27 Hen. 8. c. 25. 1 Edw. 6. c. 3. 3 & 4 Edw. 6. c. 16. 5 & 6 Edw. 6. c. 2. 1 & 2 P. & M. c. 5. 5 Eliz. c. 3. 14 Eliz. c. 5. 18 Eliz. c. 3. See all these statutes collected in Dr. Burn's History of the Poor Laws, chap. 4. p. 60. ed. 1764.

By

By the more early of these statutes, the poor were required to remove themselves to the places pointed out for their settlement. This direction was subsequently enforced by the penalty of being punished as vagabonds, when they neglected to obey. But the law of removals directing them to be conveyed thither, as to their place of settlement, in the manner already recited in 14 Eliz. c. 5. was originally established by 1 Edw. VI. chap. 3. The 1 Jac. I. c. 7. made a further alteration, ordaining, that rogues, vagabonds, and sturdy beggars, should be sent to the place of their dwelling, if they had any, and if not, to the place where they last dwelt by the space of a year, if that can be known, by their confession or otherwise; and if that cannot be known, then to the place of their birth. Removals under vagrant acts.

These statutes draw in other respects a wide and proper distinction between rogues and vagabonds, who have recourse to begging in the love of idleness and vice; and beggars who are compelled by decrepitude to glean the necessaries of life from the pity of their fellow-creatures. But they prescribe the same places, *viz.* cities, towns, or hundreds, for the settlement of beggars of both descriptions, and establish the same criterion of settlement for both; namely, *birth*, and *dwelling* or *inhabitancy* for three years, without regard to the capacity or situation in which they lived there; and placed them equally under the jurisdiction of the justices of the peace. Distinction between rogues and vagrant beggars.

It is evident from reported cases, and the opinions of learned judges, that their sole object was to suppress vagrancy, and regulate the wandering poor. These statutes apply only to vagrants.

Thus *Flemming* Chief Justice, in a case between Weston and Cowledge, 11 James I., declared, that "young children whose parents are dead, are to be set at work, " relieved, or maintained, at the charge of the town " where they were dwelling at the time of the death of " their parents, and are not to be sent to their place " of

" of birth, &c. For if the parents are not rogues, " we may not make the children rogues except they " wander abroad and beg (1)." So it is held in the resolution ascribed to the judges in the time of Elizabeth: " That no man is to be put out of the town where he " dwelleth, nor to be sent to his place of birth or last " habitation, but a vagrant rogue; nor to be found by " the town, except the party be impotent (2)." And also, that " such persons *as be of any parish*, and have " able bodies to work, if they refuse to work at such " wages as are taxed or commonly given in those parts, " are to be sent to the house of correction, *and not to their* " *place of birth or last dwelling*, by the space of a year (3)."

Dalton, when speaking of persons who having had houses, but whose leases are expired, and of servants whose times of service were ended, observes, " that such " persons must not be sent out of the town where they " so last dwelled or served: neither are they to be sent " from thence to their place of birth or last habitation, " but are to be settled there to work, being able of body; " or being impotent, are to be there relieved: and yet " if such persons shall wander abroad begging out of " that parish, then they may be sent as vagabonds from " the place where they shall be taken wandering or begging, to their places of birth," &c. (4). So it was laid down by Sir Francis Harvey, that " justices of peace, " especially out of their session, were not to meddle " with the removal or settling of any poor, but only " of rogues (5)."

(1) Dalt. Just. tit. *Poor*. chap. 73. Fo 227. edition 1727.

(2) Resol. 9. Lamb. Eirenarch. book 2. chap. 7. p. 209. ed. 1630. Dalt. Just. *Ib*. 227.

(3) 10 Resolution of Judges, temp. Eliz. Lamb. Eirenarch. p. 209. Between the vills of Suckley and Whitborn, 14 Car. 1. 1638. 2 Bulst. 357.

(4) Dalt. Just. *Ibid*. 228. Parish of Hardingham *v* Parish of Brisley, Mich. 1649. Styles, 168. 2 Bott, 306. Pl. 345.

(5) Summer assizes at Cambridge 1629. Eod. Dalt. 228.

And

And where a perſon could not be removed as a wanderer, it is ſaid to have been the common law as far back as from the time of the Mirror, that the pariſh was to maintain him when actually chargeable (1).

Of the ſettled poor.

Parliament ſeems to have interfered no further reſpecting the *Settled Poor*, than to provide a fund for their relief. As they neither defined nor enumerated the circumſtances, which ſhould conſtitute a ſettlement and draw a diſtinction between the reſident inhabitant, and the wanderer or vagrant, it becomes difficult to trace the period at which thoſe criteria which are now held to aſcertain it were firſt eſtabliſhed.

By an old law, "a ſtranger, or he who cometh gueſtwiſe "to an houſe, and there lieth the third night, is called an "*Hogenhyne* or *Agenhine*; and after the third night, he is ac-"counted one of his family in whoſe houſe he ſo lieth (2)." And Minſhieu, verb. *Hogenhyne* & *uncouth*, ſaith, that *uncouth* ſignifieth *incognitus*, and is uſed, in ancient Saxon laws, for him who cometh to an inn gueſtwiſe, and lieth there two nights at the moſt; and that by the laws of Edward, and of the Conqueror, *hoſpes trium noctium*, if he did any harm, his hoſt was anſwerable for him as for one of his own family; and that if he tarried any longer, then he was called *Hogenhyne* or *Agenhine*, that is, *familiaris*. So that it ſeemeth in thoſe times, that to lodge in a place for three or four days together, was counted a ſettling (3).

But this law ſeems to have been made not for the purpoſe of aſcertaining the poor man's ſettlement, but as a wiſe meaſure of police and general ſecurity (4).

The firſt regular definition of lawful ſettling, other than what is declared by ſtatute for vagrants, is in the reſolutions of the judges of aſſize in 1633, which ſtate, that "the

(1) *Per* Foſter J. Rex *v.* Aythrop Rooding. Burr. S. C. 412. 2 Bott, 474. Pl. 493. But the opinion of Lord Mansfield and Denniſon ſeems contrary.

(2) Terms de la Ley, voc. *Hogenhine*. Secundum antiquam conſuetudinem dici poterit de familiâ alicujus qui hoſpitium fuerit cum alio per tres noctes; qui primâ necte dici poterit *Uncouth*; ſecundâ, *Guſt*; tertiâ nocte *Hogenhine*. Bract. de Leg. fol. 1246

(3) *Per* Forteſcue J. Rex *v.* St. Peters in Oxford, Fol. 193. 2 Bott, 275. Pl. 317.

(4) 1 Black. Com. 114.

" law unsettleth none who are lawfully settled, nor permits " it to be done by a practice or compulsion; and every one " who is settled as a native, householder, sojourner, an " apprentice, or servant for a month at the least, without " a just complant made to remove him or her, shall be " held to be settled (1)."

It seems further, that it must be an inhabiting with the purpose of making the place an home. For it is laid down in the same resolution, that " a nurse child, or " scholar at the grammar school, or at the university, or " persons sent to the common gaol, hospital, or house of " correction (being impotent), are not to be esteemed as " persons to be settled there, *more than travellers in their* " *inns*; but their settling is *where their parents are settled*; " and children born in common gaols and houses of cor- " rection, their parents being prisoners, are to be main- " tained at the charge of the county (2)."

So in a question of settlement submitted to Sir William Jonès and Sir James Whitlock, judges of assize in 1629, prior to the date of these resolutions, it appeared that a woman having young children, and travelling from A. to E., died in B. an intermediate parish, leaving her children there: the judges were of opinion, that the children were settled in the place of their birth, and not where the mother died *in transitu* (3).

Relief of persons settled.

A person who became a settled inhabitant by any of these means, could not be removed unless by his own act, and if he afterwards became impotent and poor, he was entitled to relief from the parish funds, or he might ask charitable alms for subsistence, without incurring the hazard and penalties of vagrancy, provided he kept within the district in which he was settled.

Settlement by parishes.

The district from whence the fund for maintaining the poor was raised, almost of necessity determined the limits

(1) 26 Resol. of Judges of assize 1633. Dalt. 23. Dalton recites it thus, p. 289. " Every one who is " settled as a native, an householder, " sojourner, an apprentice, or a servant " retained for one month," &c.

(2) 32 Resol. eod. Dalt. 237.

(3) 2 Bulst. 351.

limits within which those for whose use it was levied, and by whose officers it was administered, should be accounted settled. The poor's rate being raised by parishes, and placed under the control of parochial officers in the time of Queen Elizabeth, it may be safely concluded that the origin of parish settlements is to be referred to the reign of that princess, if not to an earlier period (1). It is observable, indeed, that the legal decisions and opinions already cited, although of a later date, use the word "towns," in reference to settlements; but it is plain that it is considered as a denomination synonymous with "*parishes*."

Although a person thus settled became part of the the local poor, and entitled to relief; yet if he departed voluntarily, and turned vagrant; he was liable to be removed under the statute to the place of his birth, or last dwelling for three years (2). So that the obligation to relieve might cease with the continuance to dwell in the parish. For the person removing might have resided more than a month, and less than three years; and could not, if he became a vagrant, be removed thither again.

But a class of cases occurred, which were neither provided for by the statutes of vagrancy, nor by the law of settlement as it is here explained.

Persons, not in the state of wandering, poor, might be compelled, from the urgence of accidental necessity, to ask relief in places where they were not settled. Such as children within the age of nurture, left by the death or desertion of the father or mother in a parish where they were not born, nor their parents settled; persons taken suddenly ill, when travelling from one place to another in pursuit of their lawful avocations; or who after removing for the purpose of gaining an honest livelihood in another

Relief of persons removing, who were not in a state of vagrancy.

(1) The 27 Hen. 8. c. 5. imposed the duty of maintaining the wandering poor upon cities, shires, towns, hundreds, hamlets and parishes; but it imposed the penalty for neglecting to do so, viz. 20s. a month, upon parishes only.

(2) Suckley and Whitborn, 2 Bulst. 357.

ther

ther pariſh, became actually chargeable, before their ſettlement was complete.

Hence a queſtion aroſe between pariſhes, upon whom the maintenance of poor perſons thus circumſtanced ſhould fall; whether they were to be removed to the place of ſettlement appointed for vagrants; or to that of their laſt ſettlement as inhabitants: or whether they were to be maintained as caſual poor, in the pariſh in which they had thus become ſuddenly a burthen.

First determination.

The firſt general reſolution upon the ſubject ſeems to have been made by Sir William Jones and Sir James Whitlock, in the caſe already cited from Bulſtrode (1): "that the place of their birth, or the place of their laſt "habitation, if the ſame may be known, are in judg-"ment of law ſaid to be the places of ſettling; ſo that "if one be born in ſuch a place and pariſh, and after-"wards is an inhabitant in ſervice in another place and "pariſh, and after this he becomes to be a wanderer, he is "here by the law to be ſent to the laſt place of his "ſettling, to be there kept and provided for."

Birth or laſt habitation.

This reſolution refers to the caſe of wandering poor, and ſpeaks of a ſettlement by reſidence to which the removal ſhould be made; but it does not ſpecify whether it could be gained by reſidence for a ſhorter period than is preſcribed by the ſtatutes againſt vagrancy.

But they alſo reſolved, "that an infant under the age "of ſeven years ſhall not be ſaid to be a wanderer;" and they ſent the children, being infants, whoſe mother had died *in tranſitu*, from the pariſh where they were found at their mother's death, to the ſeveral pariſhes of their births, "as poor to be by them provided for, but "not as wanderers, rogues, or vagabonds."

Settlement by ſervice.

This point appears to have been more expreſsly decided a few years afterwards in the court of King's Bench. An inhabitant in the pariſh of B. hired a maid-ſervant

(1) 2 Bulſt. 351. See *ante*, 143; and 2 Bulſt. 350. Margaret Brown's caſe. 7 Car. 1. 1631.

by

by covenant; ſhe fell ſick ſome time afterwards, and her maſter turned her out without giving her any thing; and the maid for neceſſity, in travelling from B. towards H. where ſhe was born, was forced to beg for relief; whereupon ſhe was ſent as a vagrant to H.; the vill of H. ſent her back to B., whereupon B. procured an order of ſeſſions to ſettle her at H. where ſhe was born.

The queſtion was, whether this was a good order or not, for ſettling her at H. according to the ſtatute; or whether ſhe ought to be ſettled at B. where ſhe was entertained as a covenant ſervant, and turned out of ſervice, and forced to beg by that means? And *Roll* Chief Juſtice ſaid, that there ſeems to be afraudulency in the maſter to make his ſervant a vagrant, that ſo he may be rid of her: but if one beg meat and drink for neceſſity in paſſing between one town and another, this is not begging to make one a beggar within the ſtatute: and therefore the court ordered that the party ſhould be ſettled at B. where ſhe was entertained for a covenant ſervant, and not at H. where ſhe was born (1).

Theſe caſes go ſome way to ſhew, that prior to 13 & 14 Car. II. the obligation to relieve impotent and ſettled poor, continued not only while they remained in the pariſh, but after leaving it, until they became vagrants, or had acquired other ſettlements (2).

But it is difficult to point out the origin of the power of removal, by juſtices of the peace in theſe caſes. That of removing vagrants was given by ſtatute; and magiſtrates would have to determine in all caſes of relief, whether the perſon aſking it in a foreign pariſh was a vagrant or not. But whether the practice aroſe from hence, or with the magiſtrates in ſeſſions by reaſon of their appellate juriſdiction over the pariſh rate, or in what other mode it originated, or to what extent it was exerciſed, is no where laid down precisely, **Power to remove whence.**

(1) Paroch. de Hardingham *v.* Paroch. de *Brilley*, Mich. 1649. Sty. 168.

(2) Suckley *v.* Whitborn, 2 Bulſt. 357. & *ante.*

precisely, at least so far as I have been enabled to carry my researches.

A poor man might be fairly supposed to retain his situation of a settled inhabitant in a particular place, although quitting it for a season, until he parted with the character, either by settling somewhere else, or by indicating a resolution to abandon all permanent residence when he turned vagrant. When it became a question, whether one thus circumstanced should be maintained by the parish in which he was so settled, or by one to which he became chargeable by an accidental calamity, it was more conformable to the statutes regulating the wandering poor, and to natural justice, that the former should be held liable; and it was not unreasonable to conclude, that a power to remove to the place which lay under this obligatory duty to maintain him, was impliedly given by the creation of the duty itself.

This seems to have been the opinion of Lord *Holt*, who in laying down that there is no power of removing to or from an extraparochial place, observes that, "persons in "extraparochial places must subsist on private charity, as "all persons did at common law before 43 Eliz. which "enacts that every parish shall keep their own poor, *in* "*consequence of which the jurisdiction of removals was first set* "*up before the statute of* 14 *Car. II. c.* 12. for unless the "poor were removed to their own parishes, every parish "could not maintain their own poor (1)."

Some points not touched by 13 & 14 Car. II. seem to rest even now upon these principles, as being founded in the law as it stood before the statute passed. Such are the settlement of natural children born in gaol, or in hospitals, or pending an order of removal (2); that of servants residing, during sickness, in a different parish from their masters (3). Indeed every settlement gained in right of marriage or parentage, and also removals by reason thereof, and possibly settlements on

(1) Dean *v.* Linton, 2 Salk. 487.
(2) *Post.* Chap. xix.
(3) *Post.* Chap. xx.

tenements

tenements of 10*l.* a year, or freehold estates, depend equally upon the antecedent law, as not being within the letter of the statute. But the doubt, if it did exist, is removed in other cases, by the 13 & 14 Car. II. c. 12. which recites in the preamble the grounds upon which it passed. "Whereas, by reason of some defects in the law, poor "people are not restrained from going from one parish "to another, and therefore do endeavour to settle them-"selves in those parishes where there is the best stock, "the largest commons or wastes to build cottages, and "the most woods for them to burn and destroy; and "when they have consumed it, then to another parish, "and at last become rogues and vagabonds, to the great "discouragement of parishes to provide stocks when "it is liable to be devoured by strangers: be it there-"fore enacted, by the authority aforesaid, that it shall "and may be lawful, upon complaint made by the church-"wardens, or overseers of the poor of any parish, to any "justice of the peace within forty days after any such "person or persons coming to settle as aforesaid, in any "tenement under the yearly value of ten pounds, for "any two justices of the peace, whereof one to be of "the quorum of the division, when any person or per-"sons that are likely to be chargeable to the parish shall "come to inhabit, by their warrant to remove and con-"vey such person or persons to such parish where he "or they were last legally settled, either as a native, "householder, sojourner, apprentice, or servant, for the "space of forty days at the least, unless he or they give "sufficient security for the discharge of the said parish, "to be allowed of by the said justices."

13 & 14 Car. 2. c. 12.

This statute adopts the very words used in the 26th resolution of the judges of assize in 1633, as to the modes of gaining a settlement, but alters the time of residence by which it may be acquired from "a month at the least," to "forty days at the least." It places vagrant beggars on the same footing with other impotent poor, in respect to the methods of acquiring a settlement; and puts it beyond doubt, that the settlement gained is to continue until a new one is acquired. It gives power to justices of peace in all cases of removal and settlement, and prevents a settlement

Construction of the act.

being acquired by the mere act of residence for a month, without being chargeable, as might have been done previously; for it enables two magistrates to remove not only those who become chargeable before they have resided for the space of 40 days, but such as they shall in their discretion deem likely to become so, unless they give security for the discharge of the parish. Prior to this statute, no one could be removed unless they were in a state of vagrancy, or had become actually chargeable to some other place than that of their settlement. But this act regards all persons of an inferior condition who change their habitation as vagrants and vagabonds, unless they come to reside upon a tenement of 10*l.* a year value. Lastly, it gives a right of appealing to the next quarter sessions, to those who are aggrieved by the order.

The following weighty reasons are assigned by Dalton against the policy of this act: "it is well worthy the "consideration of wise law makers to consider whether, "notwithstanding the specious allegations in the said act's "preamble, it may not be prejudicial to the common-"wealth. For that, 1. By the words *likely to be charge-"able*, too great a scope is given to any person, although "never so just and prudent, to inspect, and to determine "another man's livehood and condition. 2. A man with-"out his offence is barred of his natural liberty, and upon "a possibility remote enough, be made a beggar and a "prisoner, at the same time deprived of the company of "friends and relations, choice of air, and place of trade. "3. It tends to the discouragement of ingenuity and in-"dustry; for why should any one learn or endeavour "to be excellent in any handicraft, which he is likely to "make small use, and smaller benefit of. 4. Places and "persons are deprived of the labour and industry of "others. 5. It tends to depopulation, which is the greatest "inconvenience an island can undergo (1)."

(1) Eod. Dalt. 237. But see 35 Geo. 3. c. 101. Dr. Burn, both in his History of the Poor Laws, chap 4 and 5, and in the introduction to his title "Settlement," 3 Burn's Justice, has in my apprehension, misconceived the origin and history of settlements, which has induced me to enter more fully into the subject than I should otherwise have done; besides which, it may not prove unsatisfactory to ascertain those foundations upon which, much of the law of settlements rests at present.

CHAPTER XVI.

Of the ſeveral Kinds of Settlements, and General Rules which govern them.

THE ſeveral methods of acquiring ſettlements enumerated by 13 & 14 Car. II. c. 12. are reſidence as a native, houſeholder, ſojourner, apprentice, or ſervant for the ſpace of forty days: ſo that a perſon who remained in any pariſh unremoved for that time, gained a ſettlement in whatſoever capacity he reſided; for the juſtices were not only without power to remove, except within the firſt forty days, but the act expreſsly acknowledges a reſidence for that period, even as a ſojourner, to conſtitute a legal ſettlement. From the ſhort ſpace of time given for removal, and the ſmall notoriety with which reſidence might be attended, the burthen of large families was frequently thrown upon pariſhes, without poſſibility of redreſs or power of prevention. To remedy this inconvenience it was enacted by 1 Jac. II. c. 17. that the forty days reſidence ſhould be reckoned, not from the time of a perſon's firſt coming to inhabit, but from that of his giving notice in writing to ſome one of the pariſh officers of his place of abode, and the number of his family.

Settlements by 13 & 14 Car. 2. c. 12.

Notice by 1 Jac. 2. c. 17.

The colluſion or inattention of pariſh officers rendering this proviſion alſo inadequate to the ſuppoſed miſchief, it was further provided by 3 W. III. c. 11. that the forty days ſhould be reckoned from the publication of ſuch notice in the pariſh church, by which means every inhabitant muſt or ought to receive information of the fact.

By 3 W. 3. c. 11.

If no exception had been made to this general proviſion, all perſons to whom a reſidence for forty days was

Settlements requiring reſidence.

neceſſary

necessary in order to obtain a settlement under 13 & 14 Car. II. must have complied with the formality of notice and publication. But the legislature saw that this provision might affect particular classes, who not coming into the parish clandestinely, were not within the mischief against which it was meant to guard, and with respect to whom the provision would be nugatory, as there was no power to remove them after notice given. For these reasons, the following classes of inhabitants were altogether exempted from the necessity of publishing notices: 1. Unmarried persons not having a child, who shall be hired for a year. 2. Apprentices bound by indenture. 3. Persons paying their share towards the public taxes or levies of the town or parish. 4. Persons on their own account executing any public and annual office or charge in the said town or parish during one whole year.

35 Geo. 3. c. 101.

The 35 Geo. III. c. 101. rendered persons irremoveable until they become actually chargeable to the place they inhabit; and of necessity abolished, by express provision, the mode of acquiring a settlement by notice and residence. Otherwise a person of sufficiency to maintain himself and family for the space prescribed by the statute, might have rendered the notice an unavailing formality, and the party giving it must have gained a settlement in defiance of the wishes and vigilance of the parish.

Settlements by public taxes abolished.

But all persons exempted by 3 W. III. c. 11. from the necessity of giving notice, continue to gain a settlement by residence for forty days in any of the capacities which are there enumerated, except being rated to and paying public taxes in respect of a tenement which is not of the yearly value of 10*l.* that being likewise abolished by 35 Geo. III. c. 101.

Other Settlements.

The scope of 13 & 14 Car. II. was to suppress vagrancy in the lower ranks of society, and there were other

other methods of becoming a ſettled inhabitant in uſe before the ſtatute paſſed, which it left to the operation of theſe antecedent laws.

1. Perſons who come to reſide on a tenement of the yearly value of ten pounds, are expreſsly exempt from removal by the act itſelf. 2. Perſons who come to reſide upon their own eſtate have been held ſo, as not being within the miſchief it was deſigned to remedy (1). For they do not intrude into the pariſh as ſtrollers and vagabonds, nor come with the bad intentions mentioned in the preamble (2). By the common law, no man can be removed from his own (3); and the right is under Magna Charta, that none ſhall be diſſeiſed of his freehold (4).

But it was neceſſary by the old law, that the perſon who migrated from one pariſh to another ſhould be a ſettled inhabitant to be entitled to relief; and it has been ſhewn that he muſt reſide there for a limited period in order to become ſo. In 1633, a month's reſidence ſeems to have been ſufficient (5); this might have increaſed into one for the ſpace of forty days, previous to 13 & 14 Car. II. It does not appear whether this was ſo, or whether the enactment of that ſtatute was conſidered as affording an inference, that the legiſlature intended to make a reſidence for that time neceſſary, wherever it is at all required; but a reſidence for forty days, is now held to be neceſſary in theſe as well as in caſes of ſettlement more ſtrictly within the letter of the act. 40 days reſidence.

Beſides theſe methods of acquiring ſettlements, in which reſidence is neceſſary, there are ſome in which it is not.

(1) Harrow *v.* Edgeware, 2 Bott, 465. Pl. 485: and the ſeveral caſes cited under that title *poſt.*

(2) *Per* Yates and Wilmot J. Rex *v.* Uttoxeter, Burr. S. C. 538. 2 Bott, 479. Pl. 497.

(3) *Per* Wilmot J. *Ib.*

(4) *Per* Foſter J. Rex *v.* Aythorp Rooding, Burr. S. C. 412. 2 Bott, 474. Pl. 412.

(5) Reſol. of Judges of Aſſize 1633, *ante*, p. 140.

The

Settlements where reſidence is unneceſſary: 1. Birth:

The place where the individual is born is as it were pointed out by nature, and acknowledged by every ſtatute which regulates the ſubject, as one in which he is accounted ſettled by the mere circumſtance of birth (1).

2. Marriage:

If the ſettlement of the huſband and wife were diſtinct, it would defeat the object and law of their union; her civil exiſtence is merged in his; ſhe becomes by marriage an inſeparable part of his family, and cannot be removed from him, but muſt be ſettled where he is.

3. Parentage.

The law, with the ſame obſervance of the ſocial principle, caſts the firſt duty of watching over the child's education and providing for its ſupport upon the parents. Children, during pupilage, form natural parts of that family of which the father, and upon his deceaſe the mother, are the head; to disjoin thoſe whom nature and policy had thus united, would be equally inconvenient and cruel; and the law preſerves the œconomy of private families, in holding that the parents ſettlement, is communicated to their legitimate offspring, until they are emancipated (2).

1. Derivative Settlements.

1. Theſe ſeveral enumerated methods of acquiring ſettlements, may be divided into two general claſſes; 1. ſuch as are communicated without a reſidence of forty days; which may be called derivative, or natural ſettlements (3); and are 1. marriage; 2. parentage; 3. birth.

2 Acquired Settlements.

2. Where a reſidence of forty days is neceſſary, which may be called acquired ſettlements; and are gained,

(1) The words of the 26 Reſol. of Judges 1633, and of 13 & 14 Car. 2. ſeem at firſt view to imply that there ſhould be a reſidence by the firſt for a month, and the ſecond for 40 days in the pariſh where the individual is born, in order to confer a ſettlement; but they have been conſidered as applying not to the original birth ſettlement, but to caſes where, after that ſettlement is deſtroyed by the acquiſition of one in ſome other pariſh, the party returns to his native pariſh, and reſides there forty days.

(2) See 26 Reſol. of Judges 1633, *ante*, 140.

(3) Rex *v.* St. Matthew's Bethnal Green, Burr. S. C. 482. 2 Bott, 37. Pl. 59.

1. *by*

1. *by inhabitancy* as an hired ſervant; 2. as an apprentice; 3. ſerving an office; 4. upon a rented tenement of ten pounds a year value; 5. where the perſon has a freehold eſtate.

Previous to treating in detail of the ſeveral kinds of ſettlements, it may not be improper to mention two general rules which are to be attended to by magiſtrates in making orders of removal, and determining appeals. General rules.

Firſt, A ſubſequent ſettlement always deſtroys that which is previouſly gained by the ſame perſon, and contending pariſhes are to look to this as the only means by which a ſettlement once actually gained can be deſtroyed.

The ſecond is, that no ſettlement can be legal which is brought about by practice or compulſion (2).

(2) 26 Reſol. Judges 1633. Dalt. 236. 3 Burn's Juſt. tit. *Poor* (Settlement). But this rule is not to apply to the caſe of ſettlement by marriage, where the marriage continues good, at leaſt during the life of huſband and wife, and while they live together. See *poſt*. p. 153. n. 6.

CHAPTER XVII.

SECT. I. *Of the Settlement by Marriage.*

Husband's Settlement

WHEREVER a woman intermarries with a man who has obtained a known ſettlement, it is communicated to her, although ſhe has never been where it is gained (1).

ſuperſedes his wife's,

And every ſucceeding ſettlement that he acquires is in like manner transferred to her immediately. Wherever the huſband therefore has a ſettlement, that which the wife had previous to marriage is abſolutely ſuperſeded by virtue of the rule already mentioned (2); and ſhe cannot gain a new one by any act of her own during her huſband's lifetime, even by reſidence upon her own eſtate, after he has deſerted her and his children (3).

but is ſuſpended if he has none.

But when the huſband has no ſettlement, not being born in this country, nor having acquired one during his reſidence (4), or which is the ſame thing, if born here, that which he had cannot be diſcovered, the wife's ſettlement is not totally deſtroyed by marriage, but remains ſuſpended during his life, or perhaps more properly during cohabitation. So that if the parties cohabit together and become chargeable, ſhe cannot be ſeparated from her huſband, although he has no ſettlement to which ſhe can be ſent, and it muſt fall to the pariſh in which they dwell

(1) St. Giles *v.* Everſley, 2 Seſs. Caſ. 116. 2 Bott, 81. Pl. 117. Appotens *v.* Dunſwell, as reported, *Ib.* 80. Pl. 116. is *contra.*

(2) *Ante*, p. 151.

(3) Berkhampſtead *v.* St. Mary North Church, 2 Bott, 33. Pl. 56. Rex *v.* Aythorp Rooding, *Ib.* 81. Pl. 118. Burr. S. C. 412.

(4) Rex *v.* Wilſborough Green, Fol. 249. 2 Bott, 82. Pl. 119. St. Giles *v.* St. Margaret's Weſtminſter, *Ib.* 83. Pl. 121. Rex *v.* Chidingſtone, 1 Str. 683. 1 Seſſ. Caſ. 104, Rex *v.* St. Botolph's Biſhopgate. Burr. S. C. 367. 2 Bott, 84, Pl. 123.

to relieve them both as casual poor (1). But if the husband having no settlement, dies (2); or leaves his wife, and it is not known whether he is living or dead (3); or running away, lives separate from her (4); the settlement she had previous to marriage continues, so that she may be removed thither when chargeable. It is therefore said to be suspended under these circumstances, as being liable to be destroyed if the husband shall gain one subsequently, although he has deserted her; or to be revived, if he *die* or run away from her (5) without having done so (6).

(1) Rex *v.* Carlton, Burr. S. C. 813. 2 Bott, 87. Pl. 126.

(2) Appoteas *v.* Dunswell, 1 Sess. Cas. 80. 2 Bott, 82. Pl. 120. Rex *v.* Westerham, *Ib.* 83. Pl. 122.

(3) Rex. *v.* Ryton, Cald. 39. 2 Bott, 89. Pl. 128.

(4) Rex *v.* Willsborough Green, Gilb. Rep. 79 2 Bott, 82. Pl. 119. Rex *v.* St. Botolph's Bishopsgate, Burr. S. C. 367. 2 Bott, 84. Pl. 123; and the cases cited *supra.* But Stretton *v.* Norton, Andr. 307. Burr. S. C. 122. is *contra.*

(5) Rex *v.* Witton cum Twambrookes, 3 Term Rep. 355. 2 Bott. 53. Pl. 75. The case of a father's settlement gained after deserting his family, communicated to an unemancipated son.

(6) Mr. Const has stated in the digest of his useful book, title *Marriage*, and in his marginal abstract, Rex *v.* Edwards, 2 Bott, 68. Pl. 100. Rex *v.* Watson, *Ib.* 70. Pl. 103. Rex *v.* Tarrant, *Ib.* 74. Pl. 109. That a marriage procured by bribery or any other means, with a fraudulent design to confer a settlement, will do so. He states further in his abstract of Rex *v.* Smith, 2 Bott, 76. Pl. 113. that "the marriage of a "lunatic, though procured with the "design to change her settlement, is "good." The religion of the country intermixes itself so entirely with the contract of marriage, that when it is once celebrated, all civil rights must follow from it, whatever may be the parties motives for entering therein. Although the marriages were brought about, in the first class of cases, by the procurement of parish officers, yet the parties being *habiles ad contrahendum matrimonium*, the nuptial engagement confers upon them and their issue the right of settlement, with all others, that are consequent upon the state. But there seems considerable doubt whether the lunatic's marriage would be good, not upon the ground of the overseers having procured it, but of the lunatic's incapacity to contract. 1 Blac. Com. 439, and the cases there cited. None of the cases mentioned by Mr. C. prove either position for which he cites them, they only decide that it is punishable to procure such marriages. The legality of the marriage and settlement seems inferred, because the procurement would not be civilly punishable unless it had thrown a burthen upon the parish, to do which the marriage must be valid. But this position seems inaccurate, for the crime is complete, if the fact by possibility might have put the parish to expence, especially in cases of conspiracy, which all these seem to have been, except perhaps Rex *v.* Tarrant.

SECT.

SECT. II.

Of the Proofs necessary to establish a Settlement by Marriage.

Proofs of Settlement.

ALTHOUGH the pauper is removed as a married woman, it will be sufficient to prove her maiden settlement in the place to which she is removed, and that whether her husband is dead (1) or living (2).

But where either the appellant or respondent parish mean to rely upon a settlement by marriage, they must be prepared to prove, 1. the marriage; 2. the husband's settlement.

1. Marriage.

26 Geo. 2. c. 33.

Marriage is celebrated either by banns or licence, which are regulated so far as to effect the validity of the marriage, by 26 Geo. II. chap. 33. By sect. 1. all banns of matrimony, where the parties dwell in the same parish, are to be published in the parish church, or a public chapel belonging to the parish, in which banns of matrimony have been usually published, upon three Sundays preceding the solemnization. If they live in different parishes, the banns are to be published in both; and if one or either is an extraparochial place, then in some church or chapel belonging to an adjoining parish; and in all cases where banns have been published, the marriage shall be solemnized in one of the parish churches or chapels where such banns have been published, and in no other place.

Sect. 11.

By the same act, sect. 11. all marriages solemnized by licence, after 25th of March 1754, where either of the parties, *not being a widower or widow*, shall be under the age of twenty-one years, which shall be had without the consent of the father of such of the parties so under age (if then living) first had and obtained, or if dead, of the guardian or guardians of the person of the party so under age, lawfully appointed, or one of them; and in

(1) Rex v. Woodsford, Cald. 236. 2 Bott, 92. Pl. 132.

(2) Rex v. Hedsor, *Ib.* Pl. 135. Cald. 371.

case

case there shall be no such guardian or guardians, then of the mother (if living and unmarried); or if there shall be no mother living and unmarried, then of a guardian or guardians of the person appointed by the court of chancery; shall be absolutely null and void to all intents and purposes whatsoever.

By sect. 12. where the guardians or mother shall be *non compos mentis*, or shall refuse or withhold their consent, then the person desirous of marrying may petition the Lord Chancellor, Lord Keeper, or Lords Commissioners of the Great Seal, who may hear it in a summary way; and if they judicially declare by an order that the marriage is proper, it shall be as effectual as if the guardians had consented. Sect. 12.

By sect. 4. no licence shall be granted to solemnize matrimony in any church or public chapel, except those belonging to the parish or chapelry within which the usual place of abode of one of the persons to be married shall be for the space of four weeks immediately previous to their granting such licence. Sect. 4.

And if both or either dwell in an extraparochial place, having no church or chapel where banns have been usually published, then in a parish church adjoining: but by sect. 6. this does not extend to deprive the archbishop of Canterbury of his right to grant special licences to marry at any convenient time or place, pursuant to 25 Hen. VIII. c. 21.

By sect. 10. after solemnization of a marriage *by banns*, proof of the parties dwelling where the banns were published; or, *where it is by licence*, that the usual place of abode of one of the persons, was for four weeks in the parish or chapelry where the marriage was solemnized, shall not be necessary in support of the marriage; nor shall any evidence in either of the said cases be received to prove the contrary, in any suit touching the validity of the marriage. Sect. 10.

By

Sect. 18. By sect. 18. the act is not to extend to Scotland; nor to marriages among quakers or jews, where both parties are quakers or jews; nor to marriages solemnized beyond the seas.

All marriages celebrated since the period mentioned in this statute, in England and Wales, must conform to its provisions, or no settlement can be gained in consequence thereof; for the act declares that the marriage shall be null and void to all intents and purposes (1).

It was further determined by the court of King's Bench, with great reluctance, that a marriage regularly celebrated by banns in a chapel, erected since the passing of the statute, and not upon the site of any ancient church or chapel, was void, and that no settlement could be gained under it. The act expresly referring to churches and chapels in which marriages were usually celebrated at the time it passed (2).

21 Geo. 3. c. 53. But this disgraceful consequence of a law of very questionable policy, was remedied by 21 Geo. III. c. 53. which enacted, that all marriages solemnized in any church or public chapel, erected since the passing 26 Geo. II. shall be as valid in law as if they had been solemnized in churches or chapels, having chapelries annexed wherein banns had been usually published before or at the time of passing thereof, and that the registers of such marriages shall be received in evidence.

Sect. 4. Sect. 4. provides, that such registers shall be removed within twenty-one days after 1st Aug. 1781, to the parish church of the parish in which the chapel is situated; or if in an extraparochial place, to that which is next adjoining.

(1) Rex v. Preston, Burr. S. C. 486. 2 Bott, 70. Pl. 105.

(2) Rex v. Northfield, Dougl. 659. Cald. 115. 2 Bott, 67. n. a.

The

The 26 Geo. II. extends to all perſons married in England and Wales, except jews or quakers. Illegitimate children, although looked upon by law as not having any father, are held to be within it; a marriage therefore by licence, between two illegitimate children who were minors, without conſent of parents or guardians, was held void, and not to confer a ſettlement upon the woman or her children (1). Baſtards within 26 Geo. 2. c. 39.

The court of King's Bench were further of opinion, that the power of conſent given to the "father and mo-"ther," was intended to include reputed parents, as being intereſted in their childrens welfare, and bound to provide for them by the laws of nature; and held that the marriage of ſuch minor, with the conſent of her putative father, was valid in law, and would confer a ſettlement (2).

Subſequent to theſe deciſions, however, the caſe of Horner and Liddiard came before the Conſiſtorial court in London, 24th May 1799. Miſs Liddiard was an illegitimate minor, whoſe ſuppoſed father, John Whitelock died when ſhe was 11 years old. He left her a conſiderable fortune by will, which he directed to be paid to her when ſhe ſhould attain the age of twenty-one, or the day of marriage with the conſent and approbation of her mother Sarah Liddiard, and George Aſhley, or the ſurvivor of them; to whom he further gave the tuition and care of his daughter during her minority. Miſs Liddiard, when a minor between eighteen and nineteen years old, was married by ſpecial licence to Thomas Strangeways Horner, Eſq. who had then arrived at the years of legal diſcretion. The licence ſtated that the marriage was ſolemnized by and with the conſent of Sarah Liddiard, there ſtyled Sarah Whitelock, widow, her mother and guardian; and which conſent was in fact obtained. The report does not ſtate

(1) Rex v. Hodnett, 1 Term Rep. 96. 2 Bott, 79. Pl. 115. Rex v. Preſton, Burr. S. C. 486. 2 Bott, 70. Pl. 1.

(2) Rex v. Edmonton, Cald. 435. 2 Bott, 76. Pl. 114.

whether

whether Mr. Ashley, to whom the joint power of consenting to Miss Liddiard's marriage was given by Mr. Whitelock's will, was living or dead; and it was proved that no guardian had been appointed in Chancery.

In February 1799, Mr. Horner instituted a suit to obtain a sentence pronouncing the marriage null and void, the proper consent not being obtained under sect. 11. of the act. The learned Judge, Sir William Scott, was of opinion with the court of King's Bench, that illegitimate minors are within the statute, and therefore that consent was necessary to render the marriage valid; but he differed from that court, where they held, that the reputed parents are enabled to consent, and was of opinion that it could be lawfully given only by a guardian appointed by the court of Chancery, and that otherwise the marriage is a nullity. He observed, that the court of Chancery considered this to be the law, by uniformly appointing guardians to consent to the marriage of bastards, although the father and mother were living; that the Ecclesiastical court followed the court of Chancery in adopting that construction, and has always refused to grant licences upon the mere consent of the natural father or mother, and unless it is stated that they are the lawful father and mother; and he had always understood that the form of the affidavit upon which licences are now granted was originally settled at the time of passing the act, upon great consideration, and by eminent lawyers of both professions: for want of which consent, he annulled the marriage in the case before him (1).

(1) Dr. Croke's Report of Horner *v.* Liddiard, determined 24th May 1799. The learned Judge adhered to this opinion in the case of Daniel *v.* Cooke. It is observable however among other things which might be urged in support of the judgment of the court of King's Bench in Rex *v.* Edmonton, that the power of consent given to the chancery guardian depends upon the *precedent* condition, that the father is deceased, no guardian appointed by him, and "no mother *living and unmarried*." It seems rather a strained construction therefore to consider these words as signifying the same as if they were, "and if there shall be "*no father and no mother* then," &c. The condition being made to depend *on the life or death* of the parents, seems to afford a strong inference that the legislature meant to give the power to the chancery guardian, only in cases where the parents if living would possess the right of assenting.

But

But though the marriage, if celebrated in England, must comply with the provisions of the act, yet if minors domiciled in England, withdraw themselves into Scotland, or places beyond the seas, even for the purpose of evading and as it were in fraud of the statute, the marriage is good to all intents and purposes (1).

Direct proof of marriage, 1 Copy of register.

The marriage may, for the purposes of a settlement, be proved several ways: 1st. By an examined copy of the register, and some evidence of the identity of the parties, as if the hand-writing of the husband and wife to the register is proved (2); or by people who came to the wedding dinner, or who were paid by them for ringing the bells for the wedding, or any other circumstances sufficient to satisfy the court that they were the same persons (3).

Entry in register.

The 26 Geo. II. c. 33. requires that marriages shall be solemnized in the presence of two or more credible witnesses, besides the minister who shall celebrate the same; and that it shall be entered in the registry, in which entry shall be expressed, whether the marriage was celebrated by banns or licence, and signed by the minister and the parties married, and attested by two witnesses; but this entry in the register is not of the essence of the marriage; so that where there was an entry of a marriage by banns, and neither the minister, the parties, nor the witnesses had signed it, the marriage was held valid for the purposes of settlement (4).

not essential to its validity.

Even where the witnesses do sign, it is not necessary to produce them, as it would be in the cases of deeds or any other attested instrument that is adduced in evidence (5).

(1) Crompton v. Bearcroft, Bull. L. N. P. 113. 2 Bott, 75. Pl. 121.

(2) But the register itself must be produced in this case.

(3) Birt v. Barlow, Dougl. 162. Bull. L. N. P. 27.

(4) Rex v. St. Devereux, Burr. S. C. 506. S. P. *Per* Lord Kenyon, Read v. Passer. Peake's Ni. Pri. Ca. 231.

(5) Bull. L. N. P. 27.

2d. The

2. By persons present.

Husband and wife when witnesses, &c.

3. Their declaration.

When not.

2. The marriage may be proved by any person present at the ceremony (1); even the husband and wife; and these last are also competent witnesses to disprove the fact (2): or their declarations after their death (3), or reputation in the family (4). But neither husband nor wife are admissible to prove the fact of marriage, where it might tend to criminate the other: and upon this principle of public policy, it shall not be admitted, when it tends that way, even in collateral cases. Where therefore a marriage in fact was proved between two paupers, a former wife was held not to be a competent witness to establish her previous marriage with the husband (5). But this seems to depend entirely on the principle of moral convenience, for if the husband is dead the first wife may prove the marriage (6).

4. Cohabitation.

4. By the presumption arising from the conduct of the parties to each other, as where they cohabited together for the space of thirty years, and treated each other as man and wife (7).

5. By admission when conclusive.

1. Certificate.

2. Order of removal unappealed from.

5. The strongest of all proofs is when the parish against which it is sought to establish the marriage, have so far admitted the fact as to be estopped from controverting it. As where it has granted a certificate in which it acknowledges the parties to be man and wife (8); or where the man and woman have been removed as husband and wife (9); or where the woman is removed as married,

(1) Bull. L. N. P. 27

(2) Standen *v.* Standen. Peake's Ni. Pri. Cas. 32. Rex *v.* St. Peters, Worcestershire, Burr. S. C. 25. 2 Bott, 6. Pl. 14. Rex *v.* Stockland, *Ib.* 72. Pl. 167. Burr. S. C. 508. Henley *v.* Chesham, 2 Bott, 75. Pl. 112.

(3) Rex *v.* Bramley, 6 Term. Rep. 330. 2 Bott, 743. Pl. 831.

(4) Reed *v.* Passer Peake's Ni. Pri. Cas. 231.

(5) Rex *v.* Cliviger, 2 Term. Rep. 263. See also Davis *v.* Dinwoody, 4 Term. Rep. 678. Bentley *v.* Cooke, 2 Term. Rep. 265. 269.

(6) Henley *v.* Chesham, 2 Const. 75. Pl. 112.

(7) Rex. *v.* Stockland, *ut supra* n. (2).

(8) Rex *v.* Headcorn, Burr. S. C. 253, 2 Bott, 70. Pl. 104. Rex *v.* Ullesthorpe. 8 Term. Rep. 465.

(9) Rex *v.* Silchester, Burr. S. C. 551. 2 Bott, 673. Pl. 734. Rex *v.* Berkswell, 2 Bott, 69. Pl. 102.

without

without her ſuppoſed huſband, and that to which the removal is made, has not appealed againſt the order (1). So if ſhe is removed by the name and deſcription of "E. Smith, widow," it is concluſive of her huſband's ſettlement, if he is then alive, and the order unappealed from (2): for the preſumptive concluſion to be drawn from her being removed as a married woman, or as a widow, where nothing is ſtated in the order to contradict it, is, that ſhe is removed to her huſband's ſettlement; and if the pariſh did not mean to acquieſce in that concluſion, they ſhould have controverted it by an appeal.

This evidence is ſo ſtrong between the parties giving and receiving the certificate, or thoſe removing and receiving the pauper, that it is concluſive of the fact, ſo that it cannot be controverted, although the marriage has never taken place (3). When concluſive.

As between other pariſhes it is ſtrong preſumptive evidence, but not ſo concluſive as to exclude proof to contradict it. When preſumptive.

It is ſufficient *prima facie* evidence of a regular marriage, to eſtabliſh the fact by any of the modes of proof already ſtated; it follows from thence, as matter of legal aſſumption, until the contrary appears, that all circumſtances neceſſary to render it valid did take place. Proof of marriage.

The party therefore who is intereſted to controvert it, muſt come prepared to prove what he relies on to impeach Proof to impeach its validity.

(1) Rex *v.* Hinxworth, Cald. 42 2 Bott, 89. Pl. 129. Rex *v.* Leigh, *Ib.* 91. Pl. 130. Dougl. 45. Rex *v.* Towceſter, 2 Bott, 679. Pl. 740. Rex *v.* St. Mary Lambeth, 6 Term Rep. 615. 2 Bott, 683. Pl. 744.

(2) Rex *v.* Rudgely, 8 Term Rep. 620.; and as to the effect of orders of removal unappealed from, ſee *poſt.*

(3) Caſes, n. (1); (2).

peach the validity (1), unless he can extract it by cross examination or otherwise from such evidence as the adversary has produced.

1. Where void *ab initio*.

These facts are, 1st, that the provisions established by the marriage-act have not been complied with, as where it is by banns, and they were not duly published three several times (2). 2d, Where the marriage is null and void *ab initio* without the sentence of a court ecclesiastical, as where one of the parties was previously married to a person living at the time of the second marriage (3), or where he who pretends to perform the ceremony is not in holy orders (4). These circumstances may be proved by oral testimony.

But it is not expressly decided, whether any other cause which renders a marriage null and void *ab initio* without sentence in an ecclesiastical court, can be given in evidence in a temporal one, without producing a judgment of the ecclesiastical court, or the bishop's certificate. It seems however most reasonable that all disabilities by which the marriage is rendered void, may be examined into upon the same principle; and therefore that no settlement can be gained by marriage with an idiot, or an insane person, unless celebrated dur-

Lunatics.

ing a lucid interval (5). By 15 Geo. II. c. 30. if persons found lunatics, or committed to the care of trustees by any act of parliament, marry before they are declared

(1) *Per* Lord Mansfield, Rex *v.* St. Devereux, Burr. S. C. 506. 2 Bott, 71. Pl. 106.

(2) Standen *v.* Standen, Peake's Ni. Pri. Ca. 32. See also Wilkinson *v.* Payne, 4 Term Rep. 468.

(3) Westbrook *v.* Strutville, 1 Str. 79.

(4) *Sembl.* Rex. *v.* Luffington, Burr. S.C. 232. 2 Bott, 69. Pl. 102. where the ceremony was performed prior to the marriage-act. *Quære tamen*, and by Lord Kenyon, C. J. before 26 G. 3. c. 33. I think (though I do not speak meaning to be bound) that even an agreement between the parties *per verba de præsenti* was *ipsum matrimonium*. Reed *v.* Passer, Peake's Ni. Pri. Ca. 232. See also Holt *v* Ward, 2 Stra, 937. Swinb. 74. 2 Salk. 438. 6 Mod. 155.

(5) 1 Black. Com. 439.

of

of ſound mind by the chancellor, or the majority of ſuch truſtees, the marriage is totally void.

2. Sentence of eccleſiaſtical court.

But where the ſentence of an eccleſiaſtical court of competent authority is neceſſary to annul the marriage, it being good unleſs a judgment is pronounced during the lives of both parties, the ſentence muſt be produced; and it is concluſive evidence of that fact, where the ſuit was inſtituted for the expreſs purpoſe of annulling the marriage, and its validity cannot be controverted in a civil ſuit, except on the ground of colluſion between the parties (1).

There are no caſes reported ſince the marriage-act, in which ſuch a ſentence has been held equally concluſive of its validity; but upon principle it ſeems not leſs effectual to eſtabliſh than to annul the marriage.

3. Sentence of a foreign court.

3. The ſentence of a foreign court of competent authority, where the parties were domiciled at the time; that is, where they abide with the purpoſe of permanent reſidence; or any other form of divorce eſtabliſhed there between perſons of the ſame religious perſuaſion (2).

4. Statute.

4. Divorce by act of parliament.

For proof of the various ways by, which the huſband's ſettlement is to be eſtabliſhed, ſee the ſubſequent titles of ſettlement.

(1) Ducheſs of Kingſton's Caſe, 11 St. Tri. 198. Amb. 756. S. C. Dacoſta and Villa Real, 2 Stra. 961. and the caſes cited in the note to the 3d. edit. Hume v. Burton. App. to Cruiſe on Fines, &c. 46. See alſo Croſs v. Salter, 3 Term Rep. 639.

(2) Ganer v. Lady Laneſborough, Peake's Ni. Pri. Ca. 17.

CHAPTER XVIII.

Of the Settlement of Legitimate Children by Birth.

1. The father's settlement at the birth.

THE second species of derivative settlement is acquired by relationship between parent and child. The original settlement of legitimate children being that which the father has at the time of their birth, and it makes no difference that the child is born in another parish (1), or that the father dies previous to the birth (2), or that neither he nor the son have subsequently visited the place of settlement (3).

The manner in which the parental settlement has been acquired is equally immaterial. It may be gained by the father's own act, or derived from his father or grandfather, or any other more remote relation to whom a settlement is first traced in the direct ascending line (4).

2. Gained after.

But although the father's settlement at the time of birth is the original settlement of his legitimate offspring, it is superseded if the parent gains one subsequently, while the child continues to form a part of his family (5).

The mother's at time of birth.

Where the father has not a known settlement before his child becomes chargeable, that which the mother had previous to her marriage is communicated in the same manner, and subject to the same rules (6).

(1) Coxwell *v.* Shillingford, Fort. 313. 2 Bott, 23. Pl 42.

(2) Regina *v.* Clifton, *Ib.* 24. Pl. 44. 19 Vin. Abr 382; and see Cunmer *v.* Milton, 6 Mod. 87. 2 Bott, 16. Pl. 38.

(3) St. Giles Reading *v.* Eversley Blackwater, 1 Str. 580. 2 Bott, 24. Pl. 44.

(4) Rex *v.* St. Mathew's Bethnal Green, *Ib.* 37. Pl. 59. Burr. S. C. 482.

(5) See *post.* 267.

(6) Rex *v.* St. Botolph's, Burr. S. C. 367. 2 Bott, 25. Pl. 46. Tynton *v.* King's Norton, *Ib.* 31. Pl. 54; and see 36 Resol. of Judges of Assize 1633, *ante*, 140.

But

But as the father's ſettlement where he has one muſt always fix that of his child, it is obvious that recourſe ſhould be had to the ſettlement of the father's mother, prior to that of the pauper's own mother, for it is the father's ſettlement, if his father have none; and upon the ſame principle, that of the father's grandfather's mother precedes that of his own mother, and ſo on to the more remote degrees of lineal anceſtry.

Thus where Elizabeth Taylor was born in St. Katherine's, and married Edward Brazier, whoſe ſettlement was unknown; his widow afterwards married Iſaac Coiffeau a Frenchman, who never gained a ſettlement. She had by him Abraham Coiffeau, born in the pariſh of Bethnal Green. Abraham married Mary Dormer, whoſe ſettlement was in St. Leonard's Shoreditch. Abraham died, and Mary his widow, with her children, becoming chargeable, they were held to be ſettled in St. Katherine's, being the birth ſettlement of Abraham's mother; for there is no diſtinction between an acquired ſettlement and a derivative one; the poſitive law in theſe caſes of ſettlements is, that the child's ſettlement follows that of its father, if the father's can be found (1).

But the right of ſettlement is only gained by the heads of families for their lineal deſcendants, and is not tranſmiſſible through collateral branches, as from uncles or couſins; nor in the aſcending line, from child to parent; as real property would in the firſt caſe, and perſonal in both.

The ſettlement which a child derives from its mother during the father's lifetime, muſt be acquired previous to her exiſting marriage, for ſhe can acquire none during coverture except through her huſband (2). 1. Settlement from the mother.

(1) Rex v. St. Matthew's Bethnal Green, Burr. S. C. 482. 1 Bott, 37. Pl. 59.

(2) Berkhampſtead v. St. Mary North-Church, 2 Bott, 33. Pl. 56.

2. After widowhood.

But if the father die, the mother becomes the head of the family, in which event nature and the law casts the obligation to provide for it upon her. A settlement therefore gained in her own right during widowhood, is communicated to her unemancipated children (1), although past the age of nature (2). But if she acquire a settlement by another marriage, it is not gained as the head of the family, but as a subordinate part of some other, and therefore is not communicated to her former offspring (3).

The rules respecting the transmission of parental settlements acquired previous to the child's birth, are too clear to generate much doubt or discussion; it arises from the relationship, and cannot be defeated by the parent's misconduct.

Father attainted.

A father who gained a settlement was attainted for felony: he married afterwards and had children, but received no pardon. It was held, that the settlement gained before attainder was communicated to his children born afterwards; for a settlement is not the property of any man, it cannot escheat, nor be called a franchise (4).

Neither will any incapacity in the child to sustain the civil duties of life prevent it. Thus it has been decided (and it seems surprising that such a question should be made), that an idiot, if legitimate, is settled where his parents are (5).

(1) By renting a tenement of 10*l.* a year. St. George *v.* St. Catherine's, 2 Lord Raym. 1474. 2 Bott, 29. Pl. 52. Or on lands in which she had a freehold estate in her own right, 2 Ld. Raym. 1475. 2 Bott, 30. Pl. 53. Rex *v* Oulton, Burr. S.C. 64. 2 Bott, 37. Pl. 68. Or by residence on her husband's estate, although he could not gain one by a like residence in his lifetime. Rex *v.* Long Wittenham, 2 Bott, 38. Pl. 60.

(2) Rex *v.* Barton Tuffe, Burr. S.C. 49. 2 Bott, 34. Pl. 57.

(3) Rex *v.* St. Giles's in the Fields, 2 Bott, 31. Pl. 55.

(4) Rex *v.* St. Mary Cardigan, 6 Term Rep. 116.

(5) Hard's Case, 2 Salk. 427. 2 Bott, 21. Pl. 38.

But

But the communication of ſettlements gained ſubſequent to the child's birth, takes place only whilſt it continues a member of the parent's family. When it ceaſes to be ſo, or (to uſe the phraſe borrowed from the Roman law, and not very properly applied by us) after it is emancipated, any ſettlement which the parent may acquire ſubſequently is not tranſmiſſible. 3. Parental ſettlements gained after birth, communicated.

There are two caſes in which the child is conſidered as being ſevered from the parent's family, without any reference to a ſeparation in fact. Of emancipation.

1. When a child has gained a ſettlement in its own right, that previouſly acquired from the parents is ſuperſeded, and the privilege of following one ſubſequently gained is taken away (1). When child gains a ſettlement.

The age at which a child is ſaid to be capable of acquiring a ſettlement by its own act, is ſeven years and forty days (2).

2. Where it becomes the head or part of another family by marrying, that being a relation inconſiſtent with a ſubordinate ſituation in that of its parents. Thus a ſon who being of full age and married, afterwards removed into another pariſh with his father, where he continued to live with him; was held not to follow a ſettlement which the father afterwards acquired there (3). But marriage ſeems neceſſary to make him the head of a family when there is no ſeparation. A ſon who continued to live with his mother after he was of age (his father being dead), does not become the head of a new family, nor is he emancipated, by ſetting up in buſineſs for himſelf and hiring ſervants of his own (4). When it marries.

(1) Rex *v.* Witten cum Twambrookes, 3 Term Rep. 355. 2 Bott, 53. Pl. 75. Rex *v.* Silton, 1 Wilſ. 184. 2 Bott, 41. Pl. 65.

(2) 3 Burn's Juſt. tit. *Poor.* 3 & 4 Edw. VI. c. 16. and 14 Eliz. c. 5. permit the ſeperation of children from vagrant parents at the age of five. See 23 Reſol. of Judges 1633, Dalt. 236.

(3) Rex *v.* Everton, Eaſt, 526.

(4) Rex *v.* Sowerby, 2 Eaſt, 276.

Separation after 21.

But actual ſeparation is neceſſary in all other caſes; for a child may, after attaining the age of twenty-one, derive a ſettlement from its parent, provided it remain at the time a member of the father's family, with an unbroken continuance (1).

Where a ſeparation has taken place, this diſtinction as to when it ſhall emancipate the child, or otherwiſe, has been laid down: "If a child under the age of twenty-" one years leave his father's houſe, and is thereby *quâ* "ſevered from his father's family; and returns to his "father during a ſtate of pupilage, during which time "policy requires that the child ſhould be under the pro-"tection of his father, he muſt be conſidered as incorpo-"rated with his father's family, unleſs he has gained a "diſtinct ſettlement of his own, or has become the head "of a family himſelf (2)."

But if the child after a ſtate of pupilage ſever himſelf from the father's family, as where the father removed into another pariſh, and the ſon, being above twenty-one, ſtayed behind and married, and lived ſeparate with his wife and family, and was deemed emancipated; he cannot afterwards be incorporated with it (3). In this caſe there was a marriage, which has been ſince held to emancipate, without ſeparation.

But the mere circumſtance of ſeparation by a child of full age has been alſo held ſufficient. A daughter, 22 years old, hired herſelf in the ſame pariſh in which her father lived, as a wet-nurſe at weekly wages, and after continuing but eight weeks in her place, returned to her father; and was held thereby emancipated (4).

(1) *Per* Lord Kenyon C. J. Rex *v.* Roach. 2 Bott, 57. Pl. 78. 6 Term Rep. 247.

(2) *Ante*, n. (1).

(3) Eaſtwoodhey *v.* Weſtwoodhey, 1 Stra. 438. 2 Bott, 39. Pl. 62. See alſo Bugden *v.* Ampthill, Burr. S. C. 270. 2 Bott, 42. Pl. 66. Rex *v.* Heath, 5 Term Rep. 583. 2 Bott, 615. Pl. 627.

(4) Rex *v.* Roach, *ante*, n. (1).

So

So alſo, if the child has ſeparated during its minority, and continued ſo after it has attained the age of diſcretion; it is emancipated. As where a ſon, nineteen years old, went into another pariſh, married, and continued ſeparate forty years previous to his father gaining a new ſettlement, without having himſelf acquired one; he does not follow this new ſettlement of his father's (1). So a ſon who enliſted for a ſoldier at the age of nineteen, and ſerved abroad, but returned after four years to his father, and married; does not follow his father's ſettlement gained after enliſting (2). Likewiſe the ſon of a Scotſman, who enliſted in the army at nineteen years old, before the father had acquired any ſettlement in England, and who did not return to Great Britain until after his father's death; was held not to be ſettled in the pariſh where the father had gained one after the ſeparation; for he was emancipated ſome years before the father had acquired a ſettlement, and had put himſelf under the control and government of others, and it is immaterial whether or not he has no other ſettlement for himſelf (3).

In theſe caſes, if the ſons had quitted the army and returned home before twenty-one, they would have been conſidered as part of the father's family, and participated in any ſubſequent ſettlement acquired by the father, until a more complete emancipation (4). It ſeems unſettled, therefore, whether an emancipation, which is not completed but by the child's not returning under the age of twenty-one, is to refer to the period of its original ſeparation within the age of minority, or to that of its arrival at the years of diſcretion (5).

(1) St Michael's in Norwich *v.* St. Matthew's in Ipſwich, 2 Bott, 40. Pl. 63.

(2) Rex *v.* Walpole St. Peter's, Burr. S. C. 638. 2 Bott, 44. Pl. 68.

(3) Rex *v.* Stanwix, 5 Term Rep. 670. 2 Bott, 55. Pl. 77.

(4) *Per* Lawrence J. Rex *v.* Roach, *ante*, 168. n. (1).

(5) See the opinion of Lawrence J. Rex *v.* Woburn, 8 Term Rep. 429. 2 Bott, 726. Pl. 1008.

In

In the first supposition, the child will not follow any settlement gained during the minority, if acquired subsequent to the separation; in the second, it will.

In Rex *v.* Stanwix, the father acquired his settlement after the son came of age. In Rex *v.* Walpole St. Peter's, the time of gaining the settlement in Walpole parish is not set forth.

Separations which do not emancipate.

But every separation in fact does not amount to an emancipation, although it occurs after the age of majority. Thus where it is for an occasional purpose, as going out for a few weeks in harvest, the son continues part of the family notwithstanding (1). So where a girl having her hands burned off, was incapable of work, and her father being unable to maintain her, procured her to be maintained by the parish; and she was placed in the parish workhouse, where she continued until her father gained a settlement in another parish after she came of age; this was held to be nothing like an emancipation, but that she followed the new settlement afterwards acquired by her father (2).

For the reason of drawing the distinction between separation before and after the child has attained the years of maturity ceases, when imbecility of mind or body induce the necessity of its continuing in a state of perpetual pupilage.

Separations during minority.

The case then resembles that of a child who is separated from its parent's family during minority, and gains no settlement; when it follows that which the parents acquire *at any subsequent period of minority*, whether it returns to them before, or continues to live apart, after it has arrived at the years of legal discretion.

Thus a boy, when seven years old, resided nine or ten years with his uncle for support, returning occasionally

(1) Rex *v.* Sowerby, 2 East. 276. See Rex *v.* Roach, *ante*, 168. n. (1). But the time for which the pauper was hired did not appear in that case.

(2) Rex *v.* Broadhembury, 2 Bott, 49. Pl. 72.

to his father's houſe, particularly upon any diſagreement with his uncle, and he was looked upon as part of his father's family by all parties; he derived a ſettlement from his father, gained eighteen months ſubſequent to the going to his uncle (1). So where the father ran away when his ſon was of the age of eight; his mother dying half a year afterwards, he was ſupported by his pariſh until he was able to maintain himſelf; he follows the ſettlement gained by the father during his minority (2).

Neither does it make any diſtinction, that the father at the time of the ſeparation gives a maſter or any other perſon a degree of legal control over his child, provided he reſerves to himſelf ſo much of the parental rights as are conſiſtent with it. Thus where a father hired out his ſon at the age of thirteen for ſeveral ſucceſſive periods, but inſufficient to confer a ſettlement, until he was nineteen, received his wages and waſhed for him, and the boy never returned home during the time, except for three weeks from illneſs, and never lived with his father after his firſt leaving, until the order of removal, which was made when he was nineteen; he is not emancipated (3).

A ſon hired as a yearly ſervant, in an extraparochial place (where he could not gain a ſettlement), who returned to his father at the end of the year unſettled, under age, and unmarried (4):

A ſon bound at the age of ſixteen, under an indenture for four years, which was void for want of a ſtamp; and never after returning to his father's houſe as a home (5): were held not to be emancipated, but to follow the father's ſettlement

(1) Rex *v.* Tottington Lower End, Cald. 284. 2 Bott, 46. Pl. 7. See alſo Rex *v.* Offchurch, *Ib.* 50. Pl. 73. 3 Term Rep. 114.

(2) Rex *v.* Witton cum Twambrookes, 3 Term Rep. 355. 2 Bott, 53. Pl. 75.

(3) Rex *v.* Stretton, *Ib.* 47. Pl. 74.

(4) Rex *v.* Collingbourn Ducis, *Ib.* 54. Pl. 76. 4 Term Rep. 199.

(5) Rex *v.* Edgeworth, 3 Term Rep. 353. 2 Bott, 52. Pl. 74.

settlement subsequently acquired during the period of minority (1).

So where a son enlisted at the age of sixteen into the same regiment of militia in which his father was serving as a serjeant, and lived with him until the age of twenty-three, the father receiving his pay; it was adjudged that he followed the settlement acquired by the father during this service in the militia and residence with him: for living in the family, the parental control was not altogether destroyed, the guidance and direction of the child to a certain extent was not inconsistent with the occasional military situation in which he was (2).

The principle which prevents the child from following any settlement acquired by its parents subsequent to emancipation, must, when they have none prevent it from having recourse to that gained by the grandfather, or other persons in the ascending line, subsequent to the time when the father and mother, or other ancestors, through whom they claim, have been emancipated, and ceased to form a part of the family of their immediate parents (3).

SECT. II.

Proofs necessary to support a Settlement.

1. The marriage (4).

2. That the pauper is the issue of that marriage.

When the actual descent is proved, very slight evidence will be sufficient in the first instance to establish the legitimacy; for the law does not presume that the parents have lived in a state of concubinage criminal in them, and productive of penal disability to their innocent offspring.

(1) Rex v. Collingbourn Ducis, *ante*, n. 4. was a case of emancipation from a certificate.

(2) Rex v. Woburn, 8 Term Rep. 479. 1 Bott, App. 726. Pl. 1008. *ante*.

(3) Rex v. Darlington, 4 Term Rep. 797. 2 Bott, 587. Pl. 601.

(4) See *ante*, 154. *et seq*.

It

It lies on the other ſide to eſtabliſh the baſtardy by that evidence which will be ſtated in treating of the ſettlement of illegitimate children by birth. The evidence therefore of the father and mother; an examined copy of the pariſh regiſter of the pauper's birth or chriſtening, with evidence of his identity (1); or that his parents were conſidered as married perſons; or the teſtimony of any who knew his father and mother, and their being reputed man and wife; or of their acknowledging the pauper as their lawful child (2); and even that of the pauper himſelf, is ſufficient.

3. The parents' ſettlement.

The firſt ſettlement to be relied upon is that of the father (3), and if he has done no act to gain one, it will be neceſſary to reſort to that of his grandfather or grandmother. If no ſettlement can be proved on the ſide of the father, recourſe is to be had in the ſame way to that of the mother. In all theſe caſes, the ſettlement laſt gained before their child becomes emancipated is that of the pauper..

(1) Rex *v.* Creech, Burr. S. C. 765. 2 Bott, 16. Pl. 34.

(2) Rex *v.* Bucklebury, 1 Term Rep. 164. 2 Bott, 26. Pl. 48.

(3) *Ante*, 165. and Cripplegate *v.* St. Saviour's. Fol. 265. 2 Bott, 16. Pl. 33. See *poſt.* 74.

CHAPTER XIX.

Of the Settlement of Illegitimate Children by Birth.

SECT. I. *Of the Settlement.*

THE original settlement of a legitimate child, when that of neither parent can be ascertained, is the place of birth (1); or if that is unknown, where it is first found (2).

Bastards.

On the other hand, an illegitimate child is considered as the offspring of no one; or as it is sometimes termed, to cut off all idea and hope of peculiar relationship, the child of the people. There exists no privity of blood between it and the reputed parents, through which it can lay claim to their settlement: and it is settled in the place of its birth, as we have seen that lawful children are whose parents have none (3).

Mother residing under certificate.

It is the same if the mother come into the parish under the protection of a certificate (4); unless the parish certifying therein, expressly describes the child, and undertakes to provide for it. As where parish officers by their certificate acknowledged A. C. spinster, and the child or children which she now goeth with, to be their inhabitants, and promised to provide for them; it is settled in the parish granting the certificate (5). But the parish will not be bound

(1) Whitechapel *v*. Stepney, Carth. 433. 2 Bott, 15. Pl. 30. See also cases of Clavely and Burton, 2 Bulst. 351. 2 Bott, 13. Pl. 28.

(2) *Per* Holt. C. J. Banbury & Broughton, Comb. 364. Dalt. 168. 2 Bott, 16. Pl. 31.

(3) Whitechapel *v*. Stepney, *ante*, n. 1. Rex *v*. Spitalfields, 1 Ld. Raym. 567. 2 Bott, 3. Pl. 7. Rex *v*. St. Peter's in Worcestershire, Burr. S. C. 25. 2 Bott, 6. Pl. 14.

(4) Rex *v*. Hilton, Burr. S. C. 187. 2 Bott, 7. Pl. 16.

(5) Rex *v*. Ipsley, Burr. S. C. 650. 2 Bott, 8. Pl. 19. *Quære tamen*; and see the opinion of Lord Kenyon C. J. Rex *v*. Mathon, *post*. 175. n. (2).

bound to do ſo, where the undertaking is in general terms to provide "for the woman and her child," as that ſhall always be preſumed to ſignify her legitimate offspring (1). Even if certificate is granted when the woman is unmarried and undertakes to provide for the child ſhe is then pregnant with, and all other children that ſhe might thereafter have, until ſhe or they acquire ſubſequent ſettlements; it does not extend to an illegitimate child born eight years after the certificate is granted, but he is ſettled where born (2).

Although this is the general rule reſpecting the ſettlement of natural children, there are ſome exceptions which exiſt at the common law, and others which are created by ſtatute. **Exceptions by common law.**

The firſt exception by the common law, is where a woman with child of a baſtard is removed out of one pariſh into another, through the fraud or colluſion of its officers. In this caſe the child, whereſoever it is born, is ſettled in the pariſh from which the mother has been colluſively removed (3). But the removal of the woman, muſt have been effected with a fraudulent purpoſe; for if ſhe ſhould come accidentally into one pariſh, and in conſequence of the ſelf-ſuggeſted perſuaſions of a private pariſhioner, go into ſome other, and be there delivered (4); or if ſhe ſhould without fraud leave her own pariſh, with the knowledge of the overſeers, for the purpoſe of finding the putative father of the child with which ſhe is quick, and be ſuddenly delivered in ſome other pariſh whilſt endeavouring to reach her own, theſe form no exception to the general rule, and the birth decides the ſettlement (5). **1. Removal by fraud.**

(1) Rex *v.* Wyke, Burr. S. C. 264. 2 Bott, 8. Pl. 18.

(2) Rex *v.* Mathon, 7 Term Rep. 362. 2 Bott, 12. Pl. 27.

(3) Tewkſbury *v.* Twining, Bulſt. 349. 2 Bott, 1. Pl. 2. Maſters *v.* Child, 3 Salk. 66. 2 Bott, 3. Pl. 6.

(4) *Ante*, n. (3).

(5) Rex *v.* Aſtley, 2 Bott, 10. Pl. 23.

2. Pending an order of removal. The second exception is, where a child is born after an order has been made for the mother's removal to some other parish; here, whether it is born in one of the contending parishes (1), or in some intermediate one while the officers are in the act of removing or using reasonable diligence to remove the woman (2), it is settled in the parish against which judgment is given, if the order is contested (3); or in that to which the removal is made, where it acquiesces without appeal (4).

3. Mother in custody. The third exception is, where the child is born while the mother is in actual custody of the law; as where she is in the house of correction (5), or in the county gaol (6): here it follows the settlement of the mother; or if that cannot be known, it is to be provided for in the parish where she was apprehended (7).

Exceptions by statute. The exceptions enacted by statute are:

13 Geo. 2. c. 29. 1. By 13 Geo. III. c. 29. for regulating the Foundling Hospital, no child received there shall thereby gain a settlement in the parish where the hospital is situate.

17 Geo. 2. c. 5. 2. By 17 Geo. II. c. 5. s. 25. where a woman wandering and begging, is delivered of a child in any parish or place to which she doth not belong, and thereby becometh chargeable to the same, the churchwardens or overseers may detain her till they can safely convey her to a justice of the peace; and if she shall be detained and conveyed to a justice as aforesaid, the child of which she is

(1) Reg. *v.* Icleford 1 Sess. Cas. 32. 2 Bott, 4. Pl. 10. Much Waltham *v.* Peram, *Ib.* 2. Pl. 4. 2 Salk. 474. Boreham *v.* Waltham, Carth. 397. 2 Bott, 2. Pl. 5.

(2) Reg. *v.* Icleford, *ante*, n. (1). Reg. *v.* Jane Grey *post*. n. (4).

(3) Westbury *v.* Coston, 2 Salk. 532. 2 Bott, 4. Pl. 8. & *ante*, n. (1).

(4) Reg. *v.* Jane Grey. Sett. Rem. 41. 2 Bott, 4. Pl. 9.

(5) Suckley *v.* Whitborn. 2 Bulst. 358. 2 Bott, 2. Pl. 3. 32 Resol. Judges of assise 1633. Dalt. 237. *ante* 140.

(6) Elsing *v.* The County of Hereford. 1 Sess. Ca. 99. 2 Bott, 4. Pl. 11.

(7) 2 Bott, 16. Pl. 31. See also Banbury *v.* Broughton, Comb. 364.

delivered,

delivered, if a baſtard, ſhall not be ſettled in the place where ſo born, nor be ſent thither by a vagrant paſs; but the ſettlement of the woman ſhall be deemed the ſettlement of the child.

3. By 13 Geo. III. c. 82. ſ. 5. no baſtard child, born in a lying-in hoſpital, ſhall be legally ſettled in, or entitled to relief as a pariſhioner from the pariſh wherein the hoſpital is ſituated; but every ſuch child ſhall follow the mother's ſettlement, and ſhall immediately gain a ſettlement in the pariſh or pariſhes reſpectively where his, her, or their mothers were laſt legally ſettled. 13 Geo. 3. c. 82.

4. By 20 Geo. 3. c. 36. baſtard children born in the houſe of induſtry of any hundred or other diſtrict incorporated by act of parliament for the relief and employment of the poor, ſhall be deemed to belong to the pariſh or place where the mother of ſuch baſtard child was legally ſettled. 20 Geo. 3. c. 36.

5. By 33 Geo. III. c. 54. ſ. 25. for the encouragement and relief of friendly ſocieties, it is enacted, that every child which ſhall be born a baſtard in any pariſh, townſhip, or place, during the mother's reſidence therein under the authority of this act, ſhall have, and be deemed to have the ſame ſettlement which the mother has, or is entitled to at the time of the birth of ſuch child. 33 Geo. 3. c. 54.

6. By 35 Geo. III. c. 101. ſ. 6. if an order of removal has been obtained for the purpoſe of removing an unmarried woman who is with child, and it ſhall be ſuſpended on account of the ſickneſs or other infirmity of ſuch perſon, and during ſuch ſuſpenſion the ſaid woman ſhall be delivered of any child which by the law of this kingdom ſhall be a baſtard; every ſuch child ſhall be deemed and taken to be ſettled in the ſame pariſh, townſhip, or place in which was the legal ſettlement of the mother at the time of her delivery. 35 Geo. 3. c. 101.

SECT. II.

Of the Proofs.

THE only proof required to establish this kind of settlement is, that the pauper was actually born within the parish or township. This may be effected either by the testimony of the parents, relations, or any other person acquainted with the fact.

The most usual evidence, where the parents are dead, is the pauper, as to their declarations on the subject (1).

But although birth is *prima facie* evidence of a settlement, without any reference to the legitimacy of the pauper, yet questions on the latter point must frequently arise between contending parishes, for the purpose either of getting rid of this birth settlement by proving one by parentage; or *vice versa*, of establishing conclusively that which arises from birth, by destroying the presumption that a preferable one is derived from the parents.

Proof of Illegitimacy:

The facts upon which illegitimacy depend may be classed as follows:

1. Where no marriage.

1. Where there has been no marriage, or one that is informal before the child is born (2).

2. When the father is alive.

2. Where there has been a marriage, and the father is alive *when it is born.*

3. When dead.

3. Where he dies *before it is born.*

Access presumed.

4. Legitimacy in the second case depends chiefly upon the fact of the husband's access to his wife; for where that has taken place, the issue will be legitimate, although the woman is proved to have been ever so unfaithful to the nuptial bed (3). Access shall be presumed, even in cases where there has been a voluntary separation between husband

(1) *Post.* 181.
(2) *Ante*, p. 154, &c.
(3) Rex *v.* Brown, 2 Stra. 811. 2 Bott, 446. Pl. 557.

and

and wife; and it requires ſtrong and almoſt irrefragable evidence to ſhew that it has not taken place (1).

This evidence is reducible under four heads:

First and anciently, almoſt the only proof of non-acceſs, was the child's being conceived and born while the father continued beyond the four ſeas (2). 1. When beyond four ſeas.

Secondly, where there is a divorce *a menſâ et thoro*; for obedience to the eccleſiaſtical ſentence ſhall be preſumed (3). 2. Divorce.

The third ariſes from the exploſion of the old opinion, that if the huſband is within the four ſeas the child is legitimate. If therefore it can be proved *by clear evidence*, that the huſband has not had acceſs (4), the child is a baſtard. Neither is it neceſſary in this caſe, (at leaſt where the parties have been long dead,) to eſtabliſh non-acceſs by witneſſes who can prove *him conſtantly* reſident away from his wife. Proof that the huſband left Norwich, and went to reſide at London, that his wife remained behind, and lived with another man as his wife for years, during which time the child in queſtion was born; that this child always went by the adulterer's name, and was reputed illegitimate in the family; has been held ſufficient evidence of illegitimacy, though it did not clearly appear where the real huſband had been from the time of conception to that of delivery (5). 3. Direct evidence.

Laſtly, where there is an apparent impoſſibility of procreation on the part of the huſband, as if he be only eight years old; or if a man who is bedridden marries a pregnant woman in his chamber, and ſhe is delivered twelve 4. Inability.

(1) 1 Black. Com. 457.

(2) Rex *v.* Alberton, 1 Ld. Raym. 395. 2 Salk. 483. 1 Bott, 445. Pl. 553.

(3) 1 Black. Com. 457. Bull. N. P. 112.

(4) Rex *v.* St. Bride's, 1 Str. 51. 1 Bott, 446. Pl. 556. Pendrel *v.* Pendrel, 2 Str. 925. 2 Bott, 447. Pl. 559. Rex *v.* Bedall, 2 Str. 1073. 2 Bott, 450. Pl. 564.

(5) Thompſon *v.* Saul, 4 Term Rep. 356. 1 Bott, 454. Pl. 568.

weeks after; the iſſue is baſtard (1). But the evidence muſt go to an impoſſibility; for improbability, ariſing from a bad habit of body, is inſufficient (2).

3. When father dies before the birth.

The third ſituation which may give riſe to the queſtion of illegitimacy is, where there has been a marriage, and the father dies *before the iſſue is born*.

If the child comes into the world within the uſual period of geſtation, *i. e.* forty weeks, it is in general to be deemed legitimate; if beyond, a baſtard (3). But in the opinion of medical perſons, this period may be accelerated or retarded by accidental cauſes; and upon their teſtimony, judging from the particular facts of the caſe, a child was held legitimate, though born forty weeks and nine days after the huſband's deceaſe (4).

If a man die, and his widow ſoon after marry again, and a child is born within ſuch time as renders it dubious, from the courſe of nature, to which huſband it belongs; the iſſue is ſaid to be more than ordinarily legitimate, and may, upon arriving at the years of diſcretion, chooſe which of the fathers it pleaſes (5).

Proof, by what witneſſes.

As to the witneſſes by whom the fact of illegitimacy may be proved, not only all other perſons, but the father or mother may be called, for they are not directly intereſted in the queſtion of their child's ſettlement.

Parents' evidence.

They may therefore prove, 1. The fact or time of marriage (6).

(1) Foxcroft's caſe, 2 Roll. Abr. 353. 1 Bott, 445. Pl. 552.

(2) Lomax *v.* Holmden, 2 Str. 940. 1 Bott, 447. Pl. 560.

(3) Radwell's Caſe, Co. Litt. 124, *b.* 1 Bott, 443. Pl. 547, 548.

(4) Alſop *v.* Bowtrell, Cro, Jac. 541. 1 Bott, 444. Pl. 549.

(5) *Ib.* Pl. 550. 21 Edw. III. Pl. 39.

(6) Rex *v.* St. Peter's, *Burr.* S. C. 25. 1 Bott, 448. Pl. 561. Stapylton *v.* Stapylton, Caſ. temp. Hard. 277. May *v.* May, Bull, N. P. 112. Sacheverell *v.* Sacheverell, *Ib.* 241. 287. Lord Valentia's Caſe, Cowp. 593.

2. Its

2. Its formality or informality (1).

3. Whether a child is born subsequent or prior to a marriage had between them (2).

4. But where a child appears to have been born *in wedlock*, the evidence of the parents, especially of the mother who is the offending party, seems inadmissible to prove the non-access of the husband, and bastardize the issue (3).

5. Yet where the child is so born, the mother is an admissible witness to prove the fact of her adultery with another person, because from the nature of the transaction it is usually carried on with such secrecy, as to admit of no other evidence (4).

6. Where the parent's testimony is admissible during their lives, proof of their declaration on oath or otherwise is evidence after their decease (5).

7. Where a divorce can be proved by parol, and the production of the sentence of a court is unnecessary; as where it is done abroad by the judgment and according to the forms of some foreign law, the parents are evidence to prove the fact (6).

(1) Standen *v.* Standen, Peake's Ni. Pri. Ca. 32.; and see Wilkinson *v.* Payne, 4 Term Rep. 468. *Ante*, 160.

(2) Stevens *v.* Moss, Cowp. 591.

(3) *Per* Lord Mansfield, Stevens *v.* Moss, Cowp. 593. Rex *v.* Reading, *infra* n. (4). But see Clerk *v.* Wright, 1 Bott, 447. Pl. 558. Rex *v.* Bedall, *infra* n. (4).

(4) Rex *v.* Reading, Cas. temp. Hard. 79. 1 Bott, 448. Pl. 562. Rex *v.* Bedall, *Ib.* 450. Pl. 564. 2 Str. 1076. Stevens *v.* Moss, *ante*.

(5) *Ut in* n. (2).

(6) Ganer *v.* Lady Lanesborough, Peake's Ni. Pri. Ca. 18.

CHAPTER XX.

Of Settlement by Hiring and Service.

SECT. I.

Division of the Subject.

3 W. 3. c. 11. construction of.

THE first statute which required a further qualification beyond mere residence as a servant for the space of forty days, was 3 W. III. chap. 11. sect. 6. It enacts, that if any *unmarried* person, not having *child or children*, shall be lawfully *hired* into any parish or town for one year, *such service* shall be adjudged and deemed a good settlement therein.

This section describes, first, the persons who shall be capable of gaining a settlement by hiring; it next requires that the hiring shall be for a year; and lastly, that it shall be in a "parish or township."

But the words "such service," having no regular antecedent, it was difficult to ascertain for what period the service was intended to continue. It might, and possibly with little violence, have been construed to signify a service commensurate with, and under that yearly hiring, which is required in the very same clause, since there was nothing else in the sentence to which these words could refer. But it was held to make no further alteration in the law of settlements, than requiring a *bona fide* contract for a year's service, which the parties were left to enforce at their discretion. A settlement therefore was gained by entering into this yearly agreement as a servant, joined with residence as such for forty days.

Reference

Reference to the remaining ways of acquiring ſettlements, in which nothing is neceſſary beyond reſidence for forty days in a particular capacity, ſeems to have given riſe to this conſtruction. The caſe of apprentices regulated by the ſame ſtatute, bore a ſtrong analogy to that of ſervants. Nothing further was required to gain a ſettlement by apprenticeſhip, than a contract by indenture, and reſidence under it for forty days. A ſimilar contract for a year's ſervice, with a like performance of ſervice, was deemed equally ſufficient to confer one in the caſe of hiring and ſervice.

This interpretation produced great inconvenience. Fraudulent hirings to perſons unable to maintain or employ a ſervant were entered into, that paupers might be retained in particular pariſhes. The actual ſervice, which was the ſubſtantial conſideration ſuppoſed to be paid to the pariſh for the burthens of a ſettlement, remained unperformed. If a ſervant was diſcharged by colluſion, or through miſconduct, after the lapſe of his forty days, he was thrown a more ſpeedy and permanent incumbrance upon the pariſh than where the ſervice was honeſtly performed.

To remove theſe inconveniences, a clauſe was introduced in 8 & 9 W. III. c. 30. which provides, that no perſon ſo hired as aforeſaid, ſhall be adjudged or deemed to have a good ſettlement in any ſuch pariſh, or townſhip, "unleſs ſuch perſon ſhall continue and abide in the ſame "ſervice for the ſpace of one whole year." 8 & 9 W. 3. c. 30.

Of theſe ſtatutes, when taken ſeparately, the firſt regulates three things, namely, the deſcription of perſons by whom a ſettlement may be gained; the lawful hiring for a year; and the place into which the ſervant is to be hired. Diſtribution of ſubject.

The second prescribes the service, and the abiding and continuance therein for the space of an entire year. When considered together as part of the same code, a further question arises upon them, of how far the service made necessary by the one, need be performed under the contract of hiring required by the other?

This branch of settlement law may be considered therefore under the four following general heads:

1. What persons are capable of gaining a settlement by hiring and service.

2. The contract of hiring.

3. The year's service.

4. The residence by, and place in which the settlement is gained.

SECT. II.

What Persons are capable of acquiring a Settlement by Hiring and Service.

Unmarried. THE words of 3 W. III. 11. are, that "if any unmarried person, not having child or children, shall be lawfully hired," &c.

It has been held under this provision, that if the servant marries during service (1), or even after the hiring, but before his year begins (2), it will not prevent his settlement. Neither does it make any difference, that

(1) Farringdon *v.* Witty, Salk. 527. 2 Bott, 302. Pl. 339. Rex *v.* Clent, *Ib.* 302. Pl. 340. Fol. 148. Rex *v.* Sutton, 2 Sess. Cas. 133. Rex *v.* Hanbury, Burr. S. C. 322. See also Rex *v.* Hedsor, Cald. 51. 2 Bott, 389. Pl. 331. Rex *v.* Nymphsfield, Cald. 307. 2 Bott, 290. n. (a). Rex *v.* Great Bookham, *Ib.* 292. n. (a).

(2) Rex *v.* Allendale, 3 Term Rep. 382. 2 Bott, 275. Pl. 228. *Ib.* 305. Pl. 344.

both

both parties think the ſervant married at the time of hiring; as where the huſband being abroad, died before the wife was hired, and ſhe was unacquainted with the fact (1); or although they know that the ſervant is to be married before his ſervice commences (2).

The ſervant's being married at the time of making the agreement is likewiſe immaterial, if he be ſingle, when it becomes abſolute and complete. As where a married man was hired conditionally on the 16th, to ſerve for a year from the 24th of the month, if the ſervant ſhould approve the terms; and his wife died in the intermediate time: he was held to gain a ſettlement by a year's ſervice; for the ſervant having a power to diſſent until the 24th, when he was unmarried, the hiring was conſidered as taking place on the 24th (3).

Without children.

The ſecond qualification required by the ſtatute is, that the ſervant ſhould not have any child or children at the time of hiring. This is adjudged to mean children who, by following their parent's ſettlement, might become chargeable to that pariſh in which one may be acquired under the new ſervitude. So that, if legitimate children are emancipated at the time from which the parent engages to ſerve, he may gain a ſettlement (4). But they muſt be emancipated at the commencement of the ſervice. The child's entering into a contract by which, if completed, he may gain a ſettlement, and thereby become emancipated, does not qualify the parent for obtaining one. Thus, where a father having a ſon, who had not acquired a ſettlement, hired himſelf for a year, and the ſon was alſo hired for the ſame period, on the ſame day, and both ſerved their time; the fa-

(1) Rex *v.* Henſingham Cald. 206. 2 Bott, 91. Pl. 131. *Ib.* 175. Pl. 227.

(2) Rex *v.* Allendale, *ſupra*, n. (2).

(3) Rex *v.* Banknewton, Burr. S. C. 455. 2 Bott. 174. Pl. 225. That the ſervice for the laſt 40 days muſt be performed under a contract of hiring entered into when the pauper is unmarried, ſee *poſt.* Sect. IV.

(4) Anthony *v.* Cardigan, Fort. 309. Fol. 131. S. C. 2 Bott, 172. Pl. 222

ther

ther gains no ſettlement, as not being a perſon "not having a child" within the meaning of the act; for the ſon's contract of ſervice might not have been completed, in which event, he could not have gained a ſettlement, and therefore at the time when the father entered into the relation of ſervant, the ſon conſtituted a part of his family (1).

SECT. III.

Of the Contract of Hiring.

Parties to the contract.

MANY parts of the agreement of hiring, which are of moſt importance to the maſter and ſervant, have but ſmall relation to the queſtion of ſettlement.

All contracts are made between at leaſt two contracting parties; but it is immaterial whether the agreement be to ſerve one or more maſters (2); or is made by a third perſon, if ſubſequently ratified by the parties (3). Neither is it neceſſary that they ſhould be of full age, if the agreement is entered into with the parent's conſent (4); or that the maſter ſhould have a ſettlement in the pariſh; for the ſervant does not derive the ſettlement from the maſter, but from the ſervice (5).

The degree of relationſhip or conſanguinity alſo makes no diſtinction, unleſs, as in the caſe of huſband and wife, it is inconſiſtent with the formation of the contract itſelf. The agreement by a daughter, who was emancipated to perform the offices of a ſervant to her father for a certain reward, is equally within the ſtatute as where the parties are ſtrangers to each other in blood and connection (6).

(1) Rex *v.* New Foreſt, 5 Term Rep. 478. 2 Bott, 177. Pl. 230

(2) Rex *v.* Elderſley, 2 Bott, 274. Pl. 317.

(3) *Per* Lord Kenyon, Rex *v.* St. Matthew's Ipſwich, 3 Term Rep. 449. 2 Bott, 184. Pl. 238.

(4) See Rex *v.* Winterſett, Cald. 298. 2 Bott, 261. Pl. 309.

(5) Miſſenden *v.* Cheſham, 2 Bott, 173. Pl. 223.

(6) S. C. as 186. n. (4); and Rex *v.* Chertſey, 2 Term Rep. 37. 2 Bott, 202. Pl. 251.

The

Wages and Service.

The nature of the service is likewise immaterial. It may be extended to all sorts of work, or confined to a particular sort (1). The servant may live out of the house during the entire of his service (2); or for part of the time in, and part out (3); it is still an hiring within the statute, provided he remains under his master's control during the whole time of the contract. Equally unimportant is the nature of the wages to be received; they may be in money, or in kind, or instruction (4), or in part of the servant's earnings (5), or in victuals and clothes; or either, or even none of these, provided an actual contract exists. In the same manner they may be payable either by the week (6), the year, the piece, or the gross; and any alteration in these particulars during the year, which does not put an end to the contract, is also immaterial. These circumstances will often prove important clues towards ascertaining the time for which the hiring is made, or the degree of control which it gives the master over his servant, where they do not expressly appear from the terms of the contract itself; but where these are ascertained, the former make no variation in the law of settlement.

Requisites in a contract of hiring.

The following are the principal rules to be observed relative to the contract of hiring in cases of settlement. 1. there must be a contract; 2. it must be a contract for servitude, and intended only as such; 3. it must be an entire contract for at least a complete year's prospective service; 4. it must contain no special exception, exempt-

(1) Rex *v.* St. Agnes, Burr. S. C. 671. 2 Bott, 259. Pl. 671.

(2) Rex *v.* King's Norton, Burr, S. C. 152. 2 Bott, 208. Pl. 255.

(3) Rex *v.* Sutton, 1 East, 656.

(4) Rex *v.* Hitcham, Burr. S. C. 489. 2 Bott, 212. Pl. 258.

(5) Rex *v.* Little Bolton, Cald. 367. 2 Bott, 221. Pl. 264.

(6) Rex *v.* Winchcombe, Dougl. 391. 2 Bott, 220. Pl. 263.

ing

ing the servant from his master's control during its continuance.

1. Must be a contract.

The 3 W. & M. c. 11. s. 6. requires that the person shall be lawfully hired; it is necessary therefore that an agreement, imposing the reciprocal obligation of master and servant, should subsist between the parties (1).

Such agreement may be either *express* or *implied.*

Express contracts.

An express agreement may be in writing, or by word of mouth; it requires in neither case, any technical form of expression to render it valid. Like all other contracts, it is to be interpreted according to its genuine purport, so that if the intention to bargain for a year's service be clear, no matter in what terms it is expressed. Thus an hiring for 11 months, for 4l. 10s. it being agreed at the time between the servant and master, that the servant should give a month's service in beyond the 11 months, is an hiring for a year; for it is in substance an agreement to serve for 12 months. The variation in expression is of no significance, and cannot avail to prevent the gaining a settlement (3).

2. Implied contracts.

An implied agreement of hiring is a contract which the law infers to have taken place between the parties, where an express one does not appear. The mere exercise of control, and the performance of service between persons otherwise independent, is sufficient to support

(1) Gregory Stoke *v.* Pitminster, 2 Bott, 179. Pl. 233; and see the cases cited *infra*.

(2) Pawlet *v.* Burnham, 2 Bott, 307. Pl. 347.

(3) Rex *v.* Milwich, Burr. S. C. 413. 2 Bott, 209. Pl. 256.; and see the opinion of Lord Kenyon, Rex *v.* Macclesfield, 3 Term Rep. 76. 2 Bott, 204. Pl. 252; and of Buller J. Rex *v.* Mursley, 1 Term Rep. 694. 2 Bott, 242. Pl. 288.

this

this inference, ſince it is only from an agreement either expreſsly entered into, or tacitly underſtood, that the one can derive his right to command, or the other be induced to ſubmit to obey.

Evidence of implied hirings,

Thus the mere acts of ſervice, either in huſbandry (1), or as a menial ſervant (2), or as an oſtler (3), are ſufficient to warrant the inference of a contract of hiring. So where an expreſs contract has exiſted, and expired, if the ſervant continues the ſucceeding year with his maſter, without coming to any other agreement, the law implies, from the fact of ſervice, an agreement to ſerve for that year on the ſame terms (4).

rebutted by circumſtances.

The act of ſervitude however is no more than evidence from whence a contract of hiring may be preſumed (5); it may be rebutted therefore by a diſcloſure of any circumſtances which ſhew that the parties did not ſtand in the relation of maſter and ſervant.

A footboy reſiding with a barber.

A gentleman ſent a lad who had lived with him three years, and gained a ſettlement as his foot-boy, to reſide with a barber inhabiting another pariſh, to learn the art of ſhaving and dreſſing hair; he gave the maſter ſome money to teach him, who was alſo to have the benefit of his work. The pauper lived under this agreement for more than a year; but it conferred no ſettlement, for he was in the nature of a ſcholar and not of a a ſervant, and the barber had no remedy to compel him to ſerve (6).

(1) Rex *v*. Lyth, 5 Term Rep 327. 2 Bott, 364. Pl. 392.

(2) Rex *v*. Long Whatton, 5 Term Rep 447. 2 Bott, 366. Pl. 393. Rex *v*. Hales, *Ib*. 367. Pl. 394, 5 Term Rep. 668.

(3) Rex *v*. Holy Trinity in Wareham, Cald. 141. 2 Bott, 362. Pl. 390.

(4) Rex *v*. St. Giles Reading, Cald. 54. 2 Bott, 260. Pl. 206, & *poſt*.

(5) *Supra*, n. (1), (2).

(6) Rex *v*. Whalton, Carth. 400. 2 Bott, 178. Pl. 231.

Mr.

A boy taken in charity.

Mr. Pyke, who was mortgagee of a ſmall eſtate, took the mortgagor's ſon into his family from charity; *there was no contract as to ſervice*, or the pauper's continuance with Pyke, and he got meat, drink, lodging, and clothes, but no wages. He lived there four years, doing whatever the ſervants of the houſe thought fit to bid him, and left his maſter at the age of fourteen. It was conſidered as not being an hiring to confer a ſettlement, the juſtices having found that there was no contract (1).

A boy living with his uncle.

Where a boy had lived with his uncle *as a relation, and not under any hiring*; he was afterwards hired by another perſon as a yearly ſervant, but returned to his uncle, upon his requeſt by letter, ſaying that if he would come and live with him *as before*, he could ſurely make it better for him than a common ſervice. There was no agreement with the uncle after his return, either as to time or conſideration of ſervice; but the uncle often promiſed that if he would ſtay with him for his life, he would leave him his crop, farm, and ſtock. He lived with his uncle ſeveral years, by whom he was found in meat, clothes, and pocket-money, but received no wages. He gained no ſettlement, for there was no hiring during the firſt ſervice, and the terms of coming to live with him *as before*, negative the preſumption of ſuch a contract during the ſecond (2).

The helper to a waiter.

A waiter to an inn being taken ill, ſent for the pauper *to help him*; which he did, and continued in the inn as boot-catcher for 19 months, lodging and boarding there, and was to be ſatisfied by the gentlemen who came to the houſe. The maſter knew of his being there the night after his coming, but nothing paſſed between them at that time.

(1) Rex *v.* Weyhill, Burr. S. C. 491. 2 Bott, 182. Pl. 235.

(2) Rex *v.* Stokeſley, 6 Term Rep. 757. 2 Bott, 186. Pl. 239.

The

The waiter continued in the ſervice eleven months after the pauper came there, and the latter remained for ſix months ſubſequent to his going away; the maſter employing him occaſionally on errands, &c. The pauper on going away applied to the maſter to give him ſomething for the time he had been there, who refuſed, alleging he had made no agreement with him; but afterwards gave him two guineas. The court were of opinion that there was no hiring for a year, for during the time the waiter continued at the inn, the pauper was helper *to him*; and though the laſt ſix months of the ſervice is to be referred to an implied contract with the maſter, it is inſufficient to confer a ſettlement, being for leſs than a year (1).

The inference of a contract from the performance of acts of ſervice, may be repelled by evidence of the previous ſituation of the parties:

As where a negro woman, who had been in the condition of a ſlave in America, came to England in her maſter's family, where ſhe continued to live during his life, in the capacity of a ſervant, and for ſome time afterwards with his widow and executrix. The ſituation of the woman, previous to her arrival in England, negatived the preſumption which might have ariſen from her ſervice, and the court held that ſhe gained no ſettlement, for there was no contract of hiring (2) A negro woman.

So if the parties ſtand in a degree of relationſhip towards each other, which accounts for the reciprocal acts of ſervice and maintenance, without reference to a contract for

(1) Rex v. St. Matthew's Ipſwich, 3 Term Rep. 449. 2 Bott, 284. Pl. 328.

(2) Rex v. Thames Ditton, Cald. 536. 2 Bott, 282. Pl. 236.

ſervice,

service, it seems to have considerable weight in excluding the presumption.

Young girl residing with her relation by agreement.

As where a young girl was sent to by a relation, who told her, that if she would live with her she should have meat, drink, washing, and lodging; and the girl accepted the terms, and lived with her *as a servant* for four years. It was adjudged to be no contract to confer a settlement; for this is no agreement, but an encouragement to the poor girl, that if she would live with a relation, she would maintain her (1).

A boy with his uncle.

Likewise, when a boy went to live with his uncle, who was a taylor, at the age of eleven or twelve, worked for him two years and learned the business; when the uncle proposed to take him an apprentice, which the boy refused, but continued to work for him until he was 17 years old; the uncle providing him with board, lodging, and necessaries: the court were of opinion, without argument, that he gained no settlement, for there was no hiring (2).

2. Must be a contract for service.

The second circumstance required in this contract to confer a settlement is, that it should be for servitude, and intended only as such. An agreement designed to place the parties in the relation of master and apprentice is insufficient, although it entitles the former to exercise an equal control over the person submitted to his authority.

The 3 W. & M. c. 11. and 8 & 9 W. III. c. 3. expressly require that the party is to be *hired to serve*. Not

(1) Gregory Stoke *v.* Pitminster, 2 Bott, 179. Pl. 233. But Lord Kenyon observes upon this case, "that it "was determined early in the Reign "of George II. when these questions "were not discussed or understood so "well as they are at present." Rex *v.* Worsfield, 5 Term Rep. 506. George II. seems a mistake of the reporter for George I. in the 13th year of whose reign it is reported to have been decided. See also Rex *v.* Lyth, 5 Term Rep. 927.

(2) Rex *v.* St. Mary's Guildford, Cald. 522. 2 Bott, 184. Pl. 237.

only

only an apprentice regularly indentured, therefore, cannot during the continuance of his apprenticeship acquire a settlement as a servant; but those who serve as apprentices, without indentures, or under such as are null and void for informality, cannot claim one as if their service had taken place under a contract for servitude.

So that whenever the forms required to confer a settlement by apprenticeship have not been observed, it becomes necessary to ascertain whether the person claiming a settlement has been hired as a servant, or engaged as an apprentice. It is not always easy to ascertain this fact; for a servant may hire himself for the purpose of being instructed in some particular business, as well as an apprentice.

This subject comes more regularly under discussion in treating of settlements by apprenticeship; and it is sufficient for the present, to elucidate the rule by the following cases.

The pauper agreed to let himself to his brother, who was a carpenter, for a year; by his agreement he was to receive no money by way of wages, but his brother was to teach him as much as he could of the trade during the time, and provide him with meat, drink, washing, and lodging, the pauper to do all his brother's lawful business in the farming way. This has been held a contract for service, and an hiring for a year (1).

But an agreement with a stone mason *to take the pauper as an apprentice to teach him the trade*, and provide him with meat, drink, washing, lodging and clothing; the pauper to live and work with him as an apprentice, and *indentures to be executed between them accordingly;* will not entitle the pauper

(1) Rex v. Hitcham, Burr. S. C. 489. 2 Bott, 212. Pl. 258.

to a settlement, the indenture never having been executed (1).

These cases correspond with each other in almost every particular, except that the agreement in one, was to work as a servant, and in the other as an apprentice. Upon that distinction, the pauper in the latter, was held not to gain a settlement; because he was not an apprentice for want of a binding by deed, and therefore not settled in that capacity; and he was not an hired servant, as the agreement declares that he was to be an apprentice: he cannot therefore resort to this branch of the statute, when the terms of his contract prove that he meant to come in under another, to which different provisions are applicable.

3. Must be an entire contract for a year's prospective service.

The third circumstance essential to the validity of the contract, respects the time for which the service is to last. The distinctions upon this head have given birth to a number of denominations, which it is necessary to explain, rather to enable the reader to refer to the several collections of cases upon this subject, than for any use made of them by the learned judges in delivering their opinions. Such are *Successive or several hirings*; *Customary hirings*; *Retrospective hirings*; *Conditional hirings*; *Special or particular hirings*. These terms will be severally defined, in unfolding the distinctions from which they have originated.

Successive hirings.

There must be one entire contract for a complete year's service. Successive hirings, or such as follow each other, in uninterrupted succession, without an intervening interval of time, if *severally* less than a year, are insufficient to confer a settlement, although they

(1) Rex v. Whitechurch Canonicorum, Burr. S. C. 540. 2 Bett, 378. Pl. 405.

amount

amount to a much longer period of ſervice, when taken together.

Thus an hiring for two ſucceſſive periods of eleven months each (1); or for two ſucceſſive half-years (2); or from May-tide to Lady-day, and a new agreement on Lady-day to ſerve till the May-tide enſuing, is inſufficient (3).

The ſame point was held, when the hiring was from Whitſuntide to Martinmas, *and before the expiration of that term* there was an hiring to the ſame maſter for the ſucceeding half year, from the ſaid Martinmas to the Whitſuntide following (4). Neither did it make any difference in the latter caſe, that it was a cuſtomary or general mode of hiring ſervants in that part of the country, and that the caſe ſet forth, that in Cumberland (from whence it was ſtated), the quarter ſeſſions had by invariable practice as long as can be remembered, adjudged an hiring for two ſucceſſive half years, and ſervice under it for a whole year, to be a ſettlement, for the words of the act are poſitive that the hiring ſhall be for a year.

Cuſtomary adjudications in ſeſſions affect not.

So where there is but one contract, if it wants but a day or two of the year, it is not the hiring required by the ſtatute; therefore an hiring from the 3d of October until Michaelmas day enſuing is inſufficient (5).

Muſt be for a whole year.

Where there was an hiring three days after old Michaelmas, until the next Michaelmas, and the pauper continued in the ſervice until the day after old Michaelmas-day, which being leap-year, made a ſervice of three hundred and ſixty-five days; the court was clearly of opinion

(1) Rex *v.* Haughton, 1 Stra. 83. 2 Bott, 249. Pl. 297.

(2) Dunsford *v.* Ridgwick, Salk. 535. 2 Bott, 248. Pl. 294.

(3) Horſham *v.* Shipley, Fol, 134. 2 Bott, 228. Pl. 271.

(4) Rex *v.* Lowther, Burr. S.C. 674. 2 Bott, 232. Pl. 276.

(5) Pepperharrow *v.* Frencham, Fol. 135. 2 Bott, 229. Pl. 272.; and ſee Coombe *v.* Weſtwoodhey, 1 Stra. 143. 2 Bott, 240. Pl. 284. Rex *v.* Newton, *Ib.* 229. Pl. 273. Burr. S.C. 157.

against

against the settlement, because there was no hiring for a year; for a contract made three days after Michaelmas, to serve till the Michaelmas following, is an hiring two days short of a year (1).

Customary hirings.

And its being the customary mode of hiring in that part of the country makes no alteration in the law. Where it was the custom for servants to hire by the year at two different statutes, the one held on the Friday before and the other on the Friday after old Martinmas day, and the servant was hired from the Friday after, until the old Martinmas following; it was adjudged insufficient, although the case stated it to be the custom of the country to consider it as an hiring for a year; for such a custom originating since the statute, and therefore long within the time of memory, cannot control an act of parliament (2).

If with a view to defeat the settlement, it is not fraudulent.

Neither will it make any difference, that the avowed object for curtailing the time of service is to defeat the settlement.

Where the master told the servant that he should not gain a settlement in the parish, and hired him three days after Michaelmas to serve until the Michaelmas following, the hiring was held not to be within the statute, although the sessions found that such transactions were fraudulent on the master's part (3). For the question of fraud only arises, where in truth there is an an hiring for a year; but the parties endeavour to colour it, in order to prevent the pauper's gaining a settlement (4).

(1) Rex *v.* Ackley, 3 Term Rep. 250. 2 Bott, 239. Pl 282. Rex *v.* Mursley, 1 Term Rep. 694. S. P. 2 Bott, 242. Pl. 288.

(2) Rex *v.* Harwood, Cald. 100. 2 Bott, 237 Pl. 280. South Carney *v.* Coultsbourn; where the two mops or meetings were on the Wednesdays preceding and subsequent to Michaelmas-day, and wages were paid for the whole year. 2 Bott, 241. Pl. 286.

(3) Rex *v.* Mursley, 1 Term Rep. 694. 2 Bott, 242. Pl. 288.

(4) *Per* Buller J. *Ib.*

But

Days where inclusive.

But in favour of settlements, the day of entering upon the service, and that of leaving it, are usually considered as included in the contract; for the law makes no fraction of a day, and the servant is under his master's control during a part of each. Thus an hiring on the day after old Martinmas day *until* the old Martinmas day following, is good, and that without resorting to any particular custom in the country to explain the agreement (1).

Customary hirings.

The only cases of customary hirings which are considered as giving rise to any general distinction, are contracts for service from one moveable feast to the same in the ensuing year. Where such hirings have been interpreted by the practice of the country to mean a year, it has been held sufficient, although the intervening period of time was less than three hundred and sixty-five days; as where the hiring was from Whitsuntide to Whitsuntide (2).

I have been able to find but one case expressly deciding the point, but the principle has been acknowledged in other cases (3).

In a more recent decision, however, it has been declared a case of doubtful authority (4): and where a servant was

(1) Rex *v.* Skiplam, 3 Term Rep. 490. 2 Bott, 238. Pl. 291. S. P. Rex *v.* Sydersione *cum* Bermer, Cald. 19. Dougl. 441. S. C. 2 Bott, 235. Pl. 279. Rex *v.* Adson, 5 Term Rep. 28. See also Rex *v.* Navestock, where it was stated to be the custom and usage of the country to hire a servant at the statute fair, being the day after old Michaelmas, to serve until Michaelmas following; and that circumstance is relied upon by Lord Mansfield as material to explain the word "till," which may or may not be exclusive according to the subject matter. 2 Bott, 233. Pl. 277.

(2) Rex *v.* Newstead, Burr. S. C. 669. 2 Bott, 231. Pl 275.

(3) Rex *v.* Navestock, 2 Bott, 233. Pl. 277. Rex *v.* Harwood, Cald. 100. 2 Bott, 237. Pl. 280.

(4) *Per* Lord Kenyon, Rex *v.* Bow, 8 Term Rep. 445. 1 Bott, 717. Pl. 1001.

 hired

hired from Whitſuntide to Whitſuntide, when the interval conſiſted of more than three-hundred and ſixty-five days, and was diſcharged before the enſuing Whitſuntide for being pregnant of an illegitimate child; but after having ſerved three-hundred and ſixty-five days, the ſervice was held ſufficient to confer a ſettlement (1).

Muſt be proſpective.

The next circumſtance neceſſary to the validity of the contract, in reſpect of time, is, that it muſt be *proſpective.* The terms uſed in the ſtatute expreſs futurity, and no part of the year for which the agreement is made, ſhould be elapſed at the time when it is entered into. It may be for a year to commence at ſome future time, as a week or fortnight after (2); and the ſervice need not commence in fact at the commencement of the year, as it may be diſpenſed with by the maſter (3).

Retroſpective hirings.

But if the agreement be made ſo that by-gone time is to be calculated as part of the year, it is called a retroſpective hiring, and no ſettlement can be gained by ſervice under it. Thus were a ſervant went into a place upon liking, and after he had lived there eight weeks, his maſter hired him for a year, *to commence from the beginning of the ſaid eight weeks,* it is a retroſpective hiring (4).

The law is the ſame, though the period elapſed is only a day or two ſhort of the year. Where A. was hired ſix weeks after Michaelmas, to the Michaelmas following; and before his time was out, offered to live with B. for another year from that Michaelmas-day, if he would give him four pounds a year. That propoſal not being agreed to, he went away on Michaelmas-day; and three days after the

(1) Rex *v.* Ulverſtone, 7 Term Rep. 564. 2 Bott, 239. Pl. 283.

(2) Rex *v.* Bank Newton, Burr. S.C. 455. 2 Bott, 174. Pl. 225.

(3) Rex *v.* Iſlip, 1 Stra. 423. 2 Bott, 308. Pl. 348.

(4) Rex *v.* Ilam, Burr, S. C. 304. 2 Bott, 242. Pl. 287. Rex *v.* Hoddeſden, Cald. 23. Rex *v.* Marton, 4 Term Rep. 257.

the maſter agreed to give him the money, and he immediately entered on the ſervice: this was held not to be an hiring for a year within the ſtatute (1).

Conditional hiring.

Theſe ſort of hirings, however, are to be carefully diſtinguiſhed, from ſuch as are called conditional; that is where the contract is actually made for a year of proſpective time, but may be diſſolved upon certain terms at the reciprocal election of the parties.

Thus an agreement to live as ſervant for a quarter of a year, and if the parties liked each other, then ſhe would continue for the remainder of the year (2); to come for a quarter, after the rate of twenty ſhillings a year, and if the ſervant and his maſter liked each other, he was to continue on (3); or to go into ſervice a month upon liking, and have five pound a year wages, but to go away on a month's wages, or a month's warning on either ſide (4): or being hired for a year, at yearly wages, payable quarterly; either party to be at liberty to determine the contract, at any quarter of the year, giving a month's notice (5); are hirings ſufficiently good, where the ſervice continues for the year. And it makes no difference that the ſervant declares at the time of hiring, that the reaſon why this condition is inſerted in the contract is to avoid a ſettlement (6).

In theſe caſes, the hiring was originally conditional; but the condition went only in defeazance of the contract; and the relation of maſter and ſervant being continued for a year, the agreement muſt be taken as if the inoperative condition had never exiſted.

(1) Rex *v.* Weſtwell, 1 Barnard K. B. 354. 2 Bott, 241. Pl. 285.

(2) Rex *v.* Lidney, 2 Str. 950. 2 Bott, 243. Pl. 289.

(3) Rex *v.* St. Ebbs, Burr, S. C. 289. 2 Bott, 246. Pl. 292.

(4) Rex *v.* New Windſor, Burr, S. C. 19. 2 Bott, 245. Pl. 290.

(5) Rex *v.* Atherton, Burr, S. C. 203. 2 Bott, 246. Pl. 291. See alſo Wandſworth *v.* Putney, 2 Bott, 188. Pl. 240, *paſſ.*

(6) Rex *v.* Atherton, *ut ſupra.*

 The

General hirings.

The distinctions taken hitherto relate to cases where the time of service is specified in the agreement. There are many instances, however, in which no particular period is mentioned for the continuance of service; such cases have been distinguished by the appellation of general hirings. When the contract is thus silent, and nothing appears upon the face of the transaction, from whence its duration can be deduced, the law in conformity to the several statutes which regulate the service, especially of servants in husbandry, infers that it is made for a year (1).

This principle must of necessity attach upon all cases of implied hirings, strictly so called; that is, where no express agreement appears (2). It is equally applicable to cases where the contract is explicit in other particulars, but silent as to the time of its continuance. Where a boy was hired to serve in husbandry, and his master agreed to give him meat, drink, washing, lodging, and clothes when wanted; but no particular time was agreed on (3). Where a boy went into an inn yard, and asked the master whether he wanted a boot-catcher and driver, and being answered yes, replied he should be glad to serve him, and was ordered to take care of the horses, and not to drive them too hard, and no mention was made of meat, drink, washing, and lodging, but he was found in them, and received no wages (4). One Jones met a servant girl, then in place with one Smith, and asked her whether she was again hired to Smith; she replying in the negative; he inquired "if she would "come and live with him, and take care of his "child?" to which she consented, and soon after

(1) 24 Edw. III. c. 1. 4 Hen. IV. c. 14. 23 Hen. VI. c. 13. 5 Eliz. c. 4. "If a man retain a servant generally, without expressing any time, the law shall construe it to be for one year, for that retainer is according to law." Co. Lit. 42. b.

(2) Rex *v.* Lyth, 5 Term Rep. 327. 2 Bott, 364. Pl. 292. *Ante*, 188.

(3) Rex *v.* Wincaunton, Burr. S. C. 299. 2 Bott, 192. Pl. 241.

(4) Rex *v.* Stockbridge, Burr. S. C. 759. 2 Bott, 197. Pl. 246.

went

went to him. Two or three days after ſhe came, Jones told her that he would find her in meat, drink, and clothes, and aſked her if ſhe would be ſatisfied with that? ſhe told him ſhe would (1). Theſe have been adjudged hirings by the year; and the opinion of the maſter and ſervant as to their being entitled to ſeparate at pleaſure, or bound to continue during the year, was held to make no difference in the caſe (2).

General hiring after one for leſs than a year.

This inference of a yearly hiring is not rebutted by proof, that it was connected with previous ſervice for a leſs period. Where the pauper was hired from March till Michaelmas, and continued to ſerve until her miſtreſs died two or three years afterwards, without a ſecond hiring; it was held that the continuance in the ſervice was ſufficient evidence to infer a ſubſequent hiring for a year (3). So where, after an hiring and ſervice for eleven months, the maſter ſaid, "you have been a "good ſervant, you may *as well ſtay on an end in your* "*place*, the place ſuits you, and you ſuit the place;" and the man anſwered, "very well, I have no objection;" he ſerved a year, it was held a good yearly hiring (4).

In the former caſe, a new hiring was inferred from the continuance of ſervice, at the expiration of the firſt agreement, and no time being ſpecified, the general rule in favour of yearly hirings prevailed. In the ſecond, the terms by which the contract was created, "that he might as "well ſtay on an end," being vague and indefinite, received the ſame interpretation, and were held to refer more properly to the nature of the ſervice in which the

(1) Rex *v.* Worfield, 5 Term Rep. 506. 2 Bott, 207. Pl. 254.

(2) Rex *v.* Stockbridge, Burr. S. C. 759. See alſo Rex *v.* Bath Eaſton, Burr. S. C. 823. 2 Bott, 199. Pl. 248. *Poſt.* 204.

(3) Rex *v.* Long Whatton, 5 Term Rep 447. 2 Bott, 366. Pl. 393. See alſo Rex *v.* Hales, 5 Term Rep. 668. 2 Bott, 367. Pl. 394. *ante*, 189.

(4) Rex *v.* Macclesfield, 8 Term Rep. 76. 2 Bott, 204. Pl. 252.

pauper was before engaged than to the time for which he was originally hired, and this the rather, as the wages for the ſecond year differed from thoſe ſtipulated under the firſt agreement.

Though ſervant quits in the middle of a year.

And this preſumption is not affected by the ſervant's leaving his place in ſome ſucceeding year, at a period which does not correſpond with its regular cloſe, from the time of entry upon the ſervice; for as it was competent to the parties to put an end to the agreement at any time by mutual conſent, the law will rather ſuppoſe that they exerciſed this right, than break in upon its favourite principle (1).

Special hirings.

Several reported caſes do not come properly under the denomination of general hirings, although they bear a ſtrong analogy, inaſmuch as they contain no expreſs ſtipulation reſpecting time; but they differ in ſo much as the intended duration of the ſervice, is not altogether a concluſion of law, but may be collected from the remaining terms of the agreement, the circumſtances attending it, or the conduct of the maſter and ſervant during its continuance. As theſe hirings depend upon ſpecial or particular circumſtances, they are therefore, as I ſuppoſe, denominated ſpecial or particular hirings. Whether ſuch an agreement amounts to an hiring for a year, is rather a matter of fact to be collected by the magiſtrates from the whole tranſaction, than a queſtion of law. But the court of King's Bench, when the facts are ſtated in a caſe, will adjudge whether it is a ſufficient hiring for a year (2). This concluſion may be inferred, not only from the expreſſions uſed, but the manner in which wages are to be paid, the condition of the parties, the nature of the ſervice, its actual duration, and perhaps the general prac-

(1) Rex v. Worfield, *ſupra*, 201. n. (1); where the girl lived with Jones a year and a half, when her miſtreſs told her that her child was old enough not to require attendance, and diſmiſſed her.

(2) *Per* Lord Hardwicke, Rex v. New Windſor, Burr. S. C. 19.

tice

tice of the district in which the hiring takes place, as to the usual period of servitude. These, and many other circumstances, may enable them to ascertain the fact; and where, either from the original inaccuracy of the parties at the time of making the agreement, or their want of recollection when called upon to give it in evidence, they seem to contradict each other, magistrates must endeavour to explore their way as well as they can; yet leaning, as the cases seem to do, towards the legal presumption in favour of a yearly contract, if the conclusion is otherwise doubtful.

Some cases of this kind afford a more direct inference of an yearly hiring than where it is altogether general, because the terms used, although introduced for another purpose, prove the parties to have meant that it should continue for a year. Thus where the agreement expressed, that the servant was to have 5*l.* a year wages (1); where the master told a boy coming into his service, that if he staid a year, and behaved well, he would give him a livery and wages the next year (2); or, where a barber agreed to give his journeyman meat, drink, and lodging, but no wages, in lieu of which he was to have the Christmas boxes (3); these are clear yearly hirings, although nothing else passed about time. The reference to wages for a year in the first case, and to a conditional continuance of service for a year in the second, shews that the parties intended to continue their relation of master and servant for so long; and the agreement for an annual perquisite in lieu of wages seems equally conclusive in the last.

Special yearly hirings.

So where the head keeper of a chace, having parted with one Hill who had been many years his servant, at

(1) Rex *v.* New Windsor, Burr. S.C. 19. 2 Bott, 245. Pl. 290.

(2) Wandsworth *v.* Putney, 2 Bott, 188. Pl. 240.

(3) Rex *v.* Bath Easton, Burr. S.C. 823. 2 Bott, 199. Pl. 248.

yearly

yearly wages, and a keeper's livery, &c. aſked the pauper, "do you like the life of a keeper?" and being anſwered "*yes*;" ſaid, "then go into Ned Hill's place, and "you ſhall want no encouragement; I'll give you a ſuit "of clothes directly." Here the reference to the terms upon which the former ſervant had lived with him, maniſeſt an intention to engage the new ſervant for the ſame period as Hill had been hired, which was for a year (1).

There are however a different claſs of ſpecial hirings, in which it is more difficult to aſcertain their intended continuance, as they contain facts which contradict and claſh with each other. Theſe, ſo far as they ſeem referable to any general principles, may be divided into three kinds: 1. where the reſervation of wages is weekly; 2. where a power exiſts of terminating the ſervice within the year, but reſtricted by a condition of giving previous notice, or as it is called, warning; 3. where the court have formed their opinion upon the general circumſtances of the caſe.

Apprehenſion of parties, not evidence; It is to be obſerved, previous to entering upon theſe diſtinctions, that the court have laid it down as a general rule in conſtruing this and all other parts of the contract, that the parties apprehenſion or underſtanding of the effect and legal conſequence of their agreement, can have no weight in that judicial concluſion which is to be formed reſpecting the real import. If it were otherwiſe, paupers would be judges and not witneſſes in the cauſe (2). But any acts of theirs done during ſervice, but acts are.

(1) Rex *v.* Berwick St. John, Burr. S. C. 502. 2 Bott, 194. Pl. 242. This hiring would be good as a general one, without any reference, and was ſo conſidered by the Judges.

(2) Rex *v.* Wincaunton, 2 Bott, 192. Pl. 241. Rex *v.* Seaton and Beer, Cald. 440. 2 Bott, 200. Pl. 240. Rex *v.* Birmingham, Dougl. 233. 2 Bott, 216. Pl. 262. *ante*, 201. There are many other caſes to the ſame effect.

although

although they originate from their underſtanding of the agreement, ſeem admiſſible as helps to interpretation, where the terms are not diſtinctly proved (1); for the act done could have no reference to the queſtion of ſettlement, and is evidence by one party of the contract under which he was enabled to do it, while acquieſcence on the other ſide amounts to a virtual acknowledgment of the ſame fact.

The general rule as to the operation of weekly wages, in aſcertaining the duration of the hiring, is, that if there be any thing in the contract to ſhew that the hiring was intended to be for a year, there a reſervation of weekly wages will not control it; but if the payment of weekly wages be the only circumſtance from which the duration of the contract is to be collected, it muſt be taken to be only a weekly hiring (2), for the wages becoming due at the end of the week, the contract out of which they ariſe muſt have terminated. 2. Special hirings, with wages reſerved weekly.

Thus an agreement to live as hoſtler at an inn, " at " four ſhillings and ſixpence per week," is an hiring only for a week (3). That concluſion has been made more ſtrong in ſome caſes by additional circumſtances. As where the hiring was at one ſhilling and four-pence a week, board and lodging, *for as long a time as the maſter ſhould want a ſervant:* the ſervant was paid her wages at the end of ſeven weeks, and ſo on after two or three months, as ſhe wanted money, this is only a weekly hiring, for ſhe could not be diſcharged at the end of the year if it ſhould happen in the middle of her week (4).

(1) Rex *v.* Dedham, Burr. S. C. 653. 2 Bott, 195. Pl. 244. Rex *v.* Seaton and Beer, *ſupra*, n. (2). Rex *v.* Winterſett, Cald. 298. 2 Bott, 262. Pl. 309 *Poſt.* 206.

(2) *Per* Buller J. Rex *v.* Newton Toney, 2 Term Rep. 453. 2 Bott, 223. Pl. 266. Rex. v. Clare, *poſt.* 208.

(3) *Ibid.*

(4) Rex *v.* Elſtack or Elſlack, Cald. 489. 2 Bott, 201. Pl. 250.

But the rule ſtates that this inference, ariſing from the payment of weekly wages, may be controled by other circumſtances; in which caſe, it is conſidered as introduced to arrange the manner of paying wages, ſo as to ſuit the parties' convenience.

Thus an agreement that an innkeeper ſhould "give "the pauper one ſhilling a week, as ſhe had given the "other man or men, and the vails of the ſtables", nothing being ſaid as to the time of ſervice, but at the end of the year his miſtreſs ſaid to him, "you have been here a year, "and I will pay you;" to which he anſwered, "it is no "matter, I may ſtay with you another year;" and ſhe replied, "very well;" is a general hiring (1). The pauper in this caſe continued to ſerve for a year, which ſeems to be a material circumſtance where the agreement is otherwiſe doubtful, for it is an act done by the parties in explanation of it (2).

2. Special conditional hirings, or with warning. Where times of warning and paying wages differ.

The ſecond claſs of ſpecial hirings, is where there is a warning, or inſertion of a condition by which the parties are enabled to put an end to the ſervice at a period ſhort of a year, upon giving ſtipulated notice. Where the reſerved interval of warning is longer than the time at which the wages are payable, it is ſtrong enough to control the concluſion againſt a yearly hiring which would otherwiſe ariſe from that mode of payment. This has been held not only where it was accompanied with corroborating circumſtances, ſuch as an hiring "at 3*s*. a week *the year round*, "each to be at *liberty on a fortnight's notice*; but the ſervant "not *to go away at ſeed-time, hay-making, or harveſt* (3);" but alſo where the inſertion of the notice was the only circumſtance from whence the inference can be drawn. An

(1) Rex *v*. Seaton and Beer, Cald. 440. 2 Bott, 200. Pl. 249.

(2) See *ante*, 205, and the caſes *poſt*.

(3) Rex *v*. Birdbrooke, 4 Term Rep. 245. 2 Bott, 225. Pl. 268.

agreement

agreement therefore with a miller " to serve for three shil-" lings and nine-pence a week, or *at the rate* of four shil-" lings a week;" the parties having a liberty of parting on a month's notice on either side; is an hiring for a year: for the insertion of the liberty to separate on a month's notice shews that the insertion of weekly wages was to ascertain the period at which they were to be paid, and not to limit the duration of the contract; and as the service was to last longer than a week (1), it becomes an hiring unlimited in duration, with the insertion of a condition by which it may be dissolved on either side; which is a general hiring for a year (2).

When time of warning and of paying wages coincide.

The general rule therefore is, " that wherever the relation of master and servant is to continue for an indefinite time, and cannot be put an end to at the election of either party without notice, the hiring must be understood to be an hiring for a year (3); but where the time of notice corresponds with that at which the wages are rendered payable, the contract is no longer indefinite, but is an hiring for the precise time at which the wages are payable". Thus were the pauper agreed to work for one S. as a blacksmith, at 3 *s.* 6 *d.* a week, with meat, drink, washing, and lodging, at S.'s house, and to part on a week's notice by either party; no notice being given, he served S. for six years, without any alteration in the terms, except that after he had served about four years, the wages were raised from three and sixpence to four shillings *per* week; this is an hiring by the week (4).

Warning, coupled with other circumstances.

But this conclusion from the circumstance of a longer notice is controled where the hiring is expressly for a shorter period. Thus an agreement to live with one " *by the week,*

(1) Rex *v.* Hampreston, 5 Term Rep. 205. 2 Bott, 205. Pl. 253.

(2) *Ante*, 199.

(3) *Per* Lord Kenyon, Rex *v.* Hampreston, *supra*, n. 1.

(4) Rex *v.* Hanbury, 2 East, 423.

at

at two ſhillings and ſixpence a "week, and to part at a fortnight or month's notice," is not an obligation on the part of the pauper to ſerve for a year, but an hiring for the ſtipulated time of a week (1).

So where a journeyman miller hired himſelf "*by the* "*month*, at the wages of eight ſhillings a month, to be at "liberty to depart from his ſervice at a month's wages or "month's warning," with an agreement that if he continued in the ſervice till harveſt time, he ſhould be at liberty to let himſelf for the harveſt months to any perſon he choſe; is an expreſs hiring for a month (2).

3. Preſumption of yearly hiring negatived by other circumſtances.

Other circumſtances will ſometimes prevent the concluſion, that an indefinite hiring is for a year. Such are the nature of the trade, and the relative ſituation of the parties. Where a boy had worked from ſix to ſixteen with his ſtep-father in his trade of a button-maker, without any compenſation beſides maintenance and pocket-money; he then left him, having inſiſted upon a larger allowance, which the father refuſed. The pauper returning after ſome time, it was agreed between them, "that he ſhould live in the houſe, to work as before at "his trade, and to be paid a penny for each groſs of but-"tons (being the ſame wages as his ſtep-father paid other "workmen), deducting at the rate of five ſhillings a week "for his board, waſhing, and lodging:" this is not a hiring for a year, but of a workman to work by the piece (3). So where a plumber and glazier let himſelf at the wages of ſix ſhillings a week, board, lodging, and waſhing, ſummer and winter; and after ſerving eleven months, his maſter having taken an apprentice, told him he muſt lodge out of the houſe, upon which he demanded

(1) Rex *v.* Bradnich, Burr, S. C. 662. 2 Bott, 197. Pl. 243.

(2) Rex *v.* Clare, Burr. S. C. 819. 2 Bott, 198. Pl. 247.

(3) Rex *v.* St. Peter's Dorcheſter, Burr. S. C. 513. 2 Bott, 195. Pl. 243. See alſo Rex *v.* Wringdon, Burr. S. C. 280. 2 Bott, 180. Pl. 234.

ſixpence

ſixpence a week more, threatening otherwiſe to quit the ſervice, and was paid it. This was determined not to be a yearly hiring; for the ſtipulation of ſix ſhillings a week, wages, ſummer and winter, only imports an agreement, that the wages ſhould continue always the ſame; and the preſumption of a reciprocal obligation between the contracting *parties*, which is neceſſary to conſtitute a general hiring, is deſtroyed by a demand of an increaſe of wages, and the maſter's compliance in conſequence of a threat on the part of the ſervant, that he would otherwiſe quit the ſervice (1).

So where a boy being hired a few days before Martinmas, to ſerve from Martinmas for a year, fell ill the very night of the hiring, and did not go into ſervice for a month afterwards; when he and his mother went into the maſter's houſe, who being from home, they were ſhewn to his wife, who complained that the pauper had not come into the ſervice according to the agreement, and therefore refuſed to receive him; whereupon the pauper's mother ſaid, "we muſt fall into your way for wages, and take "what you will allow us;" and left the pauper in his ſervice, where he continued until Martinmas following, when the mother was ſent for, and received for forty-eight weeks wages, after the rate of one ſhilling and twopence per week, being leſs than the rate of the original wages. This was held not only to be a diſſolution of the original hiring, and the making of a new agreement, but that the parting at the end of the original year, and receiving wages for forty-eight weeks, proved that the ſecond hiring was not for a year (2).

Exceptive hirings.

The fourth circumſtance neceſſary to render the contract of hiring ſufficient for the purpoſe of gaining a ſettlement,

(1) Rex *v.* Dedham, Burr. S. C. 53. 2 Bott, 195. Pl. 244.

(2) Rex *v.* Winterſet, Cald. 298. 2 Bott, 262. Pl. 309.

tlement, is, that it contains no ſpecial exception to exempt the ſervant from the control and authority of his maſter, at ſpecified periods. Theſe may be denominated exceptive hirings; this rule depends upon the principle already diſcuſſed, that the agreement ſhould be for a complete year's ſervice. If particular times of the year are excepted, and the ſervant is left to his own diſpoſal, ſo that the maſter cannot exerciſe any degree of authority over him, the ſervice is juſt as much ſhort of a year, by the ſum total of theſe exceptions, as if the time contracted for had been leſs by an equal portion of connected time; the only difference is, that one is ſo much leſs by a ſpace interſected with intervals of ſervice, and the other by one equal in extent, but occurring altogether.

Whether theſe reſervations are made of particular ſeaſons, or days, or even hours of the day, the ſervant gains no ſettlement by ſervice under a contract infected with this exception. Neither does it make any diſtinction, that periods are excepted, which the law would except, ſo as not only to excuſe the ſervant from labour, but to puniſh him if he worked during the time. A ſervant is not compellable, when hired in a particular trade, to work at unſeaſonable hours of the night, and he is puniſhable, if he profanes the ſabbath-day; but an expreſs exception in the hiring, even of theſe ſeaſons will defeat a ſettlement; for the right of compelling the ſervant to work, is not the ſole power which the maſter poſſeſſes over him. In exacting labour from his ſervant, he is ſubject to the general law of the land, or poſſibly to the particular cuſtoms of the place in which the ſervice is performed (1); but with this exception, a right of control and authority, at leaſt ſo far as relates to the general diſcipline and

(1) See Rex *v.* Birmingham, Dougl. 333. 2 Bott, 316. Pl. 262. *qu. tamen ?*

government

government of the servant, must reside in the master at all times during the continuance of the service (1).

Thus an hiring to work in a silk-mill for three years, at weekly wages, without diet or lodging; the service to be only eleven hours in the six working-days, and all the rest of the time, as well as on Sundays, the servant to be at his own liberty, and his own master (2): an hiring, by agreement in writing, with a clothier for five years, to be taught the business of a sheerman, "to receive weekly wages, "and work sheerman's hours, and to be at his own liberty "at all other times (3);" or, "for five years, at weekly "wages, as a colt sheerman, to work twelve hours each "day (4)"; are exceptions in the contract, which prevent the parties from standing in the relation of master and servant, but on certain days and for particular hours of the day; wherefore the servant gains no settlement.

Exceptions of particular hours in the day.

So where a servant agreed by covenant to work and serve as an artificer, in the art of a glass-grinder, or any other art his master should think proper to employ him in for seven years; and that "he would continue and be in "the service from six o'clock in the morning till seven "in the evening of each day, during the said term, in- "cluding half an hour at breakfast, and one hour at din- "ner times, except on Sundays, if in proper health". This is a covenant to serve only thirteen hours on working-days, and to be his own master on Sundays; for the expression of so many hours is the exclusion of the rest, and therefore no settlement can be gained by service under it (5).

Exception where servant has worked during excepted hours.

(1) *Per* Foster J. Rex *v.* Wroughton, Burr. S. C. 280. 2 Bott, 180. Pl. 234.

(2) Rex *v* Macclesfield, Burr. S. C. 458. 2 Bott 210. Pl. 257

(3) Rex *v.* Buckland Denham, Burr. S. C. 694. 2 Bott, 213. Pl. 260.

(4) Rex *v.* North Nibley, 5 Term Rep. 21. 2 Bott, 226. Pl. 269.

(5) Rex *v.* Kingswinford, 4 Term. Rep. 219. 2 Bott, 224. Pl. 267.

And it was thought to make no difference, "that the ser-"vant occasionally worked in the night-time, and often went "on errands for his master on Sundays;" for where the contract is explicit, it is not how much the servant actually does, but what he has agreed to do, that is to be considered (2).

An Agreement to deduct wages, no exception.

But where there is no express exception of time in the contract, a mere agreement to deduct wages for a possible loss of time does not vitiate the hiring; for it is rather settling a rate of wages, than an exemption of the servant from his master's authority, and is like the cases where the payment was to be for spinning by the stone (2); or "for "screws by the grose, good earn good hire (3)." Thus where one clubbed or agreed to serve another for three years at weekly wages, to learn the trade of a bricklayer, "and if "prevented at any time from working by badness of wea-"ther, illness, or from his master's not having employment "for him, a proportionable deduction was to be made from "his week's wages for such loss of time;" it is a good hiring, and a year's service under it will gain a settlement, though occasional deductions were made on these accounts (4).

Exceptions of days at particular seasons.

If the exception of part of the day vitiates the contract, an exception of a particular season or number of days must do it more decisively. Thus an hiring from Michaelmas to Michaelmas, "with liberty to let himself for the harvest months to any other person (5);" or from one Harborough fair to another, being a year, "subject to a liberty "of being absent eleven or twelve days in the sheep-shear-"ing season, and to have the benefit of what he got during "that time(7);" or an exception of two days in each half year,

(1) Rex v. Kingswinford, 4 Term Rep. 219. 2 Bott, 224. Pl. 267.

(2) Rex v. King's Norton, Burr. S. C. 152. 2 Bott, 208. Pl. 255.

(3) Rex v Birmingham, Dougl. 833. 2 Bott, 216. Pl. 262.

(4) Rex v. Martham, 1 East, 239.

(5) Rex v. Bishop's Hatfield, Burr. S. C. 439. 2 Bott, 231. Pl. 274.

(6) Rex v. Empingham, Burr. S. C. 791. 2 Bott, 234. Pl. 278.

year, (the servant being a pensioner in the East India company,) to go and receive his pension (1); are not sufficient hirings; not being for a year, but for a period short of it by the time excepted in the agreement.

Service in the Militia.

Two cases have however been adjudged in which it has been held that an exception in the contract does not render it so defective as to prevent a settlement. A pauper was hired for a year, but at the time of hiring told his mistress, "that "he was in the militia and *he might be* about a month in the "year to attend in that duty, and he would pay a man to "serve in his place, or else would make her an allowance out "of his wages for the time he was absent (2)." Also where a man being hired for a year, his wages to be paid weekly, told his master that, "being a balloted man in the militia, he "should be absent for the month and in lieu of that month, "should serve another at the end of the year (3)." These hirings were held good, and the following distinctions made between them, and the preceding cases, as I have collected them from the report. 1. This is not a chasm in the contract, but a dispensation with the personal service. 2. It was not an absolute exception of a month; there was an alternative, as it might happen that the servant should not be called out. 3. The agreement as to the absence for a month in the militia, was only what would have been implied, and what the master must have consented to; for the law would have compelled the absence, and the exception was not of time, which it was in the option of either to dispense with. 4. The court ought to lean in favour of settlements, and the bad consequence would be very extensive, if they were to determine that a man should lose his settlement by serving his country in the militia.

(1) Rex v. Over, 1 East, 599.

(2) Rex v. Westerleigh, Burr. S. C. 753. 2 Bott, 214. Pl. 261.

(3) Rex v. Winchcombe, Dougl. 391. 2 Bott, 220. Pl. 263.

But a diſtinction is to be carefully obſerved between actual exceptions from ſervice in the original contract and the ſervants omitting to work during the continuance of his agreement. Whether this be in conſequence of a general lawful exemption from labour, ſuch as on days ſet apart for ſacred purpoſes; or by the uſage of particular diſtricts; or by his maſters previous permiſſion; or even by the neglect or diſobedience of the ſervant, it will not prevent a ſettlement, provided it be ſubſequently forgiven by the maſter. Theſe are caſes not of exemptions in the contract, but of diſpenſations with ſervice, and will be conſidered under the next requiſite for gaining a ſettlement, namely, the year's ſervice.

SECT. III.

Of the Year's Service.

HAVING treated of the contract of hiring for a year, we are to conſider next, what amounts to a performance, and conſtitutes the year's ſervice within 8 & 9 W 3. c. 30. which declares, that no ſervant ſhall gain a ſettlement in any pariſh or townſhip, "unleſs he ſhall *continue and abide* in the *ſame* ſervice for the ſpace of *one whole* year."

8 & 9 W. 3. c. 3.

Service for 365 days.

Service, therefore, which is but a day or two ſhort of a year, does not ſatisfy the ſtatute, nor confer a ſettlement(1). But ſervice for a year, conſiſting of 365 days, is ſufficient, although the agreement be for a longer period. A ſervant maid was hired from the moveable feaſt of *Whitſuntide* to the *Whitſuntide* following. Having ſerved more than 365 days, ſhe was diſcharged for being pregnant of a baſtard child, a few days before the coming of that following *Whitſuntide* to which ſhe had agreed to ſerve. This

(1) *Per* Lord Kenyon, C. J. Rex *v.* Grantham, 3 Term Rep. 754. 2 Bott, 343. Pl. 381. See alſo Rex *v.* Whittlebury, 6 Term Rep. 464. 2 Bott, 353. Pl. 385.

was

was adjudged to be a ſervice for a year, within the ſtatute (1).

The performance of ſervice may be either *actual*, or *conſtructive*. Where the ſervant continues perſonally to fulfil the duties of his ſtation towards his maſter in the terms of his contract, without intermiſſion, it is *actual* ſervice. Where he does not perform theſe duties, but they are diſpenſed with, the ſervice is *conſtructive*.

Service: 1. Actual.

2. Conſtructive.

It has been already ſeen, that the law inveſts the maſter with authority, to enforce performance of the ſervant's contract; but having gone thus far, it leaves him to exact or remit the ſervice as ſuits his convenience or diſcretion. He may compel his ſervant to work at all lawful ſeaſons, or ſuffer him to remain unemployed. If he ſhould prove remiſs and negligent, the maſter may puniſh remiſſneſs, and enforce attention; but this idleneſs, whether permitted or otherwiſe, has no effect on the ſettlement, whilſt he continues in the ſervice, that being all which the ſtatute requires.

Origin of diſpenſations with Conſent.

Idleneſs.

An omiſſion of actual ſervice is not confined to time, when the ſervant reſides with his maſter; he may be occaſionally abſent altogether, neither employed in his buſineſs nor ready to be ſo if called upon. Here the power of the maſter is not leſs (where exerciſed without fraud) to diſpenſe with perſonal attendance, and forgive temporary abſence, than it is to endure idleneſs or overlook negligence while the ſervant reſides on his farm, or lives in his houſe. The neceſſity of leaving ſome what of diſcretionary indulgence to the head of the family, and the impoſſibility of placing any bounds to it ſhort of fraud, require that this ſhould be conſidered as conſtructive ſervice, ſufficient to ſatisfy the ſtatute.

(1) Rex *v.* Ulverſtone, 7 Term Rep. 564. 2 Bott, 239. Pl. 283.

Dispensations in law.

The servant may be likewise absent for an excuseable cause, to which the master's consent is not required; such are illness, the master's inability or refusal to let him serve the remainder of the year. In such cases, the law does not require the master's consent, but looks upon the service as constructively performed for the purpose of a settlement, provided the servant does not agree to dissolve the contract.

Dispensations from service are therefore of two kinds; 1. such as arise out of the master's consent; 2. Such as are created by operation of law.

Dispensations with consent: 1. Express. 2. Implied.

Dispensations with the master's consent, are also of two kinds 1. express, where his leave is asked and obtained; 2. implied, or constructive, when though not given in terms, it is to be inferred from the circumstances of the case.

But this power of assent exists only during the contracts continuance: if that is dissolved, and the servant absents himself, the power to dispense is gone; for the contract being at an end, the master had no right to command attendance, and consequently no authority to dispense with it. The servant does not continue in service for *a whole year*, but a chasm is created, which no return nor subsequent act of the parties can cure.

Dissolutions: 1. By consent. 2. Order of magistrate.

A dissolution of the contract takes place two ways. 1. by mutual consent of master and servant; 2. at the desire of one of them, through the intervention of a magistrate, for some lawful cause.

1. Dissolution by consent.

Dissolutions by mutual consent, like dispensations, may be either express or implied. In many cases where the master has consented in terms to the absence, it is difficult to determine whether the contract is intended to be continued,

nued, or put an end to. Recourſe muſt be had therefore to the various circumſtances which attend the ſervant's departure, or return, in order to explain theſe equivocal expreſſions, in the ſame manner, as where the parties are entirely ſilent, and all is left to inference and conjecture.

As a ſettlement is always gained where the ſervice is diſpenſed with, and never where it is interrupted by abſence under a diſſolution of the agreement, it is uſual to conſider queſtions of conſtructive ſervice as depending upon the fact of whether there has been a *diſpenſation of the ſervice*, or an *abſolute diſſolution of the contract*. If this diſtinction be put as embracing all points that can affect the queſtion of a year's ſervice, it ſeems inaccurate. There may be an abſence which cannot be purged ſo as to permit the time to count in the year's ſervice, although no diſſolution of the contract has taken place; and there may be a diſſolution, which works no diſcontinuance of the ſervice (1).

Where the maſter's conſent is neceſſary, and not expreſsly given, it may be inferred from circumſtances; but the facts will ſometimes not only furniſh no ground for that inference, but will lead to a contrary concluſion, notwithſtanding the continuance of the contract.

Three kinds of abſence.

Abſence from ſervice therefore may, with reference to ſettlement, be diſtinguiſhed into three kinds: 1. under a a diſpenſation; 2. under a diſſolution; 3. where the contract continues, but the maſter't conſent cannot be implied. In the firſt caſe a ſettlement is acquired, in the in the two laſt it is defeated.

Whether abſence is under a diſpenſation with ſervice, or a diſſolution of the contract, is a fact depending upon the

(1) See *poſt*. Sect. VI. of this chapter.

circum-

circumſtances of each particular caſe as they appear in evidence. It is a concluſion to be drawn therefore by the juſtices (1); but the court of King's Bench will lend its aſſiſtance to the magiſtrates to correct or confirm their opinion (2).

Principle of diſtinction between diſpenſation and diſſolution.

The criterion to diſtinguiſh between the two caſes is ſaid to be; whether the ſervant continues liable to ſerve for the whole year, though the maſter diſpenſes with the actual ſervice for part of it. If he does, the ſervant gains a ſettlement, becauſe the relation of maſter and ſervant ſubſiſts all the year, and the maſter may reſume the right to the ſervice whenever he chuſes; but if the maſter has once parted with his control over the ſervant, no ſettlement is gained (3). This ſeems the leading diſtinction relied upon in moſt of the recent caſes; but it does not comprehend ſome that are more ancient; particularly where the conſent was expreſsly given (4).

Abſence in the beginning of the year, &c.

No diſtinction ariſes from abſence taking place at the beginning, in the middle, or at the end of the year (5). There may be a conſtructive ſervice, or a diſſolution of the contract, in each of theſe caſes, according to the difference of circumſtance in other reſpects.

I. Of diſpenſations.
1. Expreſs leave.

Where the leave of abſence is expreſsly given, the only queſtion that can ariſe is, whether the parties intended

(1) Rex *v.* St. Peter Mancroft, 8 Term Rep. 477. 1 Bott, 724. Pl. 1007.

(2) *Per* Lord Kenyon, C. J. Rex *v.* Whittlebury, 6 Term Rep. 464. 2 Bott, 353. Pl. 385. *Per* Lord Ellenborough, C. J Rex *v.* Corſham, 2 Eaſt, 303. There are ſeveral other caſes to the like effect.

(3) *Per* Lord Kenyon, C. J. Rex *v.* Thiſtleton, 6 Term Rep. 185. 2 Bott, 299. Pl. 338. Rex *v.* St. Peter Mancroft, 8 Term Rep. 477. 1 Bott, 724. Pl. 1007.

(4) See *poſt.* 221 *et ſeq.*

(5) *Per* Lord Kenyon, C. J. Rex *v.* Eaſt Shefford, 4 Term Rep 804. 1 Bott, 347. Pl. 383. *Per* Lord Mansfield, Rex *v.* Winterſett, Cald. 397. And ſee the ſeveral caſes, *poſt.*

that

that the contract of hiring ſhould continue during this ceſſation from ſervice. If it is given before the ſervice commences, the great point will be to diſtinguiſh it from an exception in the contract; if given afterwards, from a diſſolution.

Hiring from Michaelmas, to go into ſervice the Wedneſday after.

This is ſometimes (although very ſeldom) clear from the terms uſed by the parties. As where the pauper was hired on the Fridaybefore Michaelmas-day, from Michaelmas old ſtyle, for a year to a farmer, to be his carter, and had one ſhilling earneſt, and was to have ſix pounds wages, and to go into his maſter's ſervice the Wedneſday after Michaelmas-day old ſtyle. *Per* Lord Mansfield: It is expreſsly ſtated that on the Friday before Michaelmas-day the pauper was hired for a year from Michaelmas; it is there expreſsly ſtated, that they ſtood in the relation of maſter and ſervant from Michaelmas to Michaelmas; if ſo, it would be repugnant to ſay that this was not an hiring for a year. The caſe itſelf contradicts the idea that it was an hiring from Wedneſday after Michaelmas. Then the abſence was matter of indulgence on the part of the maſter, and whether revocable or not, is ſo common in theſe tranſactions, and ſo reaſonable upon the commencement of a ſervice, that it has never been conſidered as impeaching or affecting the validity of a contract. But under all the circumſtances of this caſe, I conſider it as an indulgence, which the maſter might revoke (1).

As the language in which the parties expreſs their meaning is uſually obſcure and diverſified, recourſe muſt be had to the different circumſtances of each caſe to interpret them. There is no particular claſs of caſes which depends upon the mere form of expreſſion.

The various deciſions, therefore, upon this very perplexed head of ſettlement law, may be better arranged by a refer-

(1) Rex v. Grendon Underwood, Cald. 359. 2 Bott, 263. Pl. 210.

a reference to other circumſtances which admit of a more natural analogy (1); but it muſt be obſerved, that the language of the parties does of neceſſity conſtitute the leading means to aſcertain the effect of every agreement.

Conſent implied by return to ſervice.

The moſt ſimple caſes of implied conſent are where nothing appears but the abſence and return of the ſervant; for although the abſence is without leave, it is cured by the ſervant's coming back, and the maſter's receiving him into his ſervice, unleſs it appears that the contract has been actually diſſolved.

Abſence in the beginning.

Thus where a ſervant was hired from Michaelmas to Michaelmas, he came three days after the firſt Michaelmas, and ſtayed one day after the latter, and was abſent at different times near a fortnight, for which an abatement was made in his wages; it was held that he gained a ſettlement by ſerving the remainder of the year, for the abſence was purged by the maſter's receiving him (2).

In the middle.

So where the ſervant went during his year, without leave, to ſee his mother, and ſtayed away four days, and then returned into the ſervice; it was adjudged that the maſter diſpenſed with the attendance by taking him again (3).

Neither does it make any difference that the abſence is partly with the maſter's leave, and partly without. As

(1) The judges have often declared that it is difficult to diſcover the principle of deciſion in ſeveral caſes upon this ſubject; and the writer is compelled to confeſs, that his own incapacity for the taſk he has undertaken, never ſtrikes him ſo forcibly, as when he conſiders his utter inability to arrange theſe deciſions into a connected ſyſtem by the means of leading principles.

(2) Rex *v.* Hanbury, Burr, S. C. 322. 2 Bott, 315. Pl. 356.

(3) Rex *v.* Iſlip, 1 Str. 423. 2 Bott, 308. Pl. 348. In Rex *v.* Eaton, Burr. S. C. 47. 2 Bott, 311. Pl. 352, the ſervant was abſent three weeks in the middle of the year, without conſent, and held to be purged by the maſter's taking him again.

where

where a maſter having little to do, agreed with his ſervant that he might have leave of abſence for ſix weeks to work for himſelf, wherever he pleaſed, allowing fifteen ſhillings out of his yearly wages; he was abſent ſeven weeks, being a week more than he had leave for, and then returned, and was received: this abſence did not prevent his ſettlement (1).

Where the abſence has been at the commencement of the year, the court ſeem rather to have leaned towards conſtruing the converſation between the parties into a leave of abſence, than an exception in the contract. **Abſence in beginning.**

As where on Thurſday before Michaelmas day, which happened on Saturday, the pauper agreed with a farmer, as carter, to go into his ſervice on the Monday following, until the enſuing Michaelmas, for ſix guineas. At the time of the agreement, his maſter deſired him to go into his ſervice before Monday: but the ſervant ſaid it would not ſuit him, as he was then in ſervice; and the maſter replied, if he would come on the Monday morning, he would ſhift till that time. The ſervice in which the pauper was at the time of making this agreement expired on the enſuing Saturday, being Michaelmas-day; he left it on that night, and went into his new maſter's ſervice on the Monday following, as agreed upon. He ſerved till the day before the enſuing Michaelmas, when he deſired leave to go and ſee his relations, before he went into another ſervice: his maſter deducted one ſhilling from his wages for that day, and paid him the reſidue. The maſter on his going away told him, that if he went before Michaelmas-day, there might be a diſpute about his ſettlement, and deſired him to come back; but he went away and returned no more. **Hiring from Saturday. Maſter deſired pauper to go into ſervice before Monday, &c.**

(1) Rex *v.* Undermilbeck, 5 Term. Rep. 387. 2 Bott, 294. Pl. 335.

7 Two

Two questions arose upon this case. First, whether this was a good hiring for a year? Secondly, whether there was a sufficient service, the servant being absent the first and last day? The court were of opinion, upon the first point, that the sessions ought to draw the conclusion that this was an hiring for a year, "else why should "the master desire him to go into his service before "Monday, or say that he would shift till that time?" It appears from this, that the master understood it to be an hiring for a year; and likewise from his desiring the pauper to come back, lest his settlement should be disputed if he quitted the service before Michaelmas-day. They were also of opinion upon the second, that there was a year's service, the servant having had leave of absence for the first and last day (1).

Absence first and last day.

Length of absence immaterial.

Neither will the length of the absence prevent the settlement; the law is the same, whether it be for three days, or so many months.

Absence 13 weeks.

A servant hired for a year, ran away after serving eight weeks; he was absent for thirteen weeks, working with and receiving wages from another person; when his master apprehended him *by a warrant*, but in his way to a justice, asked whether he would *come back* to his place, or go to prison? and if he would come back *and go on* as he ought to do, he might. He said he would come back; and his master asked him then, what he would be willing to abate for the time he had been absent? He said he thought a shilling a week would not hurt him, which was agreed to. He served the remainder of the year, and received all his wages, but the thirteen shillings agreed to be deducted. The court were of opinion, that the length of the absence was immaterial; as was also the period of the service at which it took

(1) Rex v. Bray, Burr. S. C. 682. 2 Bott, 324. Pl. 363.

place.

place. The only queſtion was, whether the pauper's ſervice was performed under the old, or under a new contract; but there was no pretence to ſay he entered into a new contract, the maſter's object in apprehending him by a warrant being to compel him to complete the ſervice under the old (1).

Abſence laſt day of year.

But where abſence continues during the laſt days of the year, the maſter's permiſſion cannot be implied from a ſubſequent return to the ſervice; it is more difficult therefore to determine in theſe caſes, how far the abſence is by reaſon of a diſpenſation, or under the diſſolution of the relation between them.

Abſence, putting another in his place.

In the firſt deciſions in favour of diſpenſations at the end of the ſervice, it was evident that the relation of maſter and ſervant was not determined by the abſence. Where the ſervant aſks leave to go, and puts another in his place to perform thoſe duties, which he muſt otherwiſe have done, and the maſter aſſents upon that condition, they acknowledge the continuance of their contract, by the terms under which they diſpenſe with its perſonal execution.

Thus a ſervant hired for a year, ſerved until within three weeks of the end of it; when he aſked his maſter's leave to go to the herring fiſhery; the maſter conſented if he could get a man in his place to do his work to the maſter's liking. The ſervant procured ſuch a ſubſtitute, whom he agreed with and paid; he received part of his wages when going, and the remainder for the whole year on his return, which was three weeks after the expiration of his

(1) Rex v. Eaſt Shefford, 4 Term Rep. 804. 2 Bott, 347. Pl 383. See alſo Rex v. Grantham; an abſence of 13 weeks, with the maſter's conſent, 3 Term Rep. 754. 2 Bott, 343. Pl. 381.

year.

year. It was held that there was no diſſolution of the contract, but a conſtructive ſervice under it (1).

So if the ſervant works with another, with his maſter's conſent, *to whom he makes a compenſation, and is bound to return when called upon;* it is in fact nothing more than leave given by the original maſter to work with ſome one elſe, and is ſubſtantially ſervice done with the former. As where a ſervant, five weeks before the expiration of the year, went with his miſtreſs's leave to work in a different pariſh, and received his year's wages after the expiration of the year, when he voluntarily returned the amount of the money he had earned during his abſence; and it was further found that if his miſtreſs had required him to return during the five weeks, he would have done ſo. The contract ſubſiſted, and the ſervice was diſpenſed with; for the ſervant paid the miſtreſs, or what is the ſame thing, voluntarily deducted from the wages his miſtreſs owed him, *what he had earned* during his abſence, and would have returned during the five weeks, if ſhe had required it. This therefore was ſervice done for her, ſince if the contract had been diſſolved, the ſervant would not have returned, and the ſum deducted ſhould not have been the amount of his earning, but a part of his year's wages proportioned to his abſence (2).

It ſeems alſo to make no difference, if the pauper is not bound to return within the period of abſence, provided the parties clearly acknowledge the continuance of the contract, by giving a licence to depart, and receiving a recompenſe for that time. The pauper was hired to Ann Tyler to ſerve for a year, at which time he told her, that he was in the militia, and *might be abſent* about a month in the year to attend in that duty; and at the ſame time he told her that he would pay a man to ſerve in his place, or elſe would make her an allowance in his wages for the

(1) Rex *v.* Goodneſton, Burr. S. C. 251. 2 Bott, 313. Pl. 354.

(2) Rex *v.* Nether Heyford, Burr. S. C. 479. 2 Bott, 328. Pl. 358.

time

time he was abſent. Having ſerved till May, he then joined the militia for thirty days, and afterwards returned to his ſervice, and continued until the end of the year, and then made his miſtreſs an abatement of eight ſhillings of his wages, for the time he was abſent. The court were of opinion, that the year's ſervice was completed. "In the preſent caſe, the man is hired for a year, to ſerve for a year, but mentions an event that might happen, of his being called out to attend his militia duty; and told his miſtreſs that if it ſhould ſo happen, he would either pay a man to ſerve in his place, or make an allowance out of his wages." This is not a chaſm in the contract, but a diſpenſation with the perſonal ſervice. It was at the election of the miſtreſs, either to diſpenſe with his attendance, and have a ſubſtitute, or to have an abatement out of his wages, and ſhe preferred the latter (1).

So where a yearly ſervant ſerved the laſt half year with the aſſignee of his maſter's ſtock and farm, there being no converſation about diſſolving the contract with the old, and no freſh contract with the new (2): and where a ſervant with his maſter's conſent worked with different maſter's, receiving their wages, and making an allowance to his original maſter for abſence from him (3): theſe abſences were held to be diſpenſed with, and the ſervice virtually performed to the firſt maſter (4).

Where maſter's conſent appears, and nothing more. Poſt 243.

And where the maſter's conſent appears to have been aſked, and given, and nothing more; it is to be intended that the abſence is in conſequence of a diſpenſation, and not of a diſſolution. As where a yearly ſervant, three days before the expiration of his year, went to

(1) Rex v. Weſterleigh, Burr. S. C. 753. 2 Bott, 214. Pl. 261.

(2) Rex v. Ivinghoe, 1 Str. 10. 2 Bott, 296. Pl. 336.

(3) Rex v. Beccles. Burr. S. C. 230. 2 Bott, 298. Pl. 337.

(4) Rex v. Undermilbeck, 5 Term Rex. 387. 2 Bott, 294. Pl. 335.

his father's, with his maſter's conſent, and whilſt he continued there, his year's ſervice expired; after which he went to receive his wages, when his maſter deducted for a former abſence, but not for the latter. It was deemed a good conſtructive ſervice (1).

Leave of abſence for a fortnight at the end of a year to get what he can.

So alſo a diſpenſation has been inferred from circumſtances, although the maſter had expreſsly parted with his power of control for the remainder of the year (2).

As where the pauper was hired in February till the Michaelmas following, and ſerved accordingly. On the Friday before old Michaelmas, his maſter aſked him if he would ſtay again; the pauper ſaid he would, if they could agree about wages, and aſked five guineas, which the maſter thought too much. The pauper immediately ſet out to go to a ſtatute, and having gone about ten yards, returned for ſomething he had forgotten. He then met his maſter, who ſaid he would give him five guineas, and gave him one ſhilling earneſt. The maſter, while he was putting his hand in his pocket for the ſhilling, ſaid, "you ſhall go away a fortnight at *Michaelmas*, becauſe of your ſettlement; I will give you that fortnight to get what you can:" to which the pauper then agreed. The pauper accordingly went and ſtayed a fortnight at his father's, during which time he worked for another perſon, digging ſand at one ſhilling *per* day. At the end of the fortnight he returned to his maſter, and continued to ſerve him till Lady-day, and until his maſter died ſoon after; he then received his wages from a relation of his miſtreſs, and believes that nothing was deducted for the fortnight; but he does not remember what ſum he received. The pauper apprehended that his maſter would not have hired him, if he had not agreed to go away for the fortnight. Aſhurſt J. "the rule eſta-

(1) Rex *v.* Undermilbeck, 5 Term Rep. 387. 2 Bott, 294. Pl. 335. See *poſt*. Sect. V.

(2) But ſee *poſt*. 252.

bliſhed

bliſhed in theſe kind of caſes isthis; when there is a *bonâ fide* exception of part of the time, at the time of the hiring, that is not an hiring for a year; but if there be no exception, at the time of making the original contract, then a permiſſive abſence is conſidered as a diſpenſation of part of the ſervice by the maſter; and it does not operate in the ſame way as an exception out of the original contract, which defeats the ſettlement. And the queſtion whether it be one or the other, muſt depend on the particular circumſtances of each caſe. In this caſe there was a complete hiring for a year at the time. The parties having diſagreed on the terms propoſed, the pauper went away; but on his return, his maſter ſaid he would give him the five guineas, which he agreed to accept, and gave him one ſhilling earneſt. It is likewiſe ſtated, that while the maſter was putting his hand into his pocket, he told the pauper he ſhould go away for a fortnight; but the contract was complete before that time, and what paſſed afterwards can only be conſidered as a diſpenſation with the ſervice; for at that time the maſter had a complete right to his ſervice for a year, and the pauper had agreed to ſerve him for that time, and the one ſhilling earneſt was to bind the agreement for a year for the five guineas; otherwiſe it appears to be giving the ſervant more than he originally aſked for the whole year, for ſerving him for a ſhorter period. If then the contract were complete before any thing was ſaid relative to the fortnight's abſence, this was a diſpenſation with the ſervice, and not an exception out of the original contract. An exception is a ſtipulation on the part of the perſon for whoſe benefit it is introduced; but here it was not made on the requeſt of the ſervant, but on the offer of the maſter; and it appears that he ſaid it was for the expreſs purpoſe of preventing the pauper's gaining a ſettlement. That is not ſuch a reaſon as the court would give much countenance to; whether indeed the ſeſſions might not have determined this on the ground of fraud, was for their conſideration, as it is, there is no occaſion to go into that ground, as we are of opinion that this was a diſpenſation with the ſervice: with reſpect to the ſervant's apprehenſion, which is ſtated in the caſe, that cannot vary the queſtion; we are to decide on the terms of the contract, and not on the apprehenſion of the pauper."—Buller and Groſe J. ſame opinion (1).

Abſence on the maſter's account and requeſt. *Poſt.* 244.

The next claſs of caſes, in which the court has inclined to infer a diſpenſation, is where the abſence takes place ſolely on the maſter's account, and at his requeſt. Here it originates with him in whom the power of diſpenſation is veſted, and is only acquieſced in by the ſervant; the contract is therefore ſuppoſed to continue notwithſtanding abſence, unleſs it appears by other circumſtances to have been diſſolved by the expreſs conſent of both parties.

A footman whoſe year would expire the thirtieth of October, married a fellow ſervant on the fourth of September preceeding; ſhe had previouſly given a month's warning to quit, and was to have left her place in September, but was deſired by her maſter to ſtay till the ſeventeenth of October; which ſhe did; when the maſter ſaid to the huſband, he ſuppoſed as his wife was going away, he would like to do ſo too. The huſband replied, he would like it better, if it was agreeable to his maſter. His maſter ſaid he had no objection, as he had another footman coming, and would pay him his whole year's wages, which he accordingly did on the ſeventeenth, in full to the thirtieth. The huſband and wife left the ſervice on the ſeventeenth, and the new footman came on the ſame night into his place. It was held that this was a diſpenſation with the ſervice from the ſeventeenth to the thirtieth; the maſter voluntarily giving him leave of abſence for the laſt thirteen days, and of his own accord offering and paying him the whole year's wages, is proof of his conſent (2).

(1) Rex *v* Sulgrave, 2 Term Rep. 376. 2 Bott, 338. Pl. 377.

(2) Rex *v*. Richmond, Burr. S.C. 740. 2 Bott, 327. Pl. 366.

The

The pauper being hired for a year. Her maſter, who when ſhe was hired, lived in London, purchaſed a manufactory in Mancheſter two months before the expiration of her year. He then told all his ſervants that he was going to reſide at Mancheſter, but did not mention any time, and that they *might look out for other ſervices if they choſe, or might ſtay with him till he went*. The pauper did not look out for any other ſervice, but continued with her maſter until within ſeven days of the expiration of her year; on the evening of which day, her maſter *paid her the whole year's wages, and gave her half a guinea over*, and went to Mancheſter the ſame evening. He did not know that morning that he ſhould go in the evening, or before the expiration of the year's ſervice; it depended upon circumſtances, which he could not at that time foreſee; but if he had remained, he would have continued the pauper in his ſervice and ſhe went into a new one two days after her maſter left London.—Lord Mansfield C. J. The only queſtion is, whether the ſervant continued *bona fide* in her ſervice during the whole year. There is a diſtinction between exceptions from the contract and diſpenſations of the ſervice; but if the caſe be of the latter deſcription, and *bonâ fide*, it can make no difference when the ſervant is engaged, or where, or whether the ſervice be in the ſame, or in another occupation. Why then does ſhe quit the ſervice? *at the deſire and for the convenience of her maſter, who gave her half a guinea beyond her wages, as an equivalent no doubt for her board: it was accidental, and a favour to the maſter*. The caſe of Rex *v.* Richmond (1) is full as ſtrong as this, for there a new ſervant came into the very place which the pauper had vacated upon a diſpenſation of his ſervice. Fraud vitiates every thing but the juſtice and reaſon of the hiring are here with the ſettlement. Suppoſe ſhe had come from a diſtant country, and had no other ſettlement, ſhall ſhe loſe her only one, which ſhe deſerves ſo well (2)?"

(1) *Ante*, 228. n. (2).

(2) Rex *v.* St. Bartholomew, Cornhill, Cald. 48. 2 Bott, 329. Pl. 368.

 These

These seem to be the two strongest cases on the subject; and in the first it was not considered as making any distinction, that the master hired another servant in the footman's place; nor in the second, that the servant hired herself into a new place, two days before the expiration of the year. In this last, the servant had put it out of her power to return to the service of her original master, if he should have required it of her, by entering into a relation incompatible with it; so that it seems to resemble the cases already mentioned, where the servant worked with another master, with consent of the first.

Service by operation of law.

The next class of cases of constructive service, are such as arise by operation or inference of law. There absence or non-performance of work is excused in the servant, for some reason admitted by the law itself, without consent from the master. In requiring a complete year's service, the statute meant no more than that the servant should pay such attention to his duty as the law would compel. Service for the remainder of his time must therefore confer a settlement.

Service at all lawful times.

Thus if servant is hired by the year, to work as a weaver or carpenter, at yearly wages; his master cannot compel him to work on Sundays, and he will be held to have served a year, notwithstanding that absence from labour, which is in obedience to the law (1).

According to the custom of the country.

If there are any cases also, where a servant cannot be compelled by his master to labour during the usual seasons of the week, by reason of the usage of a particular place, they are to be classed under this head of dispensation. As where a pauper was hired for a year, at yearly wages, to work at stamp mills used for the purpose of cleansing and manufacturing tin and worked

(1) Per Willes, J. Rex v. Birmingham, post. 231. n. (1)

therein

therein daily, except holidays, and Sundays, according to the cuſtom of tinners; this is a ſufficient ſervice, being according to the cuſtom of the country (1).

So where a ſervant was hired by a wood-ſcrew-maker for a year, "good earn, good hire," to work for him and no other maſter, to make ſcrews at ſo much a groſe. By good earn good hire, is meant that his wages were to depend upou his work; he was to have nothing, if he got nothing. The ſervant abſented himſelf without leave for a week or a fortnight at a time, to drink or play. His maſter on his return was angry and checked him, *but always received him again.* It was held that a ſettlement was gained by ſuch ſervice for a year, for whatever conſtitutes a ſufficient performance of the contract, from the cuſtom of the country or nature of the ſervice, is ſufficient (2).

Caſes where the maſter is unable to keep his ſervant any longer, from a ſudden change in his circumſtances, ſeem reducible to this head; the law conſidering the ſervice as performed, which the ſervant was only prevented from diſcharging by the maſter's misfortunes. As where a ſervant, hired at yearly wages, continued in the ſervice till within four or five days of the expiration of a year, when her maſter becoming a bankrupt, and the meſſenger taking poſſeſſion of the houſe, her miſtreſs diſcharged her, paying her the whole year's wages. Bankruptcy does not diſſolve the contract of hiring, without the ſervant's conſent, and therefore the pauper gained a ſettlement (3).

Abſence, from maſter's inability to keep the ſervant.

A bankrupt.

A maid ſervant, hired for a year, ſerved until within ſeven days of the end of it; when an information having

Information againſt.

(1) Rex *v.* St. Agnes, 2 Bott, 322. Pl. 362.

(2) Rex *v.* Birmingham, Dougl. 333. 2 Bott, 216. Pl. 262. Both th s and the preceding caſe may be ſupported as caſes of diſpenſation with the maſter's conſent, for it is found that the maſter always received the ſervant back into his ſervice.

(4) Rex *v.* St. Andrew's Holborn, 2 Term Rep. 627. 2 Bott, 343. Pl. 380.

been laid against her master for keeping a gaming-house, he quitted his house, and told his servants that he had no longer occasion for their services, and then paid the pauper her whole year's wages. The master would have kept the pauper, except on account of his being so obliged to quit his house; and the pauper was unwilling to leave his service. This was held to be a mere dispensation with the service, the contract not being dissolved with the consent of both parties (1).

Absence from sickness.

The next instance is, where the absence happens on account of sickness. Here also it is immaterial whether it is with (2), or without the master's consent (3). Neither will it make any difference, that the master does all in his power to put an end to the contract (4): or whether the servant is paid the whole year's wages (5), or has a deduction made (6); provided it does not appear to be the intention of *both* parties to dissolve it (7).

It is also clear that it is immaterial, whether absence on this account be *temporary* in the middle of the year, or

(1) Rex *v.* St. Mary Lambeth, 8 Term Rep. 236. 2 Bott, 357. Pl. 388.

(2) Rex *v.* Christchurch. Where the servant was frightened into fits, 17 days before the expiration of her year, and was sent first to Mr. L's. a private house, and if Mr. L. refused to admit her, she was to be brought back to her master's house again. She resided at L's five days, and then went to an hospital. On the day after her departure, she went back to fetch her clothes, and received her full year's wages but no words of discharge passed. Burr. S. C. 494. 2 Bott, 319. Pl. 359. Rex *v.* Ozleworth; an absence for three months, and the pauper received again into the service. 2 Bott, 324. Pl. 315.

(3) Rex *v.* Islip, 1 Str. 423. 2 Bott, 308. Pl. 348. Rex *v.* Maddington, where a carter was kicked by one of his master's horses, five weeks before the expiration of his year, and went to his friends without his master's knowledge or asking his leave, to get his leg cured. He never returned during the remainder of the year, but went a short time after to receive his wages, when the master deducted six shillings for the absence, to which the servant consented. Burr. S.C. 675. 2 Bott, 322. Pl. 361.

(4) Rex *v.* Sharrington, Cald. 471. 2 Bott, 333. Pl. 372.

(5) Rex *v.* Christchurch, *supra*, n. (2). *post*. 247.

(6) Rex *v.* Maddington, *supra*, n. 3. Rex *v.* Sutton, 5 Term Rep. 657. 2 Bott, 349 Pl. 384.

(7) See *post*. 246.

continued

continued by reason of a continuance of sickness, until the end of it. As where a yearly servant served only seven weeks, when being in liquor, he broke his thigh by a fall from a beer waggon, and remained twenty-nine weeks in the hospital. On quitting the hospital, he returned to his master, who refused to receive him (the pauper continuing unable to work), but offered him his wages for seven weeks, and a present, which he refused to receive, and the pauper and his master went to a justice, but nothing was done. It was held that this was a service for a year (1).

But the service must have actually commenced under the contract, in order to let in the period of sickness, to count as part of the yearly service. For where the pauper, a few days before Martinmas, had been hired for a year to commence at Martinmas, but was prevented from going into his place for the first month, by reason of illness, in consequence of which his master refused to receive him, and they came to a new agreement; it was held that the month's absence could not be considered as a constructive service, for the hiring was executory, and the service had in fact never commenced under it (2).

The third class of cases of dispensation is, where the servant is absent for any other lawful cause, as to look for another service (3); or to be hired at a statute fair (4); this is no interruption of the service, although the master do not consent.

3. Absence to look for service, &c. *post*. 249.

(1) Rex *v.* Sharrington, Cald. 471. 2 Bott, 333. Pl. 372. S. P. Rex *v.* Sutton; where the pauper was deprived of his reason, two months before the expiration of his service, he was then taken away by his father, and did not return, but continued an incurable lunatic. 5 Term Rep. 657. 2 Bott, 349. Pl. 384.

(2) Rex *v.* Wintersett, Cald. 298. See this case reported more fully, *post*. 246. n. (1).

(3) Rex *v.* Potter Heigham, Burr. S. C. 690. 2 Bott, 325. Pl. 365.

(4) Rex *v.* Islip, *post*. 235. n. (2).

consent. If a short absence also takes place at the servant's request, for any other reasonable purpose, and it is agreed to by the master, the court has not been inclined to infer a dissolution from that fact only, notwithstanding the use of the word "discharge," which seems at first sight to mean a dissolution of the contract. As where a yearly servant had served till the day before the end of the year, when he desired his master to discharge him, as he had let himself for the next year to a person in a distant place, and was removing further from his friends, he wished to go and see them, and pass that day with them, and requested to have that time to himself; to which the master consented, and he was discharged, and paid his whole wages, save sixpence, which he allowed his master for that day. It was held not to be a dissolution of the contract, but an absence with leave (1).

4. Where master prevents the service. *post*. 245.

The fourth case is, where the master discharges the servant without his consent, or having lawful cause, and thus prevents the servant from performing his service.

Under this head are to be classed cases of absence, for the purpose of avoiding a settlement, when fraudulent, and the sessions find the fact of fraud. A case has been already stated, in which it was held, that if an hiring is for less than a year, it will be defective, although it should be found by the sessions to be fraudulent on the master's part (2). But with regard to service, it seems taken for granted in all the cases, that fraud, which vitiates most things, prevents absence from defeating a settlement. The court will never infer fraud, which must therefore be found specially (3).

(1) Rex v. Potter Heigham, *post* 238. n. (3).

(2) *Ante*, 196. n. (3).

(3) See Rex v. Preston, 2 Bott, 310. Pl. 351, and the cases cited n. (*a*) in margin.

Where

Where the completion of the ſervice is obſtructed by any act of violence on the maſter's part, it cannot injure the unoffending ſervant, or cauſe an interruption in his ſervice, whatever the maſter's motive may be.

As where, on the day before the ſervant's year expired, the maſter told him that to prevent his gaining a ſettlement in that pariſh, he ſhould go away immediately, which the ſervant refuſed to do, inſiſting to ſerve out the year; whereupon the maſter turned him out of doors. This was held ſuch a fraud in the maſter, as ſhall not prevent the ſettlement (1).

A ſervant, three days before his year was up, aſked leave of his maſter to go to a ſtatute fair to be hired, which the maſter refuſed; but the ſervant inſiſting that he muſt go, the maſter replied, "I am reſolved that you "ſhall gain no ſettlement in the pariſh, and therefore if you "will go, it ſhall be for good and all". "No", anſwered the ſervant, "I will ſerve out the year." And thereupon he went and never returned during the three days. Afterwards when he returned to be paid, the maſter after deducting for another abſence, to which the ſervant agreed, abated ſixpence for the three days, which the ſervant refuſed to allow; but the maſter refuſing to pay, the ſervant took the reſt of the wages. This abſence did not prevent a ſettlement; for the ſervant knew that his maſter deſigned to part with him; and his requeſt of leave of abſence in order to get another ſervice, was a reaſonable one, which the maſter ought not to have refuſed, and the ſubſequent abſence without leave is no deſertion of his former ſervice, eſpecially when his declaration that he would ſerve out the year, and refuſal to allow the deduction of the ſixpence, are conſidered, which

(1) Eaſtland v. Weſtherſley, 1 Str. 526. 2 Bott, 309. Pl. 340.

plainly

plainly ſhew the contract was not diſſolved till the end of the year (1).

So although the maſter uſe no violence, yet if he diſcharge the pauper without his conſent, and contrary to law, it will not defeat his ſettlement. The pauper was hired for a year in H. ſerved three quarters, and then married a woman with child. Of this his maſter complained to a juſtice of peace, who thought the matter complained of to be a ſufficient cauſe for the pauper's being diſcharged, and allowed of his diſcharge; but made no order in writing touching the matter. The maſter thereupon diſcharged the pauper againſt his conſent. The court were of opinion that this not being a reaſonable cauſe for diſcharge, and the pauper not having conſented, he was to be conſidered as having performed his year's ſervice in H. and gaining a ſettlement there (2).

Miſtreſs turns away her ſervant, who ſubmits.

A maid ſervant was hired for a year, and ſerved until within eight days of its expiration, when on account of ſome difference with her miſtreſs, ſhe gave her warning that ſhe ſhould leave her ſervice at the end of the year. The miſtreſs on having hired another ſervant; by reaſon of ſome impatient behaviour of the pauper, *diſcharged her* from the ſervice, but paid her the full year's wages. The pauper accepted the wages, and left the pariſh eight days before the year ended; but ſaid ſhe would have ſerved her year, if her miſtreſs would have let her. This was held to be a diſpenſation with the ſervice; and not a diſſolution of the contract. For the turning her away, was a mere wrongful act *ſubmitted* to, but not *agreed to* by the ſervant. Neither thought that they could put an end to the ſervice. The ſervant though deſirous of going, gave warning to quit *at the end* of the year, and the miſtreſs wiſhed

(1) Rex *v.* Iſlip, 1 Str. 423. 2 Bott, 308. Pl. 348.

(2) Rex *v.* Hanbury, Burr. S. C. 322. 2 Bott, 302. Pl. 342. *Poſt.* 251.

for

for her own convenience to dismiss the servant before the end of it; but was convinced that she could not dissolve the contract, and therefore paid her the whole year's wages. But it cannot be inferred from the pauper's receiving the wages, that she went away by agreement; *something should be stated to shew that it was voluntary on the part of the servant*, and that she consented to *a dissolution of the contract* (1).

Absence to avoid a settlement by mutual consent.

It is more difficult to determine how far absence for the purpose of avoiding a settlement, if unaccompanied with other circumstances, shall be deemed fraudulent, so as not to discontinue the service. It seems most reasonable, that when the proposal of absence originates with the master, who may be benefitted as a rated parishioner by defeating the settlement, and it is only acquiesced in by the servant, that the inclination should be to consider it a fraud (2). But on the other hand it is hard, if the law, which looks upon the privilege of gaining a settlement as beneficial to the servant, should not allow him the right of avoiding one at the end of his year, in a particular place, by absenting himself a day from service, when he might have originally done so by an exception in the contract. If cases of consent, be fraudulent, it is not a fraud upon the servant, but upon the parish in which he was previously settled.

The cases seem to have proceeded upon very nice grounds of distinction in this respect. A servant, ten days before the end of his year, told his master that he did not wish to be settled in the parish, and asked him leave to go and visit his relations, to which the master consented. After the year was expired, he returned to

(1) Rex *v.* St. Philip in Birmingham, 2 Term Rep. 624. 2 Bott, 341. Pl. 379.

(2) Rex *v.* Sulgrave, *ante*, 228. n. (1).

his

his maſter, and hired himſelf as a day labourer, in which capacity he ſerved for three months; ſometime after his return, he and his maſter made up their accounts, and he allowed for his abſence in the preceeding year, out of his daily wages. It was held that he gained a ſettlement, and that the leave and conſent of the maſter was fraudulent, and a mere evaſion of the ſettlement (1). We have juſt ſeen that abſence for a day, with conſent, that the ſervant might ſee his relations, was held conſtructive ſervice, where the purpoſe was not to avoid a ſettlement (2).

When the maſter does not object to the ſettlement.

A ſervant had continued in the ſervice, until within three days of the end of his year, when being unwilling to gain a ſettlement in the pariſh, where there was an houſe of induſtry, he requeſted his maſter to diſcharge him, which he accordingly did, and they parted by conſent, the pauper abating one ſhilling for theſe three days; the court took no notice of the point (3).

But where a ſervant, wiſhing to avoid acquiring a ſettlement in the pariſh where he ſerved, and to be ſettled elſewhere, went with his maſter, three days prior to the expiration of his year, before a neighbouring juſtice to be diſcharged, who diſcharged him, after hearing the maſter and ſervant; whether verbally or in writing did not appear; but the maſter told the juſtice, that he was welcome to gain a ſettlement in his pariſh if he pleaſed, and then paid him his wages; but deducted one ſhilling and ninepence for the time wanting to complete his year. It was held not to be fraudulent on the part of the maſter, for he had no objection to the ſettlement; it was a ſolemn diſcharge by the conſent of both parties (4).

(1) Rex *v.* Frome Selwood, Burr. S. C. 565. 2 Bott 321. Pl. 360.

(2) *Ante*, 234, n. (1).

(3) Rex *v.* Potter Heigham, Burr. S C. 690. 2 Bott, 325. Pl. 395.

(4) Rex *v.* North Baſham, Cald. 566. 2 Bott, 335. Pl. 374.

So

So where a ſervant had ſerved until within five or ſix days of the end of his year, which he would have alſo ſerved, but that ſome houſeholders of the pariſh gave him two guineas to leave his maſter, and go out of the pariſh before his year expired, he being about to be married. His maſter inſiſted upon deducting nine ſhillings from his wages before he would let him go; the pauper ſubmitted to the abatement, and went away. It did not appear that the maſter was privy to the two guineas being paid, which was done out of the pariſh rates, and he received no benefit therefrom, not being rated to the poor. The court intimated a ſtrong opinion, that the year's ſervice had not been completed, and could not confer a ſettlement, although the abſence was for the purpoſe of avoiding one; but they decided the caſe upon a defect in the order (1).

The court ſeem in theſe caſes to have regarded even the poſſible influence of the maſter, with a jealous eye. But where he has a right to diſcharge the ſervant, by reaſon of immoral conduct, he cannot be conſidered as guilty of fraud in exerciſing that right, although it defeats the ſervant's ſettlement, and the maſter may be eventually benefitted as a rated pariſhioner (2).

II. Of diſſolutions.

Wherever it appears that there has been an actual diſſolution of the contract, the period of abſence renders the ſervice imperfect in all caſes whatever.

Example:

A diſſolution by conſent may appear as a fact in the caſe; as where it is ſtated, " that the ſervant parted with

(1) Rex v. Preſton, 2 Bott, 310. Pl. 351. See alſo Pawlet v. Burnham, 2 Bott, 307. Pl. 347, *poſt.* 257.

(2) See *poſt.* 255, ſeveral caſes on this head.

" his

"his own consent (1)"; or that he quitted the service before the expiration of the year, "without any compulsion on the part of his master (2)." or even that "he left his master's service (3)."

Implied.

It may be likewise collected from various circumstances, indicating a determination to put an end to the contract. And lastly, it may appear by the parties coming to a new agreement, inconsistent with that under which they had previously lived, which necessarily presupposes a dissolution of the former.

By new agreement.

As where an unmarried man was hired for a year from Martinmas, as a servant in husbandry, at about eight pounds a year, with meat, washing, and lodging. In the succeeding January he married, but continued with his master as a menial servant until the ensuing May-day. Some days before which, the master and pauper agreed, that the pauper should go (with his wife) as a hind, to reside on and manage another farm of his master's in the same township. This second agreement was for a year from that May-day; the pauper to have five shillings a week, with a house to live in rent free, and some trifling perquisites. This was held by a majority of the court, not to be a prolongation of the former contract, but a new agreement to serve for a year from May-day, which put an end to the former, as being inconsistent with it (4).

Lord Kenyon C. J. who differed from the majority of the court, thought that the original contract was not dissolved,

(1) Rex *v.* Seagrave, Cald. 247. 2 Bott, 333. Pl. 371, *post.*

(2) Sheen *v.* Godalmine, 2 Bott, 310. Pl. 350. As to the effect of a request "to discharge," see *ante.*

(3) Rex *v.* Sudbrooke, 4 East. 356. See also *post.* 250. n. (2).

(4) Rex *v* Great Chilton, 5 Term Rep. 672. 2 Bott, 268. Pl. 313. Lord Kenyon, C. J. dissent.

 for

for there was no end of the relation of master and servant even for a moment, during the whole time the latter continued in service, and the subsequent alteration of situation was not sufficient to effect it.

But at all events, to annul the first hiring, the second agreement must be inconsistent with it. A variance in the nature of the service does not defeat the settlement. A footman who was converted into a butler, would gain a settlement, by completing a year's service, notwithstanding such a change in his station (1).

The pauper was hired by his uncle to serve for a year, in his trade of a turner, to be found in board, lodging, pocket-money, and clothes. After serving six months, his master finding him idle, he and the pauper came to a new agreement, by which he was to work and be paid by the piece, and find himself in board, lodging, pocket-money and clothes. Upon these terms he continued with his master till the end of the year, sometimes working by the piece, lodging and boarding out of his master's house, and at other times serving in the house as a servant, when he was lodged and boarded with his master. The court were of opinion, that the original contract was not interrupted and wholly done away, but only the terms of it varied. The servant was to work by the piece instead of the gross, and the conduct of the parties subsequent to the new agreement shews that, with respect to the mode of performing the service in the understanding of the parties, the original contract still continued to subsist (2).

So likewise a mere change of master, does not annul or dissolve the contract (3).

(1) *Per* Lord Kenyon, *ib.* 2 Bott, 222. Pl. 265.

(2) Rex *v.* Alton, Cald. 424. (3) See *ante*, 223, *et seq.*

The cases in which dissolution has been held to take place, will be arranged with reference to the same order of leading circumstances, as has been adopted in cases of dispensation, as by that means the reader will be the better able to compare them.

1. Dissolution, where a return to service. Dispensation, *ante* 220.

A return to service can have no effect in working a dispensation, when it clearly appears from other circumstances that there has been a dissolution. As where the pauper having served one quarter of his year, upon some dispute between him and his master, the latter insisted on turning him away, and threw down his quarter's wages, which the pauper took up, and went to his father's house, where he continued six days, during which time he looked upon himself as a freeman. *He then returned at his master's request*, and continued in the service to the end of the year, when the master paid him the remaining three quarters' wages. In this case the contract was absolutely dissolved, the master insisted upon turning away his servant, and paid him down all his wages that were due; the consent on the other side is by taking the money up. Then how did he come back again? It was upon the master's *request*; there is nothing by which the absence can be explained. The meaning of purging an absence, is where the act itself is doubtful (1).

The pauper being hired for a year to one Miles, served only three days; when his master, upon a difference arising between them, desired him to go about his business; on which he ran away, and then hired himself to Whitby for a year. Having served him for six months, Miles insisted that Whitby should not keep him in his service. He was then paid his wages to that time, and quitted the

(1) Rex *v.* Gresham, 1 Term Rep. 102. 2 Bott, 338. Pl. 376.

service,

service, and went as a labourer to a barge-master for a fortnight; when he returned, at the request of Whitby, into his service, with the consent of Miles, and served seven months, being a month over the year for which he was hired, in order to make up his lost time; and then received his wages. This is a very clear case; here is an absolute dissolution of the contract, by both master and servant, at the end of six months, whereas the statute requires a continuance in the same service for a whole year: the new service cannot be connected with the old hiring (1).

Where the agreement to separate is made by consent, and with a view of entering into another service before the year expires, it is a dissolution: for it presupposes an intention on both sides, that the servant should be *sui juris*, and the contract at an end; and is very distinguishable from cases, where the servant goes to work with other masters for a temporary period, by his original master's consent (2).

Dissolution at parties' request. *ante* 225.

Thus where a yearly servant before the end of his year went to a statute fair, and hired himself to another master, to go into the service three weeks before the expiration of the year he was then serving, if his master would let him come then; and if not, then at the expiration of his year. The next day the pauper asked his master whether he would let him go, who told him he could not spare him, he must get a new servant first. Some time after he hired one, and told the pauper, " I

(1) Rex *v.* Ross, Burr. S. C. 688. 2 Bott, 325. Pl. 364. Rex *v.* Caverswall, S. P. The servant served until within three weeks of the end of the year; when, on some dispute arising between him and his master, he was with his own consent discharged; and upon his mistress's request, went again into the service and completed his year. It was held a total dissolution of the contract. Burr. S. C. 461. 2 Bott, 315. Pl. 357.

(2) See *ante*, 223.

 have

"have got a new servant, you may go now, I have not "work for you both." The pauper then went to receive his wages, when the master's wife said to her husband, "dont deduct any thing from his wages," who replied, "I don't intend it." The pauper was paid his whole wages, and then went away, being about a fortnight before the expiration of his year. Lord Kenyon:—"The distinction between the different cases seems to be this; if the pauper be absent from the service, with the concurrence, remaining however subject to the control, of his master, he may acquire a settlement; because this only amounts to a dispensation with the service: but if the master ever parts with his control over the servant, then no settlement is gained; and the receiving the whole year's wages don't make any difference. Here he had given up all control over the servant; he was instrumental in enabling the servant to make another contract with another master; and from what passed between the parties, it was evidently the intention of both, that the pauper should become *sui juris*, and should be enabled to contract with another master. The relation of master and servant no longer continued, for he could not have insisted on the pauper's returning into his service, after the wages were paid (1)."

Dissolution for master's accommodation, and at his request. *ante* 228

So although the servant's absence takes place for the master's accommodation, it will not prevent a discontinuance of service, if the dissolution is satisfactorily made out from other circumstances (2). The pauper was hired at yearly wages for a year, to come into the service on the 11th of October, being old Michaelmas-day, a month's wages, or month's warning, the mistress stating that she did not wish to confine the servant for a a year. She came the 12th, and served until about a fortnight before *new* Michaelmas-day. Her mistress asked her,

(1) Rex *v.* Thistleton, 6 Term Rep. 185. 2 Bott, 299. Pl. 388.
(2) See *ante*, 228.

whether

whether ſhe choſe to go away on new or old Michaelmas-day, aſſigning as a reaſon for aſking, *that ſhe had hired a ſervant who wiſhed to come home on new Michaelmas-day*. The pauper ſaid *it was immaterial to her, as ſhe had not got a place, and agreed to go at new* Michaelmas-day at which time the other ſervant came into her miſtreſs's ſervice. Her miſtreſs was not in a condition of life to keep two ſervants. The pauper on coming into the ſervice had conſidered herſelf as being to live with her miſtreſs until old Michaelmas: ſhe was paid the whole of her year's wages, though when ſhe agreed to go away at the new Michaelmas, nothing was ſaid about it. The court held that the concluſion whether the contract was diſſolved, ought to have drawn by the quarter-ſeſſions: but they were of opinion, that there was ſtrong evidence to warrant them in holding that the contract was diſſolved before the end of the year, the ſervant not continuing liable to ſerve the remainder of the year, and the miſtreſs having parted with her right to make her re-aſſume the ſervice (1).

Diſſolution, when inſiſted by maſter without cauſe.

Neither does it make any difference that the maſter inſiſts upon diſſolving the contract without juſt cauſe, and makes uſe of undue means to influence the ſervant's conſent, provided it clearly appears that his conſent is actually obtained.

Theſe circumſtances may ſometimes have weight to induce a preſumption, that the abſence was rather ſubmitted to, than any actual conſent given to diſſolve the contract. But where it appears that it has been diſſolved before the year's ſervice is completed, a ſettlement cannot be acquired, although the law would have implied ſuch ſervice, if the maſter had refuſed to permit its being performed (2).

(1) Rex *v.* St. Peter Mancroft, 8 Term Rep. 477. 1 Bott, 724. Pl. 1007

(2) See *ante*, 234.

In ſickneſs. The pauper was hired at a ſtatute held a few days before Martinmas, for a year from Martinmas. He received one ſhilling for his god's penny, and was to have three guineas for his wages; the pauper fell ill the very night of the hiring, and continued ſick and unable to go, and did not go into his ſervice till a month after Martinmas, when the pauper and his mother went to the maſter's houſe; who being from home, they were ſhewn to his wife, who complained that the pauper had not come to his ſervice according to the agreement, and therefore refuſed to receive him. Whereupon the pauper's mother ſaid, we muſt fall into your will for wages, and take what you will allow us; and left the pauper in his ſervice, where he continued until Martinmas following: when his mother was ſent for, and received for forty-eight weeks' wages, after the rate of *1 s. 2 d. per* week, being leſs than the rate of the original wages.

Lord Mansfield C. J. The ſervice had never commenced under the firſt contract, if it had, no doubt the maſter muſt have ſupported the ſervant in his ſickneſs, but that is not the queſtion; the point is, that the agreement acted upon here was a freſh agreement when he recovered from his ſickneſs, and the beginning of his ſervice was then. Under the former the miſtreſs refuſed to receive him. Then conſidering the old contract at an end, the actual ſervice was but for eleven months; that is, to the Martinmas next, and the ſubmitting to the abatement of the month's wages at the end of the year is an affirmance of the agreement made by his mother; and this as reſcinding the original agreement, deſtroys more than the *legal and conſtructive* ſervice; it ſhews alſo that there was no hiring for a year, ſo that both the hiring and ſervice muſt be conſidered as imperfect and ineffectual (1).

(1) Rex *v.* Winterſett, Cald. 298. 2 Bott, 262. Pl. 309. See alſo the opinion of Buller J. upon that caſe Rex *v.* Grendon Underwood, Cald. 364. 2 Bott, 265.

In

In this case the pauper was disabled by misfortune from executing his part of the contract, namely, coming into the service at Martinmas; and the master refusing to receive him, they came to a new agreement, which was a dissolution of the former under the rule already mentioned (3). But although the sickness happens after the service is commenced; where the master cannot put an end to the contract, but is obliged to maintain his servant; yet if the latter consent to a dissolution, there is no legal or constructive service. For if the servant chuse on account of illness to go away; illness cannot prevent him from coming to an agreement with his master, to put an end to the contract (2).

Thus where a pauper served until within five days of of the expiration of his year, when he went to a statute fair to seek a service for next year. Being taken ill of a fever there, he went home to his mother, and continued ill for six weeks. Having no money to maintain him in his illness, he on the same night desired his mother to go to his master for his money, and to bring away his clothes; the mother went next day, and brought his money all but one shilling, which she told him his master had stopped for the remainder of the year, and gave it to him, together with his clothes, *with which he was satisfied;* and he thought himself at liberty to hire himself to another master if he had been well enough. This is a dissolution of the contract by consent, for the pauper who sent for his wages five days before the year expired, had no right to his wages, until the dissolution of the contract, or the expiration of the year; the master so far as in his power put an end to the contract by deducting the one shilling, which he had no right to do but on the ground that the pauper did not continue his ser-

(1) *Ante*, 240.
(2) *Per* Le Blanc J. Rex *v.* Sudbrooke, 4 East. 361, & *s. c. ante*, 232.

vant for the remainder of the year, and the pauper received the money, ſaying he was ſatisfied, and thereby alſo aſſenting (1).

Likewiſe where the pauper lived under a yearly hiring, till about the middle of April 1796, when being too ill of a fever to work, his maſter paid him his whole year's wages, *when he left his maſter's ſervice*, and went down to Lincoln hoſpital, and never returned into the ſervice again. It was held to be a diſſolution of the contract, and that no ſettlement was gained. For it being ſtated that he *voluntarily left his maſter's ſervice, before the end of the year*, it muſt be taken to be a relinquiſhment of the ſervice altogether, which could not be, unleſs the contract were meant to be diſſolved; neither did the payment of the whole year's wages in advance, make any difference to which, Rex *v.* Godalmin (2), & Rex *v.* Caſtlechurch (3). Rex *v.* Thiſtleton (4), are in point, and the court diſtinguiſhed this caſe from Rex *v.* Chriſtchurch (5), for it did not appear there that the ſervant left the ſervice, when ſhe quitted her maſter's houſe, and if Mr. Lemonier could not take her in, ſhe was again to return thither (6).

Abſence for a lawful cauſe. *ante* 233.

So where the diſſolution ariſes from the ſervant's abſence for any other lawful cauſe (7). A yearly ſervant abſented himſelf, telling his maſter he was going to be married, to which his maſter made no anſwer. He went and was married, and on his return, ſaid he had no intention of quitting the ſervice; but the maſter ſaid he would not employ him any longer; and he replied he would go, if he would pay him his year's wages. The maſter refuſed to pay him for more than the time he had ſerved, and aſked him if

(1) Rex *v.* Whittlebury, 6 Term Rep. 464. 2 Bott, 353. Pl. 385.
(2) *Poſt.* 252, n. (1).
(3) *Poſt.* 250, n. (2.)
(4) *Ante*, 244, n. 1.
(5) *Ante*, 232, n. (2).
(6) Rex *v.* Sudbrooke, 4 Eaſt. 356.
(7) See *ante*, 233.

he

he would take his wages, or go before a juſtice; the maſter ſet out about his buſineſs, when the pauper called him back, and ſaid he would take the money for the time he had ſerved, and *that he parted with his own conſent.* The court conſidered that theſe laſt words were ſo clear and unequivocal a diſſolution of the contract, that they would not ſuffer it to be argued (1).

The pauper having ſerved until nine days before the expiration of his year, went away on Sunday morning, in order to get another place, when his year ſhould be up, without aſking leave, or mentioning it to his maſter. He returned on the Tueſday following at ſix o'clock in the morning, and aſked his maſter what work he ſhould go about; the maſter told him he might go and ſerve the maſter he had worked for the day before. He ſaw his maſter an hour afterwards, who paid him his wages up to that time only. No converſation paſſed. He then went away, and did not return: he wiſhed to ſtay out the year, but his maſter would not let him. This was held to be a diſſolution of the contract, for the maſter refuſed to receive the pauper into his ſervice; and though the ſervant wiſhed to ſtay, it appears that he did not communicate that wiſh to his maſter. Both parties did that which put an end to the contract; the one paid, and the other received the wages; it is therefore impoſſible to ſay that the ſervant was conſtructively in the ſervice after that time (2).

Abſence to look for ſervice, *ante*, 238.

The general truth of the obſervation, that the fact, whether abſence from ſervice, is under a diſpenſation, or ſubſequent to a diſſolution, depends upon the entire circumſtances of each particular caſe, appears from the caſes which have been quoted. In arranging ſuch as have been already detailed, regard has been paid to ſome

(1) Rex *v.* Seagrave, Cald. 247. Bott, 333. Pl. 371.

(2) Rex *v.* Clayhydon, 4 Term Rep. 100. 2 Bott, 345. Pl. 382.

leading

leading feature, which may at leaſt point out a ſufficient analogy to aſſiſt the recollection; but they ſeverally contain circumſtantial particulars, which may have all thrown ſome weight, however ſmall, into the ſcale of judicial deciſion.

Grounds for diſtinguiſhing between diſpenſation and diſſolution.

The actual condition of the parties, the reaſons for leaving each other, the manner, and as it were temper of parting, are of importance in leading to ſuch a concluſion where the actual converſation between the maſter and his ſervant is equivocal and indeciſive. It is from theſe minute particulars that the concluſion muſt be drawn, if there are none of a more marked characteriſtic.

Thus it has been already ſeen, that where the ſervant paſſed the laſt three or four days of his year at his father's with his maſter's conſent, and afterwards when he received his year's wages, no deduction was made, it was conſidered as a diſpenſation with the ſervice (1). But a very ſlight alteration of circumſtances has been held to warrant a contrary determination; as where a ſervant eleven days before the expiration of his year went away with his maſter's conſent, *and took his clothes with him, and received his whole year's wages*, this was conſidered as a clear diſſolution of the contract, and that the ſervice was not conſtructively for a year (2).

But where, on the other hand, the pauper could not ſay whether he ſerved the laſt three days, or went away without ſerving them, but that he received his whole year's wages, "it was thought that this at leaſt ſeemed to imply the maſter's conſent or permiſſion (3)." Indeed this caſe might be ſupported on a further ground,

(1) Rex *v.* Undermilbeck, 5 Term Rep. 387. 2 Bott, 294. Pl. 335. *ante.*

(2) Rex *v.* Caſtlechurch, Burr, S. C. 68. 2 Bott, 312. Pl. 353.

(3) Rex *v.* Milwich, Burr. S. C. 433, 2 Bott, 209. Pl. 256.

that

that there being a doubt as to the fact of service for the last three days, the payment of the whole year's wages was proof of the service; for it is presumptive evidence, that the service is performed, since a title to the wages could only accrue to the servant thereby.

Effect of paying wages.

From these and the various other cases in which the manner of paying wages is stated, it appears that it is a circumstance which may serve to explain whether an act in itself equivocal amounts to a dispensation with service, or a dissolution of the contract. In this respect not only payment of the entire wages, or the subtracting of part, have been relied upon as material, but also whether it has been made at the time when the absence was about to take place, or delayed to the conclusion of the year. The payment of a year's wages gives rise to the presumption, that a year's service has been performed either actually or constructively; while a deduction of part gives equal strength to the contrary inference. If the payment is deferred to the expiration of the year, notwithstanding absence, it warrants a supposition, that the contract continued to subsist by which they were then made payable. On the other hand, if they have been discharged previously, they render it probable that a dissolution took place; for it is only in consequence of the agreement being terminated that the master could be compelled to make, or the servant enabled to enforce, payment. It may even afford room for some distinction, whether the deduction is made during the continuance of the year, when it is evidence of an intention on the master's part to dissolve the contract, and of an acquiescence by the servant; or at the termination, when the latter may be supposed to have surrendered his right to the whole, in the pressure of his immediate wants, or the apprehension of a tedious litigation. But

But these circumstances are only of importance where the case is doubtful in other respects.

Thus where a servant served a whole year except one week, which he neglected to serve, because he and his master could not agree respecting the wages he should have the ensuing year. He therefore quitted his service without *any compulsion* on the part of his master, a week before the year expired, but his master paid him his wages for the whole year. It was held that the words, " *without compulsion*," were to be understood that he had quitted the service by mutual consent, and therefore the service was interrupted (1).

37 Geo. 3. s. 22. Absence in militia.

By 37 Geo. III. 3. sect. 22. the inrolment of a servant as a militia-man, by virtue of that act shall not rescind the contract, or vacate the employment between him and his master, unless the militia in which he is inrolled shall be embodied or called out by his Majesty, or ordered so to be, in pursuance of the act, or unless he shall leave the service for the purpose of being trained and exercised for the space of twenty days in pursuance of the act, and shall not return to the same service at the end of such twenty days, or as soon after as reasonably may be, allowing an abatement from his wages in proportion to his absence from the service, to be settled by a justice of peace.

Dissolution by a magistrate.

It has been already shewn, that if the master applies to a justice to have his servant discharged, and his cause of complaint does not warrant it, the servant's dismissal against his consent, will not vitiate the service, where the magistrate makes no order, although he should be of opinion that it is a valid cause of discharge (2).

(1) Sheen v. Godalming, 2 Bott, 310. Pl. 350.

(2) Rex v. Hanbury, Burr. S.C. 322, *ante*, 236.

On the other hand, if the maſter and ſervant voluntarily, go before a magiſtrate, and the latter is diſcharged, it amounts to a ſolemn diſſolution of the contract (1).

The pauper was hired for a year at 55 ſhillings wages, and (if ſhe behaved well) two pounds of wool. She ſerved for about 8 months, when a diſpute happening with her maſter, about ſome ſtockings which had been burnt, he diſmiſſed her from his ſervice. She applied to a magiſtrate, and when before him was charged by her maſter, with neglecting to feed his pigs and burning the ſtockings. She was deſirous of continuing in the ſervice, but her maſter refuſed; and the magiſtrate ordered her maſter to take her back into his ſervice, *or pay her the whole of her wages*. He refuſed to take her again, but paid her the whole of the money, but not the wool. The pauper, from the time ſhe received her wages, offered herſelf as a ſervant ſoon after to ſeveral perſons. Lord Ellenborough, C. J. We are not called upon to ſay whether the magiſtrate had a right to diſcharge the ſervant from her ſervice; it is enough that he propoſed an option to the maſter, to take the ſervant back, or pay her the whole of her wages. The maſter refuſed to take her back, but agreed to pay the whole wages, and did pay them; and the ſervant ſhewed her aſſent to the diſſolution of the contract by taking the wages and offering her ſervices to other perſons. Both parties gave the magiſtrate the power of diſſolving the contract, by ſhewing their aſſent to what he directed in that reſpect. Then, after all this, could either the maſter or ſervant have maintained an action againſt each other, the one for not performing the remainder of the ſervice, the other for not employing her during that time? This is the true queſtion to be conſidered; and I ſhould not wiſh to carry the idea of diſpenſation further than it has been

(1) Rex *v.* North Baſham, Cald. 6, *ante*, 238, n. (3). As to how far a maſter can diſcharge his ſervant for immorality of conduct during ſervice, without the interference of a magiſtrate, *ſee poſt.* 255.

already

already carried : which in many of the caſes ſeems to me to have been ſtretched as far as ingenuity could go upon the falſe idea, that the ſervant had *a right* to acquire in gaining a ſettlement, as if he muſt not have a ſettlement at all events, in one place or another. I do not mean however to diſturb any of the caſes, which have been already decided ; but I am not inclined to carry the deciſions further from the plain words of 8 & 9 W. 3. c. 30. which are that no ſervant ſhall gain a ſettlement, " unleſs he ſhall continue and abide in " the ſame ſervice, during the ſpace of one whole year ; and it ſeems to me that when the parties ſtand in ſuch a ſituation, that neither the maſter can compel the ſervant to come back, nor the ſervant compel the maſter to take her back, and neither have any legal means of compelling redreſs againſt the other, that there is a diſſolution of the contract. Lawrence J. cited R. *v.* Thiſtleton, (1) R. *v.* St. Peter's (2), as deciding that if the maſter once parts with the control over his ſervant, and cannot call upon him for his ſervice, no ſettlement is gained (3).

This laſt caſe was decided upon the ground, that both parties went before a magiſtrate, *and agreed* to leave the deciſion of their diſpute to him, and he hearing what was urged on both ſides, gave an option to the maſter, to take the ſervant back, or pay her the whole year's wages, and both parties went away, acting as if they acquieſced in that determination (4).

But there has been a determination, that the contract of hiring between maſter and ſervant may be diſſolved even againſt their conſent, by an order of removal made and executed pending the ſervice, and unappealed from.

(1) *Ante*, 244. n. (1).
(2) *Ante*, 245. n. (1).
(3) Rex *v.* King's Pyon, 4 Eaſt. 351.
(4) *Per* Le Blanc J. 4 Eaſt. 355.

A ſerv-

A ſervant hired for a year ſerved till within ſix weeks of the expiration of his time, when he was taken up on a charge of baſtardy, and married next day. He then returned to his maſter, who had made no complaint, and did not diſcharge him. Two days afterwards he was removed by an order of removal to the place of his laſt ſettlement, where he continued four days, and then returned to his maſter's ſervice, who willingly received him again. He continued in his ſervice till the end of his year, which expired about a month after his return, when he was paid his full wages. Here the circumſtances of the pauper's apprehenſion on a charge of baſtardy and marriage were laid out of the queſtion, for it was competent to the maſter to receive him again after he was diſcharged out of cuſtody, if he pleaſed. But the two judges preſent thought that the order of removal being unappealed from, put an end to the ſervice, for the pauper could not legally return to the pariſh to fulfil his contract. He could not be liable to an action by his maſter for not completing it, (and if he had been indicted for diſobeying the order, it would have been no defence that he returned to complete his agreement. If the law intervenes, and ſays the party ſhall not complete the contract, it puts an end to it; and as the pauper ſerved only a month after his return, he could not gain a ſettlement; for the act ſubſequent to the order by which he was to gain a ſettlement, ſhould be complete in itſelf (1).

(1) Rex *v.* Kenilworth, 2 Term Rep. 598. 2 Bott, 340. Pl. 378. This caſe ſeems conſiderably ſhaken by Rex *v.* Fillongley, 2 Term Rep. 709. 2 Bott, 681. Pl. 743. For the magiſtrates have no right to put an end to a contract between parties without their conſent. Lord Kenyon ſtates as a diſtinction between that caſe and the preſent, that it was one of reſidence on a tenement, but this is of a maſter and ſervant, where juſtices have power to put an end to the contract. But in Rex *v.* Ozleworth, Burr. S. C. 302. 2 Bott, 314. Pl. 355, an order of removing a yearly ſervant, was quaſhed upon the ground that he was actually in the ſervice of his maſter, and could not be removed from ſuch ſervice. In Rex *v.* Marlborough, an or-

The

The ſervice hitherto ſhewn to be incomplete, is where a diſſolution of the contract had either taken place at the time when the ſervant was about to quit his maſter, or immediately upon his return; when in contemplation of law, it would be referred to the moment at which the abſence began.

III. Service incomplete, though contract continues.

We come now to conſider the third caſe of abſence during ſervice, namely, where the contract continues, but the maſter's conſent to the abſence cannot be implied (1).

That a ſettlement may be defeated by this means, ſeems to have been determined in one of the earlieſt reported caſes upon the queſtion of yearly ſervice.

Covenant ſervant.

A covenanted ſervant three weeks before the expiration of his year, quitted the ſervice with his maſter's conſent, and abated from his wages in proportion to that time. It was contended in favour of this being a good ſervice, that being a covenant ſervant, it muſt be preſumed to be by deed, which could not be diſcharged by parol conſent, and therefore he continued a hired ſervant during the year. But the court thought that for the purpoſe of ſettlement there was no difference between a covenant by deed, and an agreement by parol. If the hiring be by covenant perhaps it is not to be deſtroyed by ſuch conſent, and an

(1) *Ante*, 217.

der of removal of a maid ſervant, who had been got with child within the year of ſervice, was quaſhed, for till the year be out, none ſhall diſturb the party from ſerving; and ſince ſhe is not removeable, if ſhe leave her maſter without his conſent, ſhe may be ſent back to her ſervice. 12 Mod. 402. 2 Bott, 306, Pl. 346. See alſo Lord Mansfield, C. J. Rex *v* Brampton,' Cald. 11. 2 Bott, 323. Pl. 367. Rex *v*. Hardingham, Stiles 168. 2 Bott, 306. Pl. 345. 22 Reſol. of Judges of Aſſiſe 1633. Dalt. 235. and Rex *v*. Alvey, 3 Eaſt. 563.

action

action may be maintained on it; but as to a settlement, here is a clear discontinuance of the year's service. There is no fraud found, nor the appearance of any on the master's part: can he oblige his servant to gain a settlement *nolens volens?* The statute of 3 W. & M. c. 11. [8 & 9 W. III. c. 30.] says that he must serve a year; now this man has not served a year (1).

1. Servant's misbehaviour.

This class of cases exists only where there is no discharge by mutual consent, or a justice's order; and is reducible into two-kinds: 1. Where the servant misbehaves so as to entitle his master to discharge him, who in consequence prohibits his future service: 2. Where by reason of the master's ill conduct, the servant refuses to complete his agreement.

2. Master's misconduct.

Absence caused by the master.

According to the words of the statute, any interruption in the year's service renders it incomplete, unless there is a supposed assent by the master, or an exemption created by operation of law. Some cases seem adjudged upon this principle, although the contract for service continued to subsist; for the absence being wilful on the servant's part, and the master's assent directly negatived, there is nothing to warrant the inference of an implied consent. If the servant is guilty of such misconduct as justifies his master in forbidding the continuance of his service; as where a woman is pregnant, or a man the putative father, of a child likely to be born a bastard; and he does so, the service is incomplete, although the contract is not formally dissolved. It is no dispensation from service, for the master having a right to prevent its continuance and having done so, his consent that such absence shall be deemed service under the contract cannot be inferred against the fact. Neither is it constructive service by operation of law, for the law will not consider the service as performed during absence,

(1) Pawlet v. Burnham, 1 Geo. I. 2 Bott, 307. Pl. 347.

 where

where the master is guilty of no injustice in prohibiting, and the servant has no lawful excuse for not performing his duty (1).

Absence by the servant.

On the other hand, if the servant wilfully withdraw, either from his own, or his master's misconduct, this may be a mere interruption of service, in the first instance at the master's option, and at the servant's in the second.

But if the master request the servant to return and complete his service, and the latter refuse, it is impossible to imply the master's assent to subsequent absence, and the law can raise no inference in the servant's favour, against his refusal. Such cases may, and have occurred without an actual dissolution of the contract, since that cannot take place, unless by the interference of a magistrate, or by the parties' mutual consent (2).

The court seem however in some cases to have thought that the dismissal of a servant for immorality by the master, amounted to a dissolution of the contract, although it took place without a magistrate's intervention, and against the servant's consent.

Servant turned away with child.

A master finding his maid servant to be with child, turned her away three weeks before the expiration of the year, and paid her the whole year's wages, and half a crown over, whereupon she went home to her father's. The pauper said on her examination, that she was willing to stay her year out, if she might, as she was able to do the work; but it was immaterial to her whether she staid or went, as she had received her whole year's wages; and that she was not half gone with child when she left

(1) *Ante* 230.

(2) *Per* Lord Kenyon, Rex *v.* Grantham, 3 Term Rep. 754. 2 Bott, 343. Pl. 381, when the servant refused to stay. Temple *v.* Prescott, where the mistress discharged the servant not for immorality, but sauciness, Cald. 14, n. c.

her

her ſervice, and hoped ſhe could have done the work till the end of the year.

If the ſeſſions had ſtated as facts in this caſe what they ſet forth in evidence, there was perhaps ſufficient to warrant the inference of a diſſolution by conſent; but the court put it on the principle of an actual diſſolution by the maſter.

Lord Mansfield C. J. The queſtion then is, is this contract diſſolved within the year? the anſwer depends upon this; has the maſter done right or wrong in diſcharging the ſervant for this cauſe? I think he did not do wrong, the marginal note cited from Viner (1), whatever degree of authority it may be entitled to, is well warranted in principle, if the maſter agrees to the contract's going on, the overſeers it is true ſhall not take her away becauſe ſhe is with child; but ſhall the maſter therefore be bound to keep her in his houſe? to do ſo would be *contra bonos mores*; and in a family where there are young perſons, both ſcandalous and dangerous. Where a ſervant's abſence is ſaid to be purged (which is an improper expreſſion) by receiving him again, *the receiving only explains, and ſhews the nature of the abſence*; the conſequence of it indeed is, that ſuch a reception muſt generally be conſidered as amounting to a diſpenſation, and thereby ſubjects the maſter to the payment of the whole wages: *but the effect of a poſitive act of the maſter, i. e. the diſmiſſion of his ſervant*, ſhall never be done away by an implication ariſing from the payment of his whole wages (2).

So where a yearly ſervant in huſbandry, ſerved till three weeks before the expiration of his year, when the maſter on account of a *ſuppoſed* criminal intimacy between the pauper and a ſervant girl, then big with child, who

Servant for a ſuppoſed criminal intimacy with a girl with child.

(1) Rex *v.* Netlborough, Vin. Abr. tit. *Removal*, (c). 2 Bott, 306. Pl. 346.

(2) Rex *v.* Brampton, Cald. 11. 2 Bott, 328. Pl. 367.

had

had lived with the maſter, but was diſcharged from the ſervice, inſiſted upon his quitting the ſervice, and diſcharged him accordingly. The maſter offered him all his wages, but four ſhillings, which he inſiſted upon detaining as a ſatisfaction for the loſs of ſervice, for the three weeks. This, the pauper, who would have ſtaid if his maſter would have let him, refuſed to allow. The pauper after he was turned out, applied to a juſtice of peace to receive his full wages, but being told by him, that he could not, and having no money to ſubſiſt on, he accepted what his maſter had offered him, with the abatement for the three weeks. No order was made by a juſtice or juſtices for diſcharging him. The court ſeemed clear, that if the fact of criminality had been poſitively ſtated, it would have come within the principle of the foregoing caſe. It went down to be reſtated on that point, when the fact of criminality being poſitively found, the caſe was abandoned (1).

But ſuppoſing the maſter's right of diſſolving the contract to be eſtabliſhed by theſe deciſions, where a lawful cauſe of diſmiſſal exiſts, it will not reach caſes of abſence, by reaſon of an offence, for which the maſter has no authority to diſcharge the ſervant. Lord Mansfield and the court of King's Bench ſeem therefore to have "reſorted "in a ſubſequent caſe to the principle of incomplete ſer-"vice already ſtated" (2).

Servant hired after offences committed, and afterwards diſcharged for it.

A yearly ſervant was apprehended four days before the termination of his year, by a juſtice's warrant, charged by a woman with having gotten her with child, *which had been born a baſtard, about ſix months after the commencement of his year.* He was kept in cuſtody by the pariſh officers until the end of his year; his maſter on the day of his apprehenſion, ſettled his account of wages, ſaying he might not ſee him again: he then deducted one ſhilling

(1) Rex *v.* Walford, Cald. 57. 2 Bott, 330. Pl. 369.

(2) *Ante* 256, *et ſeq.*

on

on account of his not ſerving till the end of his year, ſaying that though he had no objection to the pauper gaining a ſettlement, yet that perhaps the other farmers might. The maſter did not in any other manner aſſent or diſſent from the abſence.

Lord Mansfield ſtated that he had no difficulty to ſay, that a maſter hiring a ſervant after an offence committed, and that not in his own houſe, ſhall not at the cloſe of the year diſcharge him under this pretence (1); I do not go upon that ground; nor upon the conſent or implied agreement, to go before the end of the year, for there was none; it was againſt the intention of both parties, that it ſhould affect the ſettlement. The true point is, ſuppoſing no wages paid, and no agreement, here are four days wanting in the ſervice, and it is by means of his own act, that the ſervant becomes incapable of completing it. His conduct is an offence againſt morality and the laws by what juriſdiction ſoever, thoſe laws are adminiſtered, and the conſequences of it are equivalent *to a wilful abſence.* If an action had been brought for his wages he could not recover upon a *quantum meruit* for thoſe four days. Buller J. There muſt be a year's ſervice either actual or implied; there is no actual ſervice, and the caſe affords no circumſtance that will warrant an implication; he did not gain a ſettlement (2).

The pauper within eight or nine days of the expiration of his year, was committed for not giving ſecurity to indemnify the pariſh as the father of a child likely to be born a baſtard, or entering into a recognizance to appear at the quarter ſeſſions, his maſter being one of the churchwardens, and one of the perſons that apprehended and went with him to Bridewell. The day on which his year

Abſence from confinement as father of a baſtard.

(1) *Quære* if this can extend to an unmarried female who is with child when hired, See Rex *v.* Brampton, *ante*, 259.

(2) Rex *v.* Weſtmeo, Cald. 129. 2 Bott, 331. Pl. 370.

 day,

expired, he gave his own bond to indemnify the pariſh, and on the ſame day, his maſter with the other officers went to diſcharge him; the maſter then paid him his wages agreed for, deducting four ſhillings (contrary to the pauper's conſent), for the time he had been in confinement; it was argued that the contract ſubſiſted till the end of the year, otherwiſe the wages would have been paid, when the pauper left the houſe, and alſo that it was a fraudulent act, in order to prevent a ſettlement.

Lord Mansfield C. J. The ſingle queſtion is whether the pauper ſerved his year? *In fact* he certainly did not. Did he then conſtructively? There is not a pretence that the maſter conſented to diſpenſe with the time, which the pauper did not ſerve: there is not a colour of fraud in the maſter's conduct. The ſervant's abſence was the conſequence of his own criminality. His impriſonment was not illegal. There is no doubt. Buller J. There muſt be either an actual or an implied ſervice; here is no actual ſervice: from whence is the court to imply one? (1).

What proves that there is no abſolute diſſolution of the contract in theſe caſes is, that abſence on this account, may be cured like any other, by the maſter's taking the ſervant back again. Thus where a yearly ſervant was apprehended on a charge of baſtardy, married the next day, and his maſter did not make any complaint, or diſcharge him from his ſervice. On the third day he was removed to his ſettlement, but returned to his maſter, (being abſent in the whole nine days), who received him and paid him his full year's wages. *Per* Buller J. the circumſtance of the pauper's having been apprehended on a charge of baſtardy, and of his marriage I lay entirely out of the queſtion, for it was competent to the maſter to receive him again after he was diſcharged out of cuſtody if he pleaſed, and the ſervant

(1) Rex *v.* North Cray Cald. 495. 2 Bott 334. Pl. 373.

might

might have ſerved his maſter after he was married as well as before (1).

There are ſome caſes however in which it was unneceſſary to reſort to this rule, in order to determine the ſettlement, becauſe a diſſolution of the contract, evidently took place by conſent. **May be a diſſolution by conſent.**

As where the pauper being hired from Michaelmas to Michaelmas, at ſeven pounds wages, ſerved till May, when hearing that there was a warrant out againſt him for getting a baſtard child; he went to his maſter, and told him, he muſt be off, and aſked him for money to go off with. His maſter gave him three guineas and a half, and he ran away, leaving ſome clothes and his threſhing tackle, but was taken up two or three days after, and obliged to marry the woman. After nine days abſence he returned to his maſter's houſe for his threſhing tackle and clothes which he had left behind; upon which his maſter ſaid, "where are you going," and the pauper anſwered, "I don't know;" upon which the maſter ſaid, "you may as well work for me again, as for any other," to which the pauper agreed, and continued to work there to the end of the year without any freſh agreement, and at the expiration received, including the three guineas and a half before paid him, his ſeven pounds wages, all but half-a-crown, which the maſter deducted for his abſence. The pauper when he ran away, never thought of going back to him again, but conſidered himſelf as diſcharged. It was conſidered that this was a diſſolution of the contract. When the ſervant deſired to be off, it meant from the ſervice, and when he went back, he does not claim to be reſtored in his ſtate as a ſervant upon the old agreement, but he comes back for his clothes; and then the conver-

(1) Rex v. Kenilworth, 2 Term Rep. 558. 2 Bott. 340. Pl. 378. ante 255.

ſation that took place on both ſides is deciſive evidence of a new contract (1).

2 Maſter's miſcon-duct (3).

The ſecond caſe is, where the ſervant refuſes to perform his contract by reaſon of the maſter's ill uſage. As where three days before the expiration of the ſervant's year, his maſter came home in liquor, abuſed the pauper, threw him down and afterwards turned him out of doors. The next morning the maſter would have had him return to his ſervice and ſtay the remainder of the year; but the pauper refuſed, and threatened, that unleſs he paid him the whole of his wages, he would complain of the ill uſage he had received to a magiſtrate. The maſter then agreed to pay him his full year's wages, and he left the ſervice contrary to the expreſs requeſt of his maſter. *Per* Lord Kenyon, C. J. It has been urged that this was an abſence for a reaſonable cauſe on account of the ill treatment of the maſter; but here there was no *animus revertendi*, which diſtinguiſhes the preſent from the claſs of caſes alluded to. The ſervant was ill uſed, though he could not have left the ſervice without his maſter's conſent, or without applying to a magiſtrate to be diſcharged, yet the maſter did conſent to the ſervant's leaving him, and both agreed to put an end to the contract. Aſhurſt, J. The paying the whole wages was not intended to operate as a diſpenſation of the remainder of the ſervice, but in redemption of the maſter's credit (2).

Servant turned out.

Servant beaten.

So where a ſervant ſixteen days before the expiration of her year was kicked and beaten by her maſter, ſhe complained to her father of the ill treatment, and in conjunction with her father, required her maſter to diſmiſs her, under a threat of applying to a magiſtrate for redreſs on account of the aſſault. The maſter then paid her the

(1) Rex *v.* Eaſt Kennet. Cald. Rep. 754. 2 Bott, 343. Pl. 381. 562. 2 Bott, 336. Pl. 37.

(2) Rex *v.* Grantham, 3 Term

(3) *Ante*, 245.

whole

whole year's wages, and told her ſhe might ſerve the remainder of the year; but ſhe refuſed ſo to do, and left the ſervice; this was conſidered as a clear agreement to put an end to the contract, before the expiration of the year, on the authority of the foregoing caſe (1).

Finally, where a yearly ſervant continued to ſerve until within a fortnight or three weeks of the expiration of the year, when in conſequence of his maſter's kicking him, he would not ſtay, but went to his father's houſe; he returned before the end of the year with his father, and received the whole of his wages, and half a crown for himſelf, his maſter aſked him to ſtay, *but he refuſed*, and went back to his father's houſe. The year's ſervice was held incomplete, upon the authority of the two preceding caſes. The payment of the whole year's wages, was to prevent an action, and argues no conſent on the maſter's part to diſpenſe with the ſervice (2).

Theſe caſes ſeem to reſt upon the ground of a diſſolution by conſent, which the ſecond appears to have been; but in the others, there was, from what Lord Mansfield calls "a wilful abſence," a defect in the ſervice, and it ſeems difficult to infer a diſſolution by conſent, eſpecially in Rex *v.* Grantham, where it is found that the pauper left the ſervice contrary to the expreſs requeſt of his maſter (3).

SECT. IV. Part II.

Of connecting Services under ſeveral Hirings.

The 8 & 9 W. 3. c. 30. enacts, that the perſon ſhall not only be hired for a year, but continue and abide in the ſame ſervice for that period. *Same ſervice what?*

(1) Rex *v.* Upwele, 7 Term Rep. 438. 2 Bott, 357. Pl. 487.

(2) Rex *v.* Corſham, 2 Eaſt. 303.

(3) Lord Kenyon ſtates however that "both parties agreed to put an "end to the contract."

the

A year's ſervice may be under different contracts of hiring, performed with different maſters, and in different places. It is therefore neceſſary to examine how far it is conſidered as *the ſame*, notwithſtanding the occurrence of any, or all theſe circumſtances.

Year's ſervice not to be under yearly hiring.

Although 3 & 4 W. 3. requires an hiring, and 8 and 9. W. 3. ſervice for a year, yet the ſervice need not be performed under the yearly hiring. They muſt be co-extenſive in duration, but need not be cotemporaneous; for the ſtatutes do not expreſsly declare that the ſervice ſhall be for that year for which the ſervant is hired, or even for a whole year afterwards. The words are ſatisfied, if there be an hiring, and a ſervice for a year; and it is ſaid that the intention is alſo complied with, " which was to prevent perſons of no credit " from intruding into pariſhes; the hiring for a year " being thought neceſſary to ſhew that the perſon had " credit enough to be hired for that time by a pariſhioner, " who had ſo much confidence in him. And another " conſideration was, the benefit received by the pariſh " from perſons' labour for a whole year." (1)

Service therefore under a yearly hiring, will connect with ſervice under other hirings, but ſubject to certain rules and reſtrictions.

Reaſon of connecting Services.

This conſtruction was given to the ſtatutes ſoon after the 8 & 9 W. 3. paſſed (2). It was founded on a ſtrict interpretation of their proviſions, which the court would

(1) *Per* Lee C. J. citing Lord Macclesfield C. J. Rex *v.* Fifehead Magdalen Burr. S. C. 116. 2 Bott, 254. Pl. 301. Rex *v.* Croſcombe, Burr. S. C. 256. 2 Bott, 279. Pl. 325.

(2) 10. W. 3. Rex *v.* Overton. Burr. S. C. 543. 2 Bott, 247. Pl. 293.

not

not carry beyond the letter, from an opinion that they were restrictive of the subject's liberty, and in derogation of a common law birth-right, (1) and that the power given to parish-officers should be confined to narrow limits, since the dread or suspicion of anticipated burthens, by reason of future poverty, might form the sole reason for removing the industrious poor (2). But judges, who have held themselves bound by the authority of this decision, have questioned its propriety (3). Indeed, the design of the statute seems to point to a contrary construction; and it has been stated, that the place of settlement can be of no consequence to the pauper, since he is equally intitled to support, wherever it may be (4).

Of connecting the year's service and hiring.

But as the law stands settled, if there is an hiring from March to Michaelmas, *and then an hiring for a year*; service, under the first hiring, may be connected with service from Michaelmas to the ensuing April, under the year's hiring, and confers a settlement, although the servant leave his place in April, and never fulfills his yearly contract (5). This is put as one of several parallel instances to be met with in the books, and

(1) Holy Trinity, *v*. Garfington, Caf. Sett. & Remov. 72. 2 Bott, 157. Pl. 201. Per Probyn J. Rex *v*. Fifehead Magdalen *ante* n. (1) Rex *v*. Aynhoe *post* n (3) *Per* Lord Mansfield, Under Barrow and Bradley, Field, Burr. S. C. 548.

Settlements are given as a reward for labour, and the poor-laws in favour of them have always been construed liberally, because they are made in restraint of liberty; every man being anciently free to go wherever he had the best probability of maintaining himself. This was decided by the court in the case of Holy Trinity *v*. Garfington." *Per* Lee J. St. Maurice *v*. St. Mary Kallendar. 2 Bott, 158. Pl. 203.

(2) *Ante* 146. But the law is altered in this respect by 35. Geo. 3, c. 101. *ante* 148.

(3) Rex *v*. Aynhoe. 2 Bott, 251. Pl. 298.

(4) *Ib. Per* Lord Raymond, &c. *Per* Lord Ellenborough. Rex *v*. King's Pyon, 4 East. 351.

(5) Rex *v*. Overton, *ante* 266. n (2)

which

which differ from each other only in accidental particulars only (1).

Duration of the minor hirings, and nature of the services immaterial.

The mere circumstances of the number and duration of the hirings are immaterial to the connection of services, provided one is for a year. The rest may be for successive years (2), or months, or even weeks (3). Neither is it necessary that the services to be performed under each should be *of the same kind.* It may be as an out-door servant under one, and a family servant under the other (4). He may be employed, first, to milk and plough, and secondly, as a carter (5).

In most of the reported cases which involve the question of connected service, the minor hirings under which the service was performed have *preceded* the contract of hiring for a year.

Qu. Whether such service may be subsequent to the yearly hiring?

But another question arises; namely, how far service under minor hirings, subsequent to the agreement for a year's service, will unite with antecedent service under that agreement. Such a case cannot occur unless there is a dissolution of the original yearly hiring, and an unbroken continuance of the service under some other. This may happen within the year for which the yearly hiring was made, as there may be a year's connected service during that period, and yet not under the yearly contract;

(1) Service under a minor hiring for 11 months was held to connect with service for eleven months under an hiring for the succeeding year. Brightwell *v.* Westhalley. 2 Bott, 249. Pl. 296. See also Hanmere *v.* Ellesmere, *ib.* 253. Pl. 299. 2 Stra. 878. Eardisland *v.* Leominster. 2 Bott, 253. Pl. 300. Rex *v.* Under. Barrow and Bradley. Field, *ante* 262. n (1). Rex *v.* Croscombe, Burr. S. C. 256 2 Bott, 279. Pl. 325.

(2) Rex *v.* Croscombe, *ante*, n (1)

(3) Rex *v.* Bagworth, Cald. 179. 2 Bott, 262. Pl. 368. Where the Minor hirings were by the week, and the wages received by the week, and the pauper considered himself at liberty to part at the end of any one week. Rex *v.* Sutton, 1 East. 656.

(4) In Rex *v.* Great Chilton. 5. Term. Rep. 672. 2 Bott, 268. Pl. 313.

(5) Rex *v.* Sutton, *ante*, n (3).

for

for the parties may diſſolve their original agreement, and enter into a new engagement on the ſame day, under which the ſervant may ſerve the remainder of his year.

Thus if a ſervant be hired for a year, and having ſerved a month, agrees to ſerve eleven under a new bargain, there is an hiring for a year, and connected ſervice for a year, but not under the yearly hiring. Looking to the principle upon which ſervices are allowed to connect with the year's hiring, there ſeems no reaſon why ſuch ſervice ſhould not confer a ſettlement, unleſs a *voluntary* diſſolution of the year's contract prevents the union of ſucceſſive ſervices.

The various caſes in which conſtructive ſervice is ſtated to depend, ſolely upon the circumſtance *whether there has been a diſpenſation with ſervice*, or *a diſſolution of the contract*, ſeem to aſſume by this ſtatement of the queſtion, that ſuch ſervices do not connect (1).

But none of the caſes upon the ſufficiency of ſervice, turn ſolely upon the point of diſſolution. A chaſm was created in the ſervice by abſence, after the contract was diſſolved (2).

This doubt, although not expreſsly decided, ſeems at leaſt, collaterally determined in Rex *v* Grendon Underwood (3). The pauper, on the Friday before Michaelmas-day, was hired from Michaelmas to be a carter, and had 1*s.* earneſt, and was to have 6*l.* wages, and go into his maſter's ſervice the Wedneſday after Michaelmas-day. The pauper accordingly came that day to his maſter's, where he had ſome refreſhment; and his maſter told him he had hired another ſervant in the place

Collateral determination. Rex v. Grendon Underwood.

(1) *Ante*, 217.
(2) *Ante*, 242 *et Seq.*
(3) Cald. 359. 2 Bott, 263. Pl. 310.

he

he had hired him to do; but that he wanted a man to milk and go to plough, and if he liked that work, he might ſtay: The pauper thinking himſelf not well uſed, refuſed that ſervice, and the maſter told him he might keep his earneſt, and go about his buſineſs; upon which the pauper ſaid, "Am I at liberty to hire my-"ſelf to any other perſon?" and his maſter anſwered him in the affirmative; both the maſter and pauper looking upon themſelves at liberty from their contract with each other. Upon this, the pauper left his maſter's houſe, taking his clothes with him, and went to an alehouſe about half a mile off in another pariſh. In the courſe of the ſame afternoon, the maſter met with him there, *and hired him to ſerve the place of milkman, and to go to plough, and gave him* 2s. 6d. *earneſt, and agreed to give him* 6l. 6s. *wages to ſerve him from that time till Michaelmas*; upon which the pauper immediately entered into his maſter's ſervice, and continued therein until the next February; when his maſter's carter having left his place, *his maſter hired him to ſerve the place of carter from that time to Michaelmas, and gave him* 1s. *earneſt, and agreed to give him* 10s. 6d. *additional wages*; and the pauper continued in the ſervice until the Michaelmas, and received his wages.

Here were three diſtinct hirings, bound by different earneſts, and at various rates of wages. The only queſtion raiſed was, whether the original hiring from Michaelmas was an hiring for a year, with a diſpenſation of ſervice until the enſuing Wedneſday; or whether it was a hiring from that Wedneſday, and therefore ſhort of a year by the interval from the preceding Michaelmas. But as it was admitted, that the year's ſervice was complete, the caſe decides, that ſervice under ſubſequent minor hirings will connect with that under the original yearly engagement.

The

The question might also have arisen in Rex *v.* Winterfett (1); but that case was decided on the ground *that no service had taken place under the original hiring.* Buller J. relied particularly upon that circumstance, as forming the distinction between it and Rex *v.* Grendon Underwood. Rex *v.* Winterfett.

The incompatibility of such services to unite, would also have decided Rex. *v.* Adson (2), in which there was a dissolution of the contract within the year, and an uninterrupted service for the remainder under a new agreement, but the point was not made. The inference, that it was not mentioned because untenable, derives much weight, from considering that the judges originally differed in opinion (3). Indeed, no solid distinction seems to exist between contracts which expire by efflux of time, and those which are put an end to by mutual consent in order to let the parties into a new agreement, and the principle which regulates their connectability in one case seems equally applicable to the other. Rex. *v.* Adson.

It may perhaps therefore be laid down in general, that services will connect in all cases of distinct contracts, so as to satisfy the statutes where the following rules are observed. Rules for connecting Service.

First, the service must constitute one entire unbroken year's service. Any interruption, though but for a single day, during which the servant is legally exempt from his master's controll, will defeat it. As where a person five days after Michaelmas was hired from thence to the Michaelmas following, on which day *he departed* from his master's service, and was paid his wages to that time. *On the day after* he returned, and covenanted 1. Service must be uninterrupted, &c.

(1) *Ante*, 246.

(2) 5 Term Rep. 98. *Post.*

(3) See also the Observations of Buller, J. in Rex *v.* Alton, as reported, 2 Bott, 222. Pl. 265, *ante*, 241.

with

with his ſaid maſter to ſerve him for another year; and lived with him for eleven months. *Per* Powis, judge of aſſize. The ſervices will not connect ſo as to give a ſettlement: there is no hiring for a year, *nor ſervice for a year purſuant to the hiring* (1). So a perſon hired for a year ſerved till within three weeks of the end of it, when with his own conſent, he was diſcharged by his maſter, on ſome diſpute between them. He was abſent a fortnight, and then went into the ſervice again, at the requeſt of his miſtreſs, his maſter being from home. Whilſt there, and within a week after the expiration of the firſt year, his maſter hired him for another year, of which he ſerved ſix months. The ſervices are not continued as is required by the ſtatute, for there is a chaſm of a fortnight between them, during which the ſervant was diſcharged from his maſter's ſervice (2).

Fraction of a day, no interruption.

But where the firſt ſervice terminates, and a new contract is made upon the ſame day, as the law makes no fraction of a day, unleſs in ſome ſpecial caſes, and the ſervant is under his maſter's control by the original agreement for the whole of that time, a departure from ſervice during that day has been held not to amount to ſuch a diſcontinuance as will diſconnect the ſervices. It is only a pauſe to enable the ſervant to conſider whether he will abſolutely quit the ſervice or not (3). Thus, a ſervant was hired, and lived with his maſter for three quarters of a year to Lady-Day. On that day he received his wages and left the ſervice. He then went to his father's houſe, not having had any diſcourſe with his maſter about continuing in the ſervice. When he had been about an hour with his father, the latter adviſed him to

(1) Wickford *v.* Bretford, Fort. 311. But the opinion as there expreſſed ſeems to go againſt the connection of ſervices under different contracts in all caſes.

(2) Rex *v.* Caverſwall. Burr. S. C. 461. 2 Bott, 256. Pl. 302, *ante* 243.

(3) *Per* Lord Kenyon, C. J. In Rex *v.* Grantham. 3 Term. Rep. 754. 2 Bott, 343. Pl. 382.

go

go to his maſter, and ſee if he could not agree with him for a year. He accordingly went thereupon, and agreed for another year, ſerved half of it, and was then turned off. It was held that he gained a ſettlement; for there was a yearly hiring, and a complete year's ſervice. It was not diſcontinued. The ſervant was a little doubtful about a new contract; he went to conſult his father, and in an hour's time returned and made one. "Upon "every new contract there is a ſort of diſcontinuance. "The laſt day of the former contract is the firſt day of "the ſecond ſervice; and this was only an hour's ab-"ſence within the ſpace of that ſame day; therefore he "remained a ſervant during the whole time of the com-"pletion of his year." (1)

Fraction of a day no diſcontinuance.

The ſame point was ſubſequently determined in another caſe. The ſervant had left the houſe and ſervice, and received his wages on the laſt day of his hiring. His maſter came to him half an hour afterwards, and deſired him to ſtay with him, but the pauper required a ſum for his wages, which the maſter refuſed, ſaying *he ſhould ſee him at the fair.* At one o'clock the ſame day he made an agreement with his maſter at the fair, and ſerved a month, which connected with his prior ſervice made up his year. The only difference between theſe caſes is, that in the laſt, the pauper made a new contract, and obtained an increaſe of wages. But there is no abandonment nor diſcontinuance of the ſervice (2).

Connecting ſervice under implied contracts.

In theſe inſtances the contracts under which the ſervice was performed were expreſs. But it does not make any difference if the minor contract exiſts by implica-

(1) Rex *v.* Fifehead Magdalen. Burr. S. C. 116. 2 Bott, 254. Pl. 301.

(2) Rex *v.* Ellisfield. Cald. 4. 2 Bott, 259. Pl. 305.

tion, or is made conditionally, since service for a year under such hirings would have been sufficient.

Service under an implied hiring.

The pauper was hired from November till Michaelmas, at six pounds ten shillings, and two or three days before the expiration of his time, his master offered him the same wages for the year ensuing, which the pauper did not think sufficient. On Michaelmas-day they had agreed for wages, all but the expence of washing. The servant had no intention of leaving his master, and he believed his master had no intention of parting with him. He continued in his master's house, and did what was to be done as usual; neither removing his clothes, nor offering himself to any other master; nor did the latter seek another servant. On the second day after Michaelmas-day he agreed to his master's terms, and served him for some months, amounting to more than sufficient to make up a year, if this service could connect with that under his former agreement. It was held to do so; for during the time between the first contract and the hiring for a year on the second day after Michaelmas, the servant continued in the same capacity, and did his work as usual. The law therefore implied that he continued under the former agreement, and was entitled to receive wages in the same proportion (1).

This case may be supported upon another principle, viz.; that on Michaelmas-day every thing was agreed upon, except the expence of washing; and as the servant continued in the service, the agreement in fact took place on Michaelmas-day, but subject to a condition by which it might be defeated; namely, if the parties could not agree as to the washing.

(1) Rex v. Sulgrave, 1. Term Rep. 778. 2 Bott, 266. Pl. 311. See also Rex v. Croscombe, Burr. S. C. 236. 2 Bott, 279. Pl. 325. *Post.*

The

The ſecond requiſite is, that the maſter ſhall have the ſame degree of control and authority over his ſervant during the entire year under all the contracts, as would be neceſſary to give a ſettlement where the ſervice is performed under one yearly hiring. II. The ſervant muſt be under the maſter's controll, &c.

They muſt contain no ſpecial exemption from labour either of days or hours, and be ſubject to the ſame rules preciſely as regulate the contract for a year's ſervice under the ſtatute of 3 & 4 W. 3. (1) Muſt contain no exemption.

A girl was hired under a weekly agreement at weekly wages to burl cloth, and when paid her wages every week on Saturday, was told "that ſhe ſhould come the "week following;" which ſhe did accordingly, *and renewed the contract* for the week enſuing. Here the ſervant was not under her maſter's controll from Saturday night until Monday morning, and therefore did not gain a ſettlement by her ſervice (2). Weekly hiring to burl cloth.

But where the pauper hired himſelf by the week, and nothing was ſaid about Sunday in the contract, but he worked on that day occaſionally, when aſked by his maſter, without receiving any additional wages, only ſometimes victuals—He received his wages weekly, and lodged and boarded himſelf. Having ſerved thus for nine months, he was hired by his maſter for a year, as a family ſervant, and ſerved eleven months. It was held that theſe ſervices did connect ſo as to form a ſettlement.—Becauſe nothing being ſaid about Sunday in the contract, it is to be inferred that it is included; and therefore the ſervant was under his maſter's controll during the whole of the week under each weekly hiring, juſt as much as he was under that for a year. But it was taken for granted, as

(1) *Ante*, 209, *et ſeq.*

(2) Rex *v.* Wrington. Burr. S. C. 280. 2 Bott, 180. Pl. 234.

T 2 beyond

beyond doubt, that if he had not been so, the services would not have connected (1).

These two rules are nothing more than an application to successive hirings of the principle so often referred to, as prevailing universally where the service is under one yearly hiring; namely, that when the contract is discontinued, and "the master has parted with all his authority, any interruption in the service incurably destroys "the settlement."

Both species of service are subject therefore to the same rules. If the parties agree that there shall be a chasm in the service, and provide for it by an exception in any of the contracts, it defeats the Settlement (2). If no such exception is made, but an interval intervene in fact, even from Saturday night to Monday morning, (as in the case of burling cloth) it equally destroys it. For this is no more than the common case of absence after a dissolution, where an intention to recommence the relation at a future period avails nothing (3).

But absence during the continuance of any minor hiring may be cured in the same manner, and upon the same principles, that apply to Cases of Dispensation under one yearly hiring.

III. Must be unmarried, &c.

The third rule necessary to render services connectable, does not apply to cases where the yearly contract and service are simultaneous. In this latter case, if the servant's marriage takes place after an agreement of hiring has been entered into, a settlement is not thereby prevented. But it has been held, that the servant must be unmarried at the commencement of that yearly hiring, by which he claims

(1) Rex *v.* Sutton. 1 East, 656.
(2) See *ante*, 209.
(3) *Ante*, 275. n. (2.)

a set-a ſettlement, as well where the contract is implied, in conſequence of ſervice protracted to a ſecond year, as where it is made in expreſs terms.

The pauper went into ſervice under a general hiring, in the pariſh of St. Mary, and ſerved there ſeven months when he married his preſent wife. After his marriage he remained in his maſter's ſervice, in the ſaid pariſh, four months, when he took lodgings in the pariſh of St. Giles, and removed thither with his wife; where he ſlept for ſeven months, and continued to ſerve his maſter without coming to any new hiring. Having ſerved for eighteen months in the whole, he left the ſervice. It was held by the judges, after taking time to conſider, that he gained no ſettlement in St. Giles's, where he reſided the laſt ſeven months.

Marriage before ſecond yearly hiring.

For 3 W. & M. c. 11. and 8 & 9 W. 3. c. 3. require that the ſervant ſhall be unmarried, and without children at the time of hiring into the pariſh. There was no reſidence for forty days in St. Giles's, under the firſt hiring, but only for a month; and there was an implied contract of ſervice for the ſecond year, under which he reſided in that pariſh for the laſt ſix months of his ſervice. If it had been expreſs, he could not gain a ſettlement under it, as he was married when he made it; and he cannot by an implied contract do that which in expreſs and direct terms he could not do (1).

This determination related only to the condition of the ſervant when hired for the year: but in a ſubſequent caſe it is laid down as a general rule; that, "in order to gain "a ſettlement by hiring and ſervice, there muſt be an "hiring for a year, and a ſervice for a year, and the "ſervice for the laſt forty days muſt be performed

(1) Rex *v.* St. Giles. Cald. 54. 2 Bott, 260. Pl. 206, *ante*, 189.

"under a contract of hiring entered into when the pauper was unmarried."

Servant marries between first and second hiring.

A man being unmarried, was hired for a year, as a servant in husbandry, to live in the house. He afterwards married, and at the end of six months service, put an end to his original contract by coming to a new agreement with his master for a year from that time; thereby agreeing to live out of the house. He removed under this last hiring to another farm, which his master had *in the same township*, and lived there for two years with his master, and was held not to acquire a settlement (1).

Here was a hiring for a year, the person unmarried at the time, service for a year, and marriage during its continuance. If the original contract had continued, the servant would have gained a settlement, notwithstanding the intermarriage. This is admitted in argument by all the judges, and expressly relied upon by Lord Kenyon C. J. who differed from the rest of the court, upon the ground that the first contract was not dissolved. If the reasoning used in the antecedent part of this section be just, it is equally clear that the mere act of dissolving the first agreement by consent, would not prevent the settlement, for there was an hiring for a year, service under it for six months, and uninterrupted service for much more than the remainder of a year under a new contract (2). The only ground then of the determination is, the circumstance of marriage relied upon by two of the learned judges in delivering their opinions. Mr. J. Ashurst states in general terms, "that if the second be a contract distinct from the former one, the services under "the two cannot be coupled, for the purpose of giving

(1) Rex v. Great Chilton, 5. Pl. 313. *ante*, 240. Term Rep. 672. 2 Bott, 268. (2) *Ante*, 269.

"the

" the pauper a ſettlement, becauſe at the time of enter-
" ing into the ſecond he was married."

Mr. J. Lawrence confining his opinion to what was required by the caſe before him, declared, " that the " ſervice for the laſt forty days muſt be performed " under a contract of hiring entered into when the " pauper was unmarried." (1)

The firſt of theſe two caſes, if literally conſidered, goes only to determine, that marriage previous to the yearly hiring, under which a ſettlement is ſought, prevents one being gained; and the laſt, that if the ſervant is married at the time of the hiring, whether yearly or otherwiſe, under which he ſerves the laſt forty days, he cannot acquire one.—But a ſervant may complete a year's ſervice under more contracts than two, and may (at leaſt in poſſibility) marry after entering into the firſt, and get quit of the diſability previous to that hiring under which his final reſidence of forty days takes place. Thus, in the laſt caſe, if the pauper's wife had died a month or two after he had made his ſecond agreement, and he had then entered into a new one, and ſerved a ſufficient time to complete his year, his ſettlement would not be expreſsly decided by theſe authorities; for he was unmarried at the time of his yearly hiring, which ſatiſfied the firſt, and alſo when he made the contract under which he reſided the laſt forty days, which is all that is required by the ſecond.

Obſervations on Rex *v.* St. Giles, and Rex *v.* Great Chilton.

The opinion of Mr. J. Aſhurſt however is expreſs; that " marriage in all caſes prevents an union between " ſervices performed under contracts antecedent and ſub- " ſequent thereto."

(1) *Ante*, 277.

Rex *v.* Great Chilton decides, that the servant must be exempt from statutory disability, not only at the time when he is hired for a year, but also when he enters into that agreement under which he completes his year's service; there seems no principle therefore which warrants a less general rule, than what is laid down by the learned judge; namely, that *the servant must be unmarried, and (upon the same ground) without unemancipated children, not only at the commencement of the first, but of every succeeding contract, under which that year's service is performed, through which* he seeks to gain a settlement (1).

What service is necessary under a yearly hiring to connect with minor hirings.

The next question is, whether any, and what service must be performed under the yearly hiring, for the purpose of connecting it with service under agreements to serve for a shorter period? It seems to have been at one time a received opinion, that there must be a service of forty days under the yearly hiring, because residence for so long was necessary, to gain a settlement under 3 W. and M. c. 4.; and the 8 and 9 W. 3. was not intended to reduce the time of residence required by that statute, but to increase the service. According to one report, Lord C. J. Parker was of that opinion, as he lays it down, that if "a servant during a whole year is hired from week "to week, then is hired for a year and serves one week; "this is no settlement, for want of a continuance in "the service forty days after the second hiring (2).

But this doctrine seems overuled; it being determined in a recent case by the two judges then upon the bench, that

(1) This rule states only that the servant must be free from statutory disability *at the commencement of each contract*. But he may marry during *the continuance of one of* them, and his wife die before he makes the other. Such would be the case if an unmarried person, having agreed to serve for eleven months, marries during this service; his wife dies before the 11 months expire, at the end of which he is hired to his master for a year, but the contract is dissolved after three months service.

(2) Rex *v.* Brightwell, 10 Mod. 287. See also the reasoning of the court in Eardisland *v.* Leominster. 2 Bott, 253. Pl. 300.

that ſervice for forty days under the yearly hiring is not neceſſary, but that ſervice under it for ten days, if coupled with antecedent ſervices under former hirings, confers a ſettlement (1). Upon the authority and principle of this caſe, ſervice for a day, under a yearly contract, will connect with prior ſervices ſo as to ſatisfy the ſtatute. But whether there muſt not be that day to connect them, is no where expreſsly decided.

It would be a ſtrong caſe, if when there had been twelve hirings of a month each, and upon the laſt day of the laſt month, a contract to ſerve for a year, and no ſervice under it, that the ſervant ſhould thereby acquire a ſettlement. It would be a ſtronger caſe, although perhaps not diſtinguiſhable in principle, if an agreement for a year's ſervice ſhould confer a ſettlement by reaſon of a diſtinct year of connected ſervice performed in the ſame pariſh, under ſeveral hirings at any interval of time, however great. The reaſons given in the books for ſeparating the ſervice from the hiring, is ſatisfied in this ſuppoſed caſe, as well as where part of the ſervice is performed under the yearly agreement. The words of the ſtatute are complied with; for there is an hiring for a year, and ſervice for a year. The pariſh has had a year's ſervice, which is the conſideration of the ſettlement, and the pauper (except in caſes of fraud) has found a pariſhioner who conſiders him a perſon of ſufficient credit to be hired for a year (2).

On the other hand there is no foreſeeing the conſequences of ſuch a deciſion, and perhaps the contract being completely executory, and never entered upon, would be conſidered as not being of that ſpecies of lawful hiring *into* a pariſh which the ſtatute requires (3).

(1) Rex *v.* Adſon, 5 Term Rep. 98. 2 Bott, 268. Pl. 312. The judges, Lord Kenyon and Groſe differed at firſt in opinion, but agreed, after taking time to conſider.

(2) *Ante*, 266.

But

Construction service sufficient.

But at all events, constructive service under these minor hirings seems sufficient (1); upon the same principles that it is held to satisfy the statute when there has been a single hiring (2).

SECT. IV. Part III.

Of Service with different Masters.

Service with different masters.

SERVICE performed with different masters is an abiding in the same service, and confers a settlement where the contract continues unaltered in other respects.

Service with an executor.

A servant hired for a year, served about half of it, when his master died. The executor asked him, if he was willing to serve him for the remainder of the year, *according to the bargain made between the testator and him.* The pauper assented, and served him in another parish, where the executor lived during the remainder of the year, when he received his wages. It was held that he gained a settlement in the executor's parish.—For the act of parliament does not require the service to be the same as to place and persons, but only a continuance of *the same service.* And this is a continuance of the same service and not a new contract—The contract was not dissolved by the master's death. The servant was obliged to serve the executor, and the executor to pay him (3).

Service with the assignee of a farm.

So where the pauper being hired as a shepherd to one Knight, for a year from Michaelmas, continued in his service till Lady-day, when Knight paid him half a year's

(1) See Rex *v.* Wintersett, *ante*, 246.

(2) Rex *v.* Grendon Underwood, *ante*, 269.

(3) Rex *v.* Ladock, Burr. S. C. 149. 2 Bott, 277. Pl. 323.

wages, and left the farm to one Smith, who entered, and took all the ſtock and ſervants. In harveſt-time Smith took the pauper off from keeping ſheep, at which he continued ſince Knight's departure, and ſet him to harveſt-work, for which he paid him five ſhillings extraordinary, and at the year's end paid him the other half-year's wages. Knight, when he left the farm, never told the pauper that he was no more his ſervant; nor was there any tranſactions between them towards diſſolving the contract. Neither did Smith ever make any new contract for the laſt half year. It was held that this was a continuance in the *ſame ſervice.* The original contract with Knight continued, and the ſervice to Smith ſhall be taken to be a ſervice to Knight; for the ſervant had never given his conſent to change his maſter, and it could not be done without it, and he had a right to look to Knight for payment of his wages. It reſembles the caſe where a maſter lends his ſervant to a neighbour for a week or longer, and he does ſuch work as the neighbour ſets him about, he is ſtill in the original maſter's ſervice. Knight's paying him the five ſhillings in harveſt-time makes no difference, any more than if the neighbour in the caſe ſuppoſed had given the ſervant a gratuity for his trouble (1).

Service with other maſters by conſent of the firſt.

So where a ſervant hired at yearly wages to a Blackſmith to be paid from time to time as he wanted, ſerved his maſter for the year, except that with his maſter's conſent he worked for a week with one perſon as a journeyman blackſmith, and for a fortnight with another, and in a fiſhing-boat at different times, for a ſpace not exceeding three days altogether. Theſe perſons paid the ſervant for the time he worked with them, it being agreed between him and his maſter at the time of his abſence, that he ſhould have all he earned, and the maſter to de-

(1) Rex *v.* Ivinghoe, 1 Stra. 90. 2 Bott, 296. Pl 336.

duct

duct a sum out of his wages in the proportion of the time of his absence to that of the whole year, which was done accordingly. Upon these facts it was adjudged that the service was sufficient to confer a settlement. For it is not necessary that the service should be with the same person, it is sufficient if it be with a successor in the farm or an assignee. It is only a licence of departure for a certain time; the contract remains; and service by the master's consent with another person is service with the master (1).

But to constitute *the same service* when the master is changed, the original contract must remain. If that is dissolved, service with a new master under a new contract, though entered into before the expiration of the original year with the first master's consent, who pays the year's wages, is not the same service, nor will it connect with that performed under the original hiring so as to confer a settlement (2). Some of these cases are mere instances of dispensation with service, and others, of a peculiar direction of the service by the first and only master, and are considered as such in a former section of this chapter (3).

They are classed together here, only in compliance with a distinction usually taken. Some of them are hardly cases of constructive service, since the labour done for another by the master's direction, is actual service done for the master himself. None of them are so strong as some dispensations which have been implied from a return to the service after absence without leave.

In some of these latter cases, the servant left the service without his master's knowledge, and worked wherever,

(1) Rex *v.* Beccles, Burr S. C. 230. 2 Bott, 298. Pl. 337, *ante*, 225.

(2) Rex *v.* Thistleton, *ante* 243.

(3) See *ante*, Sect. III. 221, *et seq.*

and

and with whom ſoever he pleaſed, intending to abandon the relation altogether; but in the inſtances mentioned here, excepting that of the executor, the maſter allowed of the abſence, and permitted the ſubordinate hiring, ſo that the parties acknowledged the continuance of the original contract by the very means they took to diſpenſe with its being literally fulfilled (1).

SECT. V.

Of the Reſidence by, and Place in which, a Settlement is gained.

THE 13 and 14 Car. 2. chap. 12. requires a reſidence of forty days in the capacity of a ſervant in order to gain a ſettlement. 13 and 14 Car. 2. c. 12.

3 W. 3. chap. 11. and 8 and 9 W. 3. chap. 30. make no alteration in this particular, but ſuperadds an hiring and ſervice for a year. The proviſions made by the acts of William have been already conſidered. Thoſe which are connected with the ſervant's reſidence, remain to be enquired into. They are three: 3 W. 3. c. 11. 8 & 9 W. 3. c. 30.

1ſt. The reſidence muſt be in a pariſh or townſhip having overſeers. 2d. The ſervant muſt reſide forty days in that place where the ſettlement is claimed. 3d. He muſt remain under the obligation of his yearly contract during ſome part of ſuch reſidence. To theſe general qualifications may be added, 4th. The enumeration of ſome particular diſabilities which prevent a ſettlement in certain ſituations. The reſidence.

(1) See *ante*, 223, *et ſeq.*

1. The

I. In what place.

1. The laws which provide for the maintenance and removal of the indigent poor, extend only to parishes and townships for which overseers are appointed (1). No settlement therefore can be gained either by residence as a servant, or in any other capacity in extra-parochial places where there are no overseers (2).

The 3 W. and M. c. 11. declares, "that the servant "shall be lawfully hired into any parish or town for one "year." This may seem to imply, that he should be hired for the purpose of serving a master who resides in such parish or town.—But it has been held that the words "parish or town" are only put for example, and that a settlement may be gained under a contract of hiring made in an extraparochial place, by serving where a settlement can be acquired (3); and the law is the same if the hiring take place in some other country (4).

II. The sort of residence.

The forty days residence required by the second rule is to be considered in a two-fold view. 1st. The time, place, and nature of the residence. 2d. The situation and condition under which the servant resides.

I. Place and time of residence.

As to the time and place of residence—He may either reside in one parish or township during his entire servitude, or in several. If he reside in different places, he may inhabit, partly where a settlement is to be acquired, and partly where it can not.

The residence also may be either during forty running days, or for the same period at unconnected intervals.

(1) *Ante*, Chap. 2. p. 7. *et seq.*

(2) Clerkenwell *v.* Bridewell. Ld. Raym. 549. 2 Bott, 389. Pl. 414. Rex *v.* St. Andrew's, Holborn. 2 Bott, 292. Pl. 334. Cald. 403.

(3) Rex *v.* St. Peter's, Oxford. Fol. 193. 2 Bott, 179. Pl. 232. *Ib.* 282.

(4) As, if a man be hired in Ireland for a year, and afterwards come within the year, and live in England the last forty days with his master, that is sufficient to gain a settlement. *Per* Eyre J. Rex *v.* St. Peter's in Oxford, *ante*, n. 2.

It is evident from the obſervations already made upon the 13 and 14 Car. 2. and 3. and 8 and 9 W. 3., That a ſervant gains a right of ſettlement by reſidence in a pariſh or townſhip for the firſt forty days of his ſervice, provided he is hired for a year, and ſerves that period. This right is only inchoate until the entire conditions impoſed by theſe ſtatutes are fulfilled, and when that is done, it becomes complete.

Place of reſidence.

As a reſidence for forty days therefore, confers a ſettlement under ſuch conditions; it follows that if a ſervant reſide for diſtinct periods of forty days in different pariſhes, his ſettlement floats during the continuance of his year, and is determined by the laſt reſidence of forty days—For each reſidence for that period confers a ſettlement conditionally, and upon the principle already ſtated, that a latter ſettlement ſuperſedes the former, it is the reſidence for the laſt forty days of the year's ſervice which confers the ſettlement (1).

But it may happen that he reſides during ſome part of the year's ſervice where a ſettlement may be acquired, and for the remainder where it cannot. Thus if he ſerve forty days in pariſh A, and the reſt of his year out of the kingdom, or in an extraparochial place, not having overſeers, or if he does not reſide forty days in any pariſh or place, except A, he is ſettled in A. For he has complied with all the ſtatutory requiſites. He has reſided forty days under 13 and 14 Car. 2. He has been hired for a year under 3 W. 3. and ſerved for a year under 8 and 9 W. 3. and the ſettlement in A not being ſuperſeded by one, gained ſubſequently during his ſervice, he is ſettled there (2).

(1) See the reaſoning of Lord Kenyon, C. J. Rex v. Brighthelmſtone. 5 Term Rep. 188. 2 Bott, 399. Pl. 427.

(2) *Ante*, 286, *et ſeq.*

The

The residence need not consist of successive days; it is sufficient if they amount to forty in the whole (1).

Last forty days how reckoned.

From the determination of this difficulty a new one arises; namely, what shall be accounted the last forty days. For as the days of residence need not be connected, and as the servant may serve less than forty days at a time in one parish, and more than forty in another, and ultimately complete his residence of forty, by dwelling for a day or two in the first; it remains to determine in which of these parishes he is settled.

If the last forty days are reckoned, counting each day backward, or as it is called day by day, the settlement will be in one parish. But if the completion of a term of forty days be sufficient, then the place of residence for the last day is alone material, and the settlement will be determined by a different rule.

Thus, if the servant reside twenty days in parish A, and afterwards ten in parish B, and then nineteen days in A, and thirty again in B, but return and spend the last night of his service in A, the settlement would be different according to these several modes of counting. If the last forty days are reckoned as they run backwards, it would be in B. the servant having resided the last forty out of the last sixty of his service there, and only twenty of that period in A. But if the forty days last completed confer the settlement, then he is settled in A, where he resided the last day.

The court determined, and not without some doubts, in favour of the latter mode of calculation, and wherever

(1) Greenwich *v.* Longdon, Burr. S. C. 243. 2 Bott, 279. Pl. 324. But the 13 and 14 Car. 2. c. 12. seems to have intended that the forty days should be successive.

a set-a ſettlement can be gained, the place of inhabitancy for the laſt day of the years' ſervice ſettles the ſervant, provided he has reſided there forty days in all during his years' ſervice (1).

Service in one place, reſidence in another.

But it ſome times happens that the ſervant may live in one pariſh, and his ſervice be performed in another.

The ſtatutes of William, refer only to the pariſh or townſhip in which the ſervice is done, regarding it as the place of ſettlement. It muſt be owned that there ſeems ſome little anomaly in the law, which connects every other requiſite for gaining this ſpecies of ſettlement with the pariſh in which the ſervant works, and yet makes the ſettlement depend upon the place where he ſleeps. The reaſon ſeems to be, that the latter is where he inhabits; and inhabitancy both in former ſtatutes, and in 13 and 14 Car. 2. c. 12. is made the criterion of ſettlement.

To ſuch a nicety has this rule been carried, that where a houſe ſtood in two pariſhes, and the maſter lay in pariſh A, where all the ſervice was done, but the maid ſlept in pariſh B, ſhe was held ſettled in B (2).

Reſidence unknown to maſter.

Neither is the maſter's knowledge or conſent to the ſervant's ſleeping away from his houſe material. If the ſervant marry during ſervice, and ſleep with his wife in another pariſh, unknown to his maſter (3), he is ſettled there (4). And whether he ſleeps there for ſucceſſive

(1) Loweſs *v.* Lanſtephan. Burr. S. C. 825. 2 Bott, 289. Pl. 330. Rex *v.* Hulland, *ib.* 292. Pl. 332. Dougl. 657. Rex *v.* Iveſton, Cald. 288. 2 Bott, 291. Pl. 333. and ſee *Ib.* 292, notis 1 and the obſervations of Lord Kenyon C. J. and Buller J. Rex *v.* Brighthelmſtone, 5 Term Rep. 188. 2 Bott, 399. Pl. 427.

(2) Feverſham *v.* Graveney. Fort. 221. 2 Bott, 275. Pl. 316.

(3) Rex *v.* Hedſor. 2 Bott, 289. Pl. 331. Cald. 51. Rex *v.* Nympſfield, *ib.* 107.

(4) *Ut in* n. (2).

nights or at intervals, his settlement is in the parish where he lodges the last night, if he has slept there forty in all (1). Upon the same principle, if he should sleep the last night in a parish where he had first served under his contract of hiring, and has resided there forty days during the entire service, he is settled there.

Servant's condition during residence.

As to the second consideration, namely, the servant's situation and condition during residence, it is in most cases immaterial. It is of no importance whether he dwell on land or water (2); or for what purpose the master comes into the parish, whether for a permanent residence, or a temporary sojournment. Thus, if the servant spend the last forty days of his service at a watering place, where his master went for the purpose of bathing (3), or at any other public place, where he is a temporary resident (4), sojourner, or visitor (5), he gains a settlement by inhabiting there.

Neither does it make any difference that the master has no real property, and does not live in the parish where his servant resides. Thus, a man hired to stay and look after horses at an inn where a stage-coach bated (6); a huntsman residing with his master's hounds (7); a warrener at a warren (8); a groom at a public place, exercising and training his master's running horses (9), were held

(1) Rex *v.* Great Bookham, Cald. 290. 2 Bott. 292. n (*a*); and the cases there cited.

(2) Rex *v.* Friendsbury, Burr. S.C. 644. 2 Bott. 284. Pl. 337. Goring *v.* Moltsworth. 1 Barnard K.B. 436. Cas. Set. & Rem. 412. 2 Bott, 277. Pl. 322.

(3) Rex *v.* Bath Easton, Burr. S. C. 774. 2 Bott, 286. Pl. 329.

(4) Alton *v.* Elvetham. 2 Bott, 280. Pl. 326. Burr. S. C. 418. 3 Burn's Just. Tit. Poor.

(5) Rex *v.* St. Peter's in Oxford, Fol. 193. 2 Bott, 275. Pl. 318.

(6) St. Peter's in Oxford *v.* Chipping, Wycomb. 1 Stra. 528. 2 Bott, 275. Pl. 318.

(7) Bishop's Hatfield *v.* St. Peter's, Fol. 197. 2 Bott, 276. Pl. 371.

(8) Rex *v.* Eldersley, *ib.* 274. Pl. 315.

(9) Rex *v.* East Ilsley, *ib.* 285. Pl. 328. Burr. S. C. 722.

to

to gain ſettlements in thoſe pariſhes which they inhabited, although their reſpective maſters neither reſided, nor had houſes, or other local property there.

So alſo a reſidence with different maſters, provided the ſervice is ſufficient in other reſpects, will confer a ſettlement (1). And theſe rules apply equally where the ſervice is diſpenſed with (2).

The only diſtinction taken on the ſubject is, that if a ſervant live apart from his maſter, from diſeaſe and diſability, he ſhall not be ſettled in the pariſh in which he dwells during illneſs, but in that where he reſided for the laſt forty days of his effective ſervice.

Reſidence in ſickneſs gives no ſettlement.

There is no expreſs deciſion upon this point; but the judges have ſtrongly inclined to it, upon the ſame principle, that a baſtard born in a houſe of correction, or a gaol, is ſettled, not where it is born, but in the mother's pariſh (3). Thus Lord Mansfield puts it as a clear caſe; "ſuppoſe a perſon in ſervice has an accident upon the "road by breaking a leg, and he ſtays forty days in a "place; ſhall that be a ſettlement (4)?" And where a yearly ſervant was deprived of reaſon about two months before the expiration of his year, and was then taken home by his father into another pariſh, where he lived until the year expired. The majority of the court intimated a ſtrong opinion, that he was ſettled in the pariſh where he had laſt lived with, and actually ſerved his maſtter, and not where he was kept as a lunatic for the laſt two months of his years' contract (5).

(1) Rex *v.* Ladock, Burr. S. C. 279. 2 Bott, 277. Pl. 323.

(2) Rex *v.* Undermilbeck, *ib.* 294. Pl. 335. 5 Term Rep. 387.

(3) *Ante*, 176.

(4) Alton *v.* Elvetham, *ante*, 290, n. (4)

(5) Rex *v.* Sutton, 5 Term Rep. 657. 2 Bott, 349. Pl. 384. So an apprentice was held not to gain a ſettlement by inhabitancy during ſickneſs. Rex *v* Titchfield, Burr. S.C. 511. 2 Bott, 404. Pl. 432. *et poſt.* But ſee Rex *v.* Charles, *poſt.*

Must reside under his yearly contract.

As the residence may be in different parishes by reason of a connected service under different contracts, the next question is, whether that circumstance makes any variation as to the settlement. A compliance with the several statutory qualifications is required in every parish into which the servant removes. It is sufficiently obvious, that if there is no more than one contract and one years' service, they are complied with in each parish in which there is a residence of forty days. But where there are more contracts than one, whether express or implied, and the servant removes into a new parish subsequent to a new agreement, it varies the case. A contract for a years' service must exist there, and must be connected with the year's service, the 3 W. & M. c. 11. s. 6. expresly enacting that the person shall be hired into the parish or town for a year (1). Thus, if there has been an hiring for a year, and service under it in parish A, and at the expiration of the years' service, the master and servant remove into parish B, where the servant serves for a whole year under *express weekly* hirings, he gains no settlement in B, because there is no yearly hiring there, although there is an yearly service.

But where a servant was hired for a year, and having served it, continued to live with his master in the parish in which he was so hired for above a quarter of a year longer without coming to any new agreement, and then the master took a house in a different parish, to which the servant removed with the rest of the family, and lived under the first contract for six months more, and was paid the same wages in proportion to his time, it was held that he was settled in this second parish (2).

For a second hiring was necessarily implied at the commencement of the second year, by virtue of which the pau-

(1) See *Ante*, 286.

(2) Rex v. Croscombe, Burr. S. C. 256. 2 Bott, 279. Pl. 325. See also the opinion of Ashurst J. Rex v. Sulgrave, 2 Term Rep. 778. 2 Bott, 266. Pl. 311.

per

per lived in the ſecond pariſh; and although the ſervice was not completed under it, yet as there was an hiring for a year in that pariſh, and continuance of the ſame ſervice in another, the impediments created by the ſtatutes of William were removed, and the pauper's reſidence for the laſt forty days determined his ſettlement upon 13 & 14 Car. 2, as it would if theſe acts had never paſſed (1).

It ſeems immaterial in this caſe whether a ſecond hiring was implied in the firſt pariſh; for it would have made no difference if there had been but one contract during his reſidence in both pariſhes, as it would have been ſor more than a year, and accompanied the ſervant's perſon wherever he reſided during its continuance. But although a contract cannot be conſidered as running into a new pariſh after it has expired, yet it has been already ſhewn that ſervice under an hiring in one pariſh will connect with ſervice under a new yearly contract in another, and confer a ſettlement if there is a year's ſervice complete, and a reſidence of forty days (2). For the principle of connecting ſervice, has no reference to the duration of prior or ſubſequent contracts, but to the contiguity of ſervice and the abſolute control of the maſter.

Settlement may be gained in A, but not in B, under the ſame yearly hiring.

It follows from theſe poſitions, that a ſervant may gain a ſettlement, under a hiring and ſervice in one pariſh who cannot do ſo by ſervice with the ſame maſter if he removes into another, and live under a different yearly hiring. For he may labour under incapacities at the time of the ſecond hiring, from which he was exempted during the firſt. Thus, if a ſervant be unmarried at the time he is hired for a year, he acquires a ſettlement by ſervice, and forty days reſidence under that years' hir-

(1) It may be neceſſary to appriſe the reader, that this is the author's inference from the caſe, and but partially collected from the reaſons aſſigned for the judgment in the report.

(2) *Ante*, 268; and Rex *v.* Croſcombe. *Ante*, 292.

ing, in every parish into which he removes, although he marries immediately afterwards (1). But if he marry during his first yearly contract, and then make one for a new year, he cannot gain a settlement in a new parish by subsequent service under the last agreement, by reason of his disability when it was made (2).

It should seem further, (although the point has never come directly before the court,) that he might acquire a settlement in the first parish by service in the second, under this latter contract, although he could not acquire one in the second. Thus, suppose him unmarried, and hired for a year in parish A; at the end of six months he marries; dissolves his original contract with his master's consent, and enters into a new one for a year, but does not interrupt the service. He forthwith removes to parish B. and continues to live there with his master for more than a year. He gains no settlement in B (3); but he seems to have obtained one in A. For there was an hiring for a year while unmarried, with residence forty days in A, and a years' service complete. This service of the last six months in a parish where he could not gain a settlement, is like serving in an extra-parochial place which does not defeat the inchoate right of settlement (4), none being subsequently gained by which it can be annulled.

Of residence under disabilities.

It having been determined also in Rex *v.* Adson (5), that the forty days residence need not be within the years' hiring, it seems as if a settlement may be gained in the new parish if a yearly contract subsists there for a single day, and the servant reside forty days under a contract en-

(1) Farringdon *v.* Witty, Salk. 527. 2 Bott, 301. Pl. 339, *ante*, 284; and the cases cited, n. (1).

(2) Rex *v.* St. Giles, Reading Cald. 54 2 Bott, 303. Pl. 343.

(3) Rex *v.* Great Chilton, 5 Term Rep. 672. 2 Bott, 268. Pl. 313. *Ante*, 278.

(4) Rex *v.* St. Andrew's Holborn. 2 Bott, 292. Pl. 334. *Ante*, 286. n. (4); and the cases there cited.

(5) 5 Term Rep. 98. 2 Bott, 268. Pl. 312. *Ante*, 281.

tered

tered into when exempted from ſtatutory diſqualifications, provided it is ſufficient for the purpoſe in other reſpects. Thus, if he ſerve his whole year but one day in A, and ſerve that one, and thirty-nine more in B, under an expreſs hiring for three months, he ſeems ſettled in B. For a contract for a year's ſervice ſubſiſts while he ſerves there, and the period of ſervice under it is immaterial; there is connected ſervice for a year, and reſidence of forty days under a contract made, while he labours under none of the diſqualifications created by 3 W. 3. & 8 & 9 W. 3. It is this laſt circumſtance which diſtinguiſhes this ſuppoſed caſe from Rex *v.* St. Giles (1), and the latter, from Rex *v.* Adſon (2). In Rex *v.* St. Giles, the pauper being an unmarried man, ſerved under a general hiring in Sherborne for ſeven months, when he married, and continued there in his maſter's ſervice four months more; he then took lodgings in St. Giles, removed there with his wife, and ſlept in the pariſh for ſeven months, during which time he continued to ſerve his maſter without coming to a new hiring, ſo that he ſerved eighteen months in all: viz. 11 in Sherborne, and 7 in St. Giles; the firſt month of the latter was under the old hiring, and the remaining ſix under a new one, implied from his continuance in the ſervice. Mr. J. Willes, who delivered the judgment of the court, was of opinion that had he reſided forty days in St. Giles, under the firſt hiring, he would have been ſettled there; but having reſided under it no more than thirty, and the remainder under a new hiring, he gained none.

This deciſion ſeems only to be reconciled with that in Rex *v.* Adſon, upon the principle laid down as a neceſſary qualification in all caſes of reſidence, by Mr. J. Lawrence, in Rex *v.* Great Chilton; that ſervice for the laſt forty days muſt be performed under a contract of hiring,

(1) *Ante,* 277. n. (1). (2) *Ante,* 281. n. (1).

 entered

entered into when the pauper was exempt from those disabilities which are created by statute (1).

Upon the whole, therefore, it may be concluded, that a yearly hiring must either be originally entered into, or at least exist in the particular parish to confer a settlement there, and that there must be a years' service connected with this hiring.

Of residence 40 interrupted days, under distinct yearly hirings.

But a further point is still left undetermined. How far interrupted residence of less than forty days under distinct hirings for a year can be connected.—Upon all points of settlement law, it is dangerous to hazard an opinion, and this seems entangled with considerable difficulties. If this residence happen during the same year's service, the principle of settlement by connecting services, would be frustrated in many instances, unless they can be connected. But if they occur not only under several hirings, but under distinct services for a year, the case differs little or nothing from one where the contracts are made, and services performed with different masters. The distinction arising from this principle, may be marked by the following case. If a yearly servant usually residing in B, inhabits in A under his year's hiring for twenty days, and no more, and then under a new hiring with the same master inhabits A for the last twenty of his service, the question is, whether he shall be settled there if he quits the service within the period of a years' service, to be counted from the commencement of that portion of his first residence in A, which is necessary to connect with his subsequent residence there, in order to make it up forty days. Or, on the other hand, if he serve out a second year in B. all but twenty days, and reside for that time in A, shall not these residences connect, because there is more than the interval of a year between them? This however comes round to the ques-

(1) *Ante*, 279.

tion

tion formerly difcuffed, how far fome fervice, although but for a day, under the yearly contract, is neceffary to connect it with other fervices (1). If it be neceffary, the refidence under different contracts, muft, like the fervice, be within the interval of a year. If there is no fuch rule, diftinct refidences in the fame parifh occurring at the interval of years, may confer a fettlement.

Particular difabilities, which prevent the fettlement of fervants in certain fituations, are created by the following ftatutes. IV. Of particular difabilities by ftatute.

1. By 9 & 10 W. 3. c. 11. Servants coming into a parifh under a certificate, fhall gain no fettlement there.

2. By 12 Ann. ft. 1. c. 18. f. 2. Perfons hired, and living with perfons who refide in the parifh under a certificate.

3. By 33 Geo. 3. c. 54. fect. 24. Servants to a certificated member of a benefit fociety.

4. By 13 Geo. 2. chap. 29. fect. 7. No child, nurfe, or fervant received, maintained, educated, or employed within the Foundling Hofpital, fhall gain any fettlement in the parifh or place where fuch hofpital is fituate, by virtue of fuch their reception, continuance, hiring, or refidence, in fuch hofpital.

5th. By 9 Geo. 3. c. 31. f. 8. No perfon, who fhall be admitted into the Magdalen Hofpital as a penitent proftitute, or who fhall be employed therein as an hired fervant, fhall, by reafon of fuch admittance or fervice, gain a fettlement in the parifh in which the faid hofpital is, or fhall be fituate.

(1) *Ante*, 280.

SECT.

SECT. VI.

Of the Proofs necessary to support this Settlement.

To establish a settlement by hiring and service, it is necessary to prove 1. An hiring for a year. 2. Service for a year. 3. Residence of forty days.

Hiring how proved. Written.

Where the agreement is in writing, it is generally necessary to produce the written instrument—But a copy or parol evidence of the contents may be given in evidence under circumstances (1), in two cases—1st, Where the writing cannot be found. 2d, Where it is in the custody of the adverse party.

Parol.

Where the agreement is not in writing, evidence may be given of the actual terms of the contract, or it may be inferred from what passed at the time of hiring (2), or from the mere fact of service.

Inferred from what circumstances?

Thus, where the pauper proved "that her husband was "abroad beyond sea, and had been so for two years past if "alive; that to her knowledge he lived in the capacity of "an ostler with Mrs. L—— of the parish of H—— (some "years since deceased) about two years, where she had "seen him brew; *but whether there was any agreement or "hiring relating to such service was not proved.*" The court was of opinion that the sessions were right in drawing the conclusion, that the husband was settled in H: for al-

(1) Rex v. St. Sepulchre's, Cald. 547. 2 Bott, 362. Pl. 391. This point will be discussed more fully in treating of the production of indentures of apprenticeship under that species of settlement.

(2) *Ante*, 203.

though

though the evidence of hiring was ſlight, there was nothing to contradict it (1).

So where the pauper was ſeen, and known to be in the ſervice of C, as a ſervant in huſbandry, and to act in that capacity for upwards of a year, it was held ſufficient evidence to enable the ſeſſions to draw the concluſion of his having been in fact hired for a year (2).

This however is only preſumptive evidence, and therefore liable to be rebutted by the peculiar circumſtances of each particular caſe (3).

Such preſumption however is not deſtroyed by the ſervant having originally agreed for a period ſhort of a year, if ſhe afterwards live in the ſame ſervice for a year, or more.—As where a female ſervant was at firſt only hired from March till Michaelmas following, but continued in the ſame ſervice for three years, it was deemed ſufficient evidence to warrant the juſtices in finding a hiring for a year (4).

So where the pauper a fortnight after Old Michaelmas 1792, heard from Miſs G—— that her father wanted a ſervant, and agreed with her to go a month upon liking: ſhe went accordingly, and in the Spring following, Miſs G—— told her that if ſhe behaved well, and did her work properly, ſhe ſhould have four pounds for a year. The pauper continued in Miſs G——'s ſervice, *without any other agreement*, until Chriſtmas following, when ſhe quitted it. About a fortnight after Michaelmas 1793, ſhe received 4*l*. for a year's wages then due, and for the remainder

(1) Rex *v*. Holy Trinity in Wareham, Cald. 141. 2 Bott, 362. Pl. 190. *Ante*, 200, *et ſeq*.

(2) Rex *v*. Lyth, 5 Term Rep. 327. 2 Bott, 364. Pl. 392. Lord Kenyon laid ſome ſtreſs on this being the caſe of a ſervant in huſbandry; but the ſubſequent deciſions here referred to, reſpect female ſervants.

(3) *Ut in* n (2).

(4) Rex *v*. Long Whatton, 5 Term Rep. 447. 2 Bott, 366. Pl. 393.

remainder of the service from that time, eighteen pence a week, being the proportion of wages then due at the rate of 4*l.* *per annum*. Lord Kenyon C. J. "At present the case is so imperfectly stated that we cannot give any judgment upon it. A retrospective hiring certainly is not sufficient to confer a settlement; but as the pauper *continued* in the same service after the expiration of the first year, there was abundant ground for the justices to have presumed a hiring for a year from that time (1)."

In this case, service for less than a year was held sufficient evidence of a yearly contract—It does not appear whether the presumption was considered as helped by the year of antecedent service under a retrospective hiring.—But the conclusion is evidently more strong in cases where there has been a prior service, and hiring for a year (2), and it is not affected by the servant quitting his place during the year (3).

Year's service inferred.

Where service for an entire year cannot be proved expresly, it seems fair matter of inference from the evidence of a yearly hiring, and some service done under it.

Residence.

Residence of forty days may likewise be inferred from the fact of service.

All matters which go to avoid a settlement are properly the evidence of the party who seeks to impeach it, and constitute his case.

But the facts necessary to establish or overthrow this species

(1) Rex *v.* Hales, 5 Term Rep. 668. 2 Bott, 367. Pl. 394. *Ante* 201, n. (3).

(2) Rex *v.* Croscombe, Burr. S. C. 256. 2 Bott, 279. Pl. 325. *Ante*, 292.

(3) Rex *v.* Hales, *ut supra*. *Ante* 202. n. (1.)

ſpecies of ſettlement are ſeldom left to inference. The witneſſes uſually called are qualified to give direct teſtimony of the fact. Such are the pauper or his maſter; their wives and fellow ſervants; for all perſons may be witneſſes who are not affected by the following grounds of incompetency. Witneſſes who may be Incompetent.

1. Imbecillity of underſtanding—Such are ideots and lunatics, while under the influence of their malady. 1. Imbecility.

2. Want of religious belief.—Such are children under fourteen, if unacquainted with the obligation of an oath (1).—Infidels profeſſing no religion that can bind their conſcience (2). But pagans are not incompetent, if ſworn according to the cuſtom and manner of their country (3); or any other who believes in God, the obligation of an oath, and a future ſtate of rewards and puniſhments (4). 2. Infidelity.

3. Perſons convicted of an infamous crime; ſuch as treaſon, felony without benefit of clergy, (5) perjury, conſpiracy, barratry, attaint of falſe verdict, &c.; (6) and judgment muſt be entered, and exiſt at the time, and muſt be proved by producing a copy thereof, formally 3. Infamy.

(1) Brazier's caſe, Bull, L. N. P. 293. See alſo the caſes collected. 1 Eaſt. Cro. Law. 441. But this objection ariſes partly from the imbecillity of the infant's underſtanding.

(2) *Ib.* 292. Co. Lit. 6. White's caſe, Leach's Crown caſes, 337.

(3) Ormichund *v.* Barker, 1 Wils. 84. 1 Atk. 19. Fachina, *v.* Sabine, 2 Str. 1104.

(4) Rex *v.* Taylor, Peake's Ni. Pri. Caſ. 11.

(5) By 31. Geo. 3. c. 35. No perperſon ſhall be incompetent as a witneſs by reaſon of a conviction for petty larceny. When the felony is within clergy competency is reſtored by the burning in the hand; for it is a ſtatute pardon, Rex. *v.* Count de Caſtlemain, after conſulting the judges of C. B.; T. Raym. 379 3 St. Tr. 36. 4 St. Tr. 393; and ſee caſes there cited. And now by 19 Geo. 3. c. 74, if perſons convicted of a clergyable offence be fined or whipped, their competency is reſtored.

(6) Pendock *v.* Mackinder, 2 Wils. 18.

authen-

authenticated (1). But the objection may be removed by a pardon under the great seal (2), except in cases where incompetency is part of the punishment, as in convictions for perjury on 5 Eliz. c. 9. (3)

4. Relationship.

Fourth general ground of incompetency is that of relationship: but as that extends to no case beyond the connection of husband and wife when interested in the suit, and as there are no other parties to questions of settlement but parishes or townships, this species of incompetence never can arise, unless where it involves the question of marriage, and then the wife shall not be admitted to give testimony that may even collaterally affect and criminate her husband; (4) and this perhaps although a divorce has taken place (5).

5. Interest.

The fifth, and only remaining ground of incompetency, arises from the witnesses being interested in the event of the suit. This, in cases of settlement, is narrowed to being rated, or paying parochial taxes in that parish or place by which he is produced in evidence; for persons rated are interested as contributing to the maintenance of paupers settled in their parish, and also in the costs of appeals respecting them (6).

Parishioners when compellable to give evidence.

But this is confined to the case of persons actually rated or paying; parishioners are otherwise good witnesses,

(1) Lee *v.* Gansel Cowp. 3. Wilkes *v.* Smallbrooke, 1 Sid. 51. But it seems as if the witness may be asked whether he has not been convicted, and suffered the judgment of the law. A man appeared to bail one charged with grand larceny, the counsel who opposed the justification, was permitted to ask, whether he had not stood in the pillory for perjury, for it could not subject him to any punishment; and he, admitting the fact, was rejected. Rex *v.* Edwards, 4 Term Rep. 440.

(2) Rex *v.* Gully, Leach's Crown Cas. 115.

(3) Rex *v.* Crosby, Salk. 289.

(4) *Ante*, 160, and the authorities cited in the notes.

(5) Sembl. *per* Lord Alvanley. Monroe *v.* Twisleton, Peake's Law of Evid. App. 44.

(6) Rex. *v.* Governors of St. Mary Magdalen, Bermondsey. 3 East. 7. Rex *v.* Little Lumley, 6 Term Rep. 468. 1 Bott, 290. Pl. 282.

neſſes, and may be compelled to give evidence, although liable to be included in future rates (1). The objection is further reſtricted to caſes where rated pariſhioners are produced by their own pariſh, for they ſeem admiſſible if called by the oppoſite ſide, as being produced againſt their intereſt, and not being immediate parties to the record (2).

But although ſuch a pariſhioner is a good witneſs if he comes voluntarily forward, he does not appear excepted from the general rule, that no man can be compelled to give evidence which is to charge (3) or criminate himſelf (4). But a further queſtion as to the protection of a civil intereſt may ariſe; namely, whether this privilege can extend beyond an intereſt exiſting at the time when the fact to be proved has happened; for if he becomes intereſted by his own act after the event, this ſubſequent intereſt ought not to deprive individuals, or the public, of his teſtimony (5).

When competent but not compellable.

It is evident from theſe rules that the pauper is in moſt caſes a good witneſs as to the circumſtances reſpecting his ſettlement; (6) but his maſter in ſome may not.

Pauper a witneſs, when maſter not.

(1) Rex *v.* Proſſer. 4 Term Rep. 17. 1 Bott, 285. Pl. 277. Note the queſtion of competency in this caſe, and thoſe cited n. (2) aroſe upon Appeals againſt Poor Rates; but the principle applies equally to orders of removal, and was ſo decided, Rex *v.* South Lynn, 5 Term Rep. 664 2 Bott, 756, 861.

(2) Aſhburton *v.* Woodland, 1 Term Rep. 261. 2 Bott, 138. Pl. 282. *Sed, Quære* whether as the extent of the intereſt is in general immaterial upon the queſtion of competency, a pariſhioner rated in the two contending pariſhes is compellable to give his evidence, as being intereſted both ways; for the extent of the intereſt may be unequal, owing to the difference of aſſeſſments, the quantity of property, and various other circumſtances. See caſe of Peterborough-bridge, 1 Vent. 351. Gilb. Law of Evid. 129. Rex *v* Inhabitants of Wilts, 6 Mod. 307. King *v.* Carpenter. 2 Show, 47.

(3) See Hawkins *v.* Perkins, 1 Str. 406. Bain *v.* Hargrave, Peake's Law of Evid. 132. Raines *v.* Towgood, *ib.* 133.

(4) Rex *v.* Portſea, Burr. S. C. 834. 1 Bott, 548. Pl. 747.

(5) Bent *v.* Baker, 3 Term Rep. 27. Barlow *v.* Vowel, Skin. 586. Rex. *v.* Fox, 1 Str. 652. Peake's Law of Evid. 157.

(6) *Per* Aſhurſt J. Rex *v.* Eriſwell, 3 Term Rep. 720.

But

Credit of witness how attacked and supported.

But a witness, although competent, may be unworthy of credit, either from his general character, or having given a different account of the transaction previously, or many other circumstances. Witnesses may be called to discredit him from general character, as if they will swear from the knowledge they have of it that they would not believe him upon his oath. But they must not give evidence to a particular fact which the man cannot come prepared to justify (1). A party may give general evidence to support the character of his own witness, but cannot produce it to discredit him, " for that would " be to enable him to destroy the witness if he spoke " against him, and to make him a good witness if he " spoke for him, with the means in his hands of de- " stroying him if he spoke against him (2)."

" But if a witness proves facts in a cause which makes " against the party who called him, yet the party may " call other witnesses to prove that those facts were other- " wise; for such facts are evidence in the cause, and the " other witnesses are not called directly to discredit the " first witness, but the impeachment of his credit is ac- " cidental and consequential only (3)."

Pauper's examination no evidence.

A further question has been made, how far the pauper's examination respecting his place of settlement taken before a magistrate upon oath, or a declaration of his to the like effect, could be received in evidence, in the event of his death, insanity, or being beyond the reach of judicial process.

It seems to have been the ancient practice of most quarter sessions to admit them as evidence; and the

(1) Bull L. N. P. 296.

(2) Hardwell *v.* Jarman, Taunton Spring assizes, 1789. Cor. Buller J. Hasting's Cas. *per* Lord Chancellor, 11 June 1789. In Dom. Proc. 12 Mod. 375, Adams *v.* Arnold, Bull. L. N. P. 297.

(3) Bull. L. N. P. 297.

 Court

Court of King's Bench was formerly of opinion that they were rightly received, confidering it as one of the excepted cafes in which evidence upon hearfay might be admitted (1).

But thefe points were afterwards elaborately difcuffed in the cafe of Rex *v.* Erifwell (2), when the judges were divided in opinion. It has however been fubfequently determined, and muft be now confidered as fettled law, that neither the ex parte examination of the pauper taken in writing on oath before two magiftrates, whether for the purpofe of inquiring into his fettlement (3), or of removing him (4), are admiffible in evidence upon a queftion of fettlement; and this, whether the pauper is infane (5), or has abfconded (6), or is dead (7); and hearfay evidence of the pauper's declarations as to his fettlement are equally inadmiffible under any circumftances (8). Nor his declaration

But examinations before two magiftrates are made evidence of fettlement by the mutiny-act (9), and the original examination has been held admiffible in evidence as well Examination under Mutiny Act.

(1) Rex *v.* Nuttley, Burr. S. C. 701. 2 Bott, 361. Pl. 389. Rex *v.* Greenwich, Burr. S. C. 243. Rex *v.* St. Michael's, Bath, *Ib.* 731. Rex *v.* Creech, St. Michael's, *ib.* 761. Rex *v* Holy Trinity in Wareham, Cald. 141. 2 Bott, 362. Pl. 390. Rex *v.* St. Sepulchre's, *ib.* 362. Pl. 391. Cald. 547.

(2) 3 Term Rep. 707.

(3) Rex *v* Erifwell, *ante*, (2).

(4) Rex *v.* Nuneham Courtney, 1 Eaft. 373, and the cafes cited in the following notes.

(5) Rex *v.* Erifwell, *ante.*

(6) Rex *v.* NunehamCourtney, *ante.*

(7) Rex *v.* Ferry Fryftone, 2 Eaft, 54. Rex *v.* Abergwilly, *ib.* 73.

(8) See the cafes cited, *ante*, n. (6) (7) (8) (9). Rex *v.* Chadderton, 2 Eaft, 27.

(9) Sect 33 enables two or more juftices for the county, where any non-commiffioned officer or foldier fhall be quartered, in cafe fuch officer or foldier has either wife or child, or children, to caufe fuch officer or foldier to be fummoned before them in the place where they are quartered, in order to make oath of the place of their laft legal fettlement; and fuch perfons are directed to obey fuch fummons, and to take oath accordingly. And fuch juftices are thereby requefted to give an attefted copy of fuch affidavit to the perfon making the fame,

 82

as the attested copy (1); but no other attested copy is legal evidence while the original is in existence, except that given to the soldier (2), and when produced, they must be proved and authenticated in the same manner as other written instruments (3).

---

to be by him delivered to his commanding officer, in order to be produced when required, which attested copy shall be at any time admitted in evidence as to such last legal settlement before any of his majesty's justices of the peace or at any general quarter-sessions of the peace; provided always that in case any such officer or soldier shall be again summoned to make oath as aforesaid, then on such attested copy of the oath by him formerly taken, being produced by him, or by any other person on his behalf, such officer or soldier shall not be obliged to take any other or further oath with regard to his legal settlement, but shall have a copy of such attested copy of examination, if required.

(1) Rex *v.* Warley, 6 Term Rep. 534. Rex *v.* Bilton, 1 East, 13.

(2) Rex *v.* Clayton Le Moors, 5 Term Rep. 704. 2 Bott, 549, Pl. 563.

(3) Rex *v.* Bilton, *ante*, n. (1).

CHAPTER XXI.

Of Settlement by Apprenticeſhip.

SECT. I.

Diviſion of the Subject and general Rules reſpecting it.

BY 13 & 14 Car. 2. c. 12. nothing more was required to ſettle an apprentice than a reſidence of forty days (1). The 3 Will. & Mar. c. 11. exempts him from the neceſſity created by different ſtatutes, that he ſhould give notice of his inhabitancy. It enacts, that "If any "perſon ſhall be bound an apprentice by indenture, and "inhabit in any town or pariſh, ſuch binding and inhabi- "tation ſhall be adjudged a good ſettlement, though no "ſuch notice in writing be delivered and publiſhed." 13 & 14. C. 2. c. 12. 3 W. & M. c. 11.

An apprentice is not encumbered like an hired ſervant, with the condition, that he ſhall be unmarried (2), and without emancipated children when he makes the contract. Apprentice need not be unmarried, &c.

It is ſufficient if he is *bound* as an apprentice, and inhabits the town or pariſh in that capacity.

But as he is enabled to become ſettled by theſe means, he is fettered from gaining one in a capacity which is inconſiſtent with the relation he has covenanted to ſtand in towards his maſter. Cannot gain ſettlement but as apprentice.

(1) *Ante*, Chap. xvi. p. 147. *et ſeq.* S. C. 512.
(2) Titchfield *v.* Milford, Burr.

This is moſt clearly ſtated by Lord Kenyon in what he conſiders as "axioms in this branch of ſettlement law." His words are; "It is clear that in general, an apprentice is not capable of contracting the relation of ſervant" (or apprentice) "to any other maſter, until the end of "the term for which he was bound. But it is equally "clear, that if the maſter and apprentice put an end to the "apprenticeſhip by mutual conſent, it is the ſame as if the "indentures had never been executed, and the latter may "gain a ſettlement by hiring and ſervice" (or under a new indenture of apprenticeſhip) (1), "with any other maſter, "before the expiration of the time which he was bound "to ſerve as an apprentice. Then there is a third caſe, "that where the apprentice leaves his maſter and enters "into the ſervice of another, if the indenture ſtill ſubſiſt, "he is not *ſui juris*, but is incapable of gaining a ſettlement by ſerving another maſter, unleſs he ſerve with "the conſent of his former maſter, and in ſuch caſe he "gains a ſettlement, not as an hired ſervant, but as an "apprentice." (2).

Rules apply to perfect apprenticeſhips.

Theſe rules depend upon the incapacity to make a new contract while the indentures continue, and reſpect an apprentice regularly and effectively bound.

Rule as to defective contracts.

But although the parties intend a contract of apprenticeſhip, it will not enure as ſuch if defective in ſubſtance or in form. Another rule is applicable therefore to perſons in this ſituation, viz: That "where a contract clearly appears to be intended as a contract of apprenticeſhip, "and not as one of hiring and ſervice as a ſervant, it ſhall "not, if defective as a contract of apprenticeſhip, be con-

(1) Rex *v.* Weddington, Burr. S.C. 56. 1 Bott, 528. Pl 715.

(2) *Per* Lord Kenyon C. J. Rex *v.* Chipping Warden, 8 Term Rep. 108. 2 Bott, 413. Pl. 439.

"verted

" verted into a contract of hiring and service, so as to gain " the party a settlement as a servant." (1)

For all the statutes acknowledge a distinction between the condition of an apprentice, and that of an hired servant, and the 3 W. & M. c. 11. regulates them by very different provisions. It is but reasonable, therefore, that " if the parties cannot avail themselves of " the consequences of the condition in which they " intended to stand, they shall not be put into another, in which they did not mean to place them- " selves." (2).

The foregoing rules neither admit of modification nor exception, and this branch of settlement law may, with reference to them, be distributed under the following heads: Division of subject.

1st, The binding necessary to confer a settlement by apprenticeship. Under this head will be considered the distinction between defective contracts of apprenticeship, and effective contracts of hiring and service.

2d, By what means indentures of apprenticeship are put an end to, so as to restore to the apprentice his capacity of entering into a fresh contract, under which a settlement can be acquired.

Further, as the party must inhabit the town or parish as an apprentice; what shall be considered as an abiding in that capacity? or in other words—

3d, Of the service necessary to confer the settlement.

4th, Of the residence by, and place in which a settlement is gained.

(1) *Verba* Le Blanc J. Rex *v.* Laindon, 8 Term Rep. 379. 1 Bott, 910. Pl. 1000. *ante*, 192, *et seq.*

(2) *Verba* Lord Kenyon, C. J. *Ib.*

SECT. II.

Of the Binding necessary to gain a Settlement by Apprenticeship.

How bound.

Apprentices are bound, 1st, By voluntary consent, without the intervention of parish officers; and this is usually under 5 Eliz. chap. 4.

2d, By virtue of the power given to parish officers by 43 Eliz. chap. 2., in which case they are called parish apprentices.

Design of the statutes.

Settlement by binding not under either.

Neither statute was enacted with a view to settlements. The first was designed to regulate trade, and the latter, to instruct and maintain children, actually settled and recognized as parochial poor. But a settlement may be gained, not only by a binding under either, but likewise by a voluntary binding, although not within the 5 Eliz. chap. 4., as also by one under 43 Eliz. c. 2. although the directions of that act are not literally fulfilled. The reason is, that some deviations from these statutes render the instrument void; while others make it only voidable. If void, no settlement can be acquired under it; if voidable, it is otherwise. Because, in the first case, the deed is bad as to the whole world, and for all purposes whatever; but in the latter it is only to be avoided at the election of the parties, and no other person can take advantage of the defect. The validity of indentures, so far as respects questions of settlement, depends upon the foregoing rule.

Binding, 1. By indenture.

The 3 Will. and Mary c. 11. s. 5. requires, in conformity to 5 Eliz. c. 4., that the binding shall be by *indentures* (1), *i. e.* by deed indented; a deed " being a writing

(1) This latter act seems only to refer to binding persons under age, which if done by deed poll is bad. Smith *v.* Birch, 1 Sess. Ca. 222. 2 Bott, 523. Pl. 706.

" sealed

"sealed and delivered by the parties" (1). Under this act it was necessary, that the instrument should be actually indented (2). But 31 Geo. 2. c. 11. enacts, that no person who shall be bound an apprentice, by any deed, writing or contract, NOT INDENTED, being first legally stamped, shall be liable to be removed from the place where he was so bound, and resident forty days, by virtue of any order of removal, or order of Sessions, by reason of such deed, writing or contract not being indented only. 31 Geo. 2. c. 11.

But this act does no more than cure the want of indenting. The binding must still be by deed. It must therefore be in writing, and have the other formalities of a deed (3). The pauper H. E. was placed out by the parish officers to a parishioner, under the following agreement, written in a leaf of the parish book: "August 7th, 1774. At "a general meeting held at the parish of B. this day, it is "agreed, that R. F. shall take H. E. and maintain her after "the manner of an apprentice, from this day until Mi-"chaelmas 1780. R. F. to have 20l. with her, and at the "expiration of her said time, to double clothe her: witness "my hand, R. F." She served a year and a half, but was held not to have gained a settlement as an apprentice, for the binding was not by deed, and having served *as an apprentice*, it could not be construed into service as an hired servant (4).

Binding, 2. By deed.

Agreement in parish books.

Both master and apprentice must be parties to the deed (5). But the master's condition is immaterial, if the binding is without fraud.

3. Who parties, and their condition.

(1) 2 Black. Com. 295.

(2) Rex *v.* Mellingham, 2 Bott, 370. Pl. 400. 1 Sess. Ca. 417.

(3) Rex *v.* Mawnam, Burr. S. C 290. 1 Bott, 527. Pl. 712. Rex *v.* Stratton, Burr. S. C. 272. 1 Bott, 526. Pl. 711. Rex *v.* Whitechurch Canonicorum, Burr. S. C. 540. 2 Bott, 378. Pl 405. Rex *v.* Margram, 5 Term Rep. 153. 2 Bott, 389. Pl. 414.

(4) Rex *v.* Ditchingham, 4 Term Rep 769. 2 Bott, 388. Pl. 413.

(5) See case of Chesterfield, 2 Salk. 479. 1 Bott, 522. Pl. 703; and Rex *v.* Ditchingham, *ante*, n. (4).

Binding to labourers, minors, &c.

Thus a female may be bound apprentice by the parish to a day-labourer, to learn the art and mystery of a house-wife (1). So it will be good, although the apprentice is bound to a master who has no right to take one under the statute (2). And the age of the master or servant is immaterial. A father, whose child was eight years old, agreed with M. H. to bind him to her son aged fourteen, and residing in her house as part of her family, without habitation or business of his own; the pauper was bound accordingly with his own free will. He gained a settlement by serving under the indenture, for it was not absolutely void (3). So in the case of a parish apprentice, it was no objection that the child was only eight years old (4). And the binding seems equally good, although the apprentice is a minor, and his parents' consent does not appear; because an infant may make an indenture for his own benefit (5).

4. Execution.

But although the master and apprentice must be parties to the deed, yet the settlement is not prevented by the master's neglect to execute, provided the apprentice is bound (6); and the law is the same whether it be a parish, or a voluntary apprentice.

The original indenture was properly executed by all the parish officers, and allowed by two justices. The counterpart was also allowed by the same justices; the master executed neither, yet the pauper gained a settlement by service under this apprenticeship, although the master had not signed the counterpart, pursuant to

(1) Rex *v.* St. Margaret's Lincoln. 1 Bott, 613. Pl. 854.

(2) Anon. 2 Bott, 370. Pl. 397. and *post* n. (3).

(3) Rex *v.* St. Petrox in Dartmouth, 4 Term Rep. 196. 2 Bott, 387. Pl. 412.

(4) Rex *v.* Saltern, Cald. 444. 2 Bott, 637. Pl 858.

(5) Newberry *v.* St. Mary's, Fol. 154. 2 Bott, 370. Pl. 398.

(6) Rex *v.* St. Peter's on the Hill, 2 Bott, 377. Pl. 403. 1 Bott, 544. Pl. 745.

8 & 9

8 & 9 W. 3. c. 30. ſ. 5. For that act was only made to remove the doubt whether perſons, to whom poor children were to be bound, were compellable to receive them, and ſubjects the maſter to a penalty upon his refuſal, but in no other reſpect confirms the power of binding, which was already eſtabliſhed (1). The law is the ſame if the indenture is duly ſigned by the maſter, and not by the apprentice (2), although put out by the pariſh (3); for his conſent ſhall be implied if he lives under the binding (4), even where he was originally carried to the maſter by his parent againſt his conſent (5).

So likewiſe, if an infant is not bound for that time which the ſtatutes direct him to be, it does not affect the ſettlement; for it only renders the indentures voidable, at the party's election. 5. Time of ſervice.

The 5 Eliz. c. 4. directs, that the binding ſhall be for ſeven years; yet a binding for a leſs time, as four years, confers a ſettlement (6). So 43 Eliz. c. 2. ſ. 5. enacts, that male apprentices ſhall be bound out by the pariſh till the age of twenty-four (7). Yet a binding till twenty-three (8) or twenty-one confers a ſettlement, for the ſtatute is only directory, and not compulſory in this reſpect (9). The ſame act directs, that *women-children* put out by the pariſh, ſhall be bound till they "ſhall come "to the age of one and twenty years, or the time of Leſs than what required by ſtatute.

(1) Rex *v.* Fleet, Ca'd. 31. 2 Bott, 381. Pl. 408.

(2) Rex *v.* Badby, 1 Bott, 547. Pl. 746.

(3) Rex *v.* St. Nicholas in Nottingham, 2 Term Rep. 726. 1 Bott, 620. Pl. 860. 2 Bott, 383. Pl. 410.

(4) *Ante*, n. (3).

(5) Rex *v.* Woolſtanton, 1 Bott, 610. Pl. 849.

(6) St. Nicholas *v.* St. Peter's, Burr. S. C. 91. 2 Bott, 370. Pl. 401. Rex *v.* Gainſborough, 1 Bott, 546. Pl. 745. *poſt* Rex *v.* Evered, Cald. 26. 1 Bott. 530. Pl. 717.

(7) But this is altered to the age of 21, by 18 Geo. 3. c. 47.

(8) Rex *v.* Chalbury, 1 Bott, 610. Pl. 848.

(9) Rex *v.* Woolſtanton, 1 Bott, 610. Pl. 849.

"their

"their marriage. But a girl bound out by the parish to "serve *for a longer period* than the statute authorizes, viz. "until she should have accomplished her full age of "twenty-one years," omitting the alternative of marriage, thereby acquired a settlement. For the indenture is not void, nor voidable by any but the parties themselves (1).

It is said further, that an indenture is good under that act, although it covenants for no certain time (2).

6. Other statutory regulations.

7 Jac. 1. c. 3. s. 2.

The remaining statutory provisions which respect apprentices, do not, at least in general, touch or affect the question of settlement. Thus 7 Jac. 1. c. 3. s. 2. requires, that all corporations of corporate places; and in towns and parishes not incorporate, the parson or vicar thereof, together with the constable or constables, the churchwarden or churchwardens, collectors and overseers for the poor, shall have the nomination and placing of apprentices, where money has been given for binding out a number of the poorest sort of children, unto needful trades and occupations. A binding out of a charity fund of this sort, was held sufficient, although made by the churchwardens and overseers, without the parson (3).

5 Eliz. c. 5. s. 12.

2 & 3, Anne, c. 6.

So one bound apprentice to a mariner was held settled by service under his indenture, although not inrolled in the town where the apprentice was then inhabiting, nor in the next corporate town to his habitation, pursuant to 5 Eliz. c. 5. s. 12. nor with the collector of the customs, pursuant to 2 & 3 Anne, c. 6. (4).

7. Parish indentures.

The indenture of apprentices who are put out by the parish, varies but little in substantial particulars from those,

(1) Rex *v.* St Petrox, Burr. S. C. 248. 2 Bott, 377. Pl. 604.

(2) Rex *v.* Woolstanton. *ante,* 311, n. (9).

(3) Rex *v.* Chalbury, 1 Bott, 643. Pl. 798.

(4) Rex *v.* Gainsborough, Burr. S. C. 586. 1 Bott, 546. Pl. 745.

under

under which minors are bound by their own free will, with their parents' consent.

The chief difference is, that the parish officers must be parties to the parish indenture, in which case, it requires the assent of two justices, which must be given in each other's presence, or the binding is void. "For in "such a most serious subject as this, the legislature intended, that the magistrate should have a check and "control over the parish officers, and they are called "upon to examine with the most minute and anxious at-"tention, the situation of the master, to whom the apprentices are to be bound, and to exercise their judg-"ment solemnly and soberly, before they allow or disallow "the act of the parish officers, for which purpose it is "necessary that they should confer together." (1). But it is sufficient although one magistrate signs the indenture when alone, provided he is present afterwards when the other signs it, for the assent of the first is also given at that time (2). As far as the matter can be traced, the assent of the justices has been always signified by signing (3). Officers parties. Assent of justices.

But the assent by the justices is only necessary when the minor is put out by the parish. It is not so when a poor person binds himself voluntarily as an apprentice; for 43 Eliz. c. 2. only extends to cases where a poor child is put out in a compulsory way (4). Voluntary binding of a pauper.

Indentures of apprenticeship must be properly stamped (5). These stamps were of two kinds previous to 44 8. Stamps on deed.

(1) Rex *v.* Hamstall Redware, 3 Term Rep. 380. 1 Bott, 386. Pl. 411.

(2) Rex *v.* Winwick, 8 Term Rep. 454. 1 Bott, 722. Pl. 1005.

(3) *Per* Buller J. Rex *v.* Saltren, Cald. 444. 1 Bott, 617. Pl. 858.

(4) Rex *v.* St. Mary's, Reading, 1 Bott, 609. Pl. 847.

(5) Salford *v.* Storeford, 2 Bott, 370. Pl. 399. Rex *v.* Holbeck in Leeds, Burr. S. C. 198. 2 Bott, 457. Pl. 478; and the cases *post.*

Geo.

Geo. 3. cap. 98. 1, The duty laid upon the deed itself by virtue of the general stamp acts. These were " where the apprentice was bound out by the parish, 6d. On all others where a sum or value, not exceeding 10*l*. was given or contracted for, with, or in relation to the apprentice 12s. And where the apprentice fee exceeds that sum or value, an additional 20s". And the indenture not only required a stamp, but that it should be the particular one which is appropriate to deeds of this species (1), or else one which, though of a different nature, was at least equal in amount, and the component parts of which were applicable in corresponding proportions to the same funds as those to which the proper stamp was appropriated by the legislature (2).

Want of Stamp how cured.

Although the want of this stamp is a fatal objection while it continues and renders the indentures void and unavailable in evidence (3); yet the defect can be cured by getting the instrument properly stamped. This may be done by paying the duty, together with a penalty for neglecting to have it done within the time limited by the legislature.

9. Stamp for apprentice fee. 8 Anne, c. 9. s. 32.

The other duty upon these indentures was imposed by 8 Anne, c. 9. s. 32. which enacts, that " the sum of *six* " *pence* for *every* twenty shillings of every sum of fifty " pounds or under; and one shilling for every twenty " shillings of every sum amounting to more than fifty " pounds, which shall be given, paid, contracted or agreed " for, with or in relation to every clerk, apprentice, or ser- " vant, which shall in the kingdom of Great Britain be

(1) Robinson *v*. Dryborough, 6 Term Rep. 317. Farr *v*. Price, 1 East, 54.

(2) Taylor *v* Hague, 2 East, 414. See a temporary act, 41 Geo. 3. c. 22.

(3) Rex *v*. Llanvair Dyffryn Cluyd, Burr S. C. 236 Rex *v*. Highnam, Cald. 491. 2 Bott, 381. Pl. 409.

" put

" put or placed to, or with any maſter or miſtreſs, to
" learn any profeſſion, trade, or employment, and pro-
" portionally for greater or leſſer ſums, ſhall be paid by
" the ſaid maſter or miſtreſs reſpectively."

By Sect. 35. the full ſum received or contracted for, is to be inſerted in words at length, in the indenture or writing containing the covenants, &c. relating to the ſervice, or the maſter or miſtreſs ſhall forfeit double the ſum, and the inſtrument ſhall bear date upon the day of the execution. Sect. 35.

By Sect. 36. two ſtamps are to be provided, one for the duty of 6d., and the other, for that of the ſhilling, with one of which the indentures or other writings ſhall be ſtamped, according to the amount of the ſum given or agreed for. Sect. 36.

Indentures ſigned in London, Weſtminſter or within the bills of mortality, ſhall be ſtamped within one month after date, Sect. 36.

Every indenture entered elſewhere in Great Britain, ſhall be either ſtamped within two months, or brought within that time to ſome collector or officer, appointed for the management of theſe duties, who ſhall endorſe a receipt for the duty paid, in words at length, bearing date on the day of the payment. Sect. 37.

By Sect. 38. where the endorſement is made within fifty miles from the bills of mortality, the indenture ſhall be ſtamped within three, and if at a greater diſtance, within ſix months after the date, or making thereof. Sect. 38.

By Sect. 39. all ſuch indentures or writings, as aforeſaid, wherein ſhall not be truly inſerted and written the full ſum and ſums of money received, with, or in rela- Sect. 39.

tion

tion to such clerk, apprentice, or servant as aforesaid, or whereupon the duties payable by this act shall not be duly paid, or lawfully tendered, or which shall not be stamped, or lawfully tendered to be stamped, according to the tenor and true meaning of this act, within the respective times herein for that purpose severally and respectively limited, *shall be void, and not available in any court or place, or to any purpose whatsoever*, and the clerk, or servant whom the same shall concern or relate to, shall in such case be utterly incapable of being free of any city, town, corporation, or company, and of following or exercising the intended profession, trade, or employment, any charter, law, or custom to the contrary notwithstanding.

Sect. 40. Sect. 40. Provided always, that nothing in this act contained, shall be construed to extend to charge any master or mistress with the payment of any of the said duties, in respect of any money by him or her received with any apprentice or servant, who shall be put or placed out at the common or public charge of any parish or township, or by or out of any public charity, or to require the stamping with any such new stamp, as aforesaid, of any indenture, articles, covenant, or contract relating to such apprentice or servant as last mentioned; any thing herein contained to the contrary notwithstanding.

Sect. 45. Sect. 45. Where any thing or things, not being lawful money of Great Britain, shall directly or indirectly be given, assigned, conveyed, delivered, contracted for, or secured, to or for the use or benefit of any master or mistress, with or in respect of any such clerk, apprentice or servant, for whom a duty is chargeable, by this act; the duties hereby granted and last mentioned, shall be answered and paid for the full value or values of such thing or things, and the same duties for the said values

 shall

ſhall be ſecured and anſwered in the ſame manner and form, and under the like pains, penalties, forfeitures, and incapacities, as are before in this act provided for ſecuring the ſaid rates upon monies given or paid, or agreed to be given or paid, with ſuch clerks, apprentices, or ſervants as aforeſaid (1).

This duty muſt be paid, where a fee of 20s., or more, is given to themaſter; and if a proper ſtamp is not affixed, in purſuance of the ſtatute, the indenture cannot be given in evidence, but is void, and no ſettlement is gained by ſerving under it (2).

Some indentures however do not require this ſtamp as not being within the ſcope of the act; and others are expreſsly exempted. Thus it ſeems hardly to have required a caſe to determine, that indentures where no conſideration money is given with the apprentice, are not within the ſtatutes (3). **Exceptions from 8 Anne, c. 9. 1. No conſideration.**

So likewiſe, ſums under twenty ſhillings are exempt from this duty; for the legiſlature, by fixing it at ſo much for every twenty ſhillings, limit that as the ſmalleſt ſum upon which the tax is payable (4). And the indentures will not be avoided if the duty is paid on a greater **2. Under 20s.**

(1) The foregoing clauſes reſpect the duty as it affects the validity of the indentures upon which the ſettlement depends. There are other ſections as well as ſubſequent ſtatutes which enforce penalties on the maſter for neglecting to pay the duty, and give the apprentice time to get his indentures ſtamped, under particular circumſtances, and upon certain conditions. But it ſeems unneceſſary to ſtate them here, as they do not affect the queſtion of ſettlement. Such are 18 Geo. 2. c. 22. ſſ. 24, 25, 26, 20 Geo. 2. c. 45. ſſ. 5, 6, 7, 8. 5 Geo. 3. c 46. ſſ. 18, 19, 41.

(2) Cueroen *v.* Ieland, 1 Bott, 541. Pl. 742. Rex *v.* Ditchingham, *ante*, 312. n. (4).

(3) Rex *v.* St. Peter's Cheſter, 1 Bott. 544. Pl. 745.

(4) Rex *v.* Yarmouth, Burr. S. C. 379. Baxter *v.* Faulam, 1 Wils. 129. 1 Bott, 545. Pl. 744; where the ſum given was 6d.

Duty paid on more than master receives.

greater sum than was actually received by the master, although sect. 39. requires, that the full sum received shall be truly inserted therein; for this only means that no part of what is paid shall be concealed. Thus, where the sum agreed to be paid was five guineas, which was inserted in the indenture; and the duty was paid on five guineas, although in fact only four guineas were paid; the apprentice gained a settlement under the indentures, because the duty was paid on the sum contracted for; and even if four guineas was all the master was to have, still the words of the act have been complied with, for the full sum paid and more has been inserted, and the duty paid upon it, and the proper stamp appropriated to this description of instruments has been used (1).

3. Things for apprentice's use.

It has been likewise held, that this act applies only to money, or things of value received by the master by way of premium for his own benefit; but that such things are exempt from duty, if given solely for the apprentice's use.

Money to clothe apprentice.

A master refused to take an apprentice because he wanted clothes, upon which the grandfather agreed to pay the master thirty shillings to clothe the boy, which he did; and no mention was made of this sum in the indenture, nor any duty paid. Yet service under this indenture gave a settlement. For the master was to be considered as an agent for the grandfather in clothing the boy. The clothing was before binding, and it is only putting a boy apprentice ready clothed. The statute means money given for the benefit of the master, but the master here had no benefit; he was not obliged to clothe the boy before he was his apprentice (2).

(1) Rex *v.* Keynsham, Trin. 44. Geo. 3. 5 East, 309.

(2) Rex *v.* North Owram. 2 Str. 1132. Burr. S. C. 145. 1 Bott, 514. Pl. 744.

A pau-

A pauper's indenture covenanted, that "sufficient "meat, drink, apparel of all kinds, physic, surgery, and "lodging, and all other necessaries, during the same term, "to be found and provided for the said apprentice *by the* "*said father*, which the said father for himself, his exe- "cutors and administrators, doth covenant and agree to "find the said apprentice during the said term: for "which purpose the said *master is to allow him, or them*, "the sum of four shillings per week, weekly during the "said term." A proportionable deduction of the weekly allowance was further agreed to be made for voluntary absence. The indenture was not stamped with a six penny or twelve penny stamp under 8 & 9 Anne. The court were unanimous, that it was unnecessary: for there was nothing before them to shew that the four shillings a week was not an equivalent. Aston J. hinted, that the 45th Sect. of 8 Anne c. 9. which says, "that "where any thing, or things, not being lawful money of "Great Britain, shall be directly or indirectly given," means such other equivalents, as a horse, or other valuable thing of that sort, and did not apply to an agreement "to "provide necessaries for a son." (1).

Meat, drink, &c. found by the father: the master allowing an equivalent.

So a pauper covenanted by his indentures, "that he "would at his own expence, provide for himself meat, "drink, washing, lodging, apparel and physic, during "the term;" and there was a covenant on the part of the master to pay the pauper for the first three years five shillings per week, six shillings per week for the succeeding two, and seven shillings a week for the remainder of the term, with a proviso, that he should not be entitled to wages during absence from sickness or negligence. *There was no stamp*, and it was held unnecessary upon the principle of the last case, that the master paid an equiva-

Apprentice finding his own meat, &c.

(1) Rex v. Portsea, Burr. S. C. 834. 1 Bott, 548. Pl. 747.

 lent

lent, and received no benefit within the meaning of the ſtatutes (1).

Meat, &c. found without ſtipulation for an equivalent.

In a latter caſe, it was held that ſuch an agreement was not ſubject to the tax, although the maſter did not ſtipulate to pay an equivalent, for thoſe things which he was exempted by covenant from ſupplying for his apprentice.

A father bound his ſon apprentice under an indenture for four years, to learn the trade of a ſhoemaker, in which was a covenant by the father of the apprentice, "that he would at his own charge find and provide "for his ſon good, competent, and ſufficient meat, drink "and lodging, on every ſunday in the year, during the "ſaid term; and would provide him with clothes and ap-"parel of all ſorts, except working aprons and ſhoes, and "alſo waſhing." There was alſo *(inter alia)* a covenant on the part of the maſter to provide for the apprentice meat, drink, and lodging, except on ſundays during the term. The indenture was properly executed and atteſted, and written on a five ſhilling ſtamp. The pauper ſerved under it for four years, for ſix days and nights each week; and went to his father's in another pariſh every ſunday. The pauper's father expended 5l. and upwards in clothing his ſon and providing meat, drink, &c. for him on ſundays during the four years under this covenant: for this no additional duty was paid according to 8 Anne c. 9.

Lord Kenyon C. J. "This has been *vexata queſtio* ever "ſince I came into Weſtminſter-hall; and various opinions "have been entertained upon it. It is true, that if an in-"denture be taken to the ſtamp office, they will ſet their "value upon every ſuppoſed benefit to the maſter for the "ſake of the revenue; but that is by no means deciſive.

(1) Rex v. Walton in Le Dale, 3 Term Rep. 515. 1 Bott, 553. Pl. 749.

"The

" The queſtion depends on the Stat. Anne c. 9. ſ. 22 & " 45; the former of which ſections impoſes a duty on all " ſums of money given with any apprentice, &c; and " the latter enacts, that where any thing, not being mo- " ney, ſhall be given, contracted for, or ſecured, to or " for the uſe or benefit of the maſter, the duty ſhall be " paid for the full value of ſuch things, in the ſame man- " ner, &c. The latter proviſion was inſerted for the " purpoſe of protecting the revenue from any fraud which " might otherwiſe be practiſed, by the parties giving " ſomething in lieu of money. For if, as in the caſe put " by Aſton, Juſtice, a horſe, or other valuable thing of " that ſort, be given by the friends of the apprentice " to the maſter, that muſt be conſidered to be a benefit " to the maſter, for which a duty ſhould be paid. It " occurred to me early in the argument that, in order to " ſee what would or would not be conſidered as a benefit " to the maſter, it was neceſſary to inquire what were " the duties that reſulted from the bare relation of maſter " and apprentice. And I think that the ſtatute of 8 & 9 " Will. 3. c. 30. ſ. 5. throws a great deal of light upon " that point; becauſe if, from the time of the ſtatute of " Elizabeth to that time, maſters could not be compelled " to provide for pariſh-apprentices, and that law was " made for the purpoſe, it ſhews that the obligation of " providing for apprentices did not reſult from the mere " relation of maſter and apprentice; for if it did, that " part of the ſtatute of Will. 3. was unneceſſary. The " caſe of pariſh apprentices is the only one where an ap- " prentice can be put out *nolens volens*; all the others " depend on the expreſs ſtipulations to be made by the " parties intereſted. It has never been held that the ob- " ligation of the maſter extended to the providing of " clothes for the apprentice, and yet I cannot diſtinguiſh " that from the obligation to provide ſuſtenance; for the " former are equally neceſſary with the latter; and in

 " other

" other cases than those of parish apprentices, clothes are " generally provided by the friends of the apprentice. " But if every thing is to be valued, and a duty set upon it, " from which a benefit arises to the master, it might be " equally said, that the earnings of the apprentice should " be liable to the duty. The argument therefore, that " every benefit which the master derives from the apprentice, by proving too much, proves nothing. The authority of *Aston, J.* Justice, is in all cases worth resorting " to, but particularly so, in cases of sessions law, in " which he was remarkably conversant. And his opinion, " in the case alluded to, is very strong to this point. I " think, therefore, that the clear meaning of the statute " of Anne is, that where money, or money's worth, is " given to the master by the friends of the apprentice, " by way of premium, a duty ought to be paid for it; " but, that where meat, clothes, &c. are to be provided " *by the master* (1), no duty is payable, because there is not " any thing given to the master (2)."

Apprentice's earnings.

In a more recent case, in addition to the pauper's agreement, to find himself in clothes, board, washing and lodging, it was stipulated, that the master should allow him full journeyman's wages, and have four pence out of every shilling of his earning. But it was thought too clear to admit of argument, that a part of the apprentice's earnings reserved to the master was not a benefit liable to duty under the statute. For by law, he was entitled to the whole, and might rather be said to have given up that part which he did not reserve, than to have acquired any thing (3).

(1) *Sic in orig*: *Qu.* If it should not be, by them for the apprentice.

(2) Rex *v.* Leighton. 4 Term. Rep. 732. 1 Bott. 559. Pl. 751.

(3) Rex *v.* Wantage, 1 East. 601.

Sect.

Sect. 40, expressly exempts from duty, money given with apprentices, in two cases.

1st, Where the apprentice or servant is "put out at "the common or public charge of any parish or town-"ship." The words comprehend not only parish apprentices, formally bound out by parish officers with the assent of two justices, but voluntary apprentices also, provided the master's fee or premium is taken from the public parish fund (1).

Apprentices put out at parish charge.

The 2d exception is, of money paid "out of any "public charity." The court has given a liberal construction to this clause. They have held therefore, that it need not be a *permanent charity*.

By public charity.

In the parish of St. John's, Wapping, there was a voluntary annual subscription by divers of the inhabitants, for putting apprentice, boys and girls brought up at the parish charity school. Four trustees and a treasurer were annually elected to manage the charity, and a number of children were annually bound out. This was held a public charity, and within the proviso. A boy, therefore, bound by indenture, whose master received five pounds from the trustees of this charity, gained a settlement, although not stamped with a stamp, denoting the receipt of this duty. For *per* Lord Mansfield, this is a public charity. *It is not necessary that it should be a permanent charity.* The reason of the distinction between a public and private charity is obvious. A private charity may be calculated to evade the act, which a public one cannot be supposed to be (2).

Charity not permanent.

(1) Rex *v.* St. Petrox in Dartmouth. 4 Term. Rep. 196. 1 Bott. 556. Pl. 750.

(2) Rex *v.* St. Mathew's Bethnal Green. Burr. S. C. 574. 1 Bott. 643. Pl. 899.

Extent of fund immaterial.

Neither is the extent of the fund, or number of its objects material. The criterion of a public charity, within this act, appears to be that the object of the charity should be general, without having any particular individuals in contemplation at the time it is created, as otherwise the duty might be easily evaded.

A woman bequeathed, among other charities, by her will, "to Clifton, (the parish in which she resided) fifty "pounds, to be given as my brother thinks fit; some of "it to put out children apprentices." Three children were put out by the brother under this bequest. Seven pound was given to the master with one of them, and it was expressed in the indenture to be charity-money, but there was no stamp denoting the payment of the six-penny duty, nor was it paid. It was argued, that this was not a public, but a private charity, being left entirely to the choice of the testator's brother, whether to put out children apprentices with this money. But the court held it a public charity, and that the pauper gained a settlement (1).

These stamp duties have been altered considerably by 44 Geo. 3. chap. 98. It was necessary however, to state th substance of the former statutes, not only because all indentures of apprenticeship made prior to the 10th of October 1804 are regulated by them, but also, because 44 Geo. 3. c. 98. provides, that they shall continue in force, except so far as any alteration is thereby expressly made (2).

From 19 Oct 1804. Duties, &c under care of commissioners of stamps, shall cease.

Sect. 1. That, from and after the tenth day of October, one thousand eight hundred and four, all and singular the duties, allowances, discounts, compensations,

(1) Rex v. Clifton upon Dunsmore. Burr. S. C. 697. 1 Bott. 645. Pl. 900.

(2) Sect. viii. *Post.*

and

and drawbacks of ſtamp duties, and other the duties under the care of the commiſſioners for managing the duties upon ſtamped vellum, parchment, and paper, granted by any act or acts of parliament now in force, ſhall ceaſe and determine, ſave and except in all caſes relating to the recovering, allowing, or paying any arrears thereof reſpectively, which may at that time remain unpaid, or to any fine, penalty, or forfeiture, fines, penalties, or forfeitures, relating thereto reſpectively, which ſhall have been incurred at any time before, or on the ſaid tenth day of October, one thouſand eight hundred and four.

Sect. 2. That, from and after the ſaid tenth day of October, one thouſand eight hundred and four, in lieu and inſtead of the ſaid duties reſpectively, by this act repealed, there ſhall be raiſed, levied, collected, and paid, in England, unto his Majeſty, his heirs and ſucceſſors, for and in reſpect of the ſeveral inſtruments, articles, matters, and things, mentioned, enumerated, and deſcribed in the ſchedules marked (A) and (B) hereunto annexed, the ſeveral ſums of money and duties as they are reſpectively inſerted, deſcribed, and ſet forth in the column of the ſaid ſchedules, marked (A) and (B), intitled "England;" and that there ſhall be raiſed, levied, collected, and paid in like manner in Scotland, the ſeveral ſums of money and duties as they are reſpectively inſerted, deſcribed, and ſet forth in the column of the ſaid ſchedules marked (A) and (B), intitled, "Scotland;" and that there ſhall be made, allowed, and paid, for or in reſpect of all ſuch articles, matters, or things, as are inſerted, enumerated, and deſcribed in the ſchedule marked (C,) hereunto annexed, the ſeveral allowances, drawbacks, or ſums of money, as the ſame are reſpectively inſerted, deſcribed, and ſet forth in the ſaid ſchedule marked (C).

From 10 Oct. 1804. duties in ſchedules A. & B. to be paid.

Sect. 8. And be it further enacted, that the ſaid ſeveral ſums of money reſpectively inſerted, deſcribed, and ſet

Duties and drawbacks to be paid and allowed.

as former duties and drawbacks; Provisions of former acts to extend to this act, except so far as hereby altered.

set forth in the said schedules marked (A) and (B) as duties payable to his Majesty, his heirs and successors, and the several allowances, drawbacks, and sums of money, for, or in respect of the several articles, matters, and things inserted, described, and set forth in the said schedule marked (C), shall and may be respectively raised, levied, collected, answered, paid, recovered, adjudged, mitigated, and allowed, except where any alteration is expresly made by this act, in such and the like manner, and in or by any or either of the general or special means, ways, or methods, by which the former duties under the management of the said commissioners of stamped vellum, parchment, or paper respectively, and the allowances and drawbacks under the management of the said commissioners respectively, were or might be raised, levied, collected, answered, paid, recovered, adjudged, mitigated, and allowed; and the several persons, and also all vellum, parchment, paper, or other material of what nature or kind soever, upon which any matter or thing shall be written, printed, or ingrossed, and by this act respectively made liable to the payment of duty, and also the several other articles, matters, and things, by this act respectively made liable to the payment of duty, or which shall be entitled to any allowance or drawback, as respectively inserted, described, and set forth in the said schedules, marked (A), (B), and (C), shall be, and the same are hereby made, except where any alteration is expresly made by this act, subject and liable to all, and every the conditions, regulations, rules, and restrictions, to which such persons, and also such vellum, parchment, paper, or other material of what nature or kind soever, upon which any such matter, or thing, as aforesaid, shall be written, printed, or ingrossed, and other articles, matters, and things as aforesaid, were generally, or specially subject and liable by any act or acts of parliament in force before or on the said tenth day of October, one housand thousand eight hundred and four, respecting the duties under the management of the said commissioners of stamped vellum, parchment, and paper; and all and every pain, penalty, fine, or forfeiture (except where any alteration is expresly made by this act), for any offence whatsoever, committed against, or in breach of any act or acts of parliament now in force, before or on the said tenth day of October, one thousand eight hundred and four, for securing the duties under the management of the said commissioners of stamped vellum, parchment, and paper, or for the regulation or improvement of the said duties, and the several clauses, powers, provisions, directions, matters, and things therein contained, (unless where expresly altered by this act), shall, and are hereby directed and declared to extend to, and shall be respectively applied, practised, and put in execution, for and in respect of the several duties by this act charged, imposed, and allowed, in as full and ample a manner, to all intents and purposes whatsoever, as if all and every the said clauses, provisions, powers, directions, fines, pains, penalties, or forfeitures, matters, and things, were particularly repeated and re-enacted in the body of this act.

Where instruments, except bills of exchange &c. have, without fraudulent intention, been written on improper stamps, the commissioners may remit the penalty, if brought to be duly stamped, within 12

Sect. 24. That in any case where it shall appear to the commissioners of his Majesty's Stamp Duties, upon oath or affirmation, to be made before any one or more of the said commissioners, (which oath or affirmation he or they is or are hereby authorised to administer), or otherwise to their satisfaction, that any Instrument, Matter, or Thing whatsoever, (except Bills of Exchange, Promissory Notes, or other Notes, Drafts, Orders, or Receipts, required by law to be ingrossed, printed, or written on stamped vellum, parchment, or paper), hath been ingrossed, printed, or written on vellum, parchment, or paper, not duly stamped with a Stamp of the value by this Act required, either months after execution. either by accident or inadvertency, or from urgent necessity, or unavoidable circumstances, and without any wilful delay or intention in any party or parties thereto, to evade the duties by this Act imposed, or to defraud his Majesty thereof; and such instrument, matter, and thing, shall be brought to the said commissioners to be stamped within twelve months after the making or execution thereof, it shall be lawful for such commissioners of his majesty's stamp duties to remit the penalty payable on stamping such instrument, matter, or thing, or any part thereof, as they shall deem expedient; and every person concerned in ingrossing, printing, or writing any such instrument, matter, or thing, or in making or executing the same, shall be, and he or she is hereby freed, discharged, and indemnified from all further penalties or forfeitures, than such penalties or forfeitures, or such parts thereof, as shall not be remitted by order of the said commissioners of his Majesty's stamp duties.

Schedule A. These stamp duties, so far as respect instruments which are executed in England, and relate to settlements by service or apprenticeship, are thus set forth in Schedule (A) to which the Act refers.

Articles to serve clerk to an attorney, in courts at Westminster. Articles or contracts whereby any person shall become bound to serve as a clerk in order to his admission as a solicitor or attorney, in pursuance of the laws now in force in any of his Majesty's courts at Westminster, £110.

Articles of clerks to attornies in other courts. Articles or contracts whereby any person shall become bound to serve as a clerk, in order to his admission as a solicitor or attorney in any of the courts of great Sessions in Wales, or in the counties palatine of Chester, Lancaster, or Durham, or in any court of record in England, holding pleas, where the debt or damage shall amount

amount to forty ſhillings or upwards, not being in any of his majeſty's courts at Weſtminſter, £55.

Aſſignment of ſuch articles or contract, or new articles or contract, for the reſidue of a term, occaſioned by the death of any former maſter, £1 10s. Aſſignments thereof.

Agreement made in England under hand only, where the matter thereof ſhall be of the value of 20l. or upwards, whether the ſame ſhall be only the evidence of a contract or obligatory upon the parties from its being a written inſtrument, upon any number of words, not amounting to thirty common law ſheets (calculated at ſeventy-two words to each ſheet) of which any ſuch agreement ſhall conſiſt, 16s. Agreements.

And for every entire quantity of fifteen common law ſheets (calculated at ſeventy-two words to each ſheet) of which any ſuch agreement, together with every ſchedule, receipt, inſtrument, or other matter put or indorſed thereon, or annexed thereto, ſhall conſiſt, over and above the firſt fifteen common law-ſheets, a further duty of 16s. Agreements.

Special Exemptions.

Memorandum or agreement for the hire of any labourer, artificer, manufacturer, or menial ſervant. Exemptions.

Indenture of apprenticeſhip where the ſum of value given, paid, contracted, or agreed for, with or in relation to ſuch apprentice, ſhall not exceed £10 £ 15s Indentures of apprenticeſhip.

		£	s
exceeding £10, and not exceeding	20	1	10
exceeding 20, and not exceeding	50	2	10
exceeding 50, and not exceeding	100	5	0
exceeding 100, and not exceeding	300	12	0
exceeding 300 - - -		20	0

Special

Special Exemption.

Exemption.

Indentures for binding poor parish children apprentices, or other children by any public charity.

Assignment of Indenture of apprenticeship, (except of poor parish children, or other children by any public charity) 15s.

II. *Of the Distinction between imperfect Contracts of Apprenticeship, and Contracts of Hiring and Service.*

It has been shewn already, that particular forms are required to render a contract of apprenticeship valid, which are unnecessary to the hiring of a servant (1).

This latter contract, however, may be executed with all the formalities incident to deeds of apprenticeship. It is sometimes difficult therefore to distinguish between them; especially as cases of imperfect apprenticeship, by reason of their defect, approach nearer in resemblance to the more loose form of contracts for service under an hiring.

No technical word to constitute a binding.

It seems at one time to have been thought necessary to use the word *apprentice*, in order to constitute a binding as such (2). But neither this, nor any other technical words are essential, provided the parties shew an evident intention to constitute the relation of master and apprentice (3).

(1) *Ante*, 188.

(2) See 3 Bac. Abr. 546, and Rex Little Bolton, *post*.

(3) *Per* Lord Kenyon C. J. Rex v. Laindon, 8 Term Rep. 379. 1 Bott, 710. Pl. 1000; and in Rex v. Rainham. 1 *East*, 531.

The

The court indeed ſeem to regret that a criterion, equally certain and more general, has not been reſorted to (1). This might have been, if regard being had to the derivation of the term (2), every contract by which the maſter engaged to teach, and the ſervant to learn a trade, had been held an apprenticeſhip (3).

But this diſtinction has been overlooked, and a ſettlement may be gained as an hired ſervant, although the object of the agreement and ſervice be to learn a trade (4). As the parties may lawfully enter into either engagement, the particular nature of the agreement is to be collected from their intention at the time of making it. Where the contract is in writing, this muſt be drawn from the words made uſe of; "for parol evidence cannot be received to "contradict a written agreement. But it may to aſcer-"tain a fact collateral to the written inſtrument, in order "to explain the intention of the parties; the written in-"ſtrument being in ſome meaſure equivocal (5)."

Upon this principle, an agreement which is defective as a contract of apprenticeſhip, from any of the following circumſtances, cannot be converted into an hiring and ſervice ſo as to confer a ſettlement.

Contracts of apprenticeſhip give no ſettlement.

If the parties uſe the term apprentice in deſcribing the relation to be created by their contract, or otherwiſe expreſsly declare their intention to ſtand in the ſituation of maſter and apprentice.

1. When term apprentice uſed.

(1) *Per* Lawrence J. Rex *v.* Laindon, *ante* 332.

(2) From *Apprendre*, to learn.

(3) *Per* Lord Ellenborough C. J. Rex *v* Eccleſton, 2 Eaſt. 298. *Per* Lord Kenyon C. J. Rex *v.* Laindon, *ante*. *Per* Lord Mansfield C. J. Rex *v.* Little Bolton, Cald. 367. But he afterward held a contrary opinion with the reſt of the court.

(4) Rex *v.* Hitcham, *ante* 293, and the caſes *poſt*.

(5) *Per* Lawrence J. Rex *v.* Laindon, *ante*.

G, aged

Binding as apprentice to stone mason, &c.

G, aged twenty-two, agreed with a stone mason to *bind himself apprentice* for six years; the master to provide him meat, drink, washing, lodging, and clothing, *during his apprenticeship*, and G to live with, and work for him, *as his apprentice during that term*, and that *indentures should be executed between them accordingly*; but no such indentures were executed. The pauper gained no settlement as an apprentice, because there were no indentures, nor as an hired servant, for he was engaged to serve as an apprentice (1).

A parol agreement was proved between the pauper's grandfather and the master, *to take the pauper as an apprentice*, and no indentures were executed.—He gained no settlement (2).

So where the agreement was in writing, "that the "pauper should be *bound apprentice*," but it was not stamped, no settlement was gained (3).

2. Premium given.

2d, Although the term apprentice is not made use of, yet if the party gives a premium to the master who engages to teach him some trade or mystery, it is a contract of apprenticeship. For a servant never gives such a consideration; and such agreements would otherwise evade the duties imposed by 8 Anne c. 9.

The Sessions found that the pauper went to his master (who was a carpenter) for the purpose of *being his apprentice*, in order to learn the trade; and to save the expence of the indenture and duty, four guineas consideration being paid by the pauper to the master, they

(1) Rex *v.* Whitchurch, Canonicorum, *ante* 193. Rex *v.* St. Mary Kallendar, Burr. S. C. 274. 1 Bott. 526. Pl. 711. S. P. Rex v. Margram. 5 Term Rep. 153. 2 Bott, 318. Pl. 414.

(2) Rex *v.* Kingsweare, Burr. S. C. 839.

(3) Rex *v.* All Saints, Hereford, Burr. S. C. 656, and the cases there cited. 2 Bott. 379. Pl. 407. S. C.

ſigned an agreement upon unſtamped paper, wherein the pauper covenanted to ſerve his maſter in the buſineſs or trade of carpenter for four years, and the conſideration of the agreement was, that the maſter do pay him ſo much a week, which wages were to be increaſed yearly, until the expiration of his time. The court thought that this was manifeſtly a fraud on the revenue, and that the relation intended was that of an apprentice, which being void for want of proper ſtamps, the pauper acquired no ſettlement by ſerving under the agreement (1).

In this caſe the intent to evade the duty was expreſsly found; but the conſtruction of the agreement is the ſame where this intention is not ſo manifeſt.

A pauper by a written agreement on unſtamped paper, " agreed to ſerve three years, to learn the buſineſs of a " carpenter, and to receive wages, which were to in- " creaſe each ſucceeding year." The pauper alſo proved by parol, that at the time of ſigning the above agreement, he agreed to give his maſter three guineas, as a premium to teach him the trade, and was not to be employed in any other work than that of a carpenter: it was held a defective contract of apprenticeſhip (2).

3d, It *ſeems* further, that wherever the contract is executed with the ſolemnities incident to a binding by deed, and the object of the agreement is to inſtruct the party ſerving, it is rather to be conſidered as a contract of apprenticeſhip, than of hiring as a ſervant. **3. Deed executed in due form.**

The pauper, M. Smith, agreed with T. Hills, a ſawyer, to ſerve him for three years, at weekly wages. " And " the ſaid T. H. doth agree and promiſe to learn the

(1) Rex *v.* Highnam, Cald. 491. 2 Bott. 381. Pl. 409.

(2) Rex *v.* Laindon, 8 Term Rep. 379. *ante.* 332.

" ſaid

"said M. Smith, the art and mystery of a sawyer, which "he now follows." It was further agreed, if he should wilfully lose any time, he was to pay H. three shillings a day; and if he repented of the agreement before the time expired, to pay him 10l.; and if he should be incapable of working, he was not to receive any wages. The agreement was signed, sealed, and delivered by both parties, and lawfully stamped, and no premium was paid by the pauper to his master.

Lord Kenyon, C. J. The legal conclusion can only be drawn in one way, namely, that this was a contract of apprenticeship. The instrument was under seal, and need not be indented. It has been determined, that the party serving need not be retained *eo nomine* as an apprentice; but that it is enough if the purpose of the contract be, that the one shall teach and the other learn the trade. That is the case here, for the master engaged to learn, *i. e.* to teach the pauper the art and mystery of a sawyer; and the object of the pauper was to be taught the business. No technical words are necessary to constitute the relation of master and apprentice; nor is it necessary that there should be any premium given to the master.

Mr. J. Le Blanc, the only remaining judge who gave an opinion, observed, that it was immaterial to the present case, whether the contract was to serve as an apprentice, or as an hired servant; for having served a year, he gained a settlement either way (1).

Contracts for service, when servants to be taught.

But where none of these circumstances occurred to determine the nature of the agreement, it has been held, that a contract to serve for the purpose of learning a trade, is an hiring as a servant.

(1) Rex v. Rainham, 1 East. 531. But it would have been necessary to determine, in what capacity the pauper served, if he had been married when he made the contract, or had not abided in the service for an entire year.

1st, If

1st, If the party engages to do the duties of a servant, ulterior to such as are incident to the trade he learns; for the extent of the service points out and explains the relation in which the parties intended to stand towards each other (1). 2. If he is to do all sorts of work.

The pauper clubbed, *i. e.* contracted to serve for the purpose of being taught the trade of a bricklayer, and to have less wages, on account of learning the trade. He was to serve three years, at six shillings a week the first year, seven shillings the second, and eight shillings the third. An agreement in writing was to be prepared, but was never drawn up. No premium was paid, and he was to do any work his master set him about, and was not to be absent from his business during any part of the time.

Lord Kenyon C. J. said, "it was impossible to raise a "doubt upon the case; the part which states that the "pauper was to do any work his master set him about *is* "*decisive* to shew, that he must be considered as an hired "servant, and although one of his objects was to learn a "trade, that was deemed an equivalent to part of his "wages (2)."

And the same was held, where, to an agreement in other respects similar to the preceding, it was added, that if the pauper was prevented from working at any time by badness of weather, illness, or his master's not having employment for him, a proportionable deduction

(1) But this rule applies only to equivocal contracts. If a yearly hiring is made out, a settlement may be gained, although the agreement be to work, only at a particular trade. Rex *v.* Buckland Denham, *ante*, 211, where the principle is not disputed. Burr. S. C. 694. Rex *v.* Birmingham, *ante*, 210-212. Doug. 533. Rex *v.* Alton, Cald. 424. 2 Bott, 222. Pl. 265.

(2) Rex *v.* Coltishall, 5 Term Rep. 193. 2 Bott, 228. Pl. 270.

should be made from his week's wages for such loss of time (1).

2. Contracts not appearing intended as an apprenticeship, and no premium given.

2d, There is a case, which, unless it is to be considered as "an anomalous case (2)," seems to go the length of establishing the following principle. That all contracts of service, for the purpose of instruction, which are informal as contracts of apprenticeship, are to be taken as contracts of hiring, where no direct circumstance appears to shew, that a contract of apprenticeship was intended, and no premium is given to the master.

This rule does not seem unreasonable, unless it leads to uncertainty.

It is an established maxim of law, that ambiguous instruments are to receive a judicial construction, ut res magis valeat quam pereat. Independent of which, the old decisions lean neither unwisely, nor unconstitutionally, in favour of settlements (3).

Service for two or three years, to be taught to weave counterpanes.

The pauper being unmarried, and having no child, went to one S. a weaver, and asked him if he would teach him to work counterpanes. S. answered he would, if he would work *with him two years and a half, or three years*; and the pauper's earnings were to be divided between them, and he to find himself with meat, drink, washing and clothes. He was engaged on these terms, and an agreement in writing was entered into accordingly. He worked under this agreement a year and an half, his master finding him in looms, loom room and materials, when he gave his master twenty shillings to be free, having then married. He continued to work

(1) Rex *v.* Martham, 1 East. 239.

(2) *Verba* Kenyon C. J. Rex *v.* Laindon, *ante*, 332, (3).

(3) See the opinion of Buller J. Rex *v.* Little Bolton, Cald. 370. *post*, 339, (1).

journey-

journey-work with the ſame maſter for a year. S. *never employed the pauper in any work but weaving.* He received the money, and paid the pauper one half, and looked on it, that he had a right to receive it, but ſometimes let the pauper do ſo. Lord Mansfield was originally of opinion, "If an indenture be not made neceſſary, (*i. e.* to conſtitute a binding as an apprentice,) there could be no doubt as to its being an apprenticeſhip; for the pauper is *to be taught*, and pays a conſideration for it, and is to do no other work: but if theſe agreements were allowed to give ſettlements, there would be an end of indentures of apprenticeſhip, and alſo of the revenue derived from thence." But Buller J. doubting, the court took time to conſider, and Lord Mansfield on another day delivered their opinion. "We have looked into the authorities, and find that all thoſe caſes of apprenticeſhips which have been holden to be defective, and not convertible into hirings and ſervices, ſpeak of the pauper as an apprentice, and that he was to ſerve as ſuch. There is no ſuch ſtatement here, and it is therefore a good hiring and ſervice (1). And in a very recent caſe, in which the circumſtances were ſimilar, but the agreement was not in writing, the court held it an hiring and ſervice upon the authority of the preceding caſe. Lord Ellenborough declared, that he was not convinced by the reaſoning of the preceding caſe, and that if the point were new, he ſhould think otherwiſe, and "that where the contract was, that the maſter ſhould teach the other a trade, *and the latter was to do nothing ulterior the employment* in that trade, it was a contract *apprendre*, in the true ſenſe of the word."

The other judges coincided in opinion upon the ſame ground, Le Blanc J. adding, "that he did not think that

(1) Rex *v.* Little Bolton, Cald. 367. 2 Bott, 222. Pl. 264.

 the

the King *v.* Little Bolton, had been overruled in principle (1)."

Immaterial covenants.

The age of the party contracting to serve, seems to have formed no ground of distinction in these cases, and it is equally immaterial, whether the master is to find diet, washing, and lodging (2), or the party to find himself (3), or that he is to receive wages (4), or to have a portion of his earnings in lieu thereof (5), or that he is to live away from his master at stated intervals (6). Neither does the time for which the engagement is to last, seem to have been relied upon. In all the cases cited, both those which have been deemed contracts of apprenticeship, and those which have been held contracts of hiring, the time for which the agreement was made was less than that prescribed for the binding of apprentices, either under 5 Eliz. chap. 4., or 43 Eliz. chap. 2.

SECT. III.

Of discharging the Apprentice from his Indentures.

Discharging apprentices.

A deed of apprenticeship may be discharged in four ways besides natural efflux of time.

1. By sessions, or two justices.

1st, By application of either party to two justices of peace, or to the court of quarter sessions.

1. Power of Sessions, 5 Eliz. c. 4. s. 35.

A more extensive power is given to the sessions than to the justices, and depends upon 5 Eliz. c. 4. s. 35; which

(1) Rex *v.* Eccleston, 2 East. 298.

(2) Rex *v.* Whitechurch, Canonicorum &c. *ante*, 312, (3). 334, (1).

(3) Rex *v.* Little Bolton, *ante*, 339, (1). Rex *v.* Highnam, *ante*, 335, (1). Rex *v.* Martham, *ante*, 338, (1).

(4) Rex *v.* All Saints Hereford, *ante*, 334, (3). Rex *v.* Highnam, and the cases *ante*, n. (3).

(5) Rex *v.* Little Bolton, *ante*, 339, (1). Rex *v.* Eccleston, *ante*, (1).

(6) Rex *v.* Portsea, *ante*, 321, (1).

enacts,

enacts, "that if any *such master* shall misuse or evil intreat his apprentice, or that the *said apprentice shall have any* just cause to complain, or the apprentice do not his duty to his master, then the *said master* or *apprentice being grieved*, and having cause to complain, shall repair unto one justice of peace, within the said county, or to the mayor, or other head officer of the city, town corporate, market-town, or other place where the said master dwelleth, who shall by his wisdom and discretion take such order and direction between the said master and his apprentice, as the equity of the cause shall require; and if, for want of good conformity in the said master, the said justice of peace, or the said mayor, or other head officer cannot compound and agree the matter between him and his apprentice, then the said justice, or the said mayor, or other head officer, shall take bond of the said master to appear at the next sessions then to be holden in the said county, or within the said city, town-corporate, or market-town, to be before the justices of the said county, or the mayor or head officer of the said town-corporate or market-town, if the said master dwell within any such; and upon his appearance, and hearing of the matter before the said justices, or the said mayor, or other head officer, if it be thought meet unto them to discharge the said apprentice of his apprenticehood, that then the said justices, or four of them at the least, whereof one to be of the quorum, or the said mayor or other head officer, with the assent of three other of his brethren, or men of best reputation within the said city, town-corporate or market-town, shall have power by authority hereof, in writing, under their hands and seals, to pronounce and declare, that they have discharged the said apprentice of his apprenticehood, and the cause thereof; and the said writing so being made and enrolled by the clerk of the peace or town-clerk, among the re-

5 Eliz. c. 4. f. 35.

cords that he keepeth, shall be a sufficient discharge for the said apprentice against his master, his executors and administrators; the indentures of the said apprenticehood, or any law or custom to the contrary notwithstanding. And if the default shall be found to be in the apprentice, then the said justices, or the said mayor or other head officer, with the assistance aforesaid, shall cause such due correction and punishment to be ministered unto him, as by their wisdom and discretion shall be thought meet."

20 Geo. 2. c. 19.

The power given over indentures of apprenticeship *to two magistrates*, is created by 20 Geo. 2. c. 19., and confined to parish apprentices, or others where the premium does not exceed five pounds.

Sect. 5.

It enacts, s. 5.—"That it shall and may be lawful to, and for two or more such justices, upon any complaint or application by any apprentice put out by the parish, or any other apprentice, upon whose binding out no larger a sum than five pounds of lawful British money was paid, touching or concerning any misusage, refusal of necessary provision, cruelty, or other ill-treatment of, or toward such apprentice, by his or her master or mistress, to summon such master or mistress to appear before such justices at a reasonable time, to be named in such summons; and such justices shall and may examine into the matter of such complaint; and upon proof thereof, made upon oath, to their satisfaction, (whether the master or mistress be present or not, if service of the summons be also upon oath proved) the said justices may discharge such apprentice, by warrant or certificate under their hands and seals; for which warrant or certificate no fees shall be paid."

Sect. 4. "That it shall and may be lawful to and for such justices, upon application or complaint made, upon oath,

oath, by any master or mistress, against any such apprentice, touching or concerning any misdemeanor, miscarriage, or ill behaviour, in such his or her service, (which oath such justices are hereby empowered to administer,) to hear, examine, and determine the same, and to punish the offender by commitment to the House of Correction, there to remain and be corrected, and held to hard labour for a reasonable time, not exceeding one calendar month, or otherwise by discharging such apprentice, in manner and form before mentioned."

Sect. 5. "If any person or persons shall think himself, herself, or themselves aggrieved by such determination, order, or warrant of such justice or justices as aforesaid, (save and except any order of commitment,) he, she, or they may appeal to the next general quarter sessions of the peace to be held for the county, riding, liberty, city, town-corporate, or place where such determination or order shall be made; which said next general quarter sessions is hereby empowered to hear, and finally determine the same; and to give and award such costs to any of the respective persons, appellant or respondent, as the said sessions shall judge reasonable, not exceeding forty shillings; the same to be levied by distress and sale, in manner before mentioned." Sect. 5. Appeal to sessions.

Sect. 6. "No writ of certiorari, or other process, shall issue, or be issuable, to remove any proceedings whatever, had in pursuance of this act, into any of his Majesty's courts at Westminster." Sect. 6.

The provisions of this statute seem clear and distinct, and have not hitherto given rise to any questions respecting their construction. The following observations relate to the 5th Eliz. c. 4. But these acts being made in pari materiâ, it is probable that decisions upon one, would be considered as affording an authoritative elucidation of similar doubts arising upon the other.

1. Sessions' power extends to all trades.

It was doubted originally whether the power of discharge given by 5 Eliz. c. 4. was not to be confined to apprentices in trades specifically mentioned in that statute (1). But the law is now settled, that it extends to every description of apprentices (2).

2. Sessions where master lives.

The statute requires, that the party grieved shall apply to one justice of the peace of the county, or to the mayor, &c. of the city, &c. where the master dwelleth; *and if he cannot compound and agree* the matter between him and the apprentice, *he* is to bind the master to appear at the next sessions, &c. A power is given therefore to the justices and sessions having jurisdiction over the place where the master lives, although the apprentice is bound elsewhere (3).

3. Must be four county justices, met in general sessions.

The power of discharge is confined in counties to four justices at the least, one being of the quorum, and they must be assembled at a general sessions. Where four justices discharged an apprentice at a private sessions, the order was set aside (4). In cities, towns corporate, or

(1) *Per* Lord Hale, Watkins *v.* Edwards, 1 Vent. 174. 2 Keb. 822. Rex *v.* Gately, 2 Salk 471. 5 Mod. 159. resolved accordingly. 1 Bott, 572. Pl. 780. Rex *v.* Furness, Cas. Sett.; and Rem 21. S. P.

(2) Rex *v.* Collingbourne, 1 Stra. 663. 1 Bott, 574. Pl. 785. Rex *v.* Taunton, cited *ib.* 575 (c). In Marg. Hawksworth *v.* Hilary, 1 Saund. 315.

(3) Rex *v.* Collingbourne, *ante*, (2). In this case the apprentice was bound in London, to one of the freemen, and the indentures were enrolled there, and the master lived in Middlesex at the time of the complaint. The court said, "they would not take away the "jurisdiction of the mayor's court, "but only give a concurrent jurisdic- "tion to the justices of the peace for "the county." The reporter, Strange adds, "the words of the statute are "very plain, for they give a juris- "diction to the justices where the ap- "prentice lives." But the report in Lord Raymond, 1410. gives no support to the foregoing dictum.

(4) Anon. Skin. 98. 1 Bott, 572. Pl. 776.

market-

market-towns, the power is given to the mayor or head officer, with the consent of his brethren or men of best reputation within the place.

It has been thought, that the legislature intended this power of dissolving the indenture to be exercised rather by way of appeal after the justice had tried in vain to compound the existing differences, than that the sessions should exercise it in the first instance, upon a direct application (1). But it was afterwards considered that the interference of a private justice was intended only to arbitrate and accommodate the dispute; and it is now settled that the sessions possess an original jurisdiction independent of any such previous application (2). 4. Sessions have an original jurisdiction.

5. Master's appearance.

The act requires the discharge to be made "upon the "master's appearance." An objection was taken to an order of sessions which discharged an apprentice, that it did not state this appearance. But the court held that the act must have a reasonable construction, so as not to permit the master to take advantage of his own obstinacy. The apprentice's remedy therefore was not confined to proceedings on the recognizance, forfeited by non-appearance; but the Sessions might proceed in the master's absence, as otherwise, if he ran away, the apprentice could not be discharged (3).

The original application was made in this case to a justice, and the parties being bound over to the sessions, must take notice, and appear without further summons (4). But where the application is in the first instance to the 6. Summons.

(1) See the opinion of Twysden and Rainsford, J. Watkins *v.* Edwards, 1 Mod. 287. Holt C. J. anon. 2 Salk. 67.

(2) Rex *v.* Johnson, 1 Salk. 68. 1 Bott, 573. Pl. 781. 2 Salk. 491. Rex *v.* Gill, 1 Str. 143. Rex *v.* Davis, *ib.* 704. Rex *v.* Hesseman, Cas. Temp. Hardw. 101. 2 Str. 1014. 1 Bott, 577. Pl. 788. S. C.

(3) Ditton's case, 2 Salk. 491. 1 Bott, 572. Pl. 777.

(4) *Ut videtur per* Lee C. J. Rex *v.* Amies, 1 Bott. 576. Pl. 787.

sessions,

sessions, the party complained against must be summoned, and if he make default, it is equal to an appearance (1).

Form of the order.

And where the master is complained against, the order must set forth either that he appeared, or that he was summoned and made default, or it will be quashed for the defect.—Because, although in cases of orders in general, the court will presume *omnia rite esse acta*; yet that presumption is only in case of orders which do not in express terms require an appearance. But it is otherwise in an act like that of 5 Eliz. c. 4., which gives the justices authority to proceed upon the appearance of the party; so that it is made an essential requisite to found their jurisdiction (2).

Order of discharge on whose application.

An order of discharge may be made upon the application of either party; "for an apprentice may be discharged from a bad master, and a bad apprentice from his master (3)." But the sessions cannot discharge without shewing some cause (4), which must be set forth in their order.

Ground of complaint.

The usual causes for which the apprentice complains against the master are, cruelty and misusing his contract, either by neglecting to instruct him, or the like; and when the master applies to get quit of his apprentice, it is generally upon the ground of incorrigible misbehaviour.

Grounds of discharge how stated in order.

If an order merely states that the master "misused his apprentice," or that the master "used him unkindly (5)," or that he refused to take him again (6), or that he re-

(1) *Per* Probyn J. Rex *v.* Amies, *ante*, 345, (*a*).

(2) Rex *v* Heaseman. 1 Bott, 577. Pl. 788, *ante*, 345, (2). See Regina *v.* Rutter, 1 Bott. 574. Pl. 782. Rex *v.* Gill, 1 Str. 143.

(3) Hawksworth *v.* Hilary, *ante*. 344, (2).

(4) Rex *v.* Heaseman, *ante*, (2). 2 Str. 1013. Rex *v.* Davis, *ib*, 704. 1 Bott, 576. Pl. 786.

(5) Rex *v.* Heaseman, *ante*, (2).

(6) Rex *v.* Davis. Str. 704. *ante*, (4).

fused

fused to entertain him according to the indentures (1), it does not shew a sufficient ground for the discharge. Neither is it enough that the apprentice has married without his master's consent (2). And there is no power to discharge for sickness, as "where the apprentice was "lame, and, in the surgeon's opinion, incurably afflicted "with the King's Evil," for the master takes him for better or worse, and is to provide for him in sickness and in health (3).

But where a boy who had been put out as a parish apprentice, plainly appeared to be an ideot, incapable of learning his trade, the court confirmed an order of sessions, discharging his master of him. For it would be hard upon the master to keep one who could do him no service, while the parish should go free (4). **Discharge for ideocy.**

A power of ordering restitution of money given with the apprentice may be exercised, upon discharging him as incident to the jurisdiction (5). **Restitution of fee.**

This order must be under the hands and seals of four justices (6), and enrolled as the act directs, or the superior court will set it aside (7). **Order under hand and seal.**

No case has occurred in which the settlement has depended upon the validity of such an order of discharge. The power of a quarter sessions over it, when trying a **Order how far conclusive.**

(1) Rex v Heaseman, *ante*, 346, (2).

(2) Stephenson v. Holditch, 2 Vern. 491. 1 Bott, 572. Pl. 779.

(3) Rex v. Hales Owen, 1 Str 99. 1 Bott, 574. Pl. 784.

(4) Anon. Skin. 114. 1 Bott, 571. Pl. 779. See also Rex v. Charles, Burr. S. C. 706.

(5) Rex v. Johnson, 1 Salk. 68. 2 Salk. 491, *ante*, 345, (2). Ditton's case, 1 Salk. 67 Duhamel's case, Skin. 108. 1 Bott, 571. Pl. 778. Rex v. Amies, *ante*, 345, (4).

(6) Anon. Salk. 470. 1 Bott, 572. Pl. 776. Rex v. St. Petrox, Burr. S. C. 248.

(7) Rex v. Hales Owen, 1 Str. 99. 1 Bott, 574. Pl. 783.

question of settlement, is therefore undecided. But it may perhaps be concluded from analogy to the proceedings of Ecclesiastical (1) and Admiralty courts (2), that being a direct judgment upon the fact by a court not only of competent, but exclusive jurisdiction, it is conclusive of the question between contending parishes, although they are not immediately parties to the sentence, unless it has been obtained by fraud (3), or appears altogether void (4).

2. Discharge of indentures by death.

2. Apprenticeship being a personal trust between the master and servant, is determinable by the death of either (5). But indentures are not cancelled by the master's failure in his business and running away (6).

3. Of minors bound beyond the legal period.

3. Persons who have been bound to serve beyond the age of twenty-one, may elect to vacate their indentures upon attaining that age, unless bound to serve beyond it under the authority of an act of parliament (7). But the apprentice must regularly declare his intention to do so. For where an infant was bound for six years by indenture, and being of age, ran away, alledging he did so with an intent

(1) Bunting's case, 4 Co. 29. Jones *v.* Bow-Carth, 225 11 St. Trial, 218, 222 Harvey's case, 11 St. Trial, 285.

(2) Lothian *v.* Henderson, in Dom. Proc. 3 Bos. and Pull. 499. Bolton *v.* Gladstone, 5 East. 155.

(3) Prudham *v.* Phillips, Amb. 762. Dutchess of Kingston's case.

(4) Chichester *v.* Phillips, T. Raym. 405. Havelock *v.* Rockwood, 8 Term Rep. 268. Case of the Flad-Oyen, *ib.* 270. n. *a.* 1. Robin's Adm. Rep. 135. *Quære tamen*, for the determinations which hold such sentences conclusive, in the case of third persons, relate only to Admiralty sentences in prize causes, and seem to have been given with much reluctance. See Lothian *v.* Henderson, *ante*, (2).

(5) Rex *v.* Peck, Salk. 66. 1 Bott, 581. Pl. 795. Rex *v.* Eskring, Burr. S. C. 320. 1 Bott, 585. Pl. 801. 2 Bott, 402. Pl. 429. But the apprentice and master's representative may continue the relation at their option. See several cases, *post*.

(6) Rex *v.* Buckington, 2 Lord Raym. 1352. 1 Str. 582. 2 Bott, 401. Pl. 428.

(7) *Ex parte* Mary Anne Davis, 6 Term Rep. 715. 1 Bott, 532. Pl. 719.

to

to avoid the apprenticeſhip, made when he was an infant, and to his prejudice, the court inclined ſtrongly to think that this running away did not avoid them, and that he could not make uſe of his offence to avoid the puniſhment that attends it (1).

4. The moſt uſual mode of diſcharging indentures is by mutual conſent. If the apprentice is an infant, his maſter cannot diſcharge them by his conſent alone (2). But it may be done with his father's (3), or any perſon having the legal ſuperintendance of his minority. 4. By conſent. Minors.

In the caſe of a pariſh apprentice under age, the indenture cannot be diſcharged by his conſent (4), though his father concur (5). As he is bound out by the pariſh officers under a ſpecial authority, they ought to be conſulted, and give their conſent to his diſcharge, otherwiſe the whole policy of the 43 Eliz. might be defeated (6). But ſuch aſſent is unneceſſary after he attains the age of twenty-one; at which time the maſter and apprentice may cancel the indentures by mutual agreement (7). But Pariſh apprentices.

(1) Rex *v.* Evered, Cald. 26. 1 Bott, 578. Pl. 789. But in this caſe the apprentice was diſcharged by conſent, there being another objection to the commitment. Aſhcroft *v.* Bertles, 6 Term Rep. 652. 2 Bott, 412. Pl. 438. See alſo Rex *v.* Buckington, *ante*, (1). But in Rex *v.* Eakring, *ante*, 348, (5). the apprentice ran away, and the maſter dying afterwards, the apprenticeſhip was held to be terminated by the death, ſo as to entitle the pauper to a ſettlement by hiring and ſervice.

(2) Rex *v.* Auſtrey, Burr. S. C. 441. 2 Bott, 404. Pl. 431. Even to enter into the king's ſervice. See Rex *v.* Hindringham, 6 Term Rep. 557. 1 Bott, 533. Pl. 720.

(3) Rex *v.* St. Mary, Kallendar, Burr. S. C. 274. 2 Bott, 402. Pl. 429. Rex *v.* Weddington. Burr. S. C. 766. 2 Bott, 406. Pl. 434.

(4) Rex *v.* Auſtrey, *ante*, n. (2).

(5) Rex *v.* Langham, Cald. 126. 2 Bott, 408. Pl. 435.

(6) *Per* Lord Manſfield C. J. Rex *v.* Weddington, *ſupra*, n. (3), decided in Rex *v.* Langham, *ſupra* n. (5).

(7) Rex *v.* Harberton, 2 Bott, 409. Pl. 436. 1 Term Rep. 139. Rex *v.* Eccleſal. Bierlow Burr. S. C. 562. 1 Bott, 612. Pl. 852.

if

if an attempt be made to cancel them before that time, it is not rendered valid merely by the apprentice's coming of age, and the indentures continue in force, unless the parties enter into a new agreement (1).

How discharged.

In order to discharge indentures, it is necessary, not only that the parties should agree to separate, but that the indentures should be actually cancelled, or given up (2); or at least, something done which the law considers as equivalent.

By whom.

And it *seems* as if they must be cancelled by the original master, and it cannot be done by a third person, whom the apprentice is serving with the consent of the first (3).

In what manner.

Where the parties have power to consent, the indentures may be discharged. 1st, By formally cancelling them. 2d, By exchange, or mutually delivering them up, and this, either with an indorsement (4), or without; "because the exchange of the indentures amounts, either "in law or in equity, (and they are the same thing in the "case,) to a cancelling of them, and a determination of "the apprenticeship under them (5)."

Lord Mansfield was of opinion, that it would have been more convenient, if the court had never gone further than to enquire whether the indentures have been actually cancelled, or given up (6).

(1) Rex *v.* Austrey, Burr. S. C. 441. 2 Bott, 420. Pl. 447.

(2) Rex *v.* St. Luke's, Burr. S. C. 562. 1 Bott, 611. Pl. 851.

(3) Rex *v.* Notton, 1 Bott, 613. Pl 853. *Quære tamen*, of the extent of the decision: and see Rex *v.* Clapham, Burr. S. C. 266. 2 Bott, 418. Pl. 445. Rex *v.* Shebbear, 1 East. 73.

(4) St. Petrox *v.* Stoke Fleming, Burr. S. C. 250. 2 Bott, 417. Pl. 444.

(5) *Per* Lee C. J. Rex *v.* St. Mary, Kalendar, Burr. S. C. 274. 1 Bott, 526. Pl. 711. Rex *v.* Titchfield, Burr. S. C. 511. 2 Bott, 404. Pl. 432.

(6) Rex *v.* Harberton, 2 Bott, 409. Pl. 436. 1 Term Rep. 139, S. C.; and the court seems to have held that opinion, Reg. *v.* Thursley, 6 Mod. 190. 1 Bott, 523. Pl. 705.

3d, But

3d, But apprentices have been held discharged in many instances, although the master has retained the custody of his indentures, and they have existed undefaced.

Rule for ascertaining what is a discharge.

Lord Mansfield has laid down the following general rule, as a clear line to go by in ascertaining whether the indentures are discharged. "Wherever the indenture is "so far made an end of, as to give the apprentice a re"medy at law, it shall be considered as a dissolution of "the apprenticeship; but if it were extended to every "case where a court of equity would relieve, the inquiry "would be endless, and different magistrates, not bred "to the profession, would, when left to decide *secundum* "*discretionem*, breed endless confusion, by frequently, in "the like cases, making very contrary determina"tions (1)."

Thus, where an apprentice lived with his master till twenty-one, and then made an agreement to give him one guinea to discharge him from his apprenticeship; the master gave him a discharge accordingly, and the pauper hired himself elsewhere. Lord Mansfield C. J. "I am of opinion, that if the indenture *had not been de*"*stroyed, but had remained in the master's hands*, the ap"prentice would have gained a settlement by a subse"quent hiring and service. The master received a gui"nea of his apprentice, then at full age, for the express "purpose of vacating the indenture. Why! could the "master, after this, have used the indenture against the "apprentice? So far from it, the apprentice might "have brought an action against the master for it (2)."

(1) Rex v. Harberton, *ante*, 350, (6).

(2) Rex v. Justices of Devonshire, Cald. 32. 1 Bott, 530. Pl. 716. But see Regina v. Thursley, 6 Mod. 290. 1 Bott, 505. Pl. 705. But no consideration given to the master.

The

The father of an apprentice, at his son's request, and with his consent, bought out his time for four guineas, the master giving a receipt, and offering to give up the indentures, which the father did not then take, not thinking it material; the master kept the indenture in custody, uncancelled, until the expiration of the whole time, when he delivered it up. The court were of opinion, that the indentures had been put an end to by the agreement (1).

Conditional agreement to cancel, insufficient.

But unless the indentures are actually cancelled, or given up, or the master agrees unconditionally to do so for a valuable consideration, they must be considered as continuing in force.

If the master agrees to cancel them conditionally, they remain in force until the apprentice performs the condition, although he is treated in the interim, as one *sui juris*, uncontroled by the obligation of his indentures.

Master retaining indentures till 7l. paid.

A pauper served two years and a half under his indentures to a blacksmith, when his master leaving off business, they agreed verbally, that the pauper should give his master seven pounds for the remainder of his time, the master not wishing to turn him over to any body. The master to keep the indentures till the seven pound was paid, which was to be discharged from time to time as the pauper could earn and make it convenient to pay it. The pauper afterwards worked with different masters until harvest time, when he served his original master for a month, at his request, receiving harvest wages from him as a labourer, which were deducted from the seven pounds he had agreed to pay his master. The master afterwards recommended the pauper to serve one Cherry

(1) Rex *v.* Harberton, *ante*, 350, (6).

a black-a blackſmith, in whoſe ſervice he continued with his maſter's knowledge, about twelve months. The court were of opinion, "that the parties did not put an end to the apprenticeſhip; but on the contrary, the apprentice agreed to pay ſeven pound to the maſter, who was to keep the indentures until that ſum was paid, the maſter all this time keeping a control over the apprentice." The indentures therefore continued in force when he went to ſerve Cherry, at his maſter's requeſt, by ſerving whom, he gained a ſettlement, not as an hired ſervant, but by ſerving him under the indentures of apprenticeſhip, with the conſent of his original maſter (1).

Agreement to let apprentice off for a guinea, and it is not paid.

So, where an apprentice who was aſſigned to S. propoſed to S. two months before the expiration of his apprenticeſhip, to let him off the remainder of his time, which he at firſt refuſed to do. The pauper then offered to give S. a guinea, if he would let him off, which S. agreed to do, and alſo to give him a new ſuit of clothes when the guinea was paid. The guinea was not paid, nor did S. give the pauper the clothes, nor were the indentures given up or cancelled. The indentures were held to ſubſiſt, and that the pauper gained a ſettlement by ſubſequent ſervice with a particular maſter, to whom S. had given his ſpecific conſent (2).

What ſhall not amount to a cancelling of the indentures.

It is manifeſt from theſe caſes, that a mere agreement, without valuable conſideration, to diſcharge the apprentice from the obligation of ſerving his maſter, does not put an end to the indentures.

An apprentice under age, met with a preſs-gang, and entered his majeſty's ſervice with his maſter's conſent. He never returned to his maſter, but the indentures were

(1) Rex *v.* Chipping Warden, 8 Term Rep. 108. 2 Bott, 413. Pl. 439.

(2) Rex *v.* Shebbear, 1 Eaſt. 73.

not delivered up, nor cancelled. The consent thus given by the master evidently implied that he did not put an end to the indentures, and they continued in force until the expiration of the term (1).

Service with one who covenants to indemnify the first master.

H. was bound by the parish of Knowstone to J. F., for an estate which he rented in that parish of J. L., who covenanted with F., "that if a second apprentice was bound to him for that estate, (which H. was), he the said J. L. and his representatives, would discharge the said J. F. from any expences he might incur thereby." Upon H. being so bound, F. applied to Mrs. L., the widow and representative of J. L., who took the pauper H. received the parish money with him, and went with him into the parish of Roseash, where he resided with her for three years, when, becoming a cripple, she sent him back to F., and insisted on his receiving the pauper. This F. refused to do, until she promised to pay him all the expences he should be at, in taking care of him. The court (2) were of opinion, that the original indenture continued, and was not discharged by any thing stated to have passed between F. and Mrs. L. (3).

(1) Rex *v.* Hindringham, 6 Term Rep. 557. 2 Bott, 411, Pl. 437. 2 Bott, 513. Pl. 720. Indeed all the cases in the next section proceed upon this principle.

(2) Lord Mansfield, absent.

(3) Rex *v.* Charles, Burr. S. C. 706. 2 Bott, 424. Pl. 451. In this latter report, the words given to Aston J. are, "F. having another "apprentice, applies to Mrs. L. to "take him, agreeable to her covenant; "she takes him with his consent, "and takes the parish money, which, "to be sure, *looks like an assignment*, "but is not one." It is to be observed further, that the apprentice, being under age, could not have consented to the discharge in either of the foregoing cases.

SECT.

SECT. IV.

Of the Service.

THE ſervice of an apprentice, is required by a different ſtatute, and governed by different rules from thoſe which regulate that of an hired ſervant. Of the ſervice.

It has been obſerved, that " the performance of actual ſervice is not the thing material: it is the reſidence, the inhabitancy of an apprentice in a town or pariſh for forty days, that gains the ſettlement (1)." But although the extent of the ſervice may be immaterial, the apprentice gains no ſettlement, unleſs he continues under the control of his indentures during ſuch reſidence, liable, not only in law, but in fact, to perform the duties preſcribed by his covenants. Otherwiſe, he does not inhabit as an apprentice. This is what ſeems meant by the term *ſervice*, as applied to apprentices.

The extent and quality of this ſervice is limited by the covenants of the deed by which he is bound, and it ſeems immaterial, whether they allow an interruption of ſervice, or exempt the apprentice from his maſter's control at ſtated periods. This has not been expreſsly decided, but the following caſe, which might have raiſed the queſtion, was brought before the court. A father covenanted to find the apprentice meat, drink, and lodging, on every ſunday in the year during the term; and the boy went home every ſunday, and ſerved his maſter the remaining ſix days of Extent of ſervice.

(1) *Per* Aſton J. Rex *v.* Charles, Burr. S. C. 708.

the week. This point was not ſtirred, but the apprentice acquired a ſettlement (1).

Service. Service under indentures may be either, 1. with the original maſter, 2. with another perſon by his conſent.

It has been obſerved, by a very learned judge, "that it would perhaps have been better to have confined the power of gaining a ſettlement to ſervice with the original maſter (2)," but the law is ſettled otherwiſe.

Conſent by whom given. Conſent may be given, not only by the original maſter, but by his executor (3), or even by his widow, before taking out adminiſtration (4).

Alſo the perſon receiving an apprentice with ſuch conſent, may transfer his ſervice to another; for his conſent includes that of the original maſter (5), and this, without the actual knowledge or conſent of the firſt (6), or of his repreſentatives, if he be dead (7).

This power of aſſent is an independant right, veſted in the perſon whom the apprentice is legally ſerving; which

(1) Rex *v.* Leighton, 4 Term Rep. 732. 1 Bott, 559. Pl. 751, *ante*, 324, (2). This caſe may perhaps be rather conſidered as one of interruption in the ſervice, than of an exception in the contract. As to exceptions in contracts of hiring, ſee *ante* 209, *et ſeq.*, and as to interruptions in ſervice under them, *ante* 224, *et ſeq.* But the words of 3 W. 3. c. 11. ſect. 6. are, that the ſervant "ſhall be hired "for a year," and of 8 and 9 W. 3. c. 30, that "he ſhall continue and "abide in the ſame ſervice for *one* "*whole year.*" There are none ſuch in the ſtatutes which reſpect ſettlements of apprenticeſhip.

(2) *Per* Lord Kenyon C. J. Rex *v.* Crediton, 1 Eaſt. 62.

(3) Rex *v.* St. Paul's Bedford, 6 Term Rep. 452. 1 Bott, 585. Pl. 802.

(4) Rex *v.* Eaſt Bridgeford, Burr. S. C. 133. 1 Bott, 583. Pl. 799. 2 Bott, 407. Pl. 443. But ſee Rex *v.* Chirk *poſt*, 362, (1); and *quære* whether the indentures were not determined. Rex *v.* Eakring, *ante*, 348, (5), and the note.

(5) Rex *v.* Taviſtock, Burr. S. C. 578. 2 Bott, 423. Pl. 440. Rex *v.* Eaſt Bridgeford, *ante*, (4). Rex *v.* Bradſtone, 2 Bott, 434. Pl. 459.

(6) Rex *v.* Langham, Cald. 126, *ante*, 349, (5). Rex *v.* St. Mary Lambeth, 2 Bott, 431. Pl. 457. Cald. 553.

(7) Rex *v.* Clapham, Burr. S. C. 266. 2 Bott, 418. Pl. 445.

which he may exercise without any other concurrence, than that of the apprentice, and which the latter may give, although under age (1), or bound out by the parish (2). But which, if once given, the master cannot afterwards recal (3).

It is not every consent to service with a third person which enables an apprentice to acquire a settlement. The distinction is laid down in a recent case. "If the master "is applied to for his consent to a particular service, "and give it, that shall be considered as a service with "the first master, and confers a settlement, but an "indiscriminate leave to serve any person will not (4)."

What consent sufficient.

To gain a settlement therefore by service with a third person. 1st, The consent must be direct and explicit. 2d, To serve a particular person; or 3d, if more general, it must be for the direct benefit of the master. 4th, It must be given by the master under a conviction, that the indentures are still in force.

Rules for consent to serve third person.

An explicit consent may be given. 1st, By assignment in writing. 2d, By parol.

1. Explicit consent how given.

An assignment, however formal, does not transfer the precise rights created by indenture, without a local custom to support it (5), and the defect is not cured by the

1. Written assignment.

(1) Rex *v.* Fremington, Burr. S C. 416. 2 Bott, 419. Pl. 446. Rex *v.* Bradninch, 2 Bott, 430. Pl. 456. and indeed almost all the cases of consent.

(2) Rex *v.* Tavistock, *post*, 364 (2). Rex *v.* St. George's Hanover Square, *post*, 359, (2).

(3) *Per* Holt C. J. Barber *v.* Dennis. 6 Mod. 69. 2 Bott, 512. Pl. 704. But this seems to extend only to cases where the licence is express, and it may be otherwise limited by the master. See the opinion of Ashurst J. Rex *v.* Holy Trinity in the minories, *post*, 362, (1).

(4) *Per* Lord Kenyon, Rex *v.* Shobbear. 1 East. 75.

(5) Dalt. 652. Batter *v.* Burfield, 1 Bott, 584. Pl. 800.

 ap-

Written assignments stamped.

apprentice's consent (1). But it is sufficient to legalize the service under it, and thereby confer a settlement (2), although the original indenture is voidable (3). This assignment, when in writing, must be stamped, for it is not within the exception 20 Geo. 3. c. 58. s. 4., which exempts "any memorandum or agreement for the use "of any labourer, artificer, manufacturer, or menial "servant (4)."

2. Parol.

2d, An unwritten consent to the service is equally good (5), and may be either express or implied.

Express consent.

1st, A master told his apprentice, "that he had no business for her, and that she should go where she would;" afterwards, meeting Mr. N., a relation, who wanted a maid servant, he told him, "he was over-"stocked with maids, and had an apprentice maid, which "he could spare him, if N. and she could agree about "terms." He afterwards told the apprentice, that she might go to Mr. N. and live with Mr. N. if they could agree (6). A person willing to take into his service, one who was an apprentice at the time, said to the master, "if things come about again, he hoped he would never "fetch her," (the apprentice) "again;" to which the

(1) Rex v. Channel, 3 Keb. 519. 1 Bott, 580. Pl 793.

(2) Caistor v. Eccles, 1 Lord Raym. 683. 1 Bott, 582. Pl 706. Holy Trinity v. Shoreditch 1 Str. 10. 2 Bott, 415. Pl. 440. Rex v. Petham, Burr. S. C. 154. 2 Bott, 439. Pl. 465.

(3) St Petrox v. Stoke Fleming, Burr. S. C. 258. 1 Bott. 611. Pl. 850. 2 Bott, 417 Pl 444. Where a female was bound out by the parish, and the original indentures had been vacated by the sessions, the girl having been bound absolutely till twenty one, without the alternative "or time of her marriage," see *ante*.

(4) Rex v. St. Paul's Bedford, *ante*, 356, (3). See also 44 Geo. 3. c. 98, *ante*, 331.

(5) St Olaves v. All Hallows, 8 Mod. 169. Str. 334. 2 Bott, 415. Pl. 441. Rex v. St. George's Hanover Square. Burr. S C 12. 2 Bott, 416. Pl 442. Rex v Stockland. Cald 60 Dougl. 70. 2 Bott, 430. Pl. 456.

(6) Rex v. Fremington, Burr. S.C. 416. 2 Bott, 419. Pl. 446, *ante*, 357, (1).

master

master replied, " he never would (1)?" these are express consents.

2d, A direct consent may be inferred, when the words used do not appear. A master hired out his apprentice to a third person by parol agreement, receiving her wages, and finding her in clothes (2). The assignee of an apprentice placed him out with a third person *as an apprentice* (3). An apprentice having stayed out all night, was told she might go look for another place, and being hired into one, her master gave her a character (4): these amount to sufficient consents to the particular service.

Implied consent.

But mere knowledge by the original master, that his apprentice is living in service with another person, does not (5). The pauper was bound as a parish apprentice to Matthews; he assigned her by parol to Stilliford. Having lived with him seven months, she ran away, and served one Hayes for nine months, with the knowledge, but without any express consent of Matthews, or Stilliford. Hayes did not know she was an apprentice. Matthews, the original master, resided in the same parish where the pauper served Hayes, and frequently saw her there, but during her residence there, applied to Stilliford to take her back, and threatened to put him to trouble if he did not. Lord Mansfield.—Here is no consent express, or implied; his mere knowledge of it does not imply his consent to it (6). Per Buller J.—All the cases shew that mere

Knowledge of service insufficient.

(1) Rex v. Langham, Cald. 126. 2 Bott, 438. Pl. 445, *ante*, 356, (6).

(2) Rex. v. St. George's Hanover Square, Burr. S. C. 12. 2 Bott, 416. Pl. 442, *ante*, 347, (2). But see Reg. v. Thursley. 1 Bott, 523. Pl. 705.

(3) Rex v. Clapham, Burr. S. C. 266. 2 Bott, 418. Pl. 445, *ante*, 356, (7).

(4) Rex v. St. Mary Lambeth, *ante*, 356, (6). 2 Bott, 436. Pl. 57.

(5) *Per* Buller J. Rex v. Holy Trinity, in the Minories, *post*, 365, (1).

(6) Rex v. Iteford, Burr. S. C. 821. 2 Bott, 427. Pl. 453.

knowledge is not sufficient; knowledge does not imply consent (1).

General consent

General consent, is rather to be considered as a renunciation and abandonment of the apprentice's service, expressed under the form of an indiscriminate leave, which sets the apprentice at liberty to work with other masters, than as a direct assent to service with other persons. But a master may give his servant a licence to work indiscriminately, without limiting him to a particular individual, and yet it shall not come within the meaning of such a general consent, as precludes a settlement. For such service may be *quâ* actual service to the master himself, if it be for his benefit, and he retains a direct control over the apprentice (2).

which give no settlement.

But where the master tells his apprentice "to go about "his business, and work for himself (3), that he must not "stay; he was at liberty to go where he thought pro- "per (4)." Or that he had no employment for him; he might go where he pleased (5), or an agreement, that the apprentice shall work and provide for himself (6). These are general consents, under which, service with a third person confers no settlement. For it cannot be deemed service with the first master, he having expressly renounced it, and they do not amount to a discharge of the indentures, so as to enable the apprentice to make a new contract of service with another person.

(1) Rex *v.* Holy Trinity, in the Minories, *post*, 365, (1); and see the opinion of Ashurst J. Rex *v.* Sandford, 1 Term Rep. 281, *post*, 368, (2); as also Rex *v.* St. Mary Lambeth, 2 Bott, 431. Pl. 457. The facts in both these cases would have raised the question, but it passed unnoticed, both at the bar, and upon the bench. See also the opinion of Lord Kenyon C. J. Rex *v.* Shebbeare, *ante*, 353, (2).

(2) Rex *v.* Offerton, *post*, 368, (3).

(3) St. Luke's *v.* St. Leonard's, *post*, 361, (2).

(4) Rex *v.* Chirk, Burr. S. C. 782. 2 Bott, 397. Pl. 425.

(5) Rex *v.* Crediton, *post*, 366, (1). Notton *v.* Royston, *ante*, 350, (3).

(6) Rex *v.* St. Helen, Stonegate. 1 East. 285.

Thus,

General discharge.

Thus, where the master of a parish apprentice, without the parish officer's consent, agreed, in consideration of forty shillings, paid by the apprentice, to discharge him from his apprenticeship, and delivered up his indentures, and the apprentice afterwards hired himself to several masters. It was held, that the indentures continued; for the pauper being under age, was incapable of consenting to the discharge; and the subsequent service under the hirings can never be considered as performed with the master's consent, and so, as being a service under the indenture; for it was no express consent given to the particular service, but was intended to be quite general, and even founded on a mistaken apprehension, that the pauper could consent to his being discharged (1). So where a master told his apprentice "to go about his business, and work for himself," and the indentures were not cancelled or given up. The pauper hired himself with several masters as a journeyman, and applied his earnings to his own use. His original master, not knowing with whom he worked after he left him, nor demanding any account of his earnings, nor making any inquiry after him, or any provision for him. It was held, that he gained no settlement by service as an apprentice, by this general leave; nor as an hired servant, for the indentures subsisting, he was not *sui juris* (2).

Likewise, where the master of an apprentice died, and he continued with the widow for a fortnight to finish his work. Having no employment afterwards for him, or any other workman, she told him that he must not stay with her, and he was at liberty to go where he thought

(1) Rex v. Austrey, Burr. S. C. 441. 2 Bott, 420. Pl. 447, *ante*, 349, (2).

(2) St. Luke's v. St. Leonard's Burr. S C. 542. See also Notton v. Royston, Burr. S. C. 629. 2 Bott 423. Pl. 450, *ante*, 350, (3). In this case, the apprentice being desirous to leave the master whom he served, with leave from his original mistress, applied to him, and the master answered, "he might go where he pleased."

proper.

proper. He quitted her, and on parting, told her, he was going to his father, who was a ſlater. But no agreement took place between the father and her, to his knowledge, nor were the indentures delivered up. He lived with his father for two or three years. It was held that he gained no ſettlement. "The widow does not appear to "have had any intereſt: no adminiſtration appears to "have been taken out (1)."

Conſent to particular ſervice.

A particular conſent is moſt naturally given before the commencement of the new ſervice (2), and previous to a general licence or conſent. It has never been decided, whether a conſent, ſubſequent to the commencement of the ſervice, would render it ſufficient upon the principle, *Quod omnis ratihabitio retrotrahitur atque mandato æquiparatur.*

After general licence.

But it may be given after a general licence of departure, and after the apprentice has commenced ſervice under ſuch a licence; for the indentures continuing to ſubſiſt, the maſter has a right to reſume his control, and claim ſervice from his apprentice for the remainder of his time (3). A ſubſequent ſervice of forty days, therefore, is under the indentures, and confers a ſettlement. This has been decided in ſeveral caſes.

Aſſent given by "you are "welcome "to keep "my apprentice, "&c."

A pariſh apprentice being regularly aſſigned to W. ſerved him till he was twenty years of age, when they agreed to part, and W. gave him permiſſion in writing, ſignifying that he had his conſent to ſerve any other maſter. The apprentice then hired himſelf for a year, and

(1) Rex *v.* Chirk, Burr. S. C. 782. 2 Bott, 397. Pl. 425. But ſee Rex *v.* Eaſt Bridgeford, *ante*, 356, (4). and the note.

(2) See the caſes, *ante* p. 358, *et ſeq.*

(3) See the opinion of Aſhurſt J. Rex *v.* Holy Trinity, in the Minories, 3 Term Rep. 603. 2 Bott, 435. Pl. 460.

when

when he had been eight months in the ſervice, his maſter met W. by accident, who ſaid: "I find you have an "apprentice of mine;" to which the maſter anſwered: "I do not know I have;" and then W. ſaid: "J. D. "(the pauper), is my apprentice, but you are welcome "to keep him as long as you pleaſe, and may have his "indentures when you pleaſe; for I ſhall think no more "of him."—He gains a ſettlement under this conſent (1).

"You may "go to B, "with all "my heart; "it will be "a good "thing "for you."

A pauper, two months previous to the expiration of his apprenticeſhip, had agreed with S. his maſter, to cancel the indentures, upon a condition which did not take effect; and the indentures were neither cancelled, nor given up. On the morning upon which the agreement was concluded, the pauper went to B. and offered to ſerve him, who ſaid, he would not take him without the conſent of S. The pauper went to S. and told him what B. had ſaid. S. replied: "you may go, with all my "heart; I think it will be a good thing for you to learn "the trade." This was held a ſufficient aſſent by S. to the ſervice with B. to enable the pauper to acquire a ſettlement as an apprentice. For the maſter was applied to for his conſent to let him ſerve the particular perſon named, and he expreſſed his approbation of that perſon ſo named; it is therefore a particular conſent to the particular ſervice (2).

Approbation after general licence to depart.

An apprentice was bound to ſerve till twenty-four, and at the age of twenty-two, his maſter agreed, that if he would give him a guinea in hand, and two guineas more, being one guinea a year during the continuance of his apprenticeſhip, he ſhould go and ſerve whom he pleaſed. But the maſter ſaid he would not deliver the inden-

(1) Rex *v.* Bradſtone, 2 Bott. 434. Pl. 459. See alſo Rex *v.* the Holy Trinity in Minories, *poſt*, 365, (2).

(2) Rex *v.* Shebbear, 1 Eaſt. 73.

indentures, nor discharge him from his apprenticeship, for he considered him as his apprentice still. The pauper agreed, and paid his master a guinea in hand, and then hired himself to Miss Sainthill. At the end of the first year, he went to his master, and paid him one guinea for that year. His master said: "you continue to "work with Miss S? I think it a very good place, and "hope you will continue in it." At the end of the second year, he went and paid his master the other guinea, when he said: "you still continue to work with "Miss S?" He replied, "he did;" when his master said, he would look out for the indenture, and give it to him. The pauper did not know that there was any conversation between the master and Miss S. respecting the apprenticeship; but Miss S. knew he was an apprentice, *and had enquired his character*. This was held a sufficient assent to entitle the party to a settlement by service with Miss S, as an apprentice (1).

A parish apprentice, under age, was assigned to one *Prout*. Afterwards he offered his service to *Mason*, who apprehending that he was an apprentice, sent to Prout to know whether it was with his consent that the pauper should live with him: to which he answered; "with all "my heart; he may live with Mason, or any body else, "provided he performs his agreement with me; which "was, *to pay one guinea a year during the remainder of his* "*apprenticeship*." This was held a consent by *Prout*, and his consent included that of the first master (2).

Service with a second master two months before indentures cancelled.

The pauper was bound apprentice to serve seven years. Having served six, and being only nineteen, the master declined business, when he informed the pauper, that he wished him to get another master for his good. The

(1) Rex *v.* Bradninch, 2 Bott, 430. Pl. 456.

(2) Rex *v.* Tavistock, Burr. S. C. 578. 2 Bott, 423. Pl. 449.

pauper

pauper went to his father, in another pariſh, with whom he ſtaid three or four weeks. Not meeting with a ſervice, he returned to his maſter, who told him, that he heard Mr. E. wanted a man, and to go to E. and make an agreement with him for his (the pauper's) good; and that he underſtood E would take him for a twelvemonth. The pauper went; and entered into an agreement, in writing, under ſeal, but without ſtamp, to ſerve for a year; to have board, lodging, and twelve pounds wages. The indentures were neither aſſigned, nor cancelled; but after he had ſerved E. two months, his firſt maſter gave him up his indentures. The ſervice with E. is by the firſt maſter's recommendation, and with his conſent, and the indentures not being given up for forty days, it was a ſervice under them, and conferred a ſettlement (1).

In theſe caſes, the leave was expreſsly given. In ſome there was an application to obtain it, while the maſter ſeems in the remainder, not only to have preſerved his control over the apprentice, but to exerciſe it with a ſolicitude for his welfare. But the great difficulty is, to diſtinguiſh in caſes where a general licence has been originally given, between expreſs conſent, which legalizes ſubſequent ſervice, and ſuch mere knowledge, that the apprentice is in a particular ſervice, as does not amount to conſent (2).

The following were conſidered as caſes of knowledge and acquieſcence, on the maſter's part, without conſent. Caſes of knowledge of ſervice, without conſent.

The maſter of an apprentice failing in buſineſs, told him he had no further employment for him, and he might go where he pleaſed. Afterwards, and before

(1) Rex *v.* Holy Trinity, in the Minories, 3 Term Rep. 605. 2 Bott, 435. Pl. 460.

(2) See *ante*, 359.

leaving

leaving his maſter, a perſon came to inform the apprentice, that one Underhill, who wanted a boy, was at an inn in the neighbourhood, and that he ſhould go to the inn. As the apprentice was going out of the houſe, his maſter met him, and aſked him where he was going? the pauper told him he was going down to Underhill. The maſter ſaid, "he might go there, or where he "pleaſed." Thereupon, the apprentice left his houſe, and went and hired himſelf, and lived with Underwood; but no communication took place between the original maſter and him. This is not ſuch an aſſent of the original maſter to ſerve with the ſecond, as enables him to gain a ſettlement thereby. For the pauper tells his maſter, on being aſked where he was going, that he is going to Underhill; on which the maſter repeats, in effect, what he had before ſaid, that he might go there, or where he pleaſed; meaning, that he no longer looked for his ſervice, nor took any concern how he diſpoſed of himſelf (1).

I have got your apprentice to work. "I "am glad "of it, he "was a bad "lad, &c."

An apprentice was aſſigned, by parol, to his brother, W. Chapman, a journeyman bricklayer. Being about to marry, he applied to W. Chapman, and told him he wiſhed to work, and provide for himſelf, to which W. C. conſented, and ſaid, he might do the beſt he could for himſelf, and did not afterwards conſider the pauper as his apprentice. But the indenture was neither delivered up, nor cancelled, nor any thing ſaid reſpecting it. In the ſame month, and three quarters of a year before the expiration of the apprenticeſhip, the pauper applied for work to T. Penyſton, who employed him in bricklayer's work, at weekly wages. About a month after, T. P. met W. C., and told him, he had got his brother at work; to which W. E. replied, "I am glad "of it; he was a bad lad, and I could make nothing of

(1) Rex v. Crediton, 1 Eaſt, 59, ante.

"him."

" him." This was held not to amount to an aſſent to the ſervice with the ſecond maſter, upon the authority of the foregoing caſe (1).

Aſſent where maſter derives benefit from ſubſequent ſervice.

It has been held, that the maſter may aſſent to the apprentice's working for himſelf, provided he is to derive a benefit from that ſervice, and his control continues; becauſe, in that caſe, it is actual ſervice done for the maſter. A pariſh apprentice, eighteen years old, agreed with his maſter, " that he, upon paying twelve " pence a week, and providing for himſelf, ſhould be at " liberty to work for his own benefit, during the re- " mainder of his apprenticeſhip." The maſter was to find him a loom, and was to " receive the twelve pence " a week as a ſatisfaction for his ſervice during the re- " mainder of his apprenticeſhip." Neither the churchwardens, nor overſeers, were privy to the agreement, nor were the indentures cancelled, or delivered up. The pauper then married, and worked for his own benefit; his maſter providing him with a loom, and receiving the one ſhilling *per* week. He worked during the laſt year at Offerton, for the ſame tradeſman who employed his maſter; but ſuch tradeſman did not ſettle, nor in any wiſe account with the maſter for the pauper's work, or earning; nor did he work with him by the maſter's particular direction or conſent; but the maſter knew, during all that time, where, and with whom he was working; and often applied to him, during the laſt year of his apprenticeſhip, for the arrears of the twelve pence *per* week, due in purſuance of the agreement, which he would have received, if the pauper had been able to pay. The court were of opinion, " that the apprenticeſhip continued; that there was no diſſolution of it, nor any intention to diſſolve it. As between the original maſter and the apprentice, the maſter knew that the apprentice

(1) Rex *v.* St. Helen, Stonegate, 2 Eaſt, 285.

worked at Offerton, and demanded the twelve pence a week for it. An apprentice may work in any pariſh, with the conſent of his maſter; and it is probable, that the tradeſman with whom he worked, knew that he was an apprentice, as he employed the maſter. They held therefore, that the ſervice in Offerton, was under the indentures of Apprenticeſhip (1)."

4. Conſent muſt be by maſter as ſuch.

The conſent muſt alſo be given by the maſter as ſuch, and while he conceives the indentures to continue in force. For if the parties ſuppoſe, even erroneouſly, that the indentures are cancelled, ſervice with a third perſon, although under an expreſs conſent, will be inſufficient. The pauper was bound by the pariſh officers, at the age of eleven, to E. S., to ſerve till twenty-four. He lived with E. S. five years; his maſter gave him up his indentures, and recommended him to live with W. V., with whom he made an agreement, as a ſervant, and ſerved three years. Here "the pauper being a minor, "could not conſent to the diſcharge of the indentures, "without the conſent of the pariſh officers (2)."

And, *per* lord Mansfield C. J. "It ſeems to me clear, that the pauper could not gain a ſettlement after the firſt five years, under the indentures, as an apprentice; becauſe neither party, in fact, conſidered the ſervice as ſuch; they conſidered the indentures as given up, and put an end to for ever; ſo that the ſervice was not, nor was intended to be, in the capacity of an apprentice (3)."

(1) Rex *v.* Offerton, Burr. S. C. 802. 2 Bott, 425. Pl. 452. 1 Bott, 615. Pl. 855.

(2) *Per* Willes J.

(3) Rex *v.* Sandford, 1 Term Rep. 281. 2 Bott, 432. Pl. 458. Buller J. puts the ſettlement on the ground "that it was a mere recommendation to ſerve W. V., which the pauper might have rejected or not, as he pleaſed." But the opinion of lord Mansfield C. J. Rex *v.* Auſtrey, *ante*, 361, (1), confirms this caſe. And in Rex *v.* Holy Trinity in the Minories, *ante*, 365, (1), lord Kenyon C. J. diſtinguiſhed that caſe, where the parties had power to cancel, from Rex *v.* Sandford, by reſting the ſettlement upon the reſidence of two months previous to giving up the indentures.

But

But no distinction arises from the parties having it in contemplation to give up the indentures (1), or the apprentice entering into a new relation of servitude, either by binding himself as an apprentice (2), or servant (3), although he does it with the master's knowledge, and under seal (4), or that the person, receiving him, knows him to be an apprentice (5). It is also unnecessary, in cases of particular consent, that the first master should derive any benefit from the service under it (6). Circumstances which do not affect the licence to work with another master.

SECT. V.

Of the Residence by, and Place in which an Apprentice acquires a Settlement.

A servant cannot gain a settlement until his year of service is complete. It floats undetermined until that expires, and he is then settled in that parish or town wherein he has served the last forty days, capable of conferring a settlement (7). Distinction between residence as an apprentice, and servant.

But forty days residence and service under indentures, confer an absolute settlement, which no subsequent disqualification by certificate, or otherwise, can defeat (8). If the apprentice reside so long in one parish, although the indentures are cancelled on the forty-first day after their execution, he has acquired a settlement (9).

(1) Rex *v.* Holy Trinity in the Minories, *ante*, 365, (1).

(2) St. Petrox *v.* Stoke Fleming, *ante*, 358, (3).

(3) Rex *v.* St. Mary, Lambeth, *ante*, 356, (6).

(4) *Ante*, n. (2).

(5) Rex *v.* Bradninch, *ante*, 364, (1).

(6) Rex. *v.* Fremington, *ante*, 358, (6). Rex *v.* Holy Trinity, in the Minories, *ante*, (1).

(7) *Ante*, 287, *et seq.*

(8) See Rex *v.* Clifthydon, Burr. S. C. 161. 2 Bott, 442. Pl. 466. St. Cuthbert's *v.* Westbury. Burr. S. C. 470. 2 Bott, 443. Pl. 468.

(9) A servant may acquire a settlement by a residence of 40 days, directly subsequent to his year's hiring, but he must have served an entire year.

It is rightly observed by Dr. Burn, therefore, "that an "apprentice may gain as many settlements as there are "spaces of forty days in the term of his apprentice-"ship (1)."

This is the principal distinction between residence as a servant, and as an apprentice.

Arrangement. The questions and cases which respect this subject, will be arranged therefore in the same order as was pursued in treating of the residence of hired servants. The reader will find in that section (2) a minute explication of the principles, which it would be useless and irksome to repeat here.

Settlement in parish or town. An apprentice can only acquire a settlement in a parish or township having overseers (3); for the 13 & 14 Car. 2. c. 12. extends only to these places, and the provisions of 3 W. & M. are expressly confined thereto.

Reside 40 days. He must reside forty days, free from incapacity to acquire one (4).

Of connecting services. But it is unnecessary that the days should run in unbroken succession. A residence at intervals will connect for the purpose (5).

(1). 3. Burn's Justice, Title Poor. Settlement by apprenticeship.

(2) *Ante*, Chap. xx. sect. v. p. 285.

(3) Clerkenwell *v.* Bridewell, 1 Lord Raym. 549. 2 Bott, 380. Pl. 414. Rex *v.* Circencester. 1 Str. 579. St. Mary Colechurch, *v.* Radcliffe, 1 Str. 60. *post* 372, (3).

(4) St. Cuthbert's *v.* Westbury. Burr. S. C. 470. 2 Bott, 462. Pl. 443. Missenden *v.* Grimsfield. Fol. 157. 2 Bott, 390. Pl. 416. But the ground of this latter determination was, that the agreement to reside alternately, was fraudulent.

(5) Rex *v.* Sandford. 2 Bott, 398. Pl. 426. Rex *v.* Brighthelmstone. 5 Term Rep. 188. 2 Bott, 399. Pl. 427. Rex *v.* Cirencester. Cast. Sett. and Rem. 119. 2 Bott, 392. Pl. 419. Rex *v.* St. George's Hanover Square, *ante*, 359, (2). Rex *v.* Fremington, *ante*, 358 (6). see *contra*; the law, however, is settled by the subsequent cases as above cited.

Neither does it make any diſtinction, that the reſidence is interrupted by intervals of inhabitancy in a place where no ſettlement can be acquired. An apprentice "ſerved his maſter moſtly on ſhip-board at ſea; but inhabited the pariſh of Weſt Stockwith the firſt fourteen days of his apprenticeſhip, and ſo many days after, at many different times, as with thoſe fourteen days amounted to upwards of forty days in the whole, and in no other pariſh for forty days during his apprenticeſhip." He was held ſettled in Weſt Stockwith (1). When inhabitancy in a place where no ſettlement is gained.

And the principle is the ſame where the incapacity ariſes, not from the place, but from a defect in the ſervice. Reſidence at any diſtance of time during the continuance of indentures, will connect, notwithſtanding the intervention of ſervice and reſidence, which confer no ſettlement, provided the relation of maſter and apprentice continues to ſubſiſt. Sage gave up the indentures to his pariſh apprentice, then aged eighteen, without the pariſh officer's conſent, and recommended him to live with Verney, with whom the pauper made an agreement as a ſervant for three years. Having ſerved that time, and reſided in another place for three months, he returned to his original maſter for a month, paying him ſixpence a week for lodging. Willes and Buller J. were of opinion, that this laſt reſidence would connect with that which took place antecedently in the pariſh with the ſame maſter, prior to giving up the indentures, ſo as to confer a ſettlement (2). When intervals of ſervice, by which no ſettlement gained.

The ſettlement of an apprentice, like that of a ſervant, is where he has laſt reſided forty complete days. He is ſettled finally therefore where he ſleeps the laſt night, in Settled where ſleeps laſt night.

(1) Rex *v.* Gainſborough. Burr. S. C. 586. 1 Bott, 546. Pl. 745.

(2) Rex *v.* Sandford. 2 Bott, 398. Pl. 426. S. C. 1 Term Rep. 281. 2 Bott, 432. Pl. 458. In the firſt of theſe reports a miſtake occurs in printing the name of Verney for Sage. See alſo Rex *v.* Charles, Burr. S. C. 706. 2 Bott, 424. Pl. 451.

 his

his condition of an apprentice, provided he has resided there forty days altogether (1).

Working without inhabitancy, insufficient.

Likewise, if the apprentice serve his master in one parish, and resides in another, the settlement is gained, not where he works, but where he sleeps; for it is there that he inhabits: and one condition of the settlement required by 3 W. & M. c. 11. s. 8. is, that the person shall be bound an apprentice, and *inhabit* in the town or parish (2).

And this is so, although the apprentice should be deprived of a settlement under his indentures, by adhering to the rule. An apprentice to a sea-captain serving his master every day on shore, and sleeping every night on board a ship, lying in an extraparochial place, gains no settlement under his indentures (3).

Master's consent unnecessary.

Neither is the master's permission to sleep in the particular parish necessary. An apprentice married during his apprenticeship, and afterwards worked, and dieted in the day-time with his master in the parish of C, (where the master lived, and carried on his trade). The master knew of the marriage, and that his apprentice lodged at nights with his wife at her father's, in the parish of H, but the master was not asked, nor did he give him leave to do so; but he knew of it. The pauper was held

(1) Rex *v.* Brighthelmstone, and the cases *supra*, 370, (5).

(2) Rex *v.* St. Peter's on the Hill. 2 Bott, 393. Pl. 422. The opinion of Parker C. J. and Pratt J. in St. Mary Colechurch *v.* Ratcliffe, *post.* (3). and that of the chief justice in Rex *v.* St. Olave's, is *contra.* But the opinions were extra judicial, and the law is now settled otherwise. Rex *v.* Spotland, Burr. S. C. 527. These cases decide, that the settlement is where the apprentice sleeps; but it was decided in several prior cases, that service, without residence, gave no settlement. See Rex *v.* St. Olave's Jewry. 2 Bott, 390. Pl. 417. St. Mary Colechurch *v.* Ratcliffe. *Ib.* 391. Pl. 418. St. John Baptist, and St. James, *ib.* 390. Pl. 420.

(3) St. Mary Colechurch *v.* Ratcliffe. 1 Str. 60. Cas. Sett. 105. 2 Bott, 391. Pl. 418.

settled

ſettled at H.; the place where an apprentice lies, being that of his ſettlement (1).

And, if we may conclude from analogy to the caſe of a ſervant, the maſter's knowledge of the fact ſeems as immaterial as his conſent (2), provided the apprentice continues under his maſter's control.

It makes no difference, likewiſe, whether he inhabits on land, or on ſhip board, if the place in which the veſſel lies, is within a town or pariſh (3), or whether the maſter has gained a ſettlement in the place, or lives as a houſekeeper, or merely ſojourns with one (4); or whether he goes there for a temporary purpoſe (5), or does not reſide in the pariſh at all (6), or is without property there (7).

Mode of inhabiting, and maſter's condition immaterial.

But the court appear inclined to make the ſame diſtinctions in the caſe of apprentices, as was taken in that of ſervants; viz. that if an apprentice live apart from his maſter through illneſs, he is not ſettled where he reſides, but where he had previouſly dwelt the laſt forty days under his indentures (8).

Except ſervant reſide from illneſs away from his maſter.

But it is otherwiſe, if he reſide with his maſter. The pauper was bound apprentice by the pariſh, to F., who applied to Mrs. L. his land-lady, to take the pauper, in conſequence of a covenant in his leaſe. Mrs. L. did ſo; received the pariſh money, and took the pauper into the

Otherwiſe if reſident with him.

(1) Rex *v.* Caſtleton, Burr. S. C. 569. 2 Bott, 397. Pl. 424.

(2) *Ante*, 371.

(3) Rex *v.* Burton Bradſtock, Burr. S. C. 531. 2 Bott, 394. Pl. 423.

(4) Stoke Fleming *v.* Berry Pomroy. 2 Bott, 392. Pl. 421.

(5) Rex *v.* Charles, *poſt*, 374, (1).

(6) Rex *v.* Caſtleton, *ante*, (1). and the caſes, *ib.* Rex *v.* St. George's Hanover Square, Burr. S. C. 12.

(7) Stoke Fleming *v.* Berry Pomroy, *ante*, (4).

(8) Rex *v.* Titchfield, Burr. S. C. 511. 2 Bott, 404. Pl. 432.

 pariſh

pariſh of Roſeaſh, where ſhe then lived, and where he reſided with her for three years. In conſequence of his becoming a cripple, Mrs. L. inſiſted upon F's taking him back, which he refuſed to do, unleſs ſhe agreed to pay him all the expences he ſhould be at, in taking care of him. Having agreed to do ſo, F. put him out to live with the apprentice's grandmother, in F's own pariſh of Knowſtone, at ſo much a week, and he reſided there forty days. The court held, that the indentures not being diſcharged, he acquired a ſettlement under this reſidence in Knowſtone, thereby ſuperſeding a prior ſettlement, gained by ſervice, under his indentures, with Mrs. L., in the pariſh of Roſeaſh (1).

The remaining circumſtances, neceſſary to the reſidence of an hired ſervant, are nearly peculiar to that ſpecies of ſettlement.

Muſt reſide under indentures.

It is evident, from the words of the ſtatute, 3 W. & M. c. 11. and the caſes already cited, that the apprentice muſt reſide in the place in which he ſeeks a ſettlement, ſubject to the binding power of his indenture, and the control of his maſter (2).

Diſtinction between ſervants and apprentices, as to reſidence under incapacities.

If he does ſo, no change in his condition creates an incapacity to acquire a ſettlement, as it may in the caſe of a ſervant (3). Thoſe points, therefore, incident to a ſervant's reſidence under incapacities, which have been formerly diſcuſſed, muſt ſeldom, or never, ariſe. Queſtions upon reſidence, under diſtinct deeds of apprenticeſhip, with the ſame, or different maſters, can hardly originate in a tranſaction of this nature. But if chance ſhould give birth to ſuch a caſe, the court would, in all probability, aſſimilate it to thoſe of hiring and ſervice.

(1) Rex *v.* Charles, Burr. S. C. 202. 2 Bott, 424. Pl. 451.

(2) *Ante*, ſect. iv. 355.

(3) *Ante*, 276. But the obſervation admits of ſome exception in the caſe of certificates. See *poſt*.

It is of the utmoſt importance, to render this part of the law, not only certain, but plain and diſtinct, and not to encumber it with nice, or numerous diſtinctions. The judges have inclined with this view, to a conformity of deciſion, between the two ſpecies of ſettlement, ſo far as the expreſs proviſions of the ſeveral ſtatutes upon which they reſpectively depend, are found to admit of it.

There are no particular ſtatutory diſabilities which reſpect ſettlements by apprenticeſhip. Such as relate to certificates, will be briefly treated of in another place.

SECT. VI.

Of the Proofs neceſſary to eſtabliſh a Settlement by Apprenticeſhip.

In order to eſtabliſh a ſettlement by apprenticeſhip, it is neceſſary to prove, 1ſt, The binding by indenture. 2d, The identity of the apprentice. 3d, His ſervice and reſidence of forty days in the town or pariſh. 4th, If the ſervice is with any other than the original maſter, his conſent. **Proof of ſettlement.**

To prove the binding, the deed of apprenticeſhip muſt be produced, if in exiſtence, and not in the hands of the oppoſite party (1). If in the cuſtody of a third perſon, he ſhould be ſerved with a *ſub pœna duces tecum*, to bring it with him on the hearing of the appeal. If poſſeſſed by the oppoſite party, they ſhould be ſerved with notice to produce it. It will appear, by the deed, whether it is properly ſtamped, without which it cannot be read in evidence (2). **1. The binding.** **Deed in cuſtody of others.**

(1) Rex *v.* Holbeck in Leeds, Burr. S. C. 198. 2 Bott, 457. Pl. 478. Rex *v*, St. Helens, Burr. S. C. 735. 2 Bott, 458. Pl. 479.

(2) Rex *v.* Holbeck, *ante*, n. (1).

Proof of execution.

The execution, or signing, sealing, and delivering, is to be proved, unless in certain cases, which will be mentioned hereafter.

How proved when no subscribing witness.

If there is no subscribing witness (1), or the name of a fictitious person has been put as such (2), or if he who subscribes the deed, denies having seen the execution (3), it is sufficient to prove the hand-writing of the parties. If a parish indenture be unattested, proof of the hand writing of the parish officers who signed it, is perhaps sufficient in a question with the parish. But, as against third persons, all signatures which appear on the deed, or those at least of the master and apprentice, should be proved.

When attested.

If the deed is regularly attested by one witness, he should be produced, unless he labours under some incapacity (4). It is unnecessary that he should *see* the party sign. If he be in an adjoining room, and brings it to the witness, acknowledging that he has signed and sealed, that is sufficient (5).

Witness incapacitated.

If the witness be dead (6), or blind (7), or mad (8), or abroad (9), whether domicilled there, or not (10), or cannot be found after diligent enquiry (11), or is incapaci-

(1) Com. Dig. Tit. Fait. (B. 4). Vide 1 Lev. 25. Rex *v.* Middlezoy, *post*, 376, (7).

(2) Fasset *v.* Brown, Peake's N. P. Cas. 23.

(3) Grellier *v.* Neale, *ib.* 146.

(4) Breton *v.* Cope, Peake's N. P. C. 30. Buckley *v.* Smith, 2 Espin. N. P. C. 697.

(5) Park *v.* Mears, 2 Bos and Pule, 219. Powell *v.* Blacket, 1 Espin. N. P. C. 97.

(6) Barnes *v.* Trompowsky, 7 Term Rep. 265.

(7) Wood *v.* Drury, 1 lord Raym. 734.

(8) 12 Vin. Abr. (T. 6. 48) Pl. 12.

(9) *i. e.* in a country out of the court's jurisdiction, Price *v.* Blackburn, 2 East, 250. Coghlan *v.* Williamson, Dougl. 93. Holmes *v.* Ponten, Peake's N. P. C. 99. Barnes *v.* Trompowsky, *ante*, (6). Adams *v.* Ker, 1 Bos and Pull, 360.

(10) Price *v.* Blackburne, *ante*, (9); and see 26 Geo. 3. f. 38, as to the testimony of persons residing in the East Indies.

(11) See Cunliffe *v.* Sefton, 2 East, 183.

tated

tated by crime (1), or interest (2), it will be sufficient to prove his hand-writing, after shewing his situation.

If there are two or more witnesses to the execution, it is sufficient to call one. If some are incapacitated, one must be called, who is not. If all labour under incapacity, it is sufficient to prove the signature of one (3). It was held in one case, that under such circumstances, the signature of the witness, and also of the party, must be proved (4). But this has since been adjudged unnecessary; for that of the attesting witness, when proved, is evidence of every thing on the face of the paper (5). Where one witness was dead, and the other denied the execution of the instrument, but acknowledged his signature, Lord C. J. Holt admitted evidence of the other's writing (6).

When two witnesses.

All proof of hand-writing must be either from having seen the party write the signature in question, or from previous acquaintance with his hand-writing. If the writer reside in this country, the witness must acquire his knowledge from having seen him write (7). If the party reside abroad, knowledge derived from correspondence is sufficient (8). But the witness must know, that the letters were written by the party, as by having received them in the course of correspondence, or the like. Having seen the superscription of letters which passed at the post-office,

Hand-writing how proved.

(1) Jones *v.* Mason, 2 Str. 833.

(2) Godfrey *v.* Norris, 1 Str. 34, Gosa. *v.* Tracey. 1 P. Wm. 289. Swire *v.* Bell, 5 Term Rep. 372.

(3) Adams *v.* Ker, 1 Bos. and Pull. 360. Cunliffe *v* Sefton, 2 East, 283. But Wallis *v.* De Lancey, 7 Term Rep. 266, n. c. is contra.

(4) Wallis *v.* De Lancey, *supra*, n. (3).

(5) Adams *v.* Ker, *supra*, (3). Cunliffe *v.* Sefton, *ib.* and see Price *v.* Blackburne, 2 East. 250.

(6) Blurton *v.* Toon Skin. 639.

(7) Willis *v.* Singer, Espin. N. P. C. 144.

(8) Gould *v.* Jones, Bull L. N. P. 236. 1 Black. Rep. 384. Lord Ferrers *v.* Shirley, Fitzg. 195. And *quære* whether the reason does not extend to correspondence in this country. See the opinion of Lord Raymond C. J. in Lord Ferrers *v.* Shirley.

office, as his franks, or papers, not received from the party by the witness, but by others, who told the witness from whom they came, is not sufficient; for they may have been forgeries (1).

Comparison of hands.

Evidence by mere comparison of hands, is inadmissible: there must be a degree of habitual acquaintance with the writing (2).

Degree of knowledge.

Slight knowledge acquired from competent sources is, *primâ facie*, sufficient. But it must be derived solely from acquaintance with the hand writing; disbelief created by extraneous circumstances, such as the witness's knowledge of the party, and the nature of the deed, are inadmissible (3).

Proof of sealing and delivery.

If the signature is proved, the sealing and delivery shall be presumed (4); at least where the attestation imports so much (5). But if by special custom any thing is equivalent to sealing a deed, that custom must be

(1) Lord Ferrers *v.* Shirley, *ante*, 377. Carey *v.* Pitt, Peakes law of Ev. App. 40.

(2) Brookbank *v.* Woodley, *coram* Yates J. 4 Supp. Vin. Abr. (A. 6. a1.) Pl. 6. Stanger *v.* Searl, 1 Espin. N. P. C. 14. Macpherson *v.* Thoytes, Peake's N. P. C. 20. Rex *v.* Cato, 4 Espin. N. P. C. 117. The point seems very clear; if the jury or other tribunal are required to find the fact by comparing the exhibit with other signatures, proved to be the hand writing of the party. But the distinction grows nice, when a witness is called to speak to it; for, unless where he has seen the instrument actually written, he must in all cases speak from a comparison which he institutes between it, and what he recollects of other pieces of the party's writing. See Bull L. N. P. 206. and a case cited there before Lord Hardwicke C. Allesbrook *v.* Roach, Peaks L. Ev. 104. Da Costa *v.* Pym. 1. Espin. N. P. C. 351. Peak. Evid. app. 22. S. C. Goodtitle *v.* Braham, 4 Term Rep. 497. and Osbourn *v.* Hosier, 6 Mod. 167.

(3) Da Costa *v.* Pym, *ante*, (2). Balcetti *v.* Serrani, Peake N. P. C. 142.

(4) Grellier *v.* Neale, Peake N. P. C. 146. Adams *v.* Ker, *ante*, 377, (3); and see Stone *v.* Grubham, Roll. Rep. 3.

(5) Even where there is no subscribing witness, the presumption seems in favour of delivery, as signing and sealing would otherwise be nugatory; and at all events this presumption may be raised or rebutted in such a case, by extrinsic circumstances, such as the custody of the deed, &c.

proved

proved (1). Actual proof may refute the preſumption of a proper delivery, which ariſes from atteſtation.

Caſting a deed upon the table, without doing more, does not amount to a delivery (2). But caſting it upon the table, ſaying, this will ſerve, is ſufficient (3). Delivery, what.

In the caſe of pariſh apprentices, the aſſent of two juſtices is neceſſary (4); and if given in writing, the ſignatures muſt be proved in the ſame manner (5), and ſubject to the ſame rules as the execution of indentures. But it is unneceſſary to prove the appointment as magiſtrates. For, "in the caſe of all peace-officers, juſtices of the peace, conſtables, &c. it is ſufficient to prove that they acted in thoſe characters, without producing their appointments; and that even in the caſe of murder (6)." And in an indictment for diſobeying a juſtice's order for diverting a road, it was held unneceſſary to produce the commiſſion of peace to prove the perſons who ſigned the order, magiſtrates (7). Aſſent of juſtices to pariſh indentures.

But where the maſter has ſigned the counterpart, he is ſtopped from ſhewing that the indenture and counterpart were at that time ſigned by one juſtice only (8).

Proof execution unneceſſary. 1. Deed coming from adverſary.

Proof of the execution is unneceſſary,

1ſt, If the deed come out of the hands of the adverſe party. For the ſide relying upon it, cannot know who are the ſubſcribing witneſſes, or come prepared to prove

(1) Adams *v.* Ker, 1 Bos & Pull. 360.

(2) Chamberlain *v.* Staunton, 1 Leon. 140. Pl. 193. Cro. Eliz. 122. S C.

(3) *Ibid.*

(4) Rex *v.* Hamſtall, Redware, 3 Term Rep. 380. 2 Bott, 386. Pl. 411. Rex *v.* Winwick, 8 Term Rep. 454. 1 Bott. 722. Pl. 454.

(5) See Rex *v.* Bilton, 1 Eaſt. 13. the examination of a ſoldier under the Mutiny Act, touching his ſettlement, *ante*, 306, (1).

(6) *Per* Buller J. Berryman *v.* Wiſe, 4 Term Rep. 366, and ſo determined by all the judges in Gordon's Caſe. Leach Cro. Law, Caſ. 278, n. *a*.

(7) *Per* Hotham B. after conference with Heath J. Rex *v.* Kingſton, Lent Aſſizes, 1801.

(8) Rex *v.* Saltren, Cald. 444.

the

the execution (1). In the case of an appeal between two parishes, it was held unnecessary to prove the execution of indentures of apprenticeship, they being in the custody of the appellant parish, and produced by them (2). But the propriety of this decision is said to be doubted by very high authority. "For, in a subsequent case, where a similar point came before the court, lord Kenyon said, it was too important a question to be discussed in a Sessions case, where the opinion of a Court of Error could not be taken; and that nothing but a solemn judgment of the House of Lords should ever persuade him that this decision was right (3)." The rule seems reasonable where those who retain the custody, appear parties to the instrument, or retain it as a document of a title or right (4).

For, in the first case, they may disprove the execution, and in the second, it derives authority from being preserved by them.

How in adversaries custody.

But it must be in their custody, or that of their agents. A deed in the hands of one who was attorney for the adverse party at the time of the execution, but who was not so at the trial, must be regularly proved (5).

2. Deed 30 years old.

It is unnecessary to prove the execution of a deed thirty years old (6), although the subscribing witness is alive (7).

(1) Rex *v.* Middlezoy, 2 Term Rep. 41. 2 Bott, 461. Pl. 481.

(2) *Ante*, 379, n. (9).

(3) Rex *v.* Dalton, Mich 41. Geo. 3. Peake's Law of Evid. 2 Edit. 309.

(4) It does not appear in Rex *v.* Middlezoy, whether the pauper was bound out by Sydburi parish, if it was so, then, the parish which produced the indentures was party to the binding. The notice also was, to produce at the trial of the appeal "a *certain* indenture of apprenticeship bearing date, on or about, &c." And being described as a valid deed, the opposite party by producing it under that description, seemed to admit it to be so. Vide Passal *v.* Gudsal, 2 Term Rep. 44. But no such notice is stated in Thompson *v.* Jones, *ib.* Yet the lease was held admissible, "as coming out of the hands of the other party."

(5) Leith *v.* Post, 1 Espin. N. P. C. 196.

(6) Bull, L. N. P. 255.

(7) In Marsh *v.* Culnett, 2 Espin. Ni. Pri. Cas. 666.

But

But some account is usually given, of where it has been kept or found, &c. (1); and if there be any blemish, by erasure, or interlineation, it seems prudent to prove the execution by the witnesses, if living; or if dead, by proving the hand writing of, at least, one of them; and also that of the party, in order to encounter the presumption arising from such blemishes (2).

When necessary to prove signatures to old instruments.

But it was held to be sufficient to produce a parish certificate, more than thirty years old, at the hearing of an appeal, and that the parties producing it, need not shew from whence it came (3).

Parish certificate 30 years old.

If the deed appears cancelled, or the seal torn off, that is *prima facie* evidence of its being no longer in force. But proof may be given, that it was cancelled by ill practice (4), or that the seal was torn off by accident (5). If the contract be joint, and the seal of one obligor is torn off, it destroys the obligation; but if they be severally bound, it continues as to the other, whose seal was not torn off (6). But if two men be jointly and severally bound, and the seal of one is torn off, this is a discharge of the obligee; for the manner of the obligation is destroyed *by the act of the obligee* (7).

Seal torn off.

If a deed be altered by a stranger in an immaterial point, it does not avoid the deed; but otherwise, if he alter it in one that is material. But if the party himself alter it in one that is immaterial, it avoids the deed (8). And if one covenant be altered, it destroys the deed (9). And if

(1) Bull, L. N. P. 255.

(2) Chettle *v.* Pound, *ib.*

(3) Rex *v.* Ryton, 5 Term Rep. 259.

(4) Buckrow's case, Hetl. 138.

(5) Anon. Latch. 226. Palm. 403. *Per* Twisden J. Clerk *v.* Heath, 1 Mod. 11.

(6) Bull, L. N. P. 268, cites 5 Co. 23. 11 Co. 28. *b.* 2 Lev. 220. 2 Show. 28, 29.

(7) Bull, L. N. P. 268, cites March. 125.

(8) Bull, L. N. P. 267.

(9) Bull, L. N. P. 267, cites 11 Co. 27.

 there

there be blanks left in material places, and filled up afterwards by assent of parties, yet is the obligation void, for it is not the same contract that was sealed and delivered. As if a bond were made to C., with a blank left for his christian name, and addition, which is afterwards filled up. But if A. with a blank left after his name, be bound to N., and if C. is added as a joint obligor, it does not avoid the bond; for it does not alter the contract of A., who was bound to pay the whole money, before any such addition (1). But a deed, although purposely defaced, will be good evidence (where duly proved) to establish all the legal consequences from the time of delivery, until that of cancelling (2).

How far evidence when cancelled.

Deed lost.

Where an original deed is lost, or destroyed by time or accident (3), or is in the custody of the adverse party, who refuses to produce it (4), "the counterpart may be read (5); and if there is no counterpart forth coming, then a copy (6) may be admitted: and even if there should be no copy, there may be parol evidence (7) of the deed (8)."

Where the deed is lost or destroyed, it will be necessary to prove the loss of the original, and that it was a

(1) *Ib.* 281, note (8).

(2) *Ib.* 267, and the cases cited.

(3) Doctor Leyfield's case, 10 Co. 92*b*. Underhill v. Durham, Freem. 509. Meddlicott v. Joyner, 1 Mod. 4. 2 Keb. 546. S.C. Whitfield v. Fausset, 1 Ves. 389. Thurston v. Delahay, Bull, L. N. P. 254. Pritchard v. Symonds, *ib.* Goodier v. Lake, 1 Atk. 446. Lynch v. Clerk, 3 Salk. 154.

(4) Young v. Holmes, 1 Str. 70. Clayt. 15. Pl. 2. Negus v. Reynal, Keb. 22. Basset v. Basset, 1 Mod 266. Anon. Lord Raym. 731. Gilb. Law Evid. 3d. Ed. 97. Sturt v. Mellish, 2 Atk. 612.

(5) *Per* Grose J. Rex v. Middlezoy, *ante*, 379, (8), and the cases *post*.

(6) Thurston v. De la Hay, Bull, L. N. P. 254.

(7) Sir Edw. Seymour's case, 10 Mod. 8. *post*, 385, (6) Rex v. Metheringham, *post*, 385, (8).

(8) *Per* Lord Hardwicke, C. Villiers v. Villiers, 2 Atk. 71.

genuine

genuine inſtrument (1). For this purpoſe, it muſt be ſhewn, that enquiry has been made after it (2); and the loſs muſt be proved by the perſon to whoſe cuſtody it is traced. In order to eſtabliſh an apprenticeſhip in a queſtion of ſettlement, it was proved that the indenture was of two parts; that one had been deſtroyed, and the other had come into the hands of A., who was then living. But A. was not ſubpœna'd to give evidence, or produce it; and therefore it was held, that the indenture had not been proved loſt, or deſtroyed, ſo as to let in other evidence of the contents (3).

But where there was but one copy of an agreement to rent a land ſale collery as tenants for one year, and it was depoſited in the hands of the landlord, who upon application made ſeveral times before his death, by the tenant, refuſed to produce to him the agreement. The landlord died three years previous to the appeal, which was heard ten years after executing the agreement; and the tenant ſwore at the hearing, that he did not know in whoſe cuſtody the agreement now is, or whether it is in being or not. Neither has he made any enquiry for it ſince the landlord's death. The court were of opinion, that parol evidence of this inſtrument had been properly admitted by the Seſſions. *Per* Willes J. "It had expired many years; the leſſee had been dead three years, and in his life had repeatedly refuſed a ſight of it to the pauper, who knew not where it was, or whether it exiſted. In this ſtate of things, there was ſo little proſpect of

(1) Goodier *v.* Lake, 1 Atk. 446.; and ſee lord Peterborough *v.* Mordant, 1 Mod. 94. But Page and Chapple J. were of opinion, "that after length of time, parol proof of indentures ſhall be ſufficient; becauſe in all probability, theſe indentures may be loſt; and indeed they are frequently burned when delivered up by the maſter at the end of the term." Rex *v.* Eaſt Knoyle, Burr. S. C. 151. 1 Bott, 543. Pl. 745.

(2) Rex *v.* St. Sepulcher's, 2 Bott, 362. Pl. 391.

(3) Rex *v.* Caſtleton, 6 Term Rep. 236. 2 Bott, 461. Pl. 482. See alſo Rex *v.* St. Helens, Burr. S. C. 715. 2 Bott, 458. Pl. 479.

of effecting any thing by further pursuit, that I think the evidence was properly admitted." Buller J. "Had it been in proof, that the executor of the lessee had been in possession of this instrument, it might have varied the case. After the expiration of the lease, the lessee, the pauper, was entitled to it, in strictness; but he neither had it, nor knew whether it existed; and it was now nine years after its expiration. Under such circumstances, parol evidence was properly resorted to (1)."

Upon a question of settlement of the wife and children of a militiaman, it appeared by his examination, taken in writing, under the Mutiny Act, that he went apprentice to J. M., and served five years and an half. The pauper, who was his wife, proved her marriage, and that he ran away from her, and that she had neither seen, heard from, or known, what was become of him since. This was held a reasonable presumption of a binding, although some circumstantial evidence was produced by the other side, to shew that J. M. never had an apprentice; "for every thing is to be presumed in favour of a settlement (2)."

If two parts, both must be proved lost, to let in secondary evidence.

It is an universal rule, that the best evidence which can be given by the party, must be produced (3). If two or more parts are executed therefore, the loss or destruction of all must be proved before a copy can be allowed as evidence (4).

Copy evidence when.

In order to let in a copy where the original is in the adverse party's custody, that fact must be proved. And proof of delivery to his servant is insufficient without

(1) Rex v. North Bedburn, Cald. 452. 2 Bott, 101. Pl. 147. S. C.

(2) Rex v. St. Michael's Bath, 2 Bott, 459. Pl. 480. But the authority of this case seems questioned in Rex v. Clayton Le Moore, 5 Term Rep. 704.

(3) Bull, L. N. P. 293.

(4) Pritchard v. Symonds, Bull L. N. P. 254, and see Rex v. Castleton, *ante*, 383, (3).

calling

calling the ſervant (1). But a copy may be read, after proof that the original came into the hands of defendant's brother, under whom defendant claimed; even though the defendant has ſworn, in an anſwer in chancery, that he has not got the original (2). It is alſo neceſſary to prove that he or his attorney has been ſerved with notice to produce it (3).

A counterpart of a deed is not properly a duplicate original, for it is executed only by one party. It is admiſſible evidence againſt him who ſigns it, without giving him notice to produce the original; for it recites the execution of the original, and is executed by the party (4). But it cannot be read in evidence againſt any other perſon, without accounting for the want of the original (5).

Counterpart.

Slighter evidence is required to eſtabliſh the contents of a deed, which is proved to be in the hands of the oppoſite party, than if it is ſhewn to be loſt or deſtroyed; for in the former caſe, if the party is wronged by the evidence, he may ſet it right, by producing the real inſtrument (6). But parol evidence is ſufficient, where a deed of indenture (7) or order of removal is loſt (8); and where parol evidence is given of an indenture, and a conſideration paid with the apprentice, the Seſſions ſhould

Deed in hands of adverſary, ſlighter evidence required.

(1) Rex *v.* Pearce, Peake's Ni. Pri. Caſ. 75. But ſee Col. Gordon's caſe, Leach Cr. Law. Caſ. 244.

(2) Bartlet *v.* Gawler, Bull, L. N. P. 254.

(3) Attorney General *v.* Le Merchant, 2 Term Rep. 201, (*a*). *Per* Buller J. Rex *v.* Watſon, *ib.* Leach's Cro. Caſ. 214. Cotes *qui tam v.* Winter, 3 Term Rep. 306.

(4) Burleigh *v.* Stubbs, 5 Term Rep. 465. But ſee Yelverton *v.* Cornwallis, Noy. 53.

(5) *Per* Holt C. J. Anon. Salk. 287. 6 Mod. 225. Sir Wm. Poole's caſe, 12 Vin. (Ab. 27). Pl. 4. *Per* Groſe J. Rex *v.* Middlezoy, *ante*,

(6) Sir Edw. Seymour's caſe, 10 Mod. 8. 12 Vin. (T. b. 65). Pl. 22. Eccleſton *v.* Speke, Carth. 80. Young *v.* Holmes, 1 Str. 70.

(7) Rex *v.* Badby, 2 Bott, 547. Pl 746 Rex *v.* Little Bolton, Cald. 367, *ante*, 339, (1). Rex *v.* Wantage, 1 Eaſt. 601.

(8) Rex *v.* Metheringham, 6 Term Rep. 556.

take

take it for granted that they were stamped, and the duty paid (1): for a fraud is not to be presumed (2).

Parol evidence inadmissible to contradict a written agreement.

It is a general rule, that parol evidence is inadmissible to contradict (3), or substantially to vary a deed, or other written instrument (4), or to explain an ambiguity that is patent, *i. e.* apparent, on perusal of the instrument itself; such as the total omission of a devisee's name in a will (5).

But, 1st, may explain a latent ambiguity.

But it may be given, 1st, To explain a latent ambiguity, that is, where the uncertainty does not appear upon the face of the writing, but is raised by extrinsic circumstances. For, being let in by parol evidence, the same kind of evidence that introduced the doubt, may be admitted to explain it (6). Such are imperfect and equivocal descriptions of persons, parties, or places mentioned in the instrument (7). A. devised an estate to her cousin J. C., and had two of that name, father and son: parol evidence was admitted to shew the son was intended (8). So, if the devisee is mentioned by a nickname (8); or, if a wrong name is inserted by mistake (9). So whether parcel or not of the thing demised is matter of evidence (10).

(1) Rex *v.* Badby, *ante*, 385, (7).

(2) Rex *v.* East. Knoyle, Burr. S. C. 151. 1 Bott, 543. Pl. 743.

(3) Lord Bacon's Maxims. Reg. 23. p 99.

(4) Meres & Al' *v.* Ansell, & Al. 3 Wils 275. Clifton *v.* Walmsley, 5 Term Rep. 564. Gunnis & Al' *v.* Erhart, 1 H. Black. 289. Wilson *v*, Poulter, 2 Str. 794.

(5) Ballis & Church *v.* Attorney General. *Per* Hardwicke C. Bull, L. N. P. 298, *post.*

(6) *Per* Lord Kenyon C. J. Lord Walpole *v.* Lord Cholmondeley. 7 Term Rep. 138. *post*, 389.

(7) Jones *v* Newman, 1 Black. Rep. 60. 3 Wils. 276. Cheyney's case, 5 Co. 68. S. P.

(8) Baylis & Al' *v.* the Attorney General, 2 Atk. 239.

(9) Beaumont *v.* Fell, 2 P. Wm. 141. See also Thomas *v.* Thomas, 6 Term Rep. 671.

(10) Doe *ex dem.* Freeland *v.* Burt. 1 Term Rep. B. R. 70. But this evidence seems admissible only to explain, and not to contradict the description which is given by bounderies in a lease.

2d, Parol

2d, Parol evidence may be given to ascertain a fact which does not contradict, but is collateral to the deed.

2d, To explain a fact collateral to the deed.

Upon a question of settlement, it appeared, that the pauper had made the following agreement in writing. "I J. M. do hereby agree with J. C. *to serve me* (1) three years, to learn the business of a carpenter; the first year, to have one shilling and two pence per day; the second, one shilling and six pence per day; the third year, one shilling and ten pence;" which agreement was signed by both parties. Parol evidence was admitted to prove, that at the time of signing the agreement, J. C. agreed to give J. M. three guineas, and that he was not to be, and never was employed in any other work, than that of a carpenter (2). "For it was not offered to contradict the written agreement, but to ascertain a fact collateral *thereto, in order to explain the intention of the parties*, the instrument being in some measure equivocal (3)."

Parol evidence of a further agreement.

In order to save expences, a written agreement was entered into, upon unstamped paper, whereby the pauper agreed to serve four years, at weekly wages, which were to increase annually. Evidence was admitted by the sessions to shew, that, at the time of signing, it was further agreed by parol, between the pauper and his master, that the pauper should find his own diet and lodging, be his own master on sundays, and not be paid for the time he should play. The court of King's Bench gave no opinion as to the admissibility of the evidence, but they made no objection to its having been so received (4).

Parol evidence of a further consideration.

The pauper claimed a settlement by residence on an estate, acquired by purchase. The consideration ex-

(1) *Sic in orig. Quære him?*

(2) Rex *v.* Laindon, 8 Term Rep. 379. 1 Bott, 710. Pl. 1000.

(3) *Per* Lawrence J. *ib.*

(4) Rex *v.* Highnam, Cald. 481. 2 Bott, 381. Pl. 409.

preffed in the deed of conveyance, was only 28l. Parol evidence was admitted to prove, that 30l. was the confideration actually paid (1).

To explain the direction of a parifh certificate.

A parifh confifted of feveral hamlets, having feparate churchwardens and overfeers. A certificate under 8 & 9 W. 3. c. 30. was granted by the officers of one hamlet, in which they defcribed themfelves as churchwardens and overfeers of the poor of the parifh, and acknowledged the pauper to be fettled within the parifh. Parol evidence was held admiffible to fhew, that they were officers of that particular hamlet; for it does not contradict, but explains the certificate (2).

3d, To fhew fraud in executing the deed.

3d, Parol evidence is alfo admiffible to fhew fraud or impofition practifed on the party, in executing the inftrument, upon the fame principle that it is admiffible to prove a defective execution. Thus, where it was fought to fet afide a fecond will on the ground of fraud, it was held, that parol evidence might be given of a queftion afked by the teftator, at the time of executing it, whether the contents were the fame as thofe of the former will? and his being anfwered in the affirmative, although it was in fact different; for it is evidence, that one paper was obtruded on the teftator for another (3).

Nine general rules of evidence.

It may not be wholly ufelefs, to fet forth the nine general rules refpecting evidence, as they are laid down by an eminent judge (4), moft of which are exemplified in what has been already ftated.

1ft Rule. You muft give the beft evidence that the nature of the thing is capable of: that is, no fuch evi-

(1) Rex *v.* Scammonden, 3 Term Rep. 474. 2 Bott, 519. Pl. 528. Filmer *v.* Gott, cited 3 Term Rep. 475. 7 Bro. Par. Caf. 70.

(2) Rex *v.* Samborn, 3 Term Rep. 609. 2 Bott, 571. Pl. 584.

(3) Doe on the dem. of Small *v.* Allen, 8 Term Rep. 147.

(4) Buller, L. N. P. 293, *et feq.*

dence

dence shall be brought that *ex naturâ rei*, supposes still a greater (1) evidence behind, in the parties possession or power.

2d Rule. No person interested shall be a witness (2).

3d Rule. Hearsay is no evidence, except as to the facts of *legitimacy*, *relationship*, *pedigrees*, rights of common rights of way, and all rights depending upon custom, or prescription (3).

4th Rule. In all cases where a general character or behaviour is put in issue, evidence of particular facts " (to affect it)" may be admitted: but not where it comes in collaterally (4).

5th Rule. Ambiguitas verborum latens verificatione suppletur, nam quod ex facto oritur ambiguum verificatione facti tollitur (5).

6th Rule. In every issue, the affirmative must be proved, unless where the law presumes the affirmative contained in the issue.

7th Rule. No evidence need be given of which is agreed in the pleadings.

8th Rule. Where special matter cannot be taken advantage of by pleading, it may be given in evidence, on the general issue.

9th Rule. If the substance of the issue is proved, it is sufficient.

(1) i. e. Evidence of an higher order, *ex. gr.* no body shall give evidence by parol of what appears to have been reduced into writing. See *ante*, 384.

(2) See *ante*, 302.

(3) See *ante*, 304.

(4) *Ante*, 304.

(5) *Ante*, 386.

The

Other requisites of the settlement how proved.

The remaining circumstances, necessary to establish a settlement by apprenticeship may be proved, either by direct testimony, or by inference, as is done in fixing the settlement of an hired servant (1). But if the original master's consent to service with another, is by assignment, that must be proved in the same manner as the original indentures (2); and if it be by a less formal writing, that is likewise subject to the foregoing rules.

(1) *Ante*, 298, *et seq.* 6 Term Rep. 451. 2 Bott, 463.
(2) Rex *v.* St. Paul's Bedford, Pl. 483.

END OF THE FIRST VOLUME.

Printed by Strahan and Preston,
New-Street Square, London.